Guide to Programs

In Linguistics:

1974-75

Center for Applied Linguistics
and the
Secretariat of The Linguistic Society of America

Eighth revised edition, 1975 [Former Titles, University Resources in the United States for Linguistics and the Teaching of English as a Foreign Language; University Resources in the United States and Canada for the Study of Linguistics.]

A joint publication of the Center for Applied Linguistics and the Secretariat of the Linguistic Society of America
1611 North Kent Street, Arlington, Virginia 22209

International Standard Book Number: 87281-038-0
Library of Congress Catalog Card Number: 75-13738

Printed in the United States of America

PREFACE

This eighth revised edition, listing linguistic programs in the United States and Canada, has both a new name and a new format. Guide to Programs in Linguistics (formerly University Resources in the United States and Canada for the Study of Linguistics) now includes a brief essay on the program and facilities of each institution. Also new with this edition is the departmental phone number, information on financial support available, the academic calendar for 1974-75, and increased information about faculty members and their fields of specialization. We hope that these additions make the Guide more useful.

In 1962, when the Center for Applied Linguistics researched and published the first University Resources, 33 schools were listed as having courses in linguistics and/or teaching English to speakers of other languages. By 1970, when the Linguistic Society of America began to co-sponsor this work, the number of schools had risen to 146. The 1971-72 edition of University Resources listed over 200 schools, and it looked at that time as if the growth had not yet peaked. Between 1972 and the present, a tapering off did occur and the current edition lists 167 schools. While linguistic courses are still taught at many of the institutions omitted from this latest edition (See Appendix C), the number of formal departments, interdisciplinary programs, ad hoc committees, etc. has decreased.

We would like to thank the department and program chairmen for their cooperation in providing the information in this volume. We would also like to thank the staff members of the Center for Applied Linguistics and the Secretariat of the Linguistic Society of America who helped in the preparation of the Guide. Data collection and interpretation for a work of this size is no small task, and it was only through the combined effort of many people that this volume could appear.

Rudolph C. Troike
Director
Center for Applied Linguistics

Arthur S. Abramson
Secretary-Treasurer
Linguistic Society of America

Coverage

Included in the present edition are those institutions which, on the basis of available information, offer five or more courses broadly defined as "linguistics," and which offer, as well, a degree in linguistics or a degree in a related area with either a major or minor in linguistics. The information listed for each college or university was supplied by the institution itself through a questionnaire prepared and mailed out by the Center for Applied Linguistics. In some cases, though, this had to be supplemented by information from college catalogues or other descriptive material.

Information about annual summer institutes is contained in Appendix A. Appendix B is a tabular index of universities and their degree offerings, arranged by state, and Appendix C lists schools which teach at least three courses in linguistics, but did not qualify for inclusion in the main text. Appendix D is an index of uncommonly-taught languages, Appendix E is an index of staff, and Appendix F is an index of linguists in other departments.

Arrangement

The institutions are listed in alphabetical order and under each entry is given all or part of the following information:

- Name of department, committee, program, etc.; name of chairman or executive officer; degrees offered; degrees granted 1972-73; number of present majors.
- A brief essay describing the program and facilities.
- Course offerings or course areas.

- Courses offered in linguistics and/or linguistics and related disciplines. Realizing that exact course titles and content vary from school to school, we have placed courses under seventeen categories. Some linguists may disagree with our categories or our placement of specific courses, and we are open to suggestions for changes for the next edition. Categories and a sampling of courses placed under them are as follows: INTRODUCTORY: Introduction to linguistics, Descriptive linguistics, Nature of language; PHONOLOGY: Phonetics, Phonemics, Articulatory Phonetics, Acoustics, Audiology; THEORETICAL MODELS: Generative syntax, Structural linguistics, Discourse analysis, Case grammar, Prague school; SEMANTICS AND LOGIC: Generative semantics, Philosophy of language, Meaning, Semiology; SOCIOLINGUISTICS: Sociology of language, Ethnolinguistics, Anthropological linguistics, Language contact, Language variation, Language attitudes, Language and culture/society, Language and the law; DIALECTOLOGY: Linguistic geography, Areal linguistics, Vernacular Black English; PSYCHOLINGUIS-TICS: Child language acquisition, Speech perception, Verbal behavior, Language learning theory, Linguistics and reading, Communication processes, Language of the deaf; NEUROLINGUISTICS: Biology of language, Language pathology; Electro-myography; MATHEMATICAL AND COMPUTATIONAL LINGUISTICS: Machine language/communi-cation, Formal approaches to linguistics, Automatic language processing; HISTORICAL LINGUISTICS: Indo-European linguistics, Comparative linguistics, Philology, Etymology, History of x language; HISTORY OF LINGUISTICS: Development of linguistic science; LINGUISTICS AND LITERATURE: Stylistics, Poetics, Rhetoric, Metrics; LANGUAGE PEDAGOGY: Foreign/Second language learning, Contrastive analy-sis, Bilingualism, Language teaching methodology, Teaching English as a foreign/ second language; APPLIED LINGUISTICS: Language testing, translation; LANGUAGE AREAS: Linguistics, phonology, or structure of x language or language family; OTHER: Lexicography/Lexicology, Writing systems. The number following each category indicates the number of courses offered at least once in a two-year period.

- Courses in ancient languages (other than Greek and Latin) or modern foreign languages not commonly taught in the United States. These are listed in alphabetical order, and the level (graduate or undergraduate), as well as semesters or quarters taught, is indicated where known.

- Staff, with information on highest academic degree, institution in which earned, year in which earned, present rank and principal areas of interest or specialization.
- Financial support available.
- Academic calendar for 1974-1975, including application deadlines.
- Name and address of the office from which to obtain brochures, catalogues, etc., which give full descriptions of programs and degree requirements.

Language and Foreign Studies
Vadim Medish, Chairman
Degrees: MA. Degrees Granted 72-73: 9 MA. Majors: 24 g, 24 MA.

An evening program of study open to both full-time and part-time student. The program
is offered in cooperation with graduate evening courses in foreign area studies and
day-and-evening instruction in several foreign languages. (Chinese, Czech, French,
German, Greek, Hebrew, Hindi, Japanese, Latvian, Russian, Polish, Spanish, Thai).
    Graduate assistantships in foreign language teaching (including English to
Foreigners) are available to fulltime students.
    A three-course certificate program in Teaching English as a Foreign Language may
be taken as part of the M.A. in Linguistics. It is also available to other qualified
degree and non-degree students.
    Summer offerings include introductory courses in linguistics and a special Foreign
Language Teacher's Institute.
    Main thrust in applied research is on the development and use of time-compressed
multi-media language courses based on a systematic use of television.

COURSE OFFERINGS

Introductory, 1u 2g; Theoretical Models, 1u 3g; Sociolinguistics, 1u; Applied Ling.,
1g; Psycholinguistics, 2u; History of Linguistics 1g; Language Pedagogy 2g.

UNCOMMONLY-TAUGHT LANGUAGES

Chinese (2 yr.)	Greek (1 yr.)	Hindi (2 yr.)	Latvian (1 yr.)
Czech (1 yr.)	Hebrew (3 yr.)	Japanese (2 yr.)	Polish (1 yr.)
			Thai (2 yr.)

STAFF

Edward Burkart (Ph.D., U. of Penn., 1960; Assoc Prof) General and Formal Linguistics.
Gisela Huberman (Ph.D., George Washington U., 1971; Asst Prof) Applied Linguistics.
Grace Mancill (Ph.D., Georgetown U., 1960; Assoc Prof) Applied Linguistics.
Vadim Medish (Ph.D., The American U., 1963; Prof) Applied Linguistics.
Hugo J. Mueller (Ph.D., U. of Hamburg, Germany; Prof) History of Linguistics (Part Time).

Linguists in other Departments or Schools

Robert Fox (Ph.D., U. of Illinois, 1971; Assoc. Prof.) English for Foreigners,
    English Language Institute.
William J. Leap (Ph.D., Southern Methodist, 1970; Assist. Prof.) Anthropology.

Support Available

Graduate Assistanceships in Foreign languages (including English for Foreigners)-
$2500 per year plus remitted tuition.

Academic Calendar 1974-1975

Fall Semester: September 1; Spring Semester: January 1; Summer Session: May 14.

DESCRIPTIVE MATERIAL: Write: Office of Graduate Admissions, The American University,
    Mass. and Nebraska Aves., N. W., Washington, D. C. 20016.

English Department
John D. Waller, Chairman
Degrees: B.A., M.A.T. in Teaching English as a Second Language.

The BA and MAT programs are designed to provide certification both for teaching English
and English as a second language. Practice teaching is done in both areas. The program is intended as preparation for those planning to teach either in this country
where teaching English as a second language is needed or for those desiring to teach
abroad where both regular English classes and English as a second language are needed.

COURSE OFFERINGS

Introductory, 2; Theoretical Models, 1; Applied Ling. 1; Language Pedagogy 2.

STAFF

Luanne Bauer (MATESL, St. Michael's College; Instructor) Applied linguistics, Teach-
   ing English as a Second Language (1/2 time) (Communications Department).
Elaine Giddings (Ph.D., University of Michigan; Prof.) Phonetics (1/3 time) (Com-
   munications Department).
Edith Stone (Ph.D., University of Michigan; Prof.) Applied linguistics, Syntax,
   Historical Linguistics (1/2 time) (English Department).

Academic Calendar 1974-1975

Fall Quarter: Oct. 3 - Dec. 18; Winter Quarter: Jan. 7 - March 19; Spring Quarter:
March 28 - June 4; Summer Quarter: June 12 - Aug. 8.

DESCRIPTIVE MATERIAL: Write: Admissions Office, Andrews University, Berwin Springs,
   Michigan 49104.

UNIVERSITY OF ARIZONA   Tucson, Arizona 85721   Tel. (602) 884-3362

Committee on Linguistics
Paul R. Turner, Chairman
Degrees: MA, Ph.D. Degrees Granted 72-73: 3 MA. Majors: 27 g, 13 MA, 14 Ph.D.,
          24 Graduates in Residence.

The program in linguistics is offered under the auspices of the Graduate College and
through the cooperation of the departments represented on the interdepartmental Committee below. There is a set of core courses involving introductory linguistics, the
history of a language, and a linguistic seminar that all students must take. The
balance of a student's program consists of courses selected by him and approved by
his advisor.
    There is a strong emphasis on the practical and social relevance of the study of
language to the language problems of ethnic minority groups in the State of Arizona.
All majors study jointly in linguistics and one other related field. The training
is oriented toward developing the application of linguistic skills and knowledge to
the related areas of bilingualism, child development, speech, education, social work,
measurement and evaluation.

COURSE OFFERINGS

Introductory, 2; Phonology, 3; Theoretical Models, 4; Semantics & Logic, 3; Sociolinguistics, 3; Dialectology, 1; Field Methods, 1; Psycholinguistics, 5; Historical
Linguistics, 4; Language Pedagogy, 1. Language Areas: Old French, 2; German, 2;

COURSE OFFERINGS (continued)

Chinese, 2; Japanese, 5; Russian, 5; Spanish, 5; Romance Philology, 2; Gothic, 7; Slavic Philology, 1; Old Spanish, 1.

UNCOMMONLY-TAUGHT LANGUAGES

Akkadian (gr., 2 sem.)	Arabic (un., 2 sem.) Hebrew (un., 2 sem.)	Hindi (un., 2 sem.) Hopi (gr., 2 sem.)	Papago (gr., 1 sem.) Persian (un., 2 sem.)

STAFF

A. Delores Brown (Ph.D., Wisconsin, 1957; Prof) Spanish Grammar, Dialectology, Historical Linguistics.

Anoop C. Chandola (Ph.D., Chicago, 1963; Prof) Hindi Language and Literature, Sanskrit, Indo-European Linguistics.

Mary Jane Cook (Ph.D., University of Texas at Austin, 1961; Assoc Prof) Linguistics, Modern Grammar and Usage (English Linguistics), TESL.

Robert D. Hubbell (Ph.D., Kansas University, 1969; Asst Prof) Children's Language Acquisition, Language Disorders, Psycholinguistics.

Joan M. Martin (Ph.D., University of Michigan, 1970; Asst Prof) Historical Linguistics, Germanic Linguistics, Applied Linguistics in German.

Cecil A. Rogers, Jr. (Ph.D., Tulane, 1965; Assoc Prof) Psychology and Physiology of Verbal Learning and Memory; Computer Applications.

Paul R. Turner (Ph.D., Chicago, 1966; Prof) (Chairman) Descriptive Linguistics, Field Methods, Sociolinguistics.

Patricia Downer Van Metre (Ph.D., University of Arizona, 1972; Visiting Asst Prof) Language Acquisition, Bilingualism, Phonetics.

Nicholas Vontsolos (Ph.D., Ohio State University, 1974; Lecturer) Indo-European Comparative Linguistics, Comparative Slavic Linguistics, History of Russian Language.

Linguists in other Departments or Schools

Anthropology
  Keith H. Basso (Ph.D., Stanford, 1967; Assoc Prof) North American Indian Languages (especially Athapascan), Ethnographic Semantics, Sociolinguistics.
  Daniel S. Matson (M.A., San Luis Rey Seminary, 1944; Lecturer) Pima/Papago Language and Culture, Research in Mission/Contact History of Northwest Mexico (1/4 time).
  Norman Yoffee (Ph.D., Yale, 1973; Asst Prof) Mesopotamian Languages (Akkadian, Sumerian) and Culture, Near Eastern Archaeology.
English
  Tom J. Collins (M.A., University of Arizona, 1971; Lecturer) Testing English as a Second Language, Methods in the Teaching of ESL/EFL (1/3 time).
  William M. Christie, Jr. (Ph.D., Yale, 1973; Asst Prof) Stratificational Theory, Historical Linguistics, Indo-European.
  Charles E. Davis (Ph.D., University of Arizona, 1967; Assoc Prof) Applied Linguistics in Teacher Training.
  Frank Pialorsi (Ph.D., University of Arizona, Asst Prof) Applied Linguistics, Modern Grammar, Center for English as a Second Language.
Philosophy
  Robert M. Harnish (Ph.D., M.I.T., 1972; Asst Prof) Semantics, Mathematical Linguistics.
Oriental Studies Department
  Timothy Light (Ph.D., Cornell, 1974; Asst Prof) Chinese Language, General Linguistics, Linguistic Theory.
  Hamdi A. Qafisheh (Ph.D., University of Michigan, 1968; Assoc Prof) Arabic Language and Linguistics.
Department of Romance Languages
  Jack Emory Davis (Ph.D., Tulane, 1956; Prof) Dialectology of American (i.e., New World) Spanish.
  H. Reynolds Stone (Ph.D., University of North Carolina, 1965; Assoc. Prof) Comparative Romance Philology, History of the Old Spanish Language.

Support Available

The only support available is through the cooperating departments in the form of teaching assistantships.

Academic Calendar 1974-1975

Fall Semester: August 26; Spring Semester: January 15; Summer Session: June 2-July 3.

DESCRIPTIVE MATERIAL: Write: Admissions Office, Graduate College, University of Arizona, Tucson, Arizona 85721.

BALL STATE UNIVERSITY   Muncie, Indiana 47306   Tel. (317) 285-1138

Department of English, Language
  and Linguistics Committee
Dick A. Renner, Chairman
Degrees: MA. Degrees Granted 72-73: 17 Ph.D. Majors: 12 MA, 3 in residence.

At Ball State University a student may pursue graduate study in linguistics through two degree programs: M.A., Major in Linguistics and M.A., Major in English. Under each program he can select from three curricula: Major in Linguistics, Specialization in English Language, and Specialization in Teaching English as a Foreign Language. Twenty-eight to forty-five quarter hours, including thesis or research paper are required for the M.A., Major in Linguistics and twenty-four to forty-five quarter hours, including thesis, research paper, creative project, or two graduate papers are required for M.A., Major in English.
    There is a language laboratory and opportunity for observation of classes in English for Foreign students.

COURSE OFFERINGS

Introductory, 1; Phonology, 2; Theoretical Models, 3; Sociolinguistics, 1; Dialectology, 1; Field Methods, 1; Historical Linguistics, 2; Language Pedagogy, 2. Language Areas: Old English. Other: Applied English ling.

STAFF

Keith D. Cox (Ph.D., Michigan State U., 1965; Assoc Prof) History of the English
    Language, Introduction to Linguistics, Applied English linguistics (1/12 time).
Robert E. Evans (Ph.D., U. of Iowa, 1961; Prof) History of the English Language,
    Old English, Language and Culture (1/3 time).
Merle Fifield (Ph.D., U. of Illinois, 1960; Assoc Prof) History of the English
    Language, Old English (1/12 time).
Irma F. Gale (Ed.D., Ball State U., 1967; Assoc Prof) English syntax (1/12 time).
Charles L. Houck (Ph.D., U. of Iowa, 1969; Assoc Prof) English syntax, Intro-
    duction to Linguistics, Dialectology.
Bruce W. Hozeski (Ph.D., Michigan State U., 1969; Asst Prof) History of the English
    Language, Old English (1/12 time).
Robert J. Reddick (Ph.D., U. of Minnesota, 1974; Asst Prof) History of the English
    Language, Old English, Field Methods (2/3 time).
Janet Ross (Ph.D., U. of Iowa, 1960; Prof) TEFL.
Michael F. Stewart (Ph.D., U. of Michigan, 1971; Asst Prof) Theoretical syntax,
    semantics, and phonology; Logic and language.

Support Available

Graduate assistantships--$2800 for academic year. Would teach freshman composition.

4

BALL STATE UNIVERSITY   (Continued)

Academic Calendar 1974-1975

Fall Quarter: 10 Sep to 22 Nov; Winter Quarter: 3 Dec to 28 Feb; Spring Quarter:
11 Mar to 23 May; Summer Quarter: 9 Jun to 11 Jul; 15 Jul to 15 Aug. Deadline:
16 Sep.

<u>DESCRIPTIVE MATERIAL</u>: Write: Dr. Charles L. Houck, Dept. of English, Ball State
University, Muncie, Indiana 47306.

BARNARD COLLEGE   New York, New York 10027   Tel. (212) 280-5403/5417

Department of Linguistics
Joseph L. Malone, Chairman
Degrees: BA. Degrees Granted 72-73: 9 BA. Majors: 12 u.

Since the major program in linguistics of the Barnard Linguistics Department is fully
integrated with that of Columbia College, and there is a policy of open cross-
registration in all relevant courses and facilities, please see the listings of
Columbia University for details on variety of offerings and other resources.
  It will be sufficient to state here that the Barnard major in linguistics consists of a core of eight courses in linguistics and related subjects, and is
normally based on an area of specialization (e.g. a specific language; psycholinguistics; generative theory).

COURSE OFFERINGS

Introductory, 1; Theoretical Models, 2; Semantics & Logic, 1; Sociolinguistics, 3;
Historical Linguistics, 1. Language Areas: Anglo-Saxon, 1; History of English, 1; History
of French, 1.

UNCOMMONLY-TAUGHT LANGUAGES

Please see listings of Columbia University.

STAFF

Lars-Alvar Jacobson (Ph.D., University of Stockholm, 1970; Asst Prof) Psycho-
   linguistics, language acquisition, semantic theory.
Joseph L. Malone (Ph.D., University of California at Berkeley, 1967; Assoc Prof)
   Phonological theory, Semitic linguistics..
Also see listings of Columbia University.

Linguists in other Departments or Schools

Please see listings of Columbia University.

Support Available

N.Y. State Scholar Incentive Awards. N.Y. State Regents College Scholarships.
Loans & grant-and loan awards are available. Various scholarship funds and
graduate fellowships are available. Contact Committee on Financial Aid.

Academic Calendar 1974-1975

Fall Semester: September 5 - December 20, 1974; Spring Semester: January 20 -
May 9, 1975.

<u>DESCRIPTIVE MATERIAL</u>: Write: Admissions Office, Barnard College, Morningside
   Heights, New York, New York 10027.

BETHEL COLLEGE St. Paul, Minnesota 55112   Tel. (612) 641-6332

Department of Language Science
Donald N. Larson, Chairman
Degrees: BA. Majors: 11 g, 11 u.

The academic year 1974-1975 marks the beginning of the new Department of Language Science
at Bethel College. The department offers majors in Linguistics, Spanish, French and
German. Students majoring in one of the languages are required to minor in linguistics,
and those majoring in linguistics are required to minor in at least one language.

The unifying goal for courses in linguistics is stated as follows: to nurture members
of the community in such a way that they have new vistas of self-awareness as gained
through an understanding of language and are better able to cultivate their own potential
for communication. The unifying goal for courses in Spanish, French and German is as
follows: to provide experiences for living in a community as learners from people whose
cultural and linguistic background is different from their own and for involvement in
their symbol system, albeit on a temporary and superficial basis.

These emphases are therefore integral to the goals of general liberal arts education.

COURSE OFFERINGS

Sociolinguistics, 5; Psycholinguistics, 2.

UNCOMMONLY-TAUGHT LANGUAGES

<u>Non-Western Language</u>. The specific language to be taught varies with available resources.
The following languages have been taught or are on schedule for the future:

Amharic	Cebuano	New Guinea Pidgin	Thai
Cantonese	Eskimo	Tagalog	

STAFF

Edmund A. Anderson (M.A., USC; Instr) Sociolinguistics, second-language learning,
   German (1/3 time).
Donald N. Larson (Ph.D., Chicago, 1965; Prof) General linguistics, second-language
   learning, comparative syntax (full-time).

Linguists in other Departments or Schools

Thomas C. Correll (Ph.D., Minnesota, 1972; Prof) Anthropology, Anthropological
   linguistics, Eskimo (1/3 time).

Academic Calendar 1974-1975

Fall Semester: Sept. 5 - Dec. 18; Winter Quarter: Jan. 6 - Jan. 29; Spring Semester:
Feb. 4 - May 25.

DESCRIPTIVE MATERIAL: Write: James A. Bragg, Admissions Officer, Bethel College,
St. Paul, Minnesota 55112.

BOSTON COLLEGE Chestnut Hill, Massachusetts 02167   Tel. (617) 969-0100, x2570

Department of Slavic & Eastern Languages
M. J. Connolly, Chairman
Degrees: BA, MA. Degrees Granted 1972-73: 2 BA, 1 MA. Majors: 1 g, 1 MA, 5 u.

In addition to the areas expressed in its title, the Department of Slavic & Eastern Languages at Boston College also administers an undergraduate BA and a graduate MA program
in Linguistics. In both programs a heavy emphasis lies upon solid and thorough work
of a philological nature in both modern and ancient languages upon a framework of theo-

retical, historical, and semiological linguistic direction. Students must be prepared
to work on the linguistic description and history of natural languages, predominantly
Slavic, Classical, or Romance, or in the analysis of poetic texts.

The Department participates in the research activities of the Center for East Europe,
Russia and Asia (Directors: Prof Thomas Blakeley; Assoc. Director: Prof Peter S.H. Tang)
at Boston College. The CEERA numbers among its projects an interdisciplinary study in
semantics with concentration points on the theories of medieval scholasticism and early
twentieth-century East European ideas (Prague, Moscow, Vienna).

COURSE OFFERINGS

Introductory, 4; Phonology, 4; Theoretical Models, 2; Sociolinguistics, 3; Psycholinguistics, 1; Historical Linguistics, 1; Linguistics & Literature, 2; Language Pedagogy, 2.
Language Areas: Romance philology, Russian.

UNCOMMONLY-TAUGHT LANGUAGES

Clas. Armenian	Old French	Portuguese	Serbo-Croatian
Avestan	Bib. Hebrew	Provencal	Old Church Slavonic
Czech	Israeli Hebrew	Romanian	Old Spanish
Old & Mid.	Hittite	Sanskrit	Tamil
English	Old Persian	Old Russian	Runic Turkish

All above courses on upper division undergraduate/graduate level. All courses one semester (with possibility of additional tutorial continuation) except: Bib. Hebrew (2
sem), Portuguese (4 sem), Old Spanish (2 sem), Provencal (2 sem).

STAFF

Michael J. Connolly (Ph.D., Harvard, 1970; Asst Prof) Theoretical & comparative linguis-
tics, Indo-European morphophonemics, Liturgical poetics.
Yuri Glazov (Kand. filol. nauk, Akademija nauk SSSR, Institut vostokovedenija, 1962;
Senior Lecturer) Dravidian & Turkic linguistics, Semiotics of social systems, Mytho-
logy.
Lawrence G. Jones (Ph.D., Harvard, 1952; Prof) Slavic & English phonology, Poetics,
Slavic antiquities.

Linguists in other Departments or Schools

Raymond G. Biggar (Ph.D., Univ. of Wisconsin; Assoc Prof) History & structure of English,
Medieval philology.
Paul C. Doherty (Ph.D., Univ. of Missouri; Assoc Prof) Linguistics & literary criticism.
Sterling Dow (Ph.D., Harvard; Prof) Early Greek archaeology & inscriptions.
Guillermo L. Guitarte (Profesorado, Filosofia y letras, Buenos Aires; Prof) Hispanic
linguistics.
Robert F. Renehan (Ph.D., Harvard; Prof) Classical philology, etymology.
Maria Simonelli (Dottore in lettere e filosofia, Firenze; Libera docenza in filologia
romana, Roma; Prof) Romance philology.
Rebecca Valette (Ph.D., Univ. of Colorado; Prof) Applied linguistics, Language learning.

Support Available

Graduate assistantship; Graduate & undergraduate work/study; Tuition scholarship. Merit
applications directly to Department; Applications based on need to the Associate Dean,
Graduate School of Arts & Sciences; Undergraduate assistance through Student Financial
Aid Office.

Academic Calendar 1974-1975

Fall Semester: Sept. 3 to Dec. 21; Spring Semester: Jan. 9 to May 6.

DESCRIPTIVE MATERIAL: Write: Department of Slavic & Eastern Languages, Boston
College/Carney 235, Chestnut Hill, Massachusetts 02167.

Committee on Linguistics
Robert Saitz, Chairman
Degrees: No degrees in linguistics; undergraduate sub-concentration only.
Majors: 8u.

An undergraduate sub-concentration open to students with a major in some other department
(e.g., Modern Languages, Anthropology, English, etc.) or an independent major. Eight
course requirement, some of which may also serve to fulfill student's major requirements.
Choice from many university departments: English; Modern Languages; Anthropology, School
of Education, etc. Goal is to provide students a variety of experiences in different
branches of linguistics, as a complement to his major. Particular strengths at the university include an English as a second language program (Robert Saitz, director), and
a doctorate in psycholinguistics (Paula Menyuk and Bruce Fraser, directors).

COURSE OFFERINGS

Introductory, 1; Phonology, 1; Theoretical Models, 2; Semantics & Logic, 1; Sociolinguistics, 5; Psycholinguistics, 4; Historical Linguistics, 1; Linguistics & Literature, 1.
Language Areas: Romance Lgs., Lgs. of India, Russian, Spanish.

UNCOMMONLY-TAUGHT LANGUAGES

Chinese (4 sem.)   Japanese (4 sem.)   Sanskrit (4 sem.)   Tamil (4 sem.)
Hindi (4 sem.)

STAFF

Sooda Bhatt (Ph.D., Wisconsin) General Linguistics, Indian Languages.
Juan Cano (Ph.D., Munich, 1961) Spanish Language.
Eugene Green (Ph.D., Michigan; Assoc Prof) General Linguistics, Dialectology, Onomastics.
Celia Millward (Ph.D., Brown; Assoc Prof) History of the English Language, Onomastics,
   General Linguistics.
Steven Molinsky (Ph.D., Asst Prof) Russian Language, second language teaching.
Robert Saitz (Ph.D., Wisconsin, 1955) Modern English Grammar, Kinesics, English as a
   Second Language.

Linguists in other Departments or Schools

Bruce Fraser, Paula Menyuk in Psycholinguistics have their own program.

Support Available

Some scholarships, prizes and awards and loans are available. Apply to B.U. Office of
Financial Aid.

Academic Calendar 1974-1975

Fall Semester: 9/3 - 12/20; Spring Semester: 1/13 - 5/9.

DESCRIPTIVE MATERIAL: Write: Admissions, Boston University, 121 Bay State Road, Boston,
   Massachusetts 02215.

BRANDEIS UNIVERSITY Waltham, Massachusetts 02154 Tel. (617) 647-2631

Linguistics Program
Ray Jackendoff, Chairman
Degrees: BA in English and Linguistics; Ph.D. in English and Linguistics. Degrees
     Granted 1972-73: 1 BA, 1 Ph.D. Majors: 2 g, 2 Ph.D.

Brandeis offers an undergraduate program concentrating on transformational grammar. The
graduate program is marginal and is not being actively pursued at present. We offer
a couple of interdisciplinary courses such as Linguistics and Literature, and Linguistics
and Music.

COURSE OFFERINGS

Introductory, 1; Phonology, 1; Theoretical Models, 1; Semantics § Logic, 2; Sociolinguistics, 3; Psycholinguistics, 1; Historical Linguistics, 1; Linguistics § Literature, 1.
Language Areas: Unfamiliar Lg. to be Chosen. Other: Ling. § Music Theory.

UNCOMMONLY-TAUGHT LANGUAGES

Akkadian   Hebrew   Swahili   Ugaritic   Yiddish

STAFF

Ray S. Jackendoff (Ph.D., MIT, 1969; Assoc Prof) Syntactic Theory, semantics, linguistics
     and music.
Joan M. Maling (Ph.D., MIT, 1973; Asst Prof) Syntactic Theory, Old English, prosody.

Linguists in other Departments or Schools

Judith Irvine (Ph.D., Univ. of Pennsylvania, 1971) Anthropological linguistics.
James Lackner (Ph.D., MIT, 1969) Psycholinguistics.

Support Available

Some scholarships and loans available.

Academic Calendar 1974-1975

Fall Semester: September-January; Spring Semester: February-May.

DESCRIPTIVE MATERIAL: Write: Admissions Office, Brandeis University, Waltham, Massachu-
     setts 02154.

BRIGHAM YOUNG UNIVERSITY Provo, Utah 84602 Tel. (801) 374-1211, ext. 2334

Linguistics Department
Soren F. Cox, Chairman
Degrees: MA. Degrees Granted 1972-73: 6 MA. Majors: 18g, 18 MA.

The program is a graduate program only, offering an MA degree in either theoretical or
applied linguistics and an MA in Teaching English as a Second Language. Also included
is a program in computational linguistics. The latter is closely tied to the Automatic
Language Processing project, which is administered by the University Language Research
Center. This project emphasizes junction grammar, a theory of grammar developed by Professor Eldon Lytle. The program includes a core of courses emphasizing junction grammar,
socio-linguistics, and language learning.
     Facilities include the Language Research Center and the Automatic Language Processing
project (employing from 20-25 part-time student assistants).

COURSE OFFERINGS

Introductory, 4; Phonology, 4; Theoretical Models, 4; Semantics & Logic, 1; Sociolinguistics, 1; Psycholinguistics, 1; Language Pedagogy, 2.   Language Areas: Romance 1, French 1, Gothic & Comp. Gmc. 1, German 1, Spanish 1.   Other: Problems in Translation.

UNCOMMONLY-TAUGHT LANGUAGES

Akkadian	Coptic	Syriac	Turkish
Arabic	Egyptian	Thai	Ugaritic
Aramaic	Navajo		

STAFF

Rey L. Baird (Ph.D., Indiana, 1974; Asst Prof) Polynesian languages, syntax, junction grammar.

Robert W. Blair (Ph.D., Indiana, 1964; Prof) Educational linguistics, American Indian languages, language learning.

Soren F. Cox (Ph.D., Minnesota, 1964; Prof) English Language, TESL.

Maryruth Bracy Farnsworth (MA, UCLA, 1968; Instructor) TESL, Historical linguistics, phonology.

Daryl K. Gibb (MA, BYU, 1970; Instructor) Computational linguistics, automatic language processing, junction grammar.

Eldon G. Lytle (Ph.D., Illinois, Champaign-Urbana, 1971; Assoc Prof) Theoretical lingustics, computational linguistics, junction grammar.

Harold S. Madsen (Ph.D., Colorado, 1965; Assoc Prof) English language, TESL, testing.

Linguists in other Departments and Schools

J. Halvor Clegg (Ph.D., Texas, 1969; Asst Prof of Spanish) Spanish language, Romance philology.

Marvin H. Folsom (Ph.D., Cornell, 1961; Prof of German) German language, historical-comparative linguistics.

Donald K. Jarvis (Ph.D., Ohio State, 1970; Assoc Prof of Russian) Methodology of foreign language teaching, junction grammar, computational linguistics.

Melvin J. Luthy (Ph.D., Indiana, 1967; Asst Prof of English) Transformational grammar, theoretical linguistics.

Support Available

We have available from 1-3 scholarships for tuition ($960 per year). Each year there are also several research assistantships available with the Automatic Language Processing project, stipend depending upon the qualifications of the applicant and the task to be performed.

Academic Calendar 1974-1975

Fall Semester: September 3 - December 20; Winter Semester: January 6 - April 17; Spring Term: April 28 - June 19; Summer Term: June 23 - August 14. Deadline: Winter Semester November 15; Spring Term March 10; Summer Term: May 15.

DESCRIPTIVE MATERIAL: Write: Veston E. Thomas, Admissions Office, A-153 ASB, Brigham Young University, Provo, Utah 84602.

Department of Linguistics
W. Nelson Francis, Chairman
Degrees: BA, MA, Ph.D. Degrees Granted 1972-73: 5 BA, 6 MA, 4 Ph.D. Majors:
     43 g, 18 MA, 25 Ph.D., 24 Graduate in Residence, 10 u.

The department offers a full undergraduate concentration in linguistics, as well as
joint concentrations with such fields as psychology, anthropology, and mathematics.
The graduate program leads to the MA and Ph.D. in general and theoretical linguistics,
with specialties either in language areas (e.g. English, Germanic, Slavic, Indo-
European) or in special fields (e.g. generative syntax and semantics, psycholinguistics, computational and mathematical linguistics). A new series of courses in
physiologic and acoustic phonetics is being instituted in 1974-75. The department
works closely with members of the departments of anthropology, psychology, applied
mathematics, classics, and the various modern languages, and interdepartmental
programs, both undergraduate and graduate are encouraged. Courses within the department deal with such areas of primary interest as child language acquisition and
psycholinguistics, as well as the standard areas of general linguistics. It is hoped
to add sociolinguistics in the near future.
     It is emphasized that the work of the department is largely theoretical, and that
little or no work is offered in applied linguistics and language pedagogy or TESL.

COURSE OFFERINGS

Introductory, 3; Phonology, 6; Theoretical Models, 8; Semantics & Logic, 2; Dialectology, 1; Psycholinguistics, 4; Math. & Comp. Linguistics, 2; Historical Linguistics,
2; History of Linguistics, 1. Language Areas: Skt., 2.

UNCOMMONLY-TAUGHT LANGUAGES

Chinese (Mandarin) (un., 8 sem.; gr. & un., 6 sem.)	Czech (gr., 2 sem.)	Portuguese (un., 5 sem.)	Serbo-Croatian (gr. & un., 4 sems.)

Older Languages:

Akkadian (un. & gr., 4 sem.)	Old English (gr., 2 sem.)	Bib. & Patristic Greek (gr. & un., 1 sem.)	Old Icelandic (gr., 2 sem.)
Egyptian (un., 4 sem.; gr., 3 sem.)	Mid. High German (gr. & un., 2 sem.)	Bib. & Post-Bib. Hebrew (un., 4 sem.)	Sanskrit (gr. & un., 2 sem.)

Modern Hebrew, Japanese, Turkish, and Swahili are occasionally taught on an independent study basis.

STAFF

Naomi S. Baron (Ph.D., Stanford, 1972; Asst Prof) Historical English Syntax, Lan-
     guage change, Child language acquisition.
Richard C. Beck (Ph.D., Chicago, 1972; Asst Prof) Sanskrit, Indo-European, Semantics.
Sheila E. Blumstein (Ph.D., Harvard, 1970; Asst Prof) Psycholinguistics, Phonology.
Marie C. Chan (Ph.D., Univ. of Calif. Berkeley, 1973; Asst Prof) Chinese Language
     and Literature.
W. Nelson Francis (Ph.D., Univ. of Penna., 1937; Prof and Chairman) English
     linguistics, Dialectology, Introduction to Linguistics.
David Lattimore (A.B., Harvard, 1952; Assoc Prof) Chinese Language and Literature.
Philip Lieberman (Ph.D., M.I.T., 1966; Prof) Physiologic and Acoustic Phonetics,
     Origin and Evolution of Language, Primate Communication.
Robert H. Meskill (Ph.D., Texas, 1964; Prof) Phonology, Generative Grammar, Turkish.
David M. Perlmutter (Ph.D., M.I.T., 1968; Visiting Lecturer) Generative Grammar
     (1/4 time).
John R. Ross (Ph.D., M.I.T., 1967; Visiting Lecturer) Generative Syntax and
     Semantics (1/4 time).
Gerald M. Rubin (M.A., Brown, 1971; Instructor) Mathematical and Computational
     Linguistics.
James J. Wrenn (Ph.D., Yale, 1964; Prof) Chinese Language, Sinology.

Linguists in other Departments and Schools

William Beeman (Ph.D., Chicago, 1973; Asst Prof) Anthropological linguistics.
Jonathan B. Conant (Ph.D., Yale, 1969; Asst Prof) Old Icelandic, Germanic philology.
William Crossgrove (Ph.D., Texas, 1962; Assoc Prof) Old and Middle High German,
  Germanic philology.
Antonín Dóstal (Ph.D., Charles Univ., Prague, 1931; Sc.D., Charles Univ., 1957;
  Prof) Old Church Slavonic, Czech, Slavic linguistics.
Henry Kučera (Ph.D., Harvard, 1952; Prof) Slavic Linguistics, Computational lin-
  guistics, Linguistic theory.
Robert Mathiesen (Ph.D., Columbia, 1971; Asst Prof) Slavic linguistics and philology,
  History of linguistics.
Geoffrey Russom (Ph.D., SUNY Stony Brook, 1973; Asst Prof) Old English, Structure
  and history of English.
Walter J. Schnerr (Ph.D., Univ. of Penna., 1959; Prof) Romance philology.
William F. Wyatt (Ph.D., Harvard, 1962; Prof) Latin and Greek linguistics, Indo-
  European.

Support Available

Teaching Assistantships (usually given to 2nd and 3rd year students); university
fellowships, scholarships, and loans. Deadline for applications, 10 January.
G.R.E. useful but not required.

Academic Calendar 1974-1975

Fall Semester: 9 Sept. 1974 - 22 January 1975; Spring Semester: 29 January -
26 May 1975.

DESCRIPTIVE MATERIAL: Write: Chairman, Department of Linguistics, Box E, Brown
                      University, Providence, R.I. 02912.

UNIVERSITY OF CALIFORNIA, BERKELEY Berkeley, California 94720   Tel. (415) 642-2757

Department of Linguistics
Karl E. Zimmer, Chairman
Degrees: BA, MA, Ph.D., Cand. Phil. Degrees Granted 1972-73: 32 BA, 13 MA, 10
  Ph.D., 9 Cand. Phil. Majors: 68 g, 12 MA, 54 Ph.D. (course work only:
  2), 74 u.

The undergraduate major program offers a thorough grounding in general linguistics
as well as rich opportunities for specialization in a broad variety of subfields.
  The graduate program, in addition to the usual basic courses, is highly adaptable
to a wide range of needs and interests. The department has particular strength in
semantics, experimental phonetics and phonology, American Indian linguistics, Asian
linguistics, Indo-European linguistics, Romance linguistics, and the structure of
English. It is able to combine its own resources with those of other departments
to provide well-rounded interdisciplinary programs in psycholinguistics, anthropological linguistics, and sociolinguistics.
  Facilities include the Survey of California and Other Indian Languages (with
opportunities for the support of field work along with extensive library and manu-
script holdings in American Indian languages), the Phonology Laboratory, the Language
and Pragmatics Project, the Contrastive Semantics Project, and the Project on
Linguistic Analysis. The department also maintains close relationships with other
research organizations on campus such as the Language Behavior Research Laboratory,
the Institute of Human Learning, and the Center for South and Southeast Asian
Studies.

COURSE OFFERINGS

Linguistics Department: Introductory, 2; Phonology, 6; Theoretical Models, 7;
Semantics & Logic, 1; Sociolinguistics, 2; Field Methods, 2; Psycholinguistics, 2;
Historical Linguistics, 5; History of Linguistics, 1; Linguistics & Literature, 2.
Language Areas: Gmc. 1, Romance 3, Latin 1, Greek 1, SE Asia 1, Tibeto-Burma 1,
Chinese 1.
Other Departments: Introductory, 3; Theoretical Models, 1; Semantics & Logic, 5;
Sociolinguistics, 9; Dialectology, 1; Psycholinguistics, 5; Language Pedagogy, 3.
Language Areas: Gmc. 4, Romance 5, Latin 2, Greek 1, Chinese 6, French 4, German 5,
Italian 3, Syriac 1, Iranian 1, Arabic 4, Turkic 1, Hebrew 1, Oriental 1, Japanese
2, Sino-Tibetan 1, Mongolian 1, Malayo-Polynesian 1, Comp. Altaic 1, Portuguese 1,
Spanish 7, Scandinavian 2, Swedish 1, Norwegian 1, Comp. Slavic 2, Russian 1, Finno-
Ugric 1, Hindi-Urdu 1, Nepal 1, India 6.

UNCOMMONLY-TAUGHT LANGUAGES

Akkadian (u6, g6)	Danish (u4, g4)	Hittite (u3, g3)	Portuguese (u4, g4)
Arabic (u9, g9)	Dutch (elementary,	Hungarian (u6, g6)	Provençal, Old (g2)
Arabic dialectol-	intermediate,	Icelandic, Old	Russian (u9, g9)
ogy (g3)	intensive -	(g2)	Sanskrit (u3, g5)
Bulgarian (u3, g3)	u5, g5)	Iranian, Old (u3,	Saxon, Old (g1)
Chinese, Canton-	English, Old (g1)	g3)	Serbo-Croatian
ese (u3, g3)	Egyptian (u6, g6)	Japanese (u6, g6)	(u3, g3)
Chinese, Class.	German, Old High	Korean (u6, g6)	Sumerian (u6, g6)
(u2, g2)	(g1)	Mongolian (u6, g6)	Swedish (u6, g6)
Chinese, Mandarin	Gothic (g1)	Norwegian (u6, g6)	Tamil (u3, g3)
(u9, g9)	Hebrew (u12, g12)	Persian (u6, g6)	Tibetan (u6, g6)
Coptic (u3, g3)	Hindi-Urdu (u9,	Polish (u3, g3)	Turkish (u9, g12)
Czech (ue, g3)	g9)		

STAFF

Madison S. Beeler (Ph.D., Harvard, 1936; Prof) Indo-European, Languages of ancient
   Italy, California Indian languages.
Wallace L. Chafe (Ph.D., Yale, 1958; Prof) American Indian languages (esp. Iroquoian,
   Caddoan, Siouan), Psychosemantics.
Charles J. Fillmore (Ph.D., Univ. of Michigan, 1962; Prof) Semantics, Lexicology,
   Pragmatics.
Mary R. Haas (Ph.D., Yale, 1935; Prof) American Indian languages (esp. Muskogean,
   Algonkian, Hokan, Wakashan), Southeast Asian languages (esp. Thai, Burmese),
   Comparative and historical linguistics.
George P. Lakoff (Ph.D., Indiana Univ., 1966; Prof) Syntax, Semantics, Pragmatics
   (1/2 time).
Robin T. Lakoff (Ph.D., Harvard, 1967; Assoc Prof) Semantics, Pragmatics, Syntax
   (1/2 time).
Yakov Malkiel (Ph.D., Friedrich-Wilhelm Univ., Berlin, 1938; L.H.D., Univ. of
   Chicago, 1969; Prof) Romance linguistics, Comparative and historical linguistics,
   Etymology.
James A. Matisoff (Ph.D., Univ. of California, Berkeley, 1967; Prof) Southeast
   Asian languages (Tibeto-Burman, Tai, Austronesian), Chinese, Japanese.
John J. Ohala (Ph.D., Univ. of California, Los Angeles, 1969; Assoc Prof) Ex-
   perimental phonology and phonetics, Historical phonology.
Jesse O. Sawyer (Ph.D., Univ. of California, Berkeley, 1959; Senior Lecturer)
   Phonetics, Morphology, Applied Linguistics (2/3 time).
William S-Y. Wang (Ph.D., Univ. of Michigan, 1960; Prof) Language in a biological
   context, Phonetics and phonology, Language change.
Karl E. Zimmer (Ph.D., Columbia University, 1963; Assoc Prof) Turkish, Word forma-
   tion, History of linguistics.

Linguists in other Departments and Schools

Hauro Aoki (Oriental Languages).
Brent Berlin (Anthropology).
Ariel Bloch (Near Eastern Studies).
Julian Boyd (English).
Denzl Carr (Oriental Languages).
Stephen Chan (Project on Linguistic Analysis).
Kun Chang (Oriental Languages).
Y. R. Chao (Oriental Languages).
Seymour Chatman (Rhetoric).
Jerry Craddock (Spanish).
Susan Ervin-Tripp (Rhetoric).
Robert Goldman (South & Southeast Asian Studies).
Paul Grice (Philosophy).
Glen Grosjean (Language Laboratory).
John Gumperz (Anthropology).
Paul Kay (Anthropology).
June Rumery McKay (English for Foreign Students).
Johanna Nichols (Slavic Languages).
Herbert Penzl (German).
Bruce Pray (Near Eastern Studies).
Martin Schwartz (Near Eastern Studies).
John Searle (Philosophy).
Alan Shaterian (Scandinavian).
Dan Slobin (Psychology).
J. D. Staal (South & Southeast Asian Studies).
Barend van Nooten (South & Southeast Asian Studies).
F. J. Whitfield (Slavic).

Support Available

The Department of Linguistics has a limited number of Teaching Assistantships which are normally reserved for graduate students who have been in the department for at least a year. The new graduate student should apply for a fellowship or make his own arrangements for financial support. Competition for fellowships is usually keen. Part-time employment can be investigated through the Placement Center, University of California, Berkeley, Ca. 94720. Inquiries concerning loans should be addressed to the Dean of Students, University of California, Berkeley 94720.

Fellowships and graduate scholarships offered on the Berkeley campus range from about $300 to $3,600 for the academic year, the majority carrying stipends in the range of $2,000 to $2,400; some are restricted to beginning graduate students, others to advanced graduate students; some to specific fields of study, others open to all students by competition. Detailed information on awards available each year is given in the bulletin Fellowships and Graduate Scholarships issued early in the Fall.

Academic Calendar 1974-1975

Fall Quarter: September 24 - December 14, 1974; Winter Quarter: January 2 - March 22, 1975; Spring Quarter: March 27 - June 14, 1975; Summer Quarter: June 19 - August 14, 1975.

DESCRIPTIVE MATERIAL: Write: Graduate Admissions Office (California Hall), Office of Admissions (undergraduates) (Sproul Hall), University of California, Berkeley, California 94720. For catalog: Registrar's Office, Sproul Hall ($1.50 mailed), University of California, Berkeley 94720.

Committee on Linguistics
Wayne Harsh, Chairman
Degrees: BA, MA. Majors: 14 g, 14 MA, 13 Graduate in Residence, 23 u.

The linguistics program at Davis stresses applied linguistics more strongly than
theoretical linguistics, although theoretical courses are part of the required
program. Following the trend of present-day language study, much emphasis is
placed on theory and methods of transformational grammar. However, historical
linguistics and other approaches, such as structural linguistics, are a required
part of both the undergraduate and graduate programs. Comparative and contrastive
language courses are also offered as a regular part of the curriculum. Majors in
Linguistics are urged to select courses from the related and cooperating departments and also to develop individual majors in such areas as the teaching of English
as a Second Language. As one of its innovations in the effort to improve the program, the Linguistics Committee regularly cooperates in the tutorial program for
campus students enrolled in courses in English for Foreign Students. As part of
the developing program in linguistics at Davis, other innovations, both in specific
courses and in individual study arrangements, are encouraged.

COURSE OFFERINGS

Introductory, 2; Phonology, 2; Theoretical Models, 4; Semantics & Logic, 1;
Sociolinguistics, 1; Psycholinguistics, 3; Historical Linguistics, 4; Linguistics
& Literature, 2; Language Pedagogy, 3. Language Areas: Romance Ling., German,
E. Asian lang., French.

UNCOMMONLY-TAUGHT LANGUAGES

Chinese - Cantonese (6u qtr)	Chinese - Mandarin (6u qtr)	Japanese (7u qtr)	Swedish (3u qtr)
Old English	Gothic	Old High German	Old Church Slavic
Middle English	Old Saxon	Mid. High German	Old Provençal

STAFF

Ronald A. Arbini (Ph.D.) Philosophy of language.
Jarvis R. Bastian (Ph.D.) Psycholinguistics.
Martin A. Baumhoff (Ph.D.) Anthropological linguistics.
Wilbur A. Benware (Ph.D.) Germanic linguistics, history of linguistics.
Thomas P. Campbell (Ph.D.) English linguistics.
Marianne Cooley (Ph.D.) English linguistics.
Linnea C. Ehri (Ph.D.) Developmental linguistics.
Wayne C. Harsh (Ph.D.) English linguistics.
Larry N. Hillman (Ph.D.) French linguistics.
Burt Liebert (Ph.D.) Bilingualism, applied linguistics.
Wolfgang W. Moelleken (Ph.D.) German linguistics.
Jerry A. Moles (Ph.D.) Language and culture.
Richard Ogle (MA) Syntax, History of linguistics.
David L. Olmsted (Ph.D.) American Indian languages, field methods.
Lenora Timm (Ph.D.) Sociolinguistics.
Carol Wall (Ph.D.) Child language, anthropological linguistics.
Benjamin Wallacker (Ph.D.) Oriental languages.

Support Available

University Graduate Fellowships, Jan. 15 deadline. Undergraduate Scholarships,
Jan. 15 deadline.

Academic Calendar 1974-1975

Fall Quarter: Sept. 30 - Dec. 21, 1974; Winter Quarter: Jan. 2 - March 22, 1975;
Spring Quarter: Mar. 27 - June 14, 1975.

DESCRIPTIVE MATERIAL: Write: Registrar's Office, U. C. Davis, Davis, California 95616.

Program in Linguistics
Richard Barrutia, Chairman
Degrees: BA in Linguistics. Degrees Granted 1972-73: 18. Majors: 48.

<u>COURSE OFFERINGS</u>

Introductory, 1; Phonology, 3; Theoretical Models, 1; Sociolinguistics, 1; Dialectology, 1;
Psycholinguistics, 4; Historical Linguistics, 1.

<u>UNCOMMONLY TAUGHT LANGUAGES</u>

Arabic	Chinese	Hebrew	Japanese
Portuguese			

<u>STAFF</u>

Richard Barrutia (Ph.D., University of Texas at Austin, 1964; Prof) Applied Linguistics,
    Spanish.
Peter Culicover (Ph.D., MIT, 1969; Asst Prof) Syntactic Analysis.
Mary Ritchie Key (Ph.D., University of Texas at Austin, 1963; Assoc Prof) Paralanguage &
    Kinesics, Non-verbal communication.
Tracy Terrell (Ph.D., University of Texas at Austin, 1969; Asst Prof) Spanish dialectology.
Bernard Tranell (Ph.D., University of California, San Diego, 1970; Asst Prof) Syntax,
    French.
Wilfreid Voge (Ph.D., Berkeley, 1975; Asst Prof) Historical German.

<u>Linguists in other Departments or Schools</u>

William Watt (Assoc Prof) Semantics
Kenneth Wexler (Asst Prof) Psycholinguistics

<u>DESCRIPTIVE MATERIAL</u>: Write: Office of Admissions, University of California, Irvine,
                                    Irvine, California 92664.

UNIVERSITY OF CALIFORNIA, LOS ANGELES Los Angeles, California 90024
                                                    Tel. (213) 825-0634

Department of Linguistics
Victoria A. Fromkin, Chairman
Degrees: BA, MA, Ph.D. Degrees Granted 1972-73: 5 BA, 12 MA, 12 Ph.D. Majors:
119g. In Residence: 92g, 119u.

The Department of Linguistics administers programs leading to the BA, MA, and Ph.D. degrees in Linguistics, the BA degree in Linguistics and English, Linguistics and French,
Linguistics and Italian, Linguistics and Oriental Languages, Linguistics and Philosophy,
Linguistics and Psychology, and the BA in African Languages and Literature. It also
offers a wide range of languages of Africa and certain languages of South Asia, and Central, North, and South America.
    The graduate program includes courses in linguistic theory (phonology and syntax),
historical linguistics, sociolinguistics, child language acquisition, experimental phonetics, field methods, neurolinguistics, and linguistic structures of a wide area of languages and language families.

<u>COURSE OFFERINGS</u>

Introductory, 1g 2u; Phonology, 6g 2u; Theoretical Models, 3g 2u; Semantics & Logic, 1g;
Sociolinguistics, 1g; Dialectology, 1g 1u; Field Methods, 2g; Psycholinguistics, 2g 1u;
Neurolinguistics, 1g; Math. & Comp. Linguistics, 1u; Historical Linguistics, 1g 2u;

History of Linguistics, 1u; Language Pedagogy, 1u. Language Areas: Chinese, Chaddic, African Lgs., Bantu, Japanese, Mayan.

UNCOMMONLY-TAUGHT LANGUAGES

Bambara (u6)	Hindi (u3)	Quechua (u3)	Xhosa (u3)
Hausa (u9)	Navajo (u3)	Swahili (u9)	Yoruba (u6)
		Thai (u3)	Zulu (u6)

STAFF

Raimo Anttila (Ph.D.; Assoc Prof) Historical, Indo-European, Finno-Ugric.
George Bedell (Ph.D.; Asst Prof) Syntax, Phonology, Semantics.
William Bright (Ph.D.; Prof) Anthropological, Socio, Ethnolinguistics.
Karen Courtenay (Ph.D.; Asst Prof) Yoruba, Bambara.
Joseph Emonds (Ph.D., Asst Prof) Syntax, French.
Victoria Fromkin (Ph.D.; Prof) Phonetics, Phonology, Neuro-Psycholinguistics.
Talmy Givón (Ph.D.; Asst Prof) Bantu, Semantics, Historical Syntax.
Thomas Hinnebusch (Ph.D.; Asst Prof) Swahili, African Linguistics.
Peter Ladefoged (Ph.D.; Prof) Phonetics, Psycho-linguistics, Experimental Linguistics.
Alosi Moloi (Ph.D.; Lect) African Literature, Southern Bantu.
Breyne Moskowitz (Ph.D.; Asst Prof) Child Language, Phonetics, Phonology.
Paul Schachter (Ph.D.; Prof) Syntax, Phonology, African Linguistics.
Robert Stockwell (Ph.D.; Prof) Syntax, English Structure, History of English.
Sandra Thompson (Ph.D.; Asst Prof) Syntax, Semantics, Chinese Linguistics.
Theo Vennemann (Ph.D.; Prof) Phonology, Historical, Germanic.
Benji Wald (Ph.D.; Asst Prof) Sociolinguistics, Dialectology, Bantu.
William Welmers (Ph.D.; Prof) African, Historical.

Linguists in other Departments or Schools

Christiane A.M. Baltaxe (Ph.D.; Asst Prof).
Henrik Birnbaum (Ph.D.; Prof) Slavic Languages.
J. Donald Bowen (Ph.D.; Prof) English.
Georgio Buccalleti (Ph.D.; Assoc Prof) Ancient Near East.
Russell N. Campbell (Ph.D.; Prof) English.
Edward C. Carterette (Ph.D.; Prof) Psychology.
Kenneth G. Chapman (Ph.D.; Prof) Scandinavian Languages.
Keith S. Donnellan (Ph.D.; Prof) Philosophy.
Christopher Ehret (Ph.D.; Assoc Prof) History.
Michael S. Flier (Ph.D.; Assoc Prof) History.
Sandra J. Garcia (Ph.D.; Asst Prof) English.
Evelyn R. Hatch (Ph.D.; Asst Prof) English.
Harry Hoijer (Ph.D.; Emeritus Prof) Anthropology.
Robert S. Kirsner (Ph.D.; Asst Prof) Dutch, Flemish, and Afrikaans.
Wolf Leslau (Docteur-es-Lettres; Prof) Hebrew and Semitic Linguistics.
Bengt Lofstedt (Ph.D.; Prof) Medieval Latin.
Donald G. MacKay (Ph.D.; Assoc Prof) Psychology.
Marlys McClaran (Ph.D.; Asst Prof) Anthropology.
Lois McIntosh (Ph.D.; Prof) English.
C.P. Otero (Ph.D.; Prof) Spanish and Romance Linguistics.
Thomas G. Penchoen (Ph.D.; Asst Prof) Near Eastern Languages.
Clifford H. Prator (Ph.D.; Prof) English.
Jean Puhvel (Ph.D.; Prof) Indo-European Studies.
Earl Rand (Ph.D.; Assoc Prof) English.
Kelyn H. Roberts (Ph.D.; Asst Prof) Psychology.
Emanuel A. Schegloff (Ph.D.; Asst Prof) Sociology.
Margaret E. Shaklee (MA; Acting Asst Prof) English.
Michael Shapiro (Ph.D.; Assoc Prof) Slavic Languages.
Donald Stilo (Ph.D.; Assoc Prof) Persian.
Andreas Tietze (Ph.D.; Prof) Turkish.
Alan H. Timberlake (Ph.D.; Asst Prof) Slavic Languages.
Terence H. Wilbur (Ph.D.; Assoc Prof) German.
Robert Wilson (Ph.D.; Adjunct Assoc Prof) English.
Dean S. Worth (Ph.D.; Prof) Slavic Languages.

Support Available

Student support varies from year to year. The following outlines the principle sources: Chancellor's Intern Fellowships (2 yrs $2,400. & 2 yrs TA); Regents Graduate Intern Fellowships (similar to above); Doctoral and Masters Advancement Fellowships ($2000 2200/yr, & fees); Woodrow Wilson Dissertation Fellowships ($225./mo); Teaching Assistantships (normally available only to advanced students in residence).

Academic Calendar 1974-1975

Fall Semester: September 23 - December 13; Winter Quarter: January 2 - March 21; Spring Semester: March 26 - June 13; Summer Session: June 24 - Aug 2/Aug. 5 -Sept 13 (1974) 1975?. Deadline: December 31.

DESCRIPTIVE MATERIAL: Write: Department of Linguistics, UCLA, Los Angeles, California 90024.

UNIVERSITY OF CALIFORNIA, RIVERSIDE   Riverside, California 92502

Tel. (714) 787-3420

Committee on Linguistics
Steven B. Smith, Chairman
Degrees: AB. Degrees Granted 1972-73: 11 AB. In Residence: 21u.

The undergraduate progam is administered by the interdisciplinary Committee on Linguistics and provides a full range of core courses, with an emphasis on theoretical linguistics. The majority of upper division related courses are offered by committee members in participating departments (e.g., Anthropology, Spanish, Psychology), while core courses are taught by a faculty member in Linguistics. A rigorous honors program is intended to prepare students for graduate work in theoretical linguistics. There is no graduate program in linguistics at UCR. The major in linguistics leading to the A.B. degree is flexible; related courses (beyond the core) are chosen from various departments according to the student's interests and/or future plans (psycholinguistics, graduate school, speech therapy, etc.).
   Available facilities include the California School for the Deaf and the Bilingual/Bicultural Program for Mexican Americans administered by the UCR Department of Education.

Staff

Sylvia Broadbent (Ph.D., UC Berkeley, 1960; Prof) Anthropological linguistics, Southern Sierra Miwok.
Henry Decker (Ph.D., Univ. of Michigan, 1955; Assoc Prof) Theory of syntax, applied linguistics, computer-aided instruction.
David Harrah (Ph.D., Yale, 1954; Prof) Logic of natural language, text grammars.
Peter Jorgensen (Ph.D., Harvard, 1971; Assistant Prof) Germanic philology, German and Austrian dialectology, Swedish.
Terrence Keeney (Ph.D., Univ. of Minnesota, 1968; Assistant Prof) Child language acquisition, psycholinguistics, language development.
David Dronenfeld (Ph.D., Stanford, 1970; Assist Prof) Anthropological linguistics, kinship terminology.
Jules F. Levin (Ph.D., UCLA, 1971; Assistant Prof) Balto/Slavic linguistics, historical linguistics, phonology.
William Megenney (Ph.D., Univ. of New Mexico, 1969; Asst Prof) Latin American dialectology, pidgin and creole languages, Spanish and Portuguese linguistics.
Harry Singer (Ph.D., UC Berkeley, 1960; Prof) Education and language disorders, theoretical linguistics.
Steven B. Smith (Ph.D., UCLA, 1971; Assistant Professor) Theoretical syntax, semantics, phonology.
David Warren (Ph.D., Univ. of Minnesota, 1969; Assoc. Prof.) Language development.

COURSE OFFERINGS

Phonology, 1; Sociolinguistics, 2; Field Methods, 1; Psycholinguistics, 1; Historical Linguistics, 1. Language Areas: Chinese, French, German, Russian, Spanish.

DESCRIPTIVE MATERIAL: Write: Admissions Office, University of California, Riverside, California 92502

UNIVERSITY OF CALIFORNIA, SAN DIEGO   La Jolla, California 92037   Tel. (714) 452-3600

Department of Linguistics
Edward S. Klima, Chairman
Degrees: BA, MA (The MA is offered only as a degree received on the way to the Ph.D.), Ph.D. Degrees Granted 72-73: 74 BA, 3 MA, 3 Ph.D. Majors: 61 g, 61 Ph.D., 48 Graduate in Residence, 103 u.

The graduate program is aimed essentially toward the Ph.D. degree in linguistics, with provision for granting the MA and/or the C.Phil. upon completion of basic graduate requirements. The program stresses modern linguistic theory, with particularly strong offerings in transformational generative grammar. Although the program offers the student the opportunity to concentrate on particular languages, language families, or other language-related fields of specialization, such concentration must be accompanied by attainment of proficiency in general theoretical linguistics.

A rich selection of lecture courses and seminars prepares each student in phonology, syntax, and one or more special studies (among them: semantics, historical linguistics, anthropological linguistics, history of linguistics, computational linguistics, psycholinguistics, language teaching, phonetics). A psycholinguistics laboratory and a phonetics laboratory are available to students for their research. Among the languages whose structure is currently being analyzed are English, French, Diegueño, Yuman, Samoan, Japanese, Albanian, Chinese (Mandarin and Cantonese), and Uto-Aztecan.

COURSE OFFERINGS

Introductory, 5u; Phonology, 2u 5g; Theoretical Models, 1u 6g; Semantics & Logic, 2g; Sociolinguistics, 1u 2g; Field Methods, 1g; Psycholinguistics, 2u 5g; Math. & Comp. Linguistics, 1g; Historical Linguistics, 1u 1g. Language Areas (g): Romance, Chinese, Amerindian, Japanese, Polynesian.

UNCOMMONLY-TAUGHT LANGUAGES

Afrikaans	Danish	Igbo	Polish
Albanian	Dutch	Italian	Portuguese
Arabic-Eastern	Efik	Japanese	Serbo-Croatian
Arabic-Egyptian	Esperanto	Korean	Swahili
Arabic-Iraqi	Finnish	Luganda	Swedish
Basque	Modern Greek	Malay	Tagalog
Bengali	Haitian Creole	Maori	Thai
Bulgarian	Hausa	Navajo	Tibetan
Burmese	Hawaiian	Nepali	Turkish
Chinese-Amoy	Hebrew	Nigerian Pidgin	Twi
Chinese-Cantonese	Hindi	Norwegian	Vietnamese
Chinese-Mandarin	Hungarian	Panjabi	Yiddish
Czech	Icelandic	Persian	Yoruba

STAFF

Paul G. Chapin (Ph.D., MIT, 1967; Asst Prof) Theory of Syntax, Computational Linguistics, Polynesian Linguistics.

Matthew Y.-Ch. Chen (Ph.D., U Calif., Berkeley, 1971; Asst Prof) Phonological Theory, Chinese Linguistics, Comparative Dialectology.

Alice W. Grundt (Ph.D., U Calif., Berkeley, 1973; Acting Asst Prof) Historical Phonology of English, Phonological Theory.

Edward S. Klima (Ph.D., Harvard, 1965; Prof) English Grammar, Native Language Acquisition, Psycholinguistics.

Sige-Yuki Kuroda (Ph.D., MIT, 1965; Assoc Prof) Formal Theory of Grammars, Theory of Syntax, Japanese Linguistics.

Ronald W. Langacker (Ph.D., Illinois, 1966; Assoc Prof) Linguistic Theory, French and English Syntax, Uto-Aztecan.

Margaret H. Langdon (Ph.D., U Calif., Berkeley, 1966; Assoc Prof) American Indian Linguistics, Language and Culture.

Leonard Newmark (Ph.D., Indiana, 1955; Prof) Foreign Language Acquisition, Albanian.

Sanford A. Schane, (Ph.D., MIT, 1965; Prof) Phonological Theory, French Linguistics, Orthography.

Timothy S. Smith (Ph.D., UCLA, 1970; Asst Prof) Experimental Phonetics, Phonological Theory, General Linguistics.

Benjamin K. T'sou (Ph.D., U Calif., Berkeley, 1971; Asst Prof) Historical Linguistics, Chinese Linguistics, Malayo-Polynesian Linguistics.

Linguists in other Departments and Schools

Rosaura Sanchez (Ph.D., U. of Texas, 1974; Asst Prof) Spanish Linguistics, Chicano Spanish.

Support Available

Teaching, Language, and research assistantships; Regents Fellowships; San Diego Fellowships; Fee Scholarships; Tuition Scholarships; Special Scholarships; University Grant-in-aid; Loans; Nonacademic employment; Veterans benefits; Fellowships from outside the University.

Academic Calendar 1974-1975

Fall Quarter: September 16, 1974 - December 7, 1974; Winter Quarter: January 2, 1975 - March 22, 1975; Spring Quarter: March 31, 1975 - June 14, 1975; Summer Session: June 16 - September 13. Deadline: Jan. 15.

DESCRIPTIVE MATERIAL: Write: Office of the Registrars - Admissions, University of California, San Diego, La Jolla, California 92037.

UNIVERSITY OF CALIFORNIA, SANTA BARBARA Santa Barbara, California 93106
Tel. (805) 961-3776

Linguistics Program
Arthur Schwartz, Chairman
Degrees: BA. Degrees Granted 1972-73: 6 BA. Majors: 24g.

We are a rather small department and therein lies the special attraction inasmuch as the instruction is more personalized and there is more time for student/teacher contact. Since the department is small, requirements can be adjusted or modified according to the individual needs of the student.

There is ample instruction in the syntactic, phonological, and semantic structures of language and all aspects of linguistics as the professors' specialties vary and do not overlap.

COURSE OFFERINGS

Introductory, 1; Phonology, 1; Theoretical Models, 1; Semantics & Logic, 1; Socio-linguistics, 1; Psycholinguistics, 1; Math. & Comp. Linguistics, 1; Historical Linguistics, 1.

STAFF

C. Douglas Johnson (Ph.D., U Calif., Berkeley, 1968; Asst Prof) Phonology, Mathematical Linguistics.
Charles Li (Ph.D., U Calif., Berkeley, 1969; Asst Prof) Syntax, Semantics.
Arthur Schwartz (Ph.D., University of Wisconsin, 1961; Prof) Syntax, Field Methods, Language Acquisition.

Linguists in Other Departments or Schools

Andre Malecot, French.
Robert Hetzron, Eastern Languages & Literatures.

DESCRIPTIVE MATERIAL: Write: Office of Admissions, Room 1210, Administration Building, University of California at Santa Barbara, Santa Barbara, California 93106.

UNIVERSITY OF CALIFORNIA, SANTA CRUZ Santa Cruz, Calif. 95064   Tel. (408) 429-2905

Board of Studies in Linguistics
William F. Shipley, Chairman
Degrees: BA. Degrees Granted 1972-73: 12 BA.

The major program in linguistics offers the student a choice of emphasis among three alternative clusters of courses: (1) current transformational theory including a study of generative phonology, syntax, and semantics; (2) historical linguistics; and (3) ethnolinguistics, sociolinguistics and psycholinguistics. The development of the third alternative will depend upon faculty and curricular additions within the next couple of years; for the present, an interim program is provided, making use of courses now available. The major program also provides for a basic grounding in transformational syntax for all major students.

COURSE OFFERINGS

Introductory, 1; Phonology, 2; Theoretical Models, 3; Semantics & Logic, 1; Field Methods, 3; Psycholinguistics, 1; Math. & Comp. Linguistics, 2; Historical Linguistics, 3; Linguistics & Literature, 1.

STAFF

Franklin L. DeRemer (Ph.D., MIT; Asst Prof).
John T. Grinder, Jr. (Ph.D., U Calif., San Diego, 1971; Asst Prof).
John Halverson (Ph.D., U Calif., Berkeley; Assoc Prof).
William F. Shipley (Ph.D., U Calif., Berkeley, 1959; Prof) Chairman, Board of Studies in Linguistics.
Arthur K. Spears (Ph.D. Candidate, U Calif., San Diego; Acting Asst Prof).
William V. Vroman (Ph.D. Candidate, University of Michigan; Lecturer).

Linguists in Other Departments and Schools

Franklin L. DeRemer, Information Sciences.
John Halverson, English and Comparative Literature.

DESCRIPTIVE MATERIAL: Write: Registrar's Office, University of California, Santa Cruz,
Santa Cruz, California 95064

CALIFORNIA STATE COLLEGE, DOMINGUEZ HILLS   Dominguez Hills, California 90747
Tel. (213) 532-4300, Ext. 578

Linguistics Program
Caroline Duncan, Chairman
Degrees: BA, MA (in English with concentration in Linguistics). Degrees Granted
        1972-73: 12 BA, 3 MA. Majors: 7 g, 7 MA, 7 Graduate in Residence, 47 u.

The interdepartmental program in linguistics is designed to enable the student to pursue
an investigation of language as a formal system and as a psychological & historical
phenomenon. The program provides a series of courses emphasizing attempts to describe
and explain language and focusing on current theories and methods of linguistic analysis.

COURSE OFFERINGS

Introductory, 2g; Phonology, 3g 1u; Theoretical Models, 3g 2u; Sociolinguistics, 1g 1u;
Psycholinguistics, 1g; Historical Linguistics, 2g. Language Areas: Spanish, 2g.

UNCOMMONLY-TAUGHT LANGUAGES

Old Icelandic (gr. 2 quarters)

STAFF

Richard Beym (Ph.D., U of Illinois, 1952; Prof) Spanish Linguistics.
Caroline Duncan (Ph.D., Florida State U, 1969; Assoc Prof) Phonology, Historical
    Linguistics, Germanic Linguistics.
Dale E. Elliott (Ph.D., Ohio State U, 1971; Assoc Prof) Syntax, Psycholinguistics,
    French Linguistics.
Burckhard Mohr (Ph.D., U Calif., Berkeley, 1973; Asst Prof) Phonology, Historical
    Linguistics.

DESCRIPTIVE MATERIAL: Write: California State Coll-Dominguez Hills, 1000 E. Victoria St.,
Dominguez Hills, California 90747.

CALIFORNIA STATE COLLEGE, SONOMA   Rohnert Park, California 94928   Tel. (707) 795-2124

Institute of Interdisciplinary Studies: Linguistics
Eli Katz, Coordinator for Linguistics
Degrees: Minor; Special Major on approval.

The linguistics program functions under the Institute for Interdisciplinary Studies
and offers a minor in linguistics at this time. A few special majors have been
granted, and a proposal to offer a major as part of the regular curriculum is now
being prepared and is strongly supported by student petition. Since the program

was organized initially to make the greatest use of the faculty available in different departments, a wide range of options for emphasis is open to the student.

The area served by the college is of special interest linguistically since the population has representative groups of people with different language backgrounds, such as Mexican-American and Portuguese. Of especial interest is the fact that it is also the home of the Kashaya Pomo Indian tribe, whose reservation is nearby on the coast. Work is carried on in these areas in cooperation with the Anthropology and Ethnic Studies departments.

In addition the program works closely with the Education department in the teacher training program.

A research program, Kashaya-Pomo Language in Culture, will be conducted during the 1974-75 academic year under a grant from NEH. The director is Dr. Shirley Silver of the Anthropology Department.

COURSE OFFERINGS

Introductory, 1; Theoretical Models, 2; Semantics & Logic, 1; Sociolinguistics, 6; Historical Linguistics, 2; Language Pedagogy, 3; Applied Ling., 2.

UNCOMMONLY-TAUGHT LANGUAGES

Hindi (u)   Kashaya Pomo (ul)   Sanskrit (u2)

STAFF

S. Aaron Berman (MA, Michigan, 1964) Foreign Languages.
Roshni Bohn (Ph.D., U Calif., Berkeley) India Studies.
Elizabeth S. Bright (Ph.D., U Calif., Berkeley, 1967) English.
Martha Carpenter (MA, San Francisco State) English.
Gerald W. Haslam (MA, San Francisco State, 1965) English.
Richard Hendrickson (Ph.D., U of Connecticut, 1967) English.
Eli Katz (Ph.D., UCLA, 1963) Ethnic Studies (1/3 time).
Shirley Silver (Ph.D., U Calif., Berkeley, 1966).
Philip O. Temko (Ph.D., Stanford, 1968) Philosophy.

Academic Calendar 1974-1975

Fall Semester: September 5, 1974 to January 3, 1975; Spring Semester: January 27, 1975 to May 30, 1975. Deadline: Open for the school; deadlines vary for the various departments.

DESCRIPTIVE MATERIAL: Write: Admissions Office, California State College-Sonoma,
                        1801 E. Cotati Ave., Rohnert Park, California 94928

CALIFORNIA STATE UNIVERSITY, FRESNO Fresno, California 93740   Tel. (209) 487-2441

Department of Linguistics
P. J. Mistry, Chairman
Degrees: BA, MA. Degrees Granted 1973-1974: 4 BA, 6 MA. Majors: 78 g, 56 MA, 22 u.

The Department offers programs leading to a BA, an MA, or a minor in linguistics. The options available are Spanish-English Bilingualism, Black Dialectology, and Teaching English as a Second Language. The MA program with emphasis on French or German is also available to students with suitable background in these languages.

A major consists of 30 units of selected work. A thesis of 2 to 5 semester units (included in the 30 units) and a reading knowledge of one foreign language are required for the MA program. A minor requires at least 20 units of work in the department.

Courses deal with the nature and structure of language, and with the application of these findings. The department also offers courses in English for foreign students, as well as in Chinese, Hebrew and Japanese languages. These courses provide practical experience especially valuable to students with Teaching English as a Second Language option. The Bilingual program consists of a block of courses in the Foreign Language Department, in the Ethnic Studies Program and in the Linguistics Department.

Several programs to teach English to Japanese students have been conducted in the past, and a general program to teach English to foreigners is projected for the near future.

COURSE OFFERINGS

Introductory, 2; Phonology, 3; Theoretical Models, 7; Semantics & Logic, 1; Sociolinguistics, 1; Dialectology, 2; Field Methods, 1; Historical Linguistics, 3; Language Pedagogy, 4. Language Areas: Armenian, Japanese. Other: Writing Systems.

UNCOMMONLY-TAUGHT LANGUAGES

Chinese (u 6 sem)   Hebrew (u 2 sem)   Japanese (u 6 sem)   Sanskrit (g, under independent study)

STAFF

Frederick H. Brengelman (Ph.D., Washington) English Linguistics, Writing Systems.
Edward R. Gammon (Ph.D., Stanford) Psycholinguistics, Mathematical Linguistics.
Jerry D. Hopkins (BA, Indiana) Structure of English, History of English.
P. J. Mistry (Ph.D., University of California, Los Angeles) Linguistic Theories, Historical Linguistics, Indic Linguistics.
Carol W. Pfaff (Ph.D., University of California, Los Angeles) Sociolinguistics, Syntax.
George W. Raney (Ph.D., University of Southern California) Teaching English as a Foreign Language, Applied English Linguistics.
Peter C. Wang (Ph.D., Texas) Syntax, Chinese Language and Linguistics.
Raymond S. Weitzman (Ph.D., University of Southern California) Acoustic Phonetics, Phonology, Japanese Language and Linguistics.
Milton Wohl (Ph.D., Michigan) Teaching English as a Foreign Language, Bilingualism, Applied Linguistics.
Jack B. Zeldis (Ph.D., Pennsylvania) English Grammar, Dialectology, Semitic Linguistics.

Linguists in other Departments and Schools

Benjamin B. Burton (Ph.D., Claremont Graduate School) Psycholinguistics.
Carmen P. Clough (Dr. Ped., University de la Habana) Spanish Linguistics.
Marion D. Meyerson (Ph.D., University of Illinois) Linguistics and Language Therapy.
Keith Sauer (Ph.D., University of Washington) Spanish Linguistics.
Susan J. Shanks (Ph.D., Louisiana State University) Linguistics and Language Therapy.

Support Available

A limited number of graduate assistantships to advanced students.

Academic Calendar 1974-1975

Fall Semester: September 9, 1974 to January 24, 1975; Spring Semester: January 28, 1975 to June 6, 1975; Summer Session: Unknown at present time.

DESCRIPTIVE MATERIAL: Write: Admissions Office, California State University, Fresno, Shaw and Cedar Avenues, Fresno, California 93740.

CALIFORNIA STATE UNIVERSITY, FULLERTON   Fullerton, California 92634

Tel. (714) 870-2441

Department of Linguistics
Alan S. Kay, Chairman
Degrees: BA, MA. Degrees Granted 1972-73: 20 BA, 18 MA. Majors: 40g. In Residence: 70u.

The undergraduate program provides a full range of courses, enabling the student to understand the essential relationship between language and thought and language and culture. The program will enable the student with linguistic and philological interests to grasp the scope of the field and to determine more accurately the most meaningful concentrations in graduate study.

The core courses of the graduate program are devoted to an in-depth consideration of descriptive, historical and applied linguistics. A variety of approaches to descriptive analysis and several theoretical points of view including generative grammar, transformational analysis and prosodics are presented. The aim of the graduate program is to provide a thorough and well balanced training for practice and research in the several areas of linguistic studies and to prepare qualified students for careers in the communication sciences and allied disciplines.

Facilities include extensive library holdings, an experimental phonetics laboratory and a graduate internship program at Santa Ana Community College in the Career Education Center.

COURSE OFFERINGS

Introductory, 1; Phonology, 4; Theoretical Models, 2; Semantics & Logic, 3; Sociolinguistics, 4; Dialectology, 1; Psycholinguistics, 3; Historical Linguistics, 5. Other: Ling. & Other Disciplines.

UNCOMMONLY-TAUGHT LANGUAGES

Arabic (u2)   Chinese (U2)   Japanese (u2)   Sanskrit
                                                                 Swahili (u2)

Staff

Alan S. Kay (Ph.D., U.C. Berkeley, 1971) Arabic Dialectology, General and Anthropological linguistics.
Geraldine Anderson (C. Phil., Linguistics, U.C.L.A.). Transformational Grammar, California Indian Languages, Mathematical Linguistics.
James A. Santucci (Ph.D., Australian National University, 1970) Vedic Sanskrit, Asian Civilizations.
Peter C. Solon (Ph.D., Mathematics, Brown University; C. Phil., U.C.L.A.) Indo-European Linguistics, Historical and Comparative Linguistics, Greek and Latin.
Ernie A. Smith (C. Phil., U.C. Irvine). American Dialects, Black Dialectology, Psycholinguistics.
Charles Ross (MA, U.S.C. 1969) Articulatory and Acoustic Phonetics, Sociolinguistics, General Linguistics (1/4 time).

Linguists in Other Departments or Schools

Lawrence Christensen (MA, U.C.L.A.) Anthropological Linguistics.
Otto Sadovski (Ph.D., U.C.L.A.) Uralic Linguistics, California Indian Languages,
    General and Anthropological Linguistics.
Samuel Cartledge (Ph.D., Yale University) French Linguistics.
Jacqueline Kiraithe (Ph.D., U.C.L.A.) Spanish Linguistics.
Thomas Klammer (Ph.D., University of Michigan) Transformational Grammar.
Muriel Schulz (Ph.D., U.S.C.) Sex and Language.

Support Available

Graduate assistantships offered. 20, 15, and 10 hour positions; approx. $3.00/hour.
Apply to Department Chair or Advisor.

Academic Calendar 1974-1975

Fall Semester: September 3, 1974 - January 7, 1975; Spring Semester: January 27,
1975 - June 3, 1975; Summer Session: June 9, 1975 - August 29, 1975.

DESCRIPTIVE MATERIAL: Write: Office of Admissions and Records, California State
                              University at Fullerton, 800 North State College Blvd.,
                              Fullerton, California 92634.

CALIFORNIA STATE UNIVERSITY, LONG BEACH Long Beach, California 90801
Tel. (213) 498-4111

Interdisciplinary Program in Linguistics
Janet Sawyer, Chairman
Degrees: MA in linguistics.

COURSE OFFERINGS

Introductory, 2; Phonology, 4; Thoretical Models, 2; Semantics & Logic, 2;
Dialectology, 1; Sociolinguistics, 3; Field Methods, 1; Psycholinguistics, 2;
Historical Linguistics, 3; Language Pedagogy, 1; Language Areas: Structure and
Phonology courses in English, French, Spanish.

UNCOMMONLY-TAUGHT LANGUAGES

Chinese	Hebrew	Pali
Hindi	Japanese	Sanskrit

STAFF

E.J. Borowiec; Grammatical Theory, Psycholinguistics
Daniel Cardenas; Spanish-American Dialectology, Bilingualism
Jane Cooper; Social Dialectology
Robert Harmon; Anthropological Linguistics
Robert M. Hertz; Transformational Grammar
Raul Inostroza; Spanish Linguistics
Harold Key; Field Methods, Amerindian Languages
R. Clyde McCone; Ethnolinguistics, Linguistics and Prehistory
Gloria G. McCullough; English Linguistics
Akira Miyazaki; Asian Linguistics
Steve Ross; English Linguistics, Black English, ESL
Janet Sawyer; English Linguistics, Dialectology, Bilingualism
Sara Smith; Psycholinguistics

Lindsey Thomas; French Linguistics
Francisco Trinidad; Romance Linguistics

DESCRIPTIVE MATERIAL: Write: Director, Interdisciplinary Program in Linguistics,
California State University, Long Beach, Long Beach,
California 90801.

CALIFORNIA STATE UNIVERSITY, LOS ANGELES Los Angeles, California 90032
Tel. (213) 224-3722

English Department
Sidney Richman, Chairman
Degrees: BA and MA in English with concentration in linguistics.

We have no program in Linguistics as such. Particular departments, however, offer
courses which can be elected for a concentration within the major, be it English, Speech
Communications, Philosophy, Psychology, Anthropology or Foreign Languages and Literatures.

COURSE OFFERINGS

English Department: Introductory, 1; Theoretical Models, 3; Psycholinguistics, 2; Math.
& Comp. Linguistics, 1; Historical Linguistics, 1. Language Areas: Skt. 2. Other
Departments: Introductory, 1; Phonology, 3; Theoretical Models, 2; Semantics & Logic,
2; Sociolinguistics, 5; Dialectology, 1; Field Methods, 1; Psycholinguistics, 11; Neurolinguistics, 2; Language Pedagogy, 1. Language Areas: French 3, German 2, Spanish
4.

UNCOMMONLY-TAUGHT LANGUAGES

Arabic (u 6q)	Hebrew (u 4q)	Latin (u 3q)	Sanskrit (u 2q)
Chinese (u 8q)	Japanese (u 10q)	Russian (u 4q)	

STAFF

Daniel A. Amneus (Ph.D., USC, 1953; Prof) English grammar and literature.
Donald A. Bird (Ph.D., Wisconsin, 1950; Prof) English grammar and literature.
Saralyn R. Daly (Ph.D., Ohio State, 1962; Prof) English grammar and literature.
Byron Guyer (Ph.D., Stanford, 1947; Prof) English grammar and literature.
Robert S. Hodgman (Ph.D., USC, 1964; Assoc Prof) English grammar and literature.
H. Landar (Ph.D., Yale, 1960; Prof) Sanskrit, English grammar, language and culture.
Thomas H. Peterson (Ph.D., UCLA, 1971; Asst Prof) General linguistics, African
    linguistics, English grammar and literature.
Jeanette R. Witucki (Ph.D., UCLA, 1966; Asst Prof of Anthro.) General linguistics,
    language and culture, linguistic field methods.
Mary F. Woodward (Ph.D., UCLA, 1958; Assoc Prof of Anthro.) General linguistics,
    language and culture, language and the deaf.

DESCRIPTIVE MATERIAL: Write: Registrar, 5151 State University Drive, Los Angeles,
California 90032.

CALIFORNIA STATE UNIVERSITY, NORTHRIDGE   Northridge, California 91324

Tel. (213) 885-3419

Interdisciplinary Linguistics Program
Iris Shah, Coordinator
Degrees: BA, MA. Degrees Granted 1972-73: 1 MA. Majors: 25g. In residence:
20g, 20u.

COURSE OFFERINGS

Introductory, 1; Phonology, 4; Theoretical Models, 3; Semantics & Logic, 5; Sociolinguistics, 4; Field Methods, 1; Psycholinguistics, 3; Math. & Comp Linguistics, 2; Historical
Linguistics, 3; Language Pedagogy, 1; Applied Linguistics, 1. Language Areas: Romance
ling.

UNCOMMONLY-TAUGHT LANGUAGES

Chinese	Hebrew	Japanese	Swahili
	Igbo	Nahuatl	Xhosa

STAFF

Charles R. Carlton (Ph.D., Michigan; Prof) Old English, Middle English, General
  Linguistics.
Carmelo Gariona (Ph.D., Chicago, 1964; Prof) Spanish Phonetics, Spanish Structure,
  Historical Linguistics.
Mahlon C. Gaumer III (Ph.D., Washington, 1969; Assoc Prof) Old English, Middle
  English, History of English.
Elaine Hannah (Ph.D., Indiana, 1956; Assoc Prof) Language development and language
  disorders.
Alice Hawkins (Ph.D., Iowa, 1961; Assoc Prof) Psycholinguistics, Language Acquisi-
  tion.
Paul L. Kirk (Ph.D., Washington, 1966; Prof) Synchronic and Diachronic Linguistics,
  Comparative Mazatec, Language and Culture.
Jacquelin Lindenfeld (Ph.D., U.C.L.A., 1969; Asst Prof) Socio-linguistics, Ethno-
  graphy of Communication, Psycho-linguistics.
Sidney Luchenbach (Ph.D., Pittsburgh, 1969; Assoc Prof) Symbolic Logic, Logical
  Theory.
R.S. Meyerstein (Ph.D., Michigan, 1955; Prof) French Linguistics, Romance Lin-
  guistics, General Linguistics.
Robert T. Oliphant (Ph.D., Stanford, 1962; Prof) Old English, Middle English
  History of English.
Iris S. Shah (Ph.D., Cornell, 1960; Prof) General Linguistics, Modern English
  Grammar, E.S.L.
William G. Stryker (Ph.D., Stanford 1952; Prof) General Linguistics, Modern English
  Grammar, Socio-linguistics.
Gregory Truex (Ph.D., U.C.Irvine, 1963; Asst Prof) Language and Culture, Zapotec,
  Socio-linguistics.

Academic Calendar 1974-1975

Fall Semester: August 30--December 21; Spring Semester: January20--May 30.

DESCRIPTIVE MATERIAL: Write: Professor Iris Shah, English Department, California
                       State University at Northridge, 18111 Nordhoff Street,
                       Northridge, California 90049.

CENTRAL CONNECTICUT STATE COLLEGE   New Britain, Connecticut 06050
Tel. (203) 225-7481, ex. 556

English Department, Division of Humanities
James Bailey, Chairman
Degrees: Undergraduate concentration, MA in TESOL. Degrees Granted 1972-73:
3 MS; 5 MS 1973-74.

The following TESOL programs are offered: Concentration in TESOL for English majors
(18 hrs.); Concentration in TESOL for Elementary Education majors (15 hrs.); Concentration in TESOL for Spanish Majors (18 hrs.); MS in TESOL (30 hrs. plus the Comprehensive); Summer Institute in TESOL (6 hrs. credit, 3 weeks in length, 8-11 AM (un.
& gr.) and 1-4 PM for 4 days a week).
    Area Studies: East Asian, Slavic and East European Studies, Afro-American.
English is also taught to non-native speakers and there are lab facilities for this
as well as other languages taught on the campus: German, Russian, Italian, French,
Polish, Spanish, Chinese and Arabic.

COURSE OFFERINGS

Introductory, 3; Theoretical Models, 1; Sociolinguistics, 1; Language Pedagogy, 1.

UNCOMMONLY-TAUGHT LANGUAGES

Arabic (u 4s)   Chinese (u 13s)   Russian (u 8s)

STAFF

Marco A. Arenas (MA, Columbia, 1965; Asst Prof) Spanish Linguistics; Comparative
    studies, English and Spanish; second language lab.
Ralph J. Goodell (Ph.D., Edinburgh, 1965; Prof) Applied and descriptive linguistics,
    TESOL methodology, Sociolinguistics.
Gerald J. Tullai (Ph.D., Indiana, 1970; Asst Prof) Theoretical Linguistics, Lin-
    guistics and literature, componential analysis.
Symond Yavener (Ph.D., Middlebury, 1967; Assoc Prof) French, Spanish, Russian.

Linguists in other Departments and Schools

Samuel Schulman (MA, Wisconsin, 1965; Asst Prof).
Cheng Sing Lien (MA, So. Illinois, 1973; Instructor).

Support Available

A Graduate Assistantship is available each year. $1,000. ea. Semester. Applica-
tion deadline for Fall Term May 1st; for Spring Term, December 1st.

DESCRIPTIVE MATERIAL: Write: Johnie M. Floyd, Director of Admissions, Central
                       Connecticut State College, 1615 Stanley Street, New Britain,
                       Connecticut 06050.

CENTRAL MICHIGAN UNIVERSITY   Mt. Pleasant, Michigan 48859   Tel. (517) 774-3171

English Department
Hans Fetting, Chairman
Degrees: BA, MA, Interdisciplinary Major in Linguistics. Degrees Granted 1972-73:
        303 BA, 580 MA. Majors: 920 g, 24 MA, 20 Graduate in Residence, ? u.

Under the sponsorship of the Department of English, Central Michigan University offers
an Interdisciplinary Major in Linguistics in collaboration with other academic departments of the University: the Departments of Speech, Sociology and Anthropology, Philo-

sophy, Foreign languages, and Mathematics.

The emphasis is on the central role of language in relation to other disciplines. Stress is placed on both theory and application. 'Application' relates to preparing the undergraduate for cross-cultural work through course work in social dialectology; the teaching of English to speakers of other languages, and to the teaching of English to native speakers.

At the MA level, the Department of English offers a concentration in linguistics with three options: (a) Language, Literature, and Linguistics; (b) Linguistics and TESOL; (c) Interdisciplinary Studies in Linguistics. Both the undergraduate major in linguistics and the graduate concentration require that a student have a minimum of TWO years study of at least ONE foreign language, or demonstrable competence in a foreign language. The graduate concentration requires prior undergraduate work in linguistics. Students nearing completion of their degree are required to show a satisfactory knowledge of (a) theories and methods of language description; (b) development and structure of the English language, and (c) an area of special interest to the candidate.

Facilities include a Speech and Hearing Clinic, audiovisual and self-study laboratory. Program in teaching the Spanish bilingual child; program in the teaching of reading; Psycho-Educational Clinic; Psychological Training and Consultation Center; Speech and Hearing Clinic.

COURSE OFFERINGS

Introductory, 2; Phonology, 1; Theoretical Models, 5; Semantics & Logic, 3; Sociolinguistics, 2; Dialectology, 1; Historical Linguistics, 2; Language Pedagogy, 2.

STAFF

Hans Fetting (Ph.D., Michigan State University, 1970; Assoc Prof) Historical Linguistics and English (1/2 time).
Peter Fries (Ph.D., University of Pennsylvania, 1964; Assoc Prof) Tagmemic Theory, English Grammar, Applied Linguistics.
David L. Lawton (Ph.D., Michigan State University, 1963; Prof) Creolized languages, English/Spanish dialectology, General Ling.

Linguists in other Departments and Schools

Maynard Filter (Ph.D., Bowling Green; Asst Prof) Pathology and Speech Sciences.
Eric Kadler (Ph.D., University of Michigan, 1959; Prof) Contrastive Linguistics and French (1/2 time).
Nancy Leis (Ph.D., Northwestern University; Asst Prof) Cultural Anthropology.
Bernard Meltzer (Ph.D., University of Chicago; Prof) Social Psychology (1/2 time).
Gilbert G. Rau (Ed.D., University of Denver; Prof) General Semantics.
Janice Reynolds (Ph.D., Ohio State; Asst Prof) Sociological Theory.
Larry Reynolds (Ph.D., Ohio State; Assoc Prof) Sociological Theory.
Hill Rohsenow (Ph.D., University of Michigan; Asst Prof) Cultural Anthropology, China.
Douglas Smith (Ph.D., Penn. State; Asst Prof) Mathematical Logic.
Paul Yu (Ph.D., University of Michigan; Asst Prof) Philosophy of Language.
Harold Zeoli (A.M., Boston University; Prof) Computer Science.

Support Available

E. C. Beck English Scholarship Fund - to majors in English Genl. university scholarships and loans.

Academic Calendar 1974-1975

Fall Semester: August 26 - December 14; Winter/Spring Semester: January 20 - May 17; Mini-session: May 19 - June 6; Summer Session: June 24 - August 1. Deadline: July 30.

DESCRIPTIVE MATERIAL: Write: Office of Admissions (undergrad.); Dean of Graduate Studies (graduates), Central Michigan University, Mt. Pleasant, Michigan 48859.

Department of Linguistics
Howard I. Aronson, Chairman
Degrees: BA, MA, Ph.D. Degrees Granted 1972-73: 14 BA, 13 MA, 14 Ph.D. Majors:
        35 g, 21 MA, 14 Ph.D., 35 Graduate in Residence, 21 u.

The Department of Linguistics of the University of Chicago offers programs of study
leading to the degree of Bachelor of Arts in General Linguistics and to the degrees
of Master of Arts and Doctor of Philosophy in Linguistics, in Indo-European and in
Balkan Studies.
    The Department's function is to further investigation into both the nature of lan-
guage and the structure and history of individual languages. The programs for the
M.A. and Ph.D. degrees are designed to meet the needs of students who wish to combine
the general study of synchronic and diachronic linguistics with work in a particular
language or language family, or in problems involving the relations between language
and the various fields of the humanities and sciences.

COURSE OFFERINGS

Introductory, 3; Phonology, 10; Theoretical Models, 17; Sociolinguistics, 7; Field
Methods, 2; Psycholinguistics, 3; Math. & Comp. Linguistics, 3; Historical Linguistics,
5; Linguistics & Literature, 2; Language Pedagogy, 2. Language Areas: Arabic 1, Georgian
3, Mayan 1, Romanian 3, Albanian 1, Greek 2, Old Irish 1, Amerindian Lgs. 1, Chinook
1, German 1, Munda 2, Russian 1, Semitic 2, Dravidian 2, Gothic 1, Japanese 2, Malayan
1, Austroasiatic 1, Bantu 1, Romance Lgs. 2, Kartvelian 1, Akkadian 1, Hindi 1, Near
East 1, Greenlandic 1, Nahuatl 1, Balkan 1. Other: Lexicography, Origin & Development
of Writing.

UNCOMMONLY-TAUGHT LANGUAGES

Bengali (u 6q,
  g 6q)
Bulgarian (g)
Lit. Chinese
  (g 6q)
Czech (u 12q,
  g 12q)
Old English
  (u 1q, g 1q)

Georgian u 6q,
  g 6q)
Hindi (u 6q,
  g 6q)
Class. Japanese
  (g 3q)
Malayalam (g)
Marathi (g 3q)

Polish (u 12q,
  g 12q)
Prakrit (g)
Rajasthani
  (g 3q)
Sanskrit (u 6q,
  g 6q)
Serbo-Croatian
  (u 12q, g 12q)

Tamil (u 6q,
  g 6q)
Class. Tamil
  (u 6q, g 6q)
Ukrainian (u 12q,
  g 12q)
Urdu (u 6q, g 6q)
Vedic (g)

STAFF

Howard I. Aronson (Prof).
Kali Bahl (Assoc Prof).
Miguel Civil (Prof).
Bill J. Darden (Asst Prof).
Peter F. Dembowski (Prof).
Gerard Diffloth (Asst Prof).
Paul W. Friedrich (Prof).
Ignace J. Gelb (Prof).
Gene B. Gragg (Assoc Prof).
Zbigniew Golab (Prof).
Hans G. Guterbock (Prof).
Eric P. Hamp (Prof).
Kostas Kazazis (Assoc Prof).
Carolyn G. Killean (Assoc Prof).
James D. McCawley (Prof).
Noriko A. McCawley (Asst Prof).
G. David McNeill (Prof).
Raven I. McDavid (Prof).
Norman McQuown (Prof).
A. K. Ramanujan (Prof).
Erica Reiner (Prof).
Sheldon Sacks (Prof).
Jerrold Sadock (Assoc Prof).
Michael Silverstein (Assoc Prof).

Dale Terbeek (Asst Prof).
Joseph M. Williams (Assoc Prof).
Victor H. Yngve (Prof).
Norman H. Zide (Prof).

Linguists in other Departments and Schools

Robert Ebert (Assoc Prof) Germanic Lang. and Lit.
James M. Lindholm (Instr) South Asian Lang. and Civ.
Colin P. Masica (Assoc Prof) South Asian Lang. and Civ.

Support Available

The University of Chicago awards scholarships and fellowships to students in the Linguistics Department. These range from half tuition to full tuition plus a stipend
of $2000 and are awarded on the basis of ability and need. Applications should be
made by 1 January of the year of admission to the Department.

Academic Calendar 1974-1975

Fall Quarter: 30 Sept. to 14 Dec. 1974; Winter Quarter: 6 January to 22 March 1975;
Spring Quarter: 31 March to 14 June 1975; Summer Quarter: 23 June to 29 August 1975.
Deadline: 1 January is the deadline for aid and fellowship applications; admission
to the Department of Linguistics can be effective at the beginning of any academic
quarter.

DESCRIPTIVE MATERIAL: Write: Department of Linguistics, The University of Chicago,
Goodspeed Hall, Chicago, Illinois 60637.

UNIVERSITY OF CINCINNATI   Cincinnati, Ohio 45221   Tel. (513) 475-2772

Multidepartmental Committee on Linguistics
Dr. Joseph F. Foster, Chairman
Degrees: BA, MA, Ph.D. Majors: 3 g, 2 MA, 1 Ph.D., 3 Graduate in Residence, 5 u.

Graduate: individually tailored multidisciplinary programmes designed by student
with advisory committee. MA 45 quarter hours/Ph.D. 135 quarter hours. Detailed
information available from the University Dean.
   Undergraduate: 186 quarter hours of which 54 in linguistics. Programme features
core sequence in general linguistics & language with concentration in one of the
following: A. Theoretical and Analytic Linguistics, B. Philology and Applied
Linguistics.
   Facilities: a. U.C. Library (over a million volumes plus 4,000 current journals);
b. Hebrew Union College Library; c. Computer Centre including the IBM 360/65;
d. Human Relations Area Files; e. Laboratories in Experimental Phonetics and Speech
Research Instrumentation; f. Cincinnati area especially good for research in social,
regional, and migrant dialect studies.

COURSE OFFERINGS

Introductory, 2; Phonology, 6; Theoretical Models, 4; Semantics & Logic, 3; Sociolin-
guistics, 3; Dialectology, 2; Field Methods, 1; Psycholinguistics, 4; Math. & Comp.
Linguistics, 2; Historical Linguistics, 2; Applied Linguistics, 1. Language Areas:
Germanic 3, French 3, Latin 1, Spanish 3.

UNCOMMONLY-TAUGHT LANGUAGES

Chinese (u 3q)   Gaelic (Scots)   Hebrew (u 9q)   Swahili (u 6q)
Mid. English (g 1q)   (g 1q)

| Old English (u 2q, g 2q) | Mid. High German (g 3q) | Old Norse (u 2q, g 2q) | Swedish (u 3q, g 3q) |

STAFF

Joseph F. Foster (Ph.D., Illinois, 1969; Asst Prof Anthropology) General linguistics, generative grammar, typology.

Paul Gaeng (Ph.D., Columbia, 1965; Prof Romance Languages) General, structural, and applied linguistics; Romance philology.

Michael Gertner (Ph.D., Columbia, 1971; Asst Prof Romance Langs.) General and French linguistics.

Richard Honeck (Ph.D., Wisconsin; Assoc Prof Psychology) Psycholinguistics.

Leon Kinman (MA, Cornell, 1967; Instr English) General linguistics, Slavic, English.

Richard Kretschmer (Ed.D., Columbia, 1970; Assoc Prof Special Education) Language of the hearing-impaired.

William Lasher (Ph.D., North Carolina, 1970; Asst Prof English) General linguistics, transformationalist syntax, history of English.

Gottfried Merkel (Ph.D., Leipzig, 1929; Prof Germanic Langs.) Germanic Philology.

Gregory Moschetti (MA, Michigan, 1972; Asst Prof Sociology) Sociolinguistics.

Hans-Georg Richert (Ph.D., Hamburg, 1961; Assoc Prof Germanic Langs.).

Donald A. Schumsky (Ph.D., Tulane, 1962; Prof Psychology) Psycholinguistics.

Thomas Seward (Ph.D.; Asst Prof Romance Langs.) Spanish linguistics.

R. Vernon Stroud (Ph.D., Ohio State U., 1967; Prof Speech Pathology) Social dialects, speech pathology.

William Todd (Ph.D., Michigan, 1959; Prof Philosophy) Semantics, generative syntax.

James Vail (Ph.D., Assoc Prof Classics) Comparative Philology Greek, Latin, Indo-European; Semantics.

Frank Wagner (Ph.D.; Prof Mathematics) Mathematical linguistics.

Daniel Wheeler (Ph.D., Texas; Asst Prof Education & Psychology) Psycholinguistics.

Support Available

Graduate: General university scholarships, Taft Fellowships, tuition & fee waivers, graduate assistantships (consult sponsoring department). Deadlines about 15 February, but vary among departments. Competitive fellowships available for multidisciplinary students - consult Office of the University Dean.

Undergraduate: Scholarships, grants-in aid, Ohio Instructional Grants, part-time employment. Most applications due in Financial Aid Office 1 February.

Academic Calendar 1974-1975

Fall Quarter: 27 September - 14 December 1974; Winter Quarter: 6 January - 22 March 1975; Spring Quarter: 2 April - 14 June 1975; Summer Quarter: 23 June - 28 Aug. Terms: 23 Je - 15 Jy; 16 Jy - 6 Aug; 7 Aug - 28 Aug. Deadline: Graduate: three months prior to quarter intended to enroll; Undergraduate: Two months prior to quarter intended to enroll.

DESCRIPTIVE MATERIAL: Office of Admissions, 100 French Hall, University of Cincinnati, Cincinnati, Ohio 45221. Graduate Students: Office of the University Dean for Graduate Education and Research, 305 Physics, University of Cincinnati, Cincinnati, Ohio 45221.

CITY COLLEGE OF THE CITY UNIVERSITY OF NEW YORK   New York, New York 10031
Tel. (212) 690-5384

Interdepartmental Linguistics Committee
Marshall Berger, Chairman
Degrees: BA.

A student can major in either general, anthropological, Romance, Germanic, English, or Classical linguistics. A student can also put together his own program with the approval and guidance of a member of the linguistics committee.

COURSE OFFERINGS

Introductory, 1; Phonology, 5; Theoretical Models, 3; Semantics & Logic, 3; Sociolinguistics, 5; Dialectology, 2; Field Methods, 1; Psycholinguistics, 1; Historical Linguistics, 3; Linguistics & Literature, 1; Language Pedagogy, 2.

STAFF

Marshall D. Berger (Ph.D., Assoc Prof) Phonology, Dialectology, Linguistic Geography.
O. L. Chavarria-Aguilar (Ph.D., Prof) Indic Linguistics.
Sarah G. D'Eloia (M.A., Inst) Sociolinguistics.
Louis J. Gerstman (Ph.D., Prof) Psycholinguistics.
Louis G. Heller (Ph.D., Prof) Systems Analysis, Comparative & Historical Ling.
Julius Moshinsky (Ph.D., Asst Prof) Anthropological Linguistics.

Linguists in other Departments or Schools

Gloria Borden (Ph.D., Asst Prof) Experimental Phonetics.
Gary Keller (Ph.D., Asst Prof) Bilingualism.
Louis F. Sas (Ph.D., Prof) Romance Linguistics.
Rosaline Schwartz (M.A., Inst) Yiddish Linguistics.

DESCRIPTIVE MATERIAL: Write: Office of Registrar, City College of New York, Convent at 138th Street, New York, New York 10031.

CLEVELAND STATE UNIVERSITY Cleveland, Ohio 44114   Tel. (216) 687-3985

Ad Hoc Committee on Linguistics
W. S. Chisholm, Director
Degrees: Minors in linguistics within existing majors.

We have recently listed relevant (existing) courses in "linguistics" in the Bulletin under Language Studies. Our plan at first is to offer "emphases" or "minors" in Language Studies within existing majors. Key emphases are linguistics within English major, linguistics within Modern Language, linguistics within education majors. Some socio and psycho linguistics. We are just beginning.

COURSE OFFERINGS

Introductory, 3; Phonology, 3; Theoretical Models, 3; Semantics & Logic, 4; Sociolinguistics, 8; Psycholinguistics, 3; Math. & Comp. Linguistics, 4; Historical Linguistics, 1; Linguistics & Literature, 2; Language Pedagogy, 2. Language Areas: Skt. 1, Old English 1, Middle English 1, French 2, German 2, Spanish 2, Greek 5, Latin 5.

UNCOMMONLY-TAUGHT LANGUAGES

Arabic (u 5q)   Hungarian   Polish (u 5q)   Swahili (u 5q)
Chinese (u 1q)   (u 5q)

STAFF

Earl Anderson (Ph.D., Oregon, 1970; Asst Prof) Old English.
James Barthelmess (Ph.D., U. of Washington, 1970; Asst Prof) Greek.

Bruce Beatie (Ph.D., Harvard, 1970; Prof) German, Spanish, Germanic Linguistics
and Philology.
William Chisholm (Ph.D., Michigan, 1969; Prof) Theoretical Linguistics, English
grammar.
Mary Heiser (Ph.D., Michigan, 1972; Assoc Prof) French, French linguistics, Phon-
ology.
Louis Milic (Ph.D., Columbia, 1969; Prof) Stylistics.
Laura Mertin-Barber (Ph.D., U. of Florida, 1971; Asst Prof) Structuralism.
Howard Mims (Ph.D., Case-Western Reserve; Assoc Prof) Communications Theory,
Speech Pathology.
Anita Stoll (Ph.D., Case-Western Reserve, 1966; Asst Prof) Spanish Linguistics.
Willis Sibley (Ph.D., U. of Chicago, 1971; Prof) Anthropological linguistics.

Academic Calendar 1974-1975

Fall Quarter: Oct. 2 - Dec. 20; Winter Quarter: Jan. 6 - March 21; Spring Quarter:
March 31 - June 13; Summer Quarter: June 18 - Aug. 29. Deadline: Sept. 25, 1974.

DESCRIPTIVE MATERIAL: Write: Admissions Office, Cleveland State University,
                       Cleveland, Ohio 44114.

UNIVERSITY OF COLORADO Boulder, Colorado 80302   Tel. (303) 492-8041

Department of Linguistics
Luigi Romeo, Chairman
Degrees: MA, Ph.D. BA can be earned by designing an individually structured
          major. Degrees Granted 1972-73: 17 MA, 1 Ph.D. Majors: 16 MA, 22 Ph.D.

In addition to a complete and balanced program offered by the Department in cooperation with linguists in other Departments, we possess the following characteristics:
1. A research and publication project in connection with Lakhota (Director, Dr. Allan
R. Taylor); 2. A Phonetics Program supported by a modern laboratory; 3. Colorado
Research in Linguistics (CRIL), 1971-   ; 4. Stress in American-Indian linguistics,
Romance linguistics and philology, African and Semitic linguistics, History of linguistics research.

COURSE OFFERINGS

Introductory, 3; Phonology, 3; Theoretical Models, 5; Dialectology, 2; Field Methods,
3; Psycholinguistics, 2; Math. & Comp. Linguistics, 1; Historical Linguistics, 5;
History of Linguistics, 3. Language Areas: African linguistics 2, Hausa 1, Amerindian 1, Siouan 1, Skt. 2, Romance 4.

UNCOMMONLY-TAUGHT LANGUAGES

Arabic   Hebrew   Lakhota   Sanskrit

STAFF

Alan E. Bell (Ph.D., Stanford, 1971; Asst Prof) Transformational grammar, Generative
phonology. [On leave.]
James E. Dammann (Ph.D., University of Michigan, 1964; Prof-Adj) Communication
sciences, Mathematical linguistics.
Zygmunt Frajzyngier (Ph.D., University of Warsaw, 1968; Asst Prof) African lin-
guistics.
Frede Jensen (Ph.D., U.C.L.A., 1961; Prof) Romance philology.
Luigi Romeo (Ph.D., University of Washington, 1960; Prof) History of linguistics,
Romance and historical linguistics.

David S. Rood (Ph.D., University of Calif. at Berkeley, 1969; Asst Prof) Linguistics
   and Language teaching, Amerindian (Caddoan, Siouan), descriptive linguistic
   methods and theories.
Allan R. Taylor (Ph.D., University of Calif. at Berkeley, 1969; Assoc Prof) General
   linguistics, Applied linguistics, Amerindian (Algonkoan, Siouan, Caddoan).

Linguists in other Departments and Schools

Robert Abernathy (Ph.D., Harvard, 1951; Prof) Slavic linguistics, Mathematical
   linguistics.
Edward J. Crothers (Ph.D., Indiana University, 1961; Assoc Prof) Psychology Depart-
   ment, Sociolinguistics.
Robert T. Firestone (Ph.D., Indiana University, 1962; Asst Prof) Germanic languages
   and literatures.
Rodolfo Garcia (Ph.D., Ohio State University, 1973; Asst Prof) Spanish and Portuguese
   Department.
Harold J. Kane (Ph.D., University of Pennsylvania, 1968; Prof) English Department.
Dorothea V. Kaschube (Ph.D., Indiana University, 1960; Prof) Anthropology Department.
Walter Kintsch (Ph.D., University of Kansas, 1960; Prof) Psychology Department.
J. Rolf Kjolseth (Ph.D., University of Colorado, 1968; Assoc Prof) Sociology Depart-
   ment, Sociology of language, of knowledge, theory.
Brian A. Lewis (Ph.D., University of Wisconsin, 1968; Asst Prof) Germanic languages
   and literatures.
Anthony G. Lozano (Ph.D., University of Texas at Austin, 1964; Assoc Prof) Spanish
   and Portuguese Department.
Edgar N. Meyer (Ph.D., Harvard, 1952; Prof) French Department.
Edward Rose (Ph.D., Stanford, 1942; Prof) Sociology Department, Ethnography, Soci-
   ology of languages.
Kumiko Takahara (Ph.D., University of London, 1973; Asst Prof) Oriental Languages
   Department, Linguistics and Sociolinguistics.
Hans-H. Waengler (Ph.D., University of Hamburg, 1949; Dr. habil. linguistics, 1957;
   Prof) Speech Pathology and Audiology Department, Phonetics and Sociolinguistics.
Rita S. Weiss (Ph.D., University of Colorado, 1967; Assoc Prof) Speech Pathology and
   Audiology Department.

Support Available

University of Colorado Fellowships (Graduate School available yearly): deadline is
February 1st of each year.

Academic Calendar 1974-1975

Fall Semester: August 29, 1974 to December 21, 1974; Spring Semester: January 17,
1975 to May 24, 1975 (Commencement); Summer Session: June 7, 1974 to August 17,
1974 (Commencement) (or June 7, 1975 to August 17, 1975 approx.). Deadline:
Linguistics -- Fall Semester: registration deadline July 1 or until quota is filled
(whichever comes first); Spring Semester: registration deadline December 1 or until
quota is filled (whichever comes first); Summer Session: registration deadline April
15 or until quota is filled (whichever comes first).

DESCRIPTIVE MATERIAL: Write: Office of Admissions and Records, Regent Hall 125,
                       University of Colorado, Boulder, Colorado 80302.

COLUMBIA UNIVERSITY New York, New York 10027   Tel. (212) 280-3925

Department of Linguistics
Prof. Marvin I. Herzog, Chairman
Degrees: MA, Ph.D., M.Phil. Degrees Granted 1972-73: 6 MA, 4 Ph.D., 2 M.Phil.
          Majors: 32 g, 8 MA, 24 Ph.D.; 26 Graduate in Residence.

With an unparalleled diversity of languages to draw upon, the graduate Department of Linguistics at Columbia University offers programs which allow the student to combine, or select from among areal, comparative, theoretical, and interdisciplinary approaches as these suit his/her particular needs and scholarly inclinations.

Besides the opportunities for language training which support areal and comparative studies, vast resources in the form of cultural, historical, and social interdisciplinary materials exist at Columbia (e.g., in the language and cultural departments, comparative literature programs, regional institutes, Soviet nationality programs, etc.) as well as in scholarly organizations in the New York area which assist in some of the programs of the department. Thus, in addition to pursuing the more strictly linguistic historical-comparative, dialectological, or generative approaches, the student may also consider such matters as multi-ethnicity or -nationality (e.g., bilingualism, languages in contact), literary language, the languages of poetry and of folklore, the socio-cultural contexts of language, etc.

In another vein, one of the programs in the department is concerned with the development of a new theoretical framework which focuses upon the communicatory function of language as a determinant of its structure. Other scholars in the department are applying theoretical frameworks derived from generative grammar and/or psycholinguistics-to the study of cognitive structures, semantics, acquisition of first and second languages, developmental psychology of language, phonological theory, etc. Here again, in many instances, the emphasis is interdisciplinary.

Ongoing research projects: 1) Language and Culture Atlas of Ashkenazic Jewry; 2) First and second language acquisition.

COURSE OFFERINGS

Introductory, 1u 2g; Phonology, 3g; Theoretical Models, 2u 7g; Semantics & Logic, 4g; Sociolinguistics, 2u 4g; Dialectology, 2g; Field Methods 2g; Psycholinguistics, 4g; Historical Linguistics, 1u 3g; History of Linguistics, 1g; Linguistics & Literature, 1g; Language Pedagogy, 3g. Language Areas: Structure of a lang., 1u, Uralic 2g, Hungarian 3g, Finnish 3g, Semitic 1g, Yiddish 8g, Greek 2g, German 1g, Czeck 1g, Slovak 1g, Polish 1g, Russian 1g, OCS 1g, Slavic 4g, Ukrainian & Belorussian 1g, Serbo-Croatian 1g, Spanish 4g, French 1g, Japanese 3g, Tungus 1g, Amerindian 1g, Latin 1g, Oscan-Umbrian 1g.

UNCOMMONLY-TAUGHT LANGUAGES

Akkadian (g6)	Hebrew (u4, g1)	Persian (u4, g2)	Syriac (g2)
Arabic (u4, g6)	Hindi-Urdu (u4, g2) 4)		Swahili (u4)
Armenian (u4)	Hungarian (u6)	Russian (u14)	Tibetan (g4)
Chinese (u6, g2)	Iranian (g4)	Roumanian (u6)	Turkish (u4, g2)
Czech (u4)	Japanese (u6, g2)	Sanskrit (g6)	Ugaritic (g4)
Dutch (u1)	Korean (u4, g2)	Serbo-Croatian	Uzbek (u4)
Finnish (u6)	Oscan-Umbrian	(u4)	Yiddish (u6)
Greek (u2)	(1 sem. every	Sumerian (g2)	
Hausa (u4)	other year)		

STAFF

Robert Austerlitz (Ph.D., Columbia, 1955; Prof) Phonetics, history of linguistics, data-oriented study of Uralic and Paleosiberian languages.
Thomas Bever (Ph.D., M.I.T., 1967; Prof) Interactions of language, cognition, development and perception; Second language learning; phonological theory.
Alan S. Castleman (Ph.D., Princeton, 1973; Asst Prof) Germanic and German linguistics and philology (part time).
William Diver (Ph.D., Columbia, 1953; Prof) The principled basis of theory, Explanation in grammar and phonology, Historical and comparative linguistics.
Aili Flint (MA, Columbia, 1966; Lecturer) Finnish.
Marvin I. Herzog (Ph.D., Columbia, 1964; Prof) The history and structure of Yiddish, Yiddish dialectology--social and geographic, Linguistic geography.
Clifford Hill (Ph.D., Wisconsin, 1971; Asst Prof) African languages, stylistics, structural study of oral art (part time).
John L. Inniss (BA, Queens College, 1973; Assoc) Swahili.
Lars-Alvar Jacobson (Ph.D., Stockholm University, 1970; Asst Prof) Language acquisition, philosophical problems of a developmental psychology of language.

Francis J. Juhasz (Ph.D., Columbia, 1968; Lecturer) TEFL, Hungarian.
Barbara Kirshenblatt-Gimblett (Ph.D., Indiana, 1972; Vis. Assoc Prof) Folklore
    theory and methods; ethnography of communication, Yiddish folklore and culture
    (part time).
Janos Latin (Diploma, Univ. of Budapest, 1970; Assoc) Hungarian.
Joseph L. Malone (Ph.D., Univ. of California, Berkeley, 1967; Assoc Prof) Semitic
    linguistics, Phonological theory, Writing systems.
Michael J. Reddy (Ph.D., Chicago, 1972; Asst Prof) Generative semantics, theories
    of metaphor and other figures of speech, linguistic analysis of poetic form
    (part time).
Mordkhe Schaechter (Ph.D., Univ. of Vienna, 1951; Lecturer) Yiddish.
George Y. Shevelov (Ph.D., Kharkov, 1939; Ph.D. Ukrainian Free University,
    Munich, 1949; Prof) Slavic languages, historical linguistics.
Richard H. Wojcik (Ph.D., Ohio State University, 1973; Asst Prof) Generative theory
    with a specialization in syntax and semantics, natural phonology, casual speech.

Linguists in other Departments and Schools

Robert L. Allen (Ph.D., Columbia; Prof) Teachers College.
John Attinasi (Ph.D., Chicago, 1973; Asst Prof) Anthropology.
Lois Bloom (Ph.D., Columbia; Assoc Prof) Teachers College.
James Higgenbotham (Ph.D., Columbia) Philosophy.
Janellen B. Huttenlocher (Ph.D., Radcliffe, Prof) Teachers College.
Roland A. Lange (Ph.D.; Asst Prof) East Asian Languages & Cultures.
Rado L. Lencek (Ph.D., Harvard, 1962; Assoc Prof) Slavic Languages.
Harvey Pitkin (Ph.D., California, Berkeley, 1963; Assoc Prof) Anthropology.
Peter Rosenbaum (Ph.D., M.I.T.; Prof) Teachers College.
William Stewart (MA, California (Los Angeles), Lect.) Teachers College.

Support Available

Financial aid is available in the form of fellowships, readerships, and research
assistantships. We do not yet have the deadline for application for admission for
1975-1976. Specific amounts available not yet known for 75-76.

Academic Calendar 1974-1975

Fall Semester: Sept. 5, 1974 - Dec. 20, 1974; Spring Semester: Jan. 20, 1975 -May 9,
1975. Deadline: Applications for the graduate program in Linguistics are no longer
being considered for 1974-1975.

DESCRIPTIVE MATERIAL: Write: Professor Marvin I. Herzog, Chairman, Department of
                        Linguistics, Columbia University, 401 Philosophy Hall,
                        New York, New York 10027.

COLUMBIA UNIVERSITY TEACHERS COLLEGE   New York, New York 10027   Tel. (212) 678-3796

Languages, Literature, Speech and Theatre
Prof. Louis Forsdale, Chairman
Prof. Robert L. Allen, Dir. of Program in Applied Linguistics
Degrees: MA, Ph.D., M.Ed., ED.D. Degrees Granted 1972-73: 72 MA, 4 Ed.D.

The program in Applied Linguistics is offered in the Department of Languages, Literature,
Speech and Theatre. Concentration is on theory and practice in one particular field
of specialization -- whether syntactic or semantic analysis, the teaching of English
to speakers of other languages, or Afro-American/African linguistics -- and is balanced
with a great variety of courses from which the graduate student may select in such
areas as psycholinguistics, sociolinguistics, cultural anthropology, dialectology,

language as communication, communication theory, learning theory, stylistics, bilingualism, cross-cultural studies, language and reading, reading disabilities, child language, and the language of the hearing impaired, as well as recent developments in educational technology and instructional methodologies.

There is a set of core courses on grammatical theory which attempt to exemplify the application of scientific approaches to the study of linguistic structure. There is a strong emphasis on the practical relevance of the study of language, with a number of courses oriented to majors in other programs.

Each student has an adviser and works out the program that is most appropriate for his interests. The MA program does not include a thesis or extended research project. Graduate training is oriented toward developing application of linguistic skills and knowledge in related areas (e.g. child development, speech, education, social work, measurement and evaluation). Candidates for the Ed.M.: a one-hour lecture on research project, with question and answer period.

Candidates majoring in Applied Linguistics will be expected to show proficiency in the following areas: (1) the history and development of the English language; (2) the background and origins of traditional grammar; (3) the development of comparative and historical linguistics; (4) the origins and development of descriptive linguistics in the United States; and (5) the various schools of linguistics in this country and the basic tenets of each, together with the names of the leaders of each school and of the important publications pertaining to each. The student will also be expected to have some knowledge of the theories of leading European linguists; some knowledge of various areas that linguists have been concerned with in addition to those of phonology, morphology, and syntax; and some knowledge of developments in the newer branches of linguistics such as psycholinguistics and sociolinguistics. In addition, the cadidate must undertake -- and give a satisfactory report on -- a careful and detailed analysis of some aspect of language (applied to some particular language), making use of the techniques of one or more schools of modern linguistics.

COURSE OFFERINGS

Introductory, 2; Phonology, 2; Theoretical Models, 6; Semantics & Logic, 2; Sociolinguistics, 3; Dialectology, 1; Psycholinguistics, 4; Math. & Comp. Linguistics, 1; Linguistics & Literature, 3; Language Pedagogy, 3; Applied Ling.; Applications of Lx. to the Classroom.

UNCOMMONLY-TAUGHT LANGUAGES

Introductory	Intermediate	Introductory	Intermediate
Hausa	Hausa	Swahili	Swahili

STAFF

Doris A. Allen (MA, Columbia, 1971; Inst).
Robert L. Allen (Ph.D., Columbia University, 1962; Prof) Applied Linguistics.
Annette Baslaw (Ph.D., New York University, 1969; Asst Prof) Teaching of Foreign
    Languages.
Robert A. Bone (Ph.D., Yale University, 1955; Prof) Teaching of English.
Dannis Eaton (Inst).
Steven Epstein (MA, University of Illinois, 1970; Inst) Communication and Theatre
    Arts.
Ella Erway (Inst).
John Faneslow (Ph.D., Columbia University, 1971; Asst Prof) TESOL, Bilingualism.
Joan Feindler (Inst).
Erwin Flaxman (Inst).
Gloria Flórez (Inst).
Louis Forsdale (Ed.D., Columbia University, 1951; Prof) Teaching of English.
Kumiko Fujimura (Inst).
Clifford A. Hill (Ph.D., University of Wisconsin, 1971; Asst Prof) Applied Linguistics.
Milton A. Kaplan (Ph.D., Columbia University, 1946; Prof) Teaching of English.
Paul Kozelka (Ph.D., Yale University, 1943; Prof) Communication and Theatre Arts.
Eric V. Larsen (Inst).
B. Barton McIntyre (Inst).
Dale Myers (Ph.D., University of Florida, 1970; Asst Prof) Applied Linguistics, TESOL.
Donald Pace (Inst).

Peter S. Rosenbaum (Ph.D., M.I.T., 1965; Assoc Prof) Applied Linguistics, TESOL, Communication and Theatre Arts.
Mordecai S. Rubin (Ph.D., University of Maryland, 1960; Prof) TESOL, Bilingualism.
Barbara Sandberg (Inst).
Merrill Skaggs (Inst).
Arthur A. Stern (M.A., Columbia University, 1963; Lect) English Linguistics.
William A. Stewart (MA, UCLA, 1963; Lect) Dialectology, Creole Languages.

Support Available

Scholarships, fellowships and loans are available at the Office of Student Aid.

Academic Calendar 1974-1975

Fall Semester: Registration: September 3-4 Classes begin 5th Late Registration 5-6, Sat 7, 9; Spring Semester: Registration: January 16-17, Late Registration Sat 18th and 20-22; Summer Session: (2) Summer A: end of May (6 week sessions) Summer B: end of June. Deadline: August 1-Last day to complete application for admission to a degree program for Autumn Term.

DESCRIPTIVE MATERIAL: Write: Department of Languages, Literature, Speech and Theatre, Box 66-AL, Teachers College, Columbia University, New York, New York 10027.

UNIVERSITY OF CONNECTICUT   Storrs, Connecticut 06268   Tel. (203) 486-4229

Department of Linguistics
Ignatius G. Mattingly, Acting Head
Degrees: MA, Ph.D. Degrees Granted 1972-73: 2 Ph.D. Majors: 20 g, 3 MA, 17 Ph.D., 15 Graduate in Residence.

The Department has special strength in experimental phonetics. A well-equipped phonetics laboratory is available, including a NOVA 2/10 on-line computer with an A/D/A system and speech synthesizer, sound spectrographs, studio, and other equipment for detecting, recording, analyzing and displaying speech. Members of the Linguistics and Psychology Departments collaborate in a Language and Psychology graduate program emphasizing experimental work in speech production, perception, analysis and synthesis of speech.

COURSE OFFERINGS

Introductory, 1; Phonology, 8; Theoretical Models, 3; Semantics & Logic, 1; Sociolinguistics, 1; Field Methods, 1; Psycholinguistics, 6; Neurolinguistics, 2; Math. & Comp. Linguistics, 1; Historical Linguistics, 1.

STAFF

Arthur S. Abramson (Ph.D., Columbia, 1960; Prof) Experimental Phonetics: Production and perception of speech, cross-language experimental phonetics.
Franklin S. Cooper (Ph.D., M.I.T., 1936; Adjunct Prof) Experimental Phonetics: Nature of the processes involved in communication by voice.
Janet Dean Fodor (Ph.D., M.I.T., 1970; Asst Prof) Psycholinguistics, Semantics.
Thomas Gay (Ph.D., City University of New York, 1967; Assoc Prof) Speech physiology, electromyographic and radiographic phonetics.
Howard Lasnik (Ph.D., M.I.T., 1972; Asst Prof) Syntax and semantics.
Ignatius G. Mattingly (Ph.D., Yale, 1968; Prof) Speech synthesis and perception, origins of speech and language, the reading process.

David Michaels (Ph.D., University of Michigan, 1969; Assoc Prof) Phonology, syntax, phonic interference, languages in contact.
Jacqueline Sachs (Ph.D., University of California, Berkeley, 1966; Assoc Prof) Psycholinguistics, child language acquisition.

Linguists in other Departments and Schools

Anthony Kroch (Socioanthropology).
Alvin M. Liberman (Psychology).
Terrance McCormick (Germanic and Slavic Languages).
William McMunn (English).
Donald Shankweiler (Psychology).
Michael T. Turvey (Psychology).

Support Available

University Fellowships, Teaching Assistantships, Research Assistantships.

Academic Calendar 1974-1975

Fall Semester: Sept. 4, 1974 - Dec. 21, 1974; Spring Semester: Jan. 20, 1975 - May 3, 1975. Deadline: June 3, 1974.

DESCRIPTIVE MATERIAL: Write: Graduate Admissions, U-6A, University of Connecticut, Storrs, Connecticut 06268.

CORNELL UNIVERSITY Ithaca, New York 14850   Tel. (607) 256-3554

Department of Modern Languages and Linguistics
Gerald B. Kelley, Chairman
Degrees: BA, MA, Ph.D. Degrees Granted 1972-73: 7 BA, 7 MA, 13 Ph.D. Majors: 52 g, 5 MA, 47 Ph.D., 51 Graduate in Residence, 27 u.

A candidate for the MA degree is required to demonstrate a reading knowledge of one language other than his native language. The Ph.D. candidate is required to demonstrate a reading knowledge of two languages other than his native language, of which at least one must be English, German or Russian.
    For the Ph.D., a qualifying examination is required, in addition to the examinations required by the Graduate School.
    A well-qualified student with a good background in linguistics can complete an MA degree in one year and a Ph.D. degree in three years after the B.A. It is not required that an MA degree be earned prior to a Ph.D. Degree.
    A broad scope of offerings in both pure and applied linguistics is available, including not only courses in general linguistics, but also language-specific courses in East Asian linguistics (China, Japan) South Asian linguistics (Ceylon, India, Pakistan), and Southeast Asian linguistics (Burma, Indonesia, Philippines, Thailand, Vietnam).
    Specialization in linguistics is offered by several fields in the Graduate School: Asian Studies has East Asian linguistics, South Asian linguistics and Southeast Asian linguistics as minor subjects. There is a minor in Indo-European linguistics in the Field of Classics. A minor in English linguistics may be taken in the Field of English Language and Literature. The Field of Germanic Studies has majors and minors in Germanic linguistics. Under Romance Linguistics, majors and minors are offered in French, Italian, Romance, and Spanish linguistics. Majors and minors are offered by the field of Slavic Linguistics.

COURSE OFFERINGS

Introductory, 3; Phonology, 4; Theoretical Models, 9; Sociolinguistics, 4; Field Methods, 1; Psycholinguistics, 1; Math. & Comp. Linguistics, 1; Linguistics & Literature, 1;

Applied Lx., 1. Language Areas: Comp. Romance 1, Old Provençal 1, Old Irish 2, Comp. IE 2, Skt. 2, Old Javanese 2, SE Asia 2, Mon Khmer 1, Slavic 1, Pali 1, Chinese 3, E. Asia 1, Thai 2, Tibeto-Burman 1, French 6, German 5, Japanese 3, Polish 2, Quechua 1, Russian 3, Spanish 1, Sino-Tibetan 1, Malayo-Polynesian 1, Cambodian 1.

UNCOMMONLY-TAUGHT LANGUAGES

Burmese (8 sem.)	Chinese-FALCON	Japanese (8 sem.)	Quechua (2 sem.)
Cambodian (6 sem.)	Intensive Man-	Japanese-FALCON	Sinhalese (6 sem.)
Cebuano (2 sem.)	darin one year,	Intensive Japa-	Swedish (2 sem.)
Chinese-Cantonese	36 credit hrs.	nese one year,	Tagalog (4 sem.)
(4 sem.)	Hindi-Urdu (8 sem.)	36 credit hrs.	Tamil (2 sem.)
Chinese-Hokkien	Indonesian	Javanese (4 sem.)	Telugu (4 sem.)
(2 sem.)	(8 sem.)	Portuguese (6 sem.)	Thai (8 sem.)
Chinese-Mandarin			Vietnamese (8 sem.)
(8 sem.)			

STAFF

F. B. Agard: Romance linguistics, Portuguese, Rumanian.
L. H. Babby: Slavic linguistics.
N. C. Bodman: Chinese and Sino-Tibetan linguistics.
J. S. Bowers: Transformational grammar.
S. P. Durham: French linguistics.
J. M. Echols: Malayo-Polynesian linguistics.
C. E. Elliott: English linguistics, Hindi.
J. W. Gair: General linguistics, South Asian linguistics, Sinhalese.
J. E. Grimes: General linguistics, indigenous languages of the Americas, computational linguistics.
R. A. Hall, Jr.: Comparative Romance linguistics, history of Italian language and literature, pidgin and creole languages.
C. F. Hockett: Anthropological linguistics.
F. E. Huffman: Vietnamese, Cambodian, Thai.
R. B. Jones, Jr.: Descriptive and comparative linguistics of Southeast Asia.
E. H. Jorden: Japanese linguistics, language pedagogy.
R. E. Kaske: English linguistics.
G. B. Kelley: Dravidian, general linguistics, sociolinguistics.
H. L. Kufner: Germanic linguistics.
R. L. Leed: Slavic linguistics, general linguistics.
P. Lowe, Jr.: Germanic linguistics.
J. McCoy: Japanese and Chinese linguistics, Chinese dialects.
G. M. Messing: Classical linguistics.
J. S. Noblitt: Romance linguistics, programmed learning.
D. F. Solá: Spanish linguistics, Quechua.
R. D. Steele: Slavic linguistics.
G. J. Suci: Psycholinguistics and language acquisition.
M. A. Suner: Spanish linguistics.
F. van Coetsem: Germanic linguistics.
J. F. Vigorita: Celtic linguistics, Indo-European.
L. Waugh: French linguistics.
J. U. Wolff: Indonesian and Philippine linguistics.

Linguists in other Departments and Schools

R. Borker: Sociolinguistics, Religion.
J. Catlin: Psycholinguistics.
E. Lenneberg: Developmental Psychology, Experimental Psychology, Physiological Psychology.

Support Available

Teaching Assitantships, Research Assistantships, Fellowships, Tuition and Fees.

Academic Calendar 1974-1975

Fall Semester: Begins Sept. 2, 1974 - Dec. 7, 1974; Winter break Dec. 21, 1974 -
Jan. 27, 1975; Spring Semester: Begins Jan. 27, 1975 - May 10, 1974; Summer Session:
Begins May 27, 1975 - Aug. 8, 1975. Deadline: For Fall term admission - January 15;
For Spring term admission - April 15.

DESCRIPTIVE MATERIAL: Write: Cornell Graduate School, Sage Graduate Center,
Cornell University, Ithaca, New York 14850.

UNIVERSITY OF DETROIT Detroit, Michigan 48221   Tel. (313) 927-1238

Languages and Linguistics Department
Lloyd W. Wedberg, Chairman
Degrees: BA, MA with concentration in linguistics or interdisciplinary major.

Any student may take individual courses in linguistics, but two special options are
available: (1) a concentration in linguistics, for students majoring in English,
psychology, languages or other fields, but interested in gaining a deeper understanding
of language through a program of language-related courses and research; (2) an interdisciplinary major, e.g. in "English and Linguistics," "Psycholinguistics," or "Languages and Linguistics." This latter option, consisting of a minimum of 21 hours in
linguistics and 21 in another field, is planned by the student to the mutual satisfac-
tion of his advisor in both areas and approved by the interdisciplinary linguistics
committee.
     A program of Interdisciplinary Studies in Linguistics builds upon one or more basic
courses in linguistics where the student has an opportunity to demonstrate his capacity
for original research and independent study. In addition to regular course offerings
(listed each term in a special section of the schedule of classes), students who show
such ability will be encouraged to devote one or more terms to research and directed
readings.
     Many areas of specialized study and research open to the student are suggested in
the brochure "Interdisciplinary Studies in Linguistics," which may be obtained from
the Languages and Linguistics office, Briggs 319.

COURSE OFFERINGS

Theoretical Models, 4; Semantics & Logic, 1; Dialectology, 1; Applied Ling., 1; Psycholinguistics, 6; Math. & Comp. Linguistics, 1; Historical Linguistics, 2; History of
Linguistics, 1; Linguistics & Literature, 1; Language Pedagogy, 3.

STAFF

Michael Capp (Ph.D., Deutsche Karlsuniversität, Prague; Assoc Prof) Germanic
     Philology.
Theodore W. Walters, S.J. (Ph.D., Georgetown University, 1966; Assoc Prof) Lin-
     guistics - Applied Linguistics.

Linguists in other Departments and Schools

Mimi La Driere (Ph.D., Fordham University; Assoc Prof) Psychology Dept.
Ralph J. Spendal (Ph.D., University of Oregon) Medieval Literature.
Thomas Wallenmaier (M.A., Michigan State; Asst Prof) History of Philosophy,
     Philosophy and Methodology of Science.

Academic Calendar 1974-1975

Fall Trimester, Sept. 3, 1974 to December 14, 1974; Winter Trimester, Jan. 6,
1975 to April 26, 1975; Summer Session: June 20, 1975 - August 1, 1975.

DESCRIPTIVE MATERIAL: Write: Admissions Department, University of Detroit, 4001
W. McNichols Rd., Detroit, Michigan 48221.

DREW UNIVERSITY Madison, New Jersey 07940   Tel. (201) 377-9031, x258

Committee on Linguistics
Roger W. Wescott, Chairman
Degrees: BA, MA, Ph.D. in related field with emphasis in linguistics.

COURSE OFFERINGS

Introductory, 1; Theoretical Models, 1; Sociolinguistics, 1; Psycholinguistics, 1;
Historical Linguistics, 1. Language Areas: Romance 1, Semitic 1.

UNCOMMONLY-TAUGHT LANGUAGES

Ugaritic

STAFF

Robert Chapman (Ph.D., Michigan, 1952; Prof) Lexicography, History of English,
   Grammatical theories.
Carlos Fuentes (Ph.D., Villanova-Habana Cuba, 1953; Assoc Prof) Spanish, Romance
   languages, Latin American cultures.
Herbert Huffman (Ph.D., Michigan, 1963; Assoc Prof) Biblical philology, Semitic
   languages, Near Eastern writing systems.
Roger Wescott (Ph.D., Princeton, 1948; Prof) African languages, Phonology, Animal
   communication systems.

Academic Calendar 1974-1975

Fall Quarter: Sep 74 - Dec 74; Winter Quarter: Jan 75 (only); Spring Quarter:
Feb 75 - May 75.

DESCRIPTIVE MATERIAL: Write: Registrar, Drew University, Madison, New Jersey 07940.

DUKE UNIVERSITY Durham, North Carolina 27706   Tel. (919) 684-3706

Interdepartmental Committee on Linguistics
Alexander O. Hull, Chairman
Degrees: BA. Degrees Granted 1972-73: 2 BA.

Students wishing to major in linguistics may do so under the supervision of the
University Committee on Program II, and with the sponsorship of one of the established departments (usually Anthropology, English, or Romance Languages). There
are no established requirements for this program; students create their own course
of study, with the advice of the sponsoring department, and submit it to the University
Committee for approval.

COURSE OFFERINGS

Introductory, 1gu 1u; Phonology, 1gu; Theoretical Models, 1gu 1u; Semantics & Logic 1u; Sociolinguistics, 1u; Psycholinguistics, 1gu; Historical Linguistics, 1gu 1u; Applied Lx., 1u. Language Areas: Old English 1, French 2, German 2, Spanish 1.

UNCOMMONLY-TAUGHT LANGUAGES

Chinese (u 6 sem.)   Hindi-Uru   Japanese (u 7 sem.)   Swahili (u 2 sem.)
Dutch (u 2 sem.)   (u 8 sem.,
                       g 2 sem.)

STAFF

Mahadeo L. Apte (Ph.D.; Assoc Prof) Hindi-Urdu.
Ronald R. Butters (Ph.D.; Assoc Prof) American dialects, Variation theory.
Ronald W. Casson (Ph.D.; Asst Prof) Turkish, Child Language Acquisition.
Alexander Hull (Ph.D.; Assoc Prof) Romance linguistics, Variation theory.
Holger O. Nygard (Ph.D.; Prof) Old English, Middle English.
William O'Barr (Ph.D.; Asst Prof) Anthropology Dept.
Henry R. Stern (Ph.D.; Asst Prof) German.
Paul Welsh (Ph.D.; Prof) Philosophy Dept.

Academic Calendar 1974-1975

Fall Semester: September 3 - December 20; Spring Semester: January 10 - May 6.

DESCRIPTIVE MATERIAL: Write: Admissions Office, 614 Chapel Drive, Duke University, Durham, North Carolina 27706.

EAST TEXAS STATE UNIVERSITY   Commerce, Texas 75428   Tel. (214) 468-5136

Department of Literature and Languages
Fred Tarpley, Chairman
Degrees: BA, MA, MS in English language and linguistics; Ed.D. in college teaching
        of English with specialization in English language. Degrees Granted 1972-
        73: 2 MA, 3 Ph.D., Ed.D. 1. Majors: 18g. In Residence: 10g, 4 u.

The linguistic emphases at East Texas State University are on English language and bilingual methodology (Spanish-English). The university library has strong holdings in general linguistics, and seven university libraries in the Dallas/Fort Worth area are also available to students. Most of the linguistics students plan to use their training for teaching in secondary schools or colleges. Recent research has focused on analyses of Black English, regional dialectology, linguistics and composition, Chicano English, and generative grammar and rhetoric.

COURSE OFFERINGS

Introductory, 1; Phonology, 2; Theoretical Models, 2; Semantics & Logic, 1; Sociolinguistics, 2; Dialectology, 1; Historical Linguistics, 3; Language Pedagogy, 3. Language Areas: Spanish, French.

Staff

Fred Tarpley (Ph.D., LSU, 1969; Prof) English language, dialectology, grammar.
Charles Carlson (Ph.D., Indiana, 1972; Asst Prof) General linguistics, Finno-
    Ugric languages, contrastive linguistics.
Mamie Hafner (Ph.D., Wisconsin, 1965; Prof) English language, Old English, Middle
    English.

Loyd Guidry (Ed.D., Kansas, 1971; Asst Prof) Grammar, contrastive linguistics,
   bilingual methodology.
William J. Harvey (Ph.D., Texas, 1972; Asst Prof) Contrastive linguistics, general
   linguistics, German.

Support Available

Assistant instructorships are available to graduate students at the masters and
doctoral level. These graduate assistants teach two sections of freshman or
sophomore English, including English as a second language, and receive $330 per month.

Academic Calendar 1974-1975

Fall Semester: August 29-December 20; Spring Semester: January 16-May 17; Summer
Session: June 3-August 15. (Two terms)

DESCRIPTIVE MATERIAL: Write: Admissions Office, East Texas State University,
                Commerce, Texas 75428.

FEDERAL CITY COLLEGE Washington, D.C. 20001   Tel. (202) 727-2319

Communication Science
Ann Covington, Chairman
Degrees: B.A., MA in Communication Science. Degrees Granted 1972-73: 9 BA, 15 MA.
         Majors: 56 g, 56 MA, 49 Graduate in Residence, 80 u.

The undergraduate program offers introductory courses in linguistics to complement
majors in speech pathology, foreign languages, English, and Anthropology. Particular
emphasis is given to social dialectology and language and culture.
   The graduate program in Communication Sciences offers a major in Urban Language
Studies and/or Speech Pathology. As a part of both of these majors, basic courses
in phonological and grammatical theory are required, as well as representative courses
in sociolinguistics. Majors in Urban language studies take aspects of linguistic fieldwork and more advanced courses in linguistic theory and analysis. The particular orientation of the Communication Sciences program is directed toward urban areas.

COURSE OFFERINGS

Phonology, 1; Theoretical Models, 1; Sociolinguistics, 3; Dialectology, 1; Field
Methods, 1; Psycholinguistics, 2; Language Pedagogy, 1.

UNCOMMONLY-TAUGHT LANGUAGES

Chinese   Portuguese   Swahili

STAFF

Nona H. Clarke (MA, Georgetown University, 1971; Asst Prof) Syntax, Language
   Acquisition, sociolinguistics.
Faye Vaughn Cooke (MA, Georgetown University, 1972; Asst Prof) Language acquisi-
   tion, speech disorders, sociolinguistics.
Ronald Williams (Ph.D., Ohio State University, 1968; Prof) Phonetics, Sociolin-
   guistics, psycholinguistics.
Walt Wolfram (Ph.D., Hartford Seminary Foundation, 1969; Prof) Sociolinguistics,
   Variation theory, Phonology.

Linguists in other Departments and Schools

Janet McKay (Ph.D., Princeton University, 1973; Asst Prof) Department of English;
    English Grammar, History of English Language.
Marie M. Racine (Ph.D., Georgetown University, 1970; Assoc Prof) Dept. of Foreign
    Languages; Bilingualism, Pidgins and Creoles.

Support Available

Work Study Fellowships; Student training fellowships in Speech Pathology. Contact
Dr. Ann Covington, Chairman.

Academic Calendar 1974-1975

Fall Quarter: Sept. 15; Winter Quarter: Jan. 6; Spring Quarter: April 3; Summer
Quarter: July 1. Deadline: One month prior to beginning of quarter.

DESCRIPTIVE MATERIAL: Write: Dr. Ann Covington, Chairman, Communication Sciences,
                       Federal City College, 724 9th St., N.W., Washington DC 20001.

UNIVERSITY OF FLORIDA   Gainesville, Florida 32611   Tel. (904) 392-0639

Program in Linguistics
Irving R. Wershow, Acting Director
Degrees: MA, Ph.D. Degrees Granted 1972-73: 2 MA, 1 Ph.D. Majors: 22 MA, 10 Ph.D.

At this time there is no undergraduate program in Linguistics, but an interdisciplinary
degree involving eight departments is being proposed.
    The graduate program is highly flexible. Among MA's available, there are specific
programs to train TESL specialists (thesis) and reading specialists (no thesis; Florida
Certification). MA and Ph.D. degrees are available in any area(s) adequately represented by the faculty. We recommend combining theory with application: Theory with Psycho
linguistics, Phonology or Syntax with structural and practical knowledge of a language
or language family, Theory and Neurolinguistics, Anthropological linguistics with language pedagogy or bilingual education, English linguistics with TESL or bidialectal
problems are some contributions selected by one Ph.D. candidate.
    The faculty of the Program is supported by five participating departments: Anthropo-
logy, English, Germanic and Slavic Languages, Romance Languages, and Speech. Other
related units on campus are Centers for African Studies (H. Der-Houssikian, Director),
Afro-American Studies (R. C. Foreman, Director), Asian Studies (A.B. Creel, Chairman),
Neurological and Behavioral Linguistic Research (R. J. Scholes, Director), Communication
Sciences Laboratory (H. Hollien, Director), Computer and Information Sciences (G. E.
Haynam, Director), English Language Institute (J. C. Harder, Director), Foreign Lan-
guage Education (C. L. Hallman), Latin American Studies (W. E. Carter, Director), Read-
ing and Studies Skills (A. G. Cranney, Director), Soviet and East European Studies
(J. F. Morrison), Speech and Hearing Clinics (E. C. Hutchinson), Western European Studies
(Max Kele, Chairman).

COURSE OFFERINGS

Program: Introductory, 2g, 1u; Phonology, 4g; Theoretical Models, 5g; Semantics & Logic,
1g; Dialectology, 1g, 1u; Field Methods, 1g; Psycholinguistics, 1g, 1u; Neurolinguistics,
1g; Math. & Comp. Linguistics, 1g; Historical Linguistics; 4g; Applied Ling., 1g.
Related Dept.: Phonology, 1g; Theoretical Models, 1g; Sociolinguistics, 2g; Field Methods;
2g; Psycholinguistics, 4g; Math. & Comp. Linguistics, 1g. Other Dept.: Introductory,
3u; Phonology, 4u; Theoretical Models, 1u; Semantics & Logic, 2u; Psycholinguistics,
1u; Historical Linguistics, 1u; Language Pedagogy 1u. Other: Ling. in the Community

College. Language Areas: African langs. 1, German 2, Icelandic 1, Russian 2, French 3, Portuguese 1, Spanish 3, Romance 1, Swahili 1.

UNCOMMONLY-TAUGHT LANGUAGES

Aymara (u 6q)	Greek (u 5)	Latin (u 5)	Swahili (u 5)
Chinese (u 5)	Hebrew (u 3)	Polish (u 4)	Ukrainian (u 3)

STAFF

Jean Casagrande (Ph.D., Indiana, 1968; Assoc Prof) Syntax and Dialectology, French (1/2 time).

J. Wayne Conner (Ph.D., Princeton; Prof) Romance Linguistics, Linguistic Geography.

Chauncey C. Ch'u (Ph.D., Texas, 1970; Asst Prof) Linguistic Theory, Chinese Linguistics (1/3 time).

Haig Der-Houssikian (Ph.D., Texas, 1969; Assoc Prof) African Linguistics, Sociolinguistics, Generative Syntax (1/3 time).

Donald D. Dew (Ph.D., Iowa; Assoc Prof) Phonetics, Experimental Phonetics.

Christian Gellinek (Ph.D., Yale; Prof) Germanic Philology.

Jayne C. Harder (Ph.D., Florida, 1956; Assoc Prof) ESL, Standard English as a second dialect.

Martha Hardman-de Bautista (Ph.D., Stanford, 1962; Prof) Anthropological Linguistics, Field Method, Jaqian Languages (1/3 time).

Paul J. Jenson (Ph.D., Iowa, 1962; Assoc Prof) Language Acquisition, Speech Pause Phenomena (1/3 time).

Paul A. Kotey (Ph.D., Wisconsin, 1969; Asst Prof) African Linguistics, Phonology, Linguistic Problems in Africa (1/3 time).

Marion M. Lasley (Ph.D., Columbia; Assoc Prof) Romance Linguistics, Spanish.

Norman M. Markel (Ph.D., Chicago; Prof) Speech and Personality, Sociolinguistics.

Kevin M. McCarthy (Ph.D., North Carolina, 1969; Asst Prof) Historical Linguistics, English Linguistics, Stylistics (1/3 time).

Gary D. Miller (Ph.D., Harvard, 1969; Asst Prof) Language Change, Phonology, Indo-European (1/3 time).

Theron A. Nunez (Ph.D., California; Assoc Prof) Language and Culture, Anthropological Linguistics.

Arnold Paige (Ph.D., California; Assoc Prof) Phonetics, Speech Synthesis, Electrical Engineering.

Yves Rouchaleau (Ph.D., Stanford; Asst Prof) Mathematical Linguistics, Applied Mathematics.

Bohdan Saciuk (Ph.D., Illinois, 1969; Asst Prof) Phonology, Romance Dialectology, Ukrainian (1/3 time).

Robert J. Scholes (Ph.D., Indiana, 1964; Assoc Prof) Neurolinguistics, Aphasia, Linguistic Theory (1/3 time).

Stanley Y. W. Su (Ph.D., Wisconsin; Assoc Prof) Computational Linguistics, Man-Machine Communication.

William J. Sullivan (Ph.D., Yale, 1969; Asst Prof) Phonology, Stratificational Theory, Slavic (1/3 time).

Roger M. Thompson (Ph.D., Texas, 1971; Asst Prof) Sociolinguistics, Dialectology (1/3 time).

Melvin E. Valk (Ph.D., Wisconsin; Assoc Prof) Germanic Philology.

Irving R. Wershow (Ph.D., Yale; Prof) Spanish, Language Pedagogy.

J. Jay Zeman (Ph.D., Chicago; Prof) Logic, Semiotics.

Support Available

Graduate Fellowship (1. Graduate School, 2. College of Arts and Sciences); Research Assistantships (Graduate School); Teaching Assistantships (From related departments and programs).

Academic Calendar 1974-1975

Fall Quarter: September 23-December 6 & Exam Week; Winter Quarter: January 6 -March 14 & Exam Week; Spring Quarter: March 31 - June 6 & Exam Week; Summer Session: June 23 -August 22 & Exam Week.

DESCRIPTIVE MATERIAL: Write: Registrar's Office, Tigert Hall, University of Florida, Gainesville, Florida 32611.

FLORIDA ATLANTIC UNIVERSITY Boca Raton, Florida 33432   Tel. (305) 395-5100, x2507

Languages and Linguistics Department
Dr. Ernest L. Weiser, Chairman
Degrees: BA, MA. Degrees Granted 1972-73: 14 BA, 4 MA. Majors: 25 g, 25 MA,
        12 Graduate in Residence, 28 u.

The department, with a faculty of linguists and literature professors, offers MA and MAT degree programs in French linguistics, German linguistics, and Spanish linguistics. Emphasis is placed in each upon the linguistics of one of the three languages.
    The MA program has as its objectives the training of language teachers who will have a scientific knowledge of their subject and linguists who will be qualified to continue studies for the Ph.D. in theoretical or applied linguistics. Studies in the areas of phonetics and phonemics, morphology and syntax, and psycholinguistics are complemented by intensive work in the history, dialectology, phonology and structure of the target language. Electives in applied linguistics, English linguistics, and literature are also part of the program. After a minimum of one quarter and submission of a thesis proposal, students may be admitted to candidacy. The thesis, which must deal with some aspect of linguistics, such as an analysis of a dialect or a study of bilingualism, is defended in an oral. The program, which has a one quarter residence requirement, normally requires four to five quarters to complete.
    The purpose of the MAT program is to train junior college teachers. Courses in the linguistics of the target language are augmented by courses in literature and civilization. A teaching internship and courses in the junior college curriculum and testing and measurement are required. The steps are the same as in the MA program, although the MAT thesis should deal with some problem in the teaching of language or literature according to sound linguistic and pedagogical principles.
    The Department of Languages and Linguistics operates a Linguistics Research Laboratory for student and faculty research in experimental phonetics, dialectology, and psycholinguistics. Facilities include a sound spectrograph and audio recording equipment for both field work and laboratory use.
    The department also offers a BA in linguistics as well as in German, French, and Spanish: The four undergraduate programs require work in linguistics, at least two languages, and the literature of the major language being studied.

COURSE OFFERINGS

Introductory, 3; Phonology, 2; Theoretical Models, 2; Dialectology, 1; Psycholinguistics, 1; Historical Linguistics, 2; Language Pedagogy, 3. Language Areas: German 3, Spanish 3, French 3.

STAFF

Marie C. Barnes (MA, Florida Atlantic University, 1967; Interim Inst) French
    language and literature (1/2 time).
Juan Estarellas (Ed.D., Harvard University, 1956; Prof) Psycholinguistics, language
    learning, programmed instruction.
Peter C. Merrill (Ph.D., Columbia University, 1974; Asst Prof) General linguistics,
    English as a foreign language, German linguistics.
Nelida G. Norris (Ph.D., UCLA, 1970; Asst Prof) Latin-American literature (1/2 time).
Huguette H. Parrish (Ph.D., University of Florida, 1972; Asst Prof) French, French
    literature - principally of the 19th century.
Vicente H. Rangel (Ph.D., University of Virginia, 1969; Asst Prof) Spanish, Conti-
    nental Spanish literature - principally of the Golden Age.

Melvyn C. Resnick (Ph.D., University of Rochester, 1968; Assoc Prof) General and
   experimental linguistics, phonetics, Spanish linguistics and dialectology.
Robert L. Trammell (Ph.D., Cornell, 1970; Asst Prof) General linguistics, French
   linguistics, psycholinguistics.
Ernest L. Weiser (Ph.D., UCLA, 1966; Assoc Prof) German, German literature - prin-
   cipally of the 18th century.

Linguists in other Departments and Schools

Mary E. Faraci (Ph.D., University of Florida, 1972; Asst Prof) English, linguistics,
   medieval and renaissance literature.

Support Available

A comprehensive program of student financial aid includes scholarships, grants, loans,
employment, and teaching assistantships which may provide assistance from initial enrollment through graduate study. Teaching assistantships are available in French, German,
and Spanish. Out-of-state tuition may be waived for these student assistants and others
who may be considered by virtue of their special qualifications or career plans. Opportunities also exist for limited support from a federally sponsored work-study program.
Prospective graduate students should contact the chairman of the department in which
they plan to enroll regarding these fellowships and assistantships at the time they
send in their application. Financial assistance in the form of student loans and employment is administered through the Office of Student Financial Aid.

Academic Calendar 1974-1975

Fall Quarter: September 23 to December 13, 1974; Winter Quarter: January 6 to March
21, 1975; Spring Quarter: March 31 to June 12, 1975; Summer Session: June 23 to August
29, 1975. Deadline: Aug. 23, 1974.

DESCRIPTIVE MATERIAL: Write: Admissions Office or Dr. Ernest L. Weiser, Chairman,
                       Department of Languages & Linguistics, Florida Atlantic Uni-
                       versity, 500 N.W. 20th Street, Boca Raton, Florida 33432.

GALLAUDET COLLEGE   Washington, D.C. 20002   Tel. (202) 447-0707

Linguistics Research Laboratory
Wm. C. Stokoe, Jr., Director

The Linguistics Research Laboratory at Gallaudet College is primarily concerned
with the language of deaf persons, specifically their competence in sign language and
in English, as it relates to social groups of hearing and deaf. From this central
concern, the activities of the LRL lead, in one direction, to exploring basic language
theory, in the other, to application of language science to materials, curricula, and
strategies for learning.   Sign languages, especially American Sign Language, afford
a triangulation point unique in linguistic research. If language, as now is supposed,
consists of a silent, invisible, inner process of the human brain, then we usually
try to survey language from only one vantage point: our ability to hear and speak the
units of its symbolic expression. When, however, gestural signs express language,
we may be able to learn things about language hidden from its hearer-speakers.
Activities, both theoretical and applied, are reported in two periodical publications:
SIGNS FOR OUR TIMES distributed without charge monthly in the academic year to about
1,200 readers. Its brief notes help keep in touch a widely dispersed group interested
in SIGN and language. SIGN LANGUAGE STUDIES (1972--) contains articles, reviews, and
reports relating sign language research to disciplines ranging from anthropology to
zoology. This semiannual journal (Nos. 1-4 in print) is edited by William Stokoe,
director of the LRL, and published by Mouton.

Support for the LRL comes from Gallaudet College and from agencies which directly foster research. During the first two years of its full-time operation, the Laboratory has been fortunate in securing support from the National Science Foundation for a study of semantics and syntax in American Sign Language, and with the Center for Applied Linguistics, from the National Institutes of Health for a Sign-English contrastive study. These two major projects well reflect the double concern with language theory and with applying linguistic knowledge to learning.

Courses for Gallaudet College, Washington Consortium, and visiting scholars are taught by the director and associates of the LRL. Presently appearing among undergraduate and graduate offerings of the departments of audiology and speech, English, and sociology, these courses, seminars, and directed research studies are planned for increasing numbers of master's and doctoral candidates in anthropology, linguistics, sociolinguistics, and educational technology.

Visitors to the LRL are able to consult its growing collection of published and unpublished papers, and its videotaped and filmed research data. Present plans call for indexing, abstracting, and entering much of this material in the Edward Miner Gallaudet Memorial Library computer-based information system. We hope that soon remote users of LRL services may thus have access also to recent information.

COURSE OFFERINGS

Introductory, 1; Theoretical Models, 1; Sociolinguistics, 3; Psycholinguistics, 1.

UNCOMMONLY-TAUGHT LANGUAGES

American Sign Language   Pidgin Sign English

STAFF

Robbin M. Battison (MA, Univ. of Calif., San Diego, 1973; Res Assoc) Sign Languages,
    Psycholinguistics, Neurolinguistics.
Harry Markowicz (MA, Simon Fraser University, Vancouver, B.C., 1970; Res Assoc)
    Sign Languages, Sociolinguistics.
William C. Stokoe, Jr. (Ph.D., Cornell, 1946; Prof) Sign Languages, Lang. & Culture
    of the Deaf (1/3 time; 2/3 research).
James C. Woodward, Jr. (Ph.D., Georgetown; Asst Prof) Sign Languages, Sociolinguistics
    1/3 time; 2/3 research).

GEORGETOWN UNIVERSITY Washington, D.C. 20007   Tel. (202) 625-4832

School of Languages and Linguistics
Department of Linguistics
Francis P. Dinneen, S.J., Chairman [R. Ross Macdonald as of July 1975]
Degrees: BS, MS, Ph.D. Degrees Granted 1972-73: 8 BA, 47 MA, 9 Ph.D. Majors:
        184 g, 57 MA, 75 Ph.D., 138 Graduate in Residence, 66 u.

The undergraduate program stresses theoretical and applied linguistics. The freshman quota in linguistics is 15, but double majors in language and linguistics are common, and transfer students are accepted. Ten one-semester courses complete the undergraduate major requirements. Courses in other areas of linguistics are available to juniors and seniors. Teacher accreditation can be arranged for languages.

All graduate programs, except Sociolinguistics, require both languages and linguistics. Language majors minor in theoretical and applied linguistics. Linguistic majors are offered in Theoretical, Applied, Computational and Sociolinguistics. Minors are in language (optional for sociolinguistic majors) and another area of linguistics. Areas of concentration are general and theoretical linguistics, applied linguistics, TEFL, computational linguistics (IBM 370/145 available), sociolinguistics. Three Sonographs and several other instruments are available for acoustic analysis.

COURSE OFFERINGS

Introductory, 2g 3u; Phonology, 4g 1u; Theoretical Models, 5g, 1u; Semantics & Logic, 4g;
Sociolinguistics, 13g 1u; Dialectology, 1g; Field Methods, 2g; Psycholinguistics, 6g;
Math. & Comp. Linguistics, 5g; Historical Linguistics, 3g; Language Pedagogy, 5g, 3u.
Language Areas: Arabic, 2; Chinese, 6; French, 2; German, 6; Italian, 3; Japanese, 5;
Portuguese, 5; Russian, 5; Spanish, 10. Other: Lexicography, Literacy.

UNCOMMONLY-TAUGHT LANGUAGES

Arabic   Chinese   Japanese   Portuguese

STAFF

James E. Alatis (Ph.D., Ohio State, 1966; Dean, SLL and Assoc Prof) Applied Lin-
  guistics, TESOL, English Linguistics.
Walter A. Cook, S.J. (Ph.D., Georgetown, 1965; Prof) Syntax.
Daniel P. Dato (Ph.D., Cornell, 1960; Assoc Prof) Psycholinguistics.
Francis P. Dinneen, S.J. (Ph.D., London, 1961; Prof) Linguistic Theory and Semantics.
Robert J. Di Pietro (Ph.D., Cornell, 1960; Prof) Contrastive Analysis, Post-
  transformational Grammar, Bilingualism.
Ralph W. Fasold (Ph.D., Chicago, 1968; Asst Prof) Sociolinguistics, Applied Lin-
  guistics, General Linguistics.
David P. Harris (Ph.D., Michigan, 1954; Prof) Historical Linguistics, TEFL, Language
  Testing.
Charles W. Kreidler (Ph.D., Michigan, 1958; Prof) English Linguistics.
Robert Lado (Ph.D., Michigan, 1950; Prof) Applied Linguistics.
Donald Larkin (MA, Michigan, 1968; Asst Prof) Sociolinguistics, Pragmatics.
R. Ross Macdonald (Ph.D., Yale, 1955; Prof) English Linguistics and Computation.
Richard J. O'Brien, S.J. (Ph.D., Georgetown, 1965; Assoc Prof) General Linguistics,
  Latin.
Gerd Quinting (Ph.D., Rochester, 1970; Asst Prof) Psycholinguistics, English Lin-
  guistics.
Solomon Sara, S.J. (Ph.D., Georgetown, 1969; Asst Prof) Phonology, General Lin-
  guistics and Arabic.
Muriel R. Saville-Troike (Ph.D., Texas, 1968; Asst Prof) Sociolinguistics, Cultural
  Anthropology, American Indian Linguistics.
Shaligram Shukla (Ph.D., Cornell, 1968; Asst Prof) Language & Culture, Historical
  Linguistics and General Linguistics.
Roger W. Shuy (Ph.D., Case Western Reserve, 1962; Prof) Sociolinguistics.
Karl Stowasser (Ph.D., Münster, 1967; Lecturer) Lexicography (1/3 time).
Michael Zarechnak (Ph.D., Harvard, 1967; Assoc Prof) Computation, Semantics,
  General Linguistics.

Linguists in other Departments and Schools

Frederick J. Bosco (MA, Michigan, 1958; Asst Prof) Applied Linguistics and Italian.
William W. Cressey (Ph.D., Illinois, 1966; Assoc Prof) Phonology and Spanish.
Wallace Erwin (Ph.D., Georgetown, 1964; Prof) Arabic.
Flora Klein (Ph.D., Columbia, 1972; Asst Prof) Spanish.
Michael McCaskey (Ph.D., Yale, 1965; Assoc Prof) Chinese.
Gino Parisi (Ph.D., Georgetown, 1968; Asst Prof) Spanish.
Clea Rameh (Ph.D., Georgetown, 1970; Asst Prof) Portuguese.
Paul Yang, S.J. (Ph.D., Georgetown, 1967; Assoc Prof) Chinese.

Support Available

Of about 9 university fellowships and 7 scholarships, as many as 5 may be available
in a given year. Stipend: $2500. Occasional assistantships in Language Departments.

Academic Calendar 1974-1975

Fall Semester: September 5 - December 20; Spring Semester: January 15 - May 9;
Summer Session: May 20 - August 30 (varied programs). Deadline: g: February 15,

for financial aid in Fall, December 15 for Spring registration; ug: Freshmen: January 15 for following fall, Transfers: May 1 for following Fall.

DESCRIPTIVE MATERIAL: Write: (undergraduate) Office of Undergraduate Admissions, (graduate) The Graduate School, Georgetown University, Washington, D. C. 20007.

UNIVERSITY OF GEORGIA   Athens, Georgia 30602

Curriculum in Linguistics
Jane Appleby, Director
Degrees: MA, Ph.D.

The Curriculum in Linguistics at the University of Georgia offers interdepartmental study leading to the MA and Ph.D. in Linguistics. Students may take core courses in linguistics and pursue a variety of possible specializations, such as anthropological linguistics, psycholinguistics, English linguistics, pedagogical linguistics, languages, etc. The curriculum includes many courses which are open to undergraduates.

Facilities include extensive library holdings in Romance and Germanic languages, American Indian languages, Japanese, collections of colonial materials for dialect study, and a growing language laboratory. Spectographic equipment is available for work in acoustical phonetics. Computer facilities include an IBM 360-65, an IBM 370-58, and a CDC 6400.

COURSE OFFERINGS

Introductory, 2; Phonology, 3; Theoretical Models, 3; Semantics & Logic, 2; Dialectology, 1; Field Methods, 2; Psycholinguistics, 4; Historical Linguistics, 3; History of Linguistics, 1; Language Pedagogy, 2. Language Areas: Japanese 1, Skt. 1, Greek 1, Latin 1, OE 1, ME 1, German 4, Gothic 1, Spanish 2, French 2, Provencal 1, Romance 1. Other: Nature of Oral Lg.

STAFF

John T. Algeo (Ph.D., Florida, 1960; Prof) English linguistics.
Jane Appleby (Ph.D., U. Wisconsin, 1967; Assoc Prof) Historical linguistics, Dialectology, Grammar.
Maija Blaubergs (Ph.D., California, Santa Barbara, 1972; Asst Prof) Psycholinguistics, Semantics, Language Acquisition.
Lowell Bouma (Ph.D., Wisconsin, 1968; Asst Prof) Germanic linguistics, Semantics, Second language acquisition.
James M. Crawford (Ph.D., California, Berkeley, 1966; Assoc Prof) American Indian languages, General linguistics.
Ralph de Gorog (Ph.D., Columbia, 1954; Prof) Romance linguistics, Lexicology, Medieval French and Spanish.
Betty J. Irwin (Ph.D., U. Wisconsin, 1967; Asst Prof) Historical linguistics, Grammar.
Jared Klein (Ph.D., Yale, 1974; Asst Prof) Indo-European linguistics, Classical linguistics, Sanskrit.
Roy C. O'Donnell (Ph.D., George Peabody, 1961; Prof) Applied English linguistics, Developmental psycholinguistics.
Richard Rystrom (Ed.D., California, Berkeley, 1966; Assoc Prof) Applied linguistics, Reading, Dialectology.
Donald L. Smith (Ph.D., U. Michigan, 1970; Asst Prof) English and Japanese linguistics, Generative semantics, Computational.
Edward A. Stephenson (Ph.D., North Carolina, 1958; Prof) Historical linguistics, English linguistics and philology, Old and Middle English literature.
Ernst Von Glasersfeld (B.S., Zuoz College, Switzerland, 1935; Asst Prof) Psycholinguistics, Cognition, Cybernetics.

Language Department
Royce W. Miller, Chairman
Degrees: BA. Degrees Granted 1972-73: 4 BA. Majors: 12 u.

Student specializes in a foreign language, takes wide span of studies in General
Linguistics. The Wycliffe Summer Institute of Linguistics is a regular part of
our program.

COURSE OFFERINGS

Introductory, 3; Phonology, 2; Theoretical Models, 2; Psycholinguistics, 2; Historical
Linguistics, 2. Language Areas: Romance 1, Latin 1, Portuguese 1, Spanish 1, Quechua
1, French 1, German 1.

UNCOMMONLY-TAUGHT LANGUAGES

Quechua

STAFF

Marion Carter (Ph.D., Catholic U., 1945; Prof) General Linguistics.
Royce W. Miller (Ph.D., Geo. Wash. U., 1967; Prof) General Ling., Romance Ling.,
    Indo-European Ling.
Donald Stark (Ph.D., Cornell U., 1970; Prof) General Linguistics, Quechua.

Linguists in other Departments and Schools

Delvin Covey (Ph.D., U. of Illinois, 1951; Prof) Modern English Grammar.
Winifred Currie (Ed.D., Boston U., 1963; Prof) Learning Disabilities and Teaching
    of Reading.
Thomas Howard (Ph.D., N.Y.U., 1970; Prof) Hist. of English Language.

Academic Calendar 1974-75

Fall Quarter: Sept. 16; Winter Quarter: Dec. 4; Spring Quarter: Apr. 1; Summer Quarter:
June 15.

DESCRIPTIVE MATERIAL: Write: Mr. Craig Hammon, Director of Admissions, Gordon
                       College, Wenham, Massachusetts 01984.

GRADUATE SCHOOL OF THE CITY UNIVERSITY OF NEW YORK   New York, N.Y. 10036
                                                    Tel. (212) 790-4602,3

Ph.D. Program in Linguistics
D. Terence Langendoen, Chairman
Degrees: Ph.D. Degrees Granted 1972-73: 3 Ph.D. Majors: 33g, 33 Ph.D.

The Program offers training in all aspects of linguistic theory, in applied linguistics (particularly English as a Second Language), historical linguistics,
psycholinguistics, philosophy of language, linguistic approaches to literature,
and anthropological linguistics. Laboratory facilities for work in phonetics, psycholinguistics, and anthropological linguistics are available through the Programs in
Speech, Developmental Psychology and Anthropology.
    The faculty resources of the Program are extensive, thanks to the cooperation of
many departments (in various fields) of the various colleges of the City University
of New York, including Brooklyn, City, Hunter, Lehman, and Queens Colleges.
    We are currently experiencing considerable difficulty obtaining adequate financial
support for graduate students; fortunately, tuition is low ($450 per semester for full-
time students who are New York City residents), and tuition waivers are available.

COURSE OFFERINGS

Introductory, 1; Phonology, 4; Theoretical Models, 4; Semantics & Logic, 1; Dialectology, 1; Field Methods, 2; Historical Linguistics, 1; History of Linguistics, 1. Language Areas: Persian 1, Skt. 1, Hebrew 1, West Africa 7, Welsh 1.

UNCOMMONLY-TAUGHT LANGUAGES

Modern Hebrew   Modern Persian   Welsh

STAFF

Beryl Bailey (Ph.D., Columbia U., 1964; Prof) General & Comparative Linguistics, Creole Languages.
Edward Bendix (Ph.D., Columbia U., 1965; Assoc Prof) Anthropological-Linguistics, South Asian Languages, Creole Languages.
Donald Byrd (Ph.D., U. of North Carolina, 1973; Asst Prof) English as a 2nd Language.
Arthur Bronstein (Ph.D., New York U., 1949; Prof) Dialectology.
Charles Cairns (Ph.D., Columbia U., 1968; Assoc Prof) Phonological Theory.
Helen Cairns (Ph.D., U. of Texas at Austin, 1970; Assoc Prof) Psycholinguistics.
Erica Garcia (Ph.D., Columbia U., 1964; Assoc Prof) Linguistic Theory, Spanish.
Edgar Gregersen (Ph.D., Yale, 1962; Prof) Anthropological-Linguistics, African Languages.
R. M. R. Hall (Ph.D., New York U., 1967; Assoc Prof) Linguistic Theory, Historical Linguistics.
Jerrold Katz (Ph.D., Princeton U., 1960; Prof) Semantic Theory, Philosophy of Language.
Stephen Krashen (Ph.D., U.C.L.A., 1972; Asst Prof) English as a 2nd Language, Neurolinguistics.
D. Terence Langedoen (Ph.D., Mass. Inst. of Tech., 1964; Prof) Linguistic Theory, English Syntax.
Samuel Levin (Ph.D., U. of Penn., 1956; Prof) Linguistics and Poetics.
Sally McLendon (Ph.D., U. of Cal., Berkeley, 1970; Assoc Prof) Anthropological-Linguistics, Sociolinguistics, Theory of Narrative.
Julius Moshinsky (Ph.D., U. of Cal., Berkeley, 1970; Asst Prof) Anthropological-Linguistics.
John Moyne (Ph.D., Harvard, 1970; Assoc Prof) Mathematical Linguistics, Iranian Linguistics.
Miroslav Rensky (Ph.D., Charles U., Prague, 1951; Prof) History and Structure of English.
Alan Stevens (Ph.D., Yale, 1964; Phonological Theory, South Asian Languages.
Robert Vago (Ph.D., Harvard, 1974; Asst Prof) Phonological Theory.
Virginia Valian (Ph.D., Northeastern U., 1971; Asst Prof) Psycholinguistics.
Ralph Ward (Ph.D., Yale, 1935; Prof) Indo-European Linguistics.

Linguists in other Departments and Schools

O.L. Chavarria-Aguilar (Ph.D., University of Pennsylvania; Prof) Indo-Iranian Linguistics.
Lindsey Churchill (Ph.D.) Program in Sociology, Ethnography of Speaking.
George Jochnowitz (Ph.D.) Romance Linguistics, Judeo-Italic Dialects.
Arnold Koslow (Ph.D.) Program in Philosophy, Philosophy of Language.
Katherine Harris (Ph.D.) Program in Speech, Phonetics.
Harry Levitt (Ph.D.) Program in Speech, Phonetics and Instrumentation.

Support Available

Assistantships (Junior, Intermediate & Senior), $300./mo (Approx.). College Work-study Awards. Dissertation Year Fellowships, $3000/yr. (Approx.). Intermediate Year Fellowships, $2000/yr. (Approx.). National Science Foundation Award, $2000/yr. (Approx.). NDEA Fellowship $2600/yr. (Approx.). Regent War Service Scholarships. Scholar Insentive Awards. Teaching Assistantships (as either Adjunct Lecturers, Lecturer, part-time or Lecturer Full-time) $3000/yr. (Approx.). University Fellowship, $2000/yr. (Approx.).

Academic Calendar 1974-1975

Fall Semester: Sept. 10, 1974 - Jan. 14, 1975; Spring Semester: Feb. 3, 1975 -June
2, 1975. Deadline: Mar. 15, 1975 for Fall 1975.

DESCRIPTIVE MATERIAL: Write: Office of Admissions, C.U.N.Y. Graduate Center,
33 West 42 Street, New York, New York 10036.

HAMPSHIRE COLLEGE Amherst, Massachusetts 01002   Tel. (413) 542-4790

School of Language and Communication
David Kerr, Coordinator 1974-75
Ruth Hammen, Administrative Assistant
Degrees: B.A. Student can design his own interdisciplinary program.

The School of Language and Communication is an undergraduate program that brings together the disciplines that study symbolic activity. The School was founded in the
belief that the formal study of the forms and uses of symbols has emerged in this century as a major perspective in the study of human life. The program has two parts.
The first part is devoted to the study of thought and language, and is composed of
linguistics, mathematical logic, computer science, analytic philosophy, and cognitive
psychology. The second part is devoted to the study of communication both in face-
to-face social interaction and in the mass media. This part of the program is composed of mass communications, and parts of anthropology, psychology, sociology, and
American Studies, and it includes courses in television production and journalism.
The School emphasizes interdisciplinary study and undergraduate research. The student designs his own interdisciplinary program of study, which can be within the School
or include other areas such as biology or literature. The student may enroll freely
in any course at the University of Massachusetts, and Amherst, Smith, and Mount Holyoke
Colleges. The student is required to do a substantial original project in his final
year.

COURSE OFFERINGS

Theoretical Models, 4; Semantics & Logic, 14; Sociolinguistics, 5; Dialectology, 1;
Psycholinguistics, 9; Math. & Comp. Linguistics, 6; Historical Linguistics, 1; Linguistics & Literature, 2; Language Pedagogy, 1.

STAFF

Emmon Bach (Ph.D., Chicago, 1959; Prof) Theoretical linguistics, Field Linguistics
    (1/2 time).
John Brandeau (MLS, SUNY Albany, 1972; Faculty Assoc) Film (1/6 time).
Allen Hanson (Ph.D., Cornell, 1969; Asst Prof) Computer Science, Artificial Intel-
    ligence, especially visual perception and semantics.
John Hornik (Ph.D., Illinois, 1972; Visiting Assoc) Social psychology, Proxemics,
    space, and crowding.
David Kerr (MA, Vanderbilt, 1965; Asst Prof) Mass communications theory, Journalism.
James Koplin (Ph.D., Minnesota, 1962; Assoc Prof) Cognitive psychology, Psycho-
    linguistics.
J. J. LeTourneau (Ph.D., UCBerkeley, 1968; Assoc Prof) Mathematical logic, Computer
    science.
Richard Lyon (Ph.D., Minnesota, 1962; Prof) American culture, literature, philosophy.
William Marsh (Ph.D., Dartmouth, 1966; Assoc Prof) Mathematical logic, Theoretical
    linguistics, History of linguistics and related disciplines.
Stephen Mitchell (Ph.D., Indiana, 1961; Assoc Prof) Literature, Computer Science.
Richard Muller (Ph.D., Syracuse, 1972; Asst Prof) Mass communications theory and law,
    Philosophy of technology (1/2 time).

Michael Radetsky (MA, UCBerkeley, 1968; Asst Prof) Philosophy, Philosophy of action, Philosophy of science.
Robert Rardin (BA, Swarthmore, 1967; Asst Prof) Linguistics, Applied linguistics.
Neil Shister (M.Phil., Yale, 1972; Asst Prof) American popular culture, Film.
Neil Stillings (Ph.D., Stanford, 1971; Asst Prof) Cognitive psychology, Psycho-linguistics, Theory of face-to-face interaction.
Janet Tallman (BA, Minnesota, 1962; Asst Prof) Anthropology, Sociolinguistics, Structure of conversation.
Martha Teghtsoonian (Ph.D., Radcliffe, 1960; Assoc Prof) Experimental psychology, Perception and perceptual development, Behaviorism (1/2 time).
Yvette Tenney (Ph.D., Cornell, 1973; Asst Prof) Cognitive psychology, Cognitive development, reading.
Harvey Wasserman (BA, Michigan, 1967; Faculty Asso) Journalism (1/6 time).
Christopher Witherspoon (MA, UCBerkeley, 1968; Asst Prof) Philosophy, Philosophy of perception, Philosophy of language.

Support Available

All financial aid comes from Hampshire College rather than from the School of Language and Communication.

Academic Calendar 1974-1975

Fall Term: September 11 - December 13, 1974; January Term: January 1-29, 1975; Spring Term: February 5 - May 16, 1975.

DESCRIPTIVE MATERIAL: Write: Van R. Halsey, Director of Admissions, Hampshire College, Amherst, Massachusetts 01002.

UNIVERSITY OF HARTFORD West Hartford, Connecticut 06117   Tel. (203) 243-4732

Linguistics Committee
J. David Danielson, Chairman
Degrees: BA. Degrees Granted 1972-72: 3(?) BA.
          In Residence: 10(?)u.

The major program in linguistics is designed to provide instruction in the basic topics, concepts, and methodology of linguistics-the systematic study of language. Students are encouraged to approach the study of language from as many points of view as possible, including those of such cognate disciplines as anthropology, literature, mathematics, philosophy, psychology, and speech, as well as those of linguistics itself. Alternate lines of study are available for (a) those interested primarily in foreign languages, (b) those interested primarily in English, (3) those whose major interest in linguistics is seconded by a strong interest in a cognate field, (d) students preparing for graduate work in linguistics. Within the framework of the major requirements, each student is expected to plan his own course of study, in consultation with his advisor. The program is administered by the Linguistics Committe of the College of Arts and Sciences.

COURSE OFFERINGS

Introductory, 2; Phonology, 2; Theoretical Models, 1; Semantics & Logic, 1; Socio-linguistics, 1; Psycholinguistics, 1; Historical Linguistics, 1; Linguistics & Literature, 1; Language Pedagogy, 2.

UNCOMMONLY-TAUGHT LANGUAGES

Modern Hebrew (u6)   Hindi

Staff

J. David Danielson (Ph.D., Michigan, 1960; Assoc Prof) Spanish-English contrastive
    linguistics (part time).
Robert Sherman (Ph.D., Michigan, 1965; Asst Prof) Speech (Part time).
Gerald Forbes (Ph.D., Florida, 1964; Asst Prof) Speech (part time).
Norman W. Oflager (Ph.D., Cornell, 1956; Assoc Prof) Anthropology, Iroquoian (part
    time).
Bernard Den Ouden (Ph.D., Hartford Seminary Foundation, 1973; Asst Prof) Philosophy
    of Language (part time).
George M. Evica (MA, Columbia, 1965; Asst Prof) English (part time).
Leo Rockas (Ph.D., Michigan, 1960; Assoc Prof) English, Modern Greek (part time).

Academic Calendar 1974-1975

Fall Semester: 2 Sep -20 Dec; Spring Semester: 12 Jan - 14 May; Summer Session:
Day: Two 5-week sessions, beginning 2 June. Evening: one 8-week session, beginning
2 June. Deadline: 1 June for September, 1 Dec for January.

DESCRIPTIVE MATERIAL: Write: Admissions Office, Auerbach Hall, University of
                       Hartford, West Hartford, Ct. 06117.

HARVARD UNIVERSITY   Cambridge, Massachusetts 02138   Tel. (617) 495-4054, 4006

Department of Linguistics
Chairman: Susumu Kuno
Degrees: BA, MA, Ph.D. Degrees Granted 1972-73: 5 BA, 6 MA, 5Ph.D. Majors: 30g.
         In Residence: 25g, 35u.

The Undergraduate concentration requires that linguistics be combined with another subject, either a language area, or some discipline whose interests overlap with those
of linguistics (mathematics, philosophy, psychology, social relations, etc.). In addition to regular courses, the program offers three years of group and individual tutorials,
and honor candidates write a senior thesis.
    The Graduate program includes extensive course offerings both within the Department
and in related departments. The program is particularly strong in historical linguistics
(Indo-European and Semitic), Amerindian linguistics and generative theory of grammar (phonology, syntax, and language universals). Breadth of coverage both in languages and
various areas of linguistics is emphasized.
    Facilities include extensive library holdings at Widener Library and other
affiliated libraries; the Center for Middle Eastern Studies, the Harvard-Yenching
Institute, the East Asian Research Center, the Semitic Museum and the Peabody
Museum of Archaeology and Ethnology.

COURSE OFFERINGS

Introductory, 3; Phonology, 3; Theoretical Models, 8; Semantics & Logic, 4; Sociolinguistics, 4; Dialectology, 1; Field Methods, 2; Psycholinguistics, 2; Math. & Comp. Ling.,
1; Historical Ling., 6. Language Areas: Classical Lgs 1, Native N. Amerindian 2, Algonquian 1, Menomini 1, Japanese 1, Chinese 2, Latin 1, Greek 1, Scandinavian 1, Germanic
1, German 1, English 1, Russian 3, Slavic 5, Comp. Celtic 1, Irish 1, French 1, Romance
2, Spanish 2, Portuguese 1, Indo.Aryan 1, Iranian 2, Comp. Semitic 2, Hebrew 2, African
Lgs. 1; Arabic 2, Turkic 4.

UNCOMMONLY-TAUGHT LANGUAGES

Akkadian (g6)
Class. Arabic
  (u2)
Arabic (u5, g3)
Aramaic (g3)
Armenian (u2,
  g2)
Class. Armenian
  (u2, g2)
Med. Armenian
  (g1)
Avestan (g1)
Bulgarian (u1)
Chinese (u8)
Class. Chinese
  (u8)
Chuvash (g1)
Class. Ethiopic
  (u2)
Old French (g2)

Class. Georgian
  (u2)
Mid. High German
  (g1)
Old High German
  (g1)
Gothic (g1)
Hebrew (u4)
Bib. Hebrew
  (u6)
Hittite (g3)
Mod. Irish
  (u2)
Old Irish (u1)
Mid. Irish (u1)
Japanese (u8)
Class. Japanese
  (u4)
Khalkha (u2)
Korean (u6)

Kurdish (g1)
Mongolian (u2)
Class. Mongolian
  (u3)
Mid. Mongolian
  (u1)
Old Norse (g1)
Norwegian (u2)
Pali (u4)
Pashto (g1)
Persian (u2)
Old Persian (g1)
Mid. Persian
  (g2)
Portuguese (u3)
Polish (u2)
Romanian (u2)
Old Russian (g1)
Sanskrit (u5,
  g2)

Scottish Gaelic
  (u1)
Serbo-Croatian (u2)
Medieval Slavic
  (g1)
Old Church Slavonic
  (g1)
Sogdian (g1)
Sumerian (g4)
Swedish (u4)
Syriac (g3)
Class. Tibetan (u3)
Turkish (u6, g2)
Old Turkish (g1)
Mid. Turkic (g2)
Old Uighur (g2)
Ugaritic (u1)
Ukrainian (u2)
Class. Urdu (g1)
Vietnamese (u2)
Early Welsh (g2)

STAFF

Judith Aissen (Ph.D., Harvard, 1974; Lecturer) Syntax, linguistic theory (1/2 time).
Stephen R. Anderson (Ph.D., M.I.T., 1969; Assoc Prof) Phonology, linguistics theory, Scandinavian.
Anthony T. Arletto (Ph.D., Harvard, 1966; Lecturer) Historical linguistics, descriptive linguistics, Chinese.
R. H. Ives Goddard III (Ph.D., Harvard, 1969; Asst Prof) Amerindian, descriptive linguistics, historical linguistics.
Jorge Hankamer (Ph.D., Yale, 1971; Asst Prof) Syntax, linguistic theory, Turkish.
Einar Haugen (Ph.D., Univ. of Illinois, 1931; Prof) Sociolinguistics, Scandinavian.
Jay Jasanoff (Ph.D., Harvard, 1968; Prof) Syntax, Linguistic theory, Japanese.
Omelijan Pritsak (Ph.D., Univ. of Gottingen, 1948; Prof) Turkic and Altaic.
Jochem Schindler (Ph.D., University of Wurzburg, 1972; Asst Prof) Historical Linguistics, Indo-European.
Karl V. Teeter (Ph.D., U. C. at Berkely, 1962; Prof) Descriptive linguistics, Amerindian, Japanese.
Calvert Watkins (Ph.D., Harvard, 1959; Prof) Historical linguistics, Indo-European, Celtic.

Linguists in other Departments or Schools

Richard Brecht (Ph.D., Harvard, 1972; Asst Prof) Slavic.
Morton W. Bloomfield (Ph.D., Univ. of Wisconsin, 1938; Prof) English, stylistics.
Carol Chomsky (Ph.D., Harvard, 1968; Lecturer) Language acquisition.
Frank M. Cross (Ph.D., Johns Hopkins, 1950; Prof) Near Eastern Languages, Semitics.
Michael W. Freeman (Ph.D., U. C. at Santa Barbara, 1971; Asst Prof) Romance.
Richard N. Frye (Ph.D., Harvard, 1946; Prof) Near Eastern Languages, Semitics.
Thomas O. Lambdin (Ph.D., Johns Hopkins, 1952; Prof) Near Eastern Languages, Semitics.
Horace G. Lunt (Ph.D., Columbia Univ., 1950; Prof) Slavic.
David Nasjleti (Ph.D., Cornell Univ., 1971; Assist. Prof.) Romance.

Support Available

Scholarships based on needs; teaching fellowships for advanced graduate students.

Academic Calendar 1974-1975

Fall Semester: September 23, 1974 - January 29, 1975; Spring Semester: February 4, 1975 - June 3, 1975. Deadline: January 10, 1975.

DESCRIPTIVE MATERIAL: Write: Admissions Office, Graduate School of Arts and Sciences, Harvard University, Byerly Hall, Cambridge, Mass. 02138.

UNIVERSITY OF HAWAII Honolulu, Hawaii 96822   Tel. (808) 948-8374

Department of Linguistics
Byron W. Bender, Chairman
Degrees: BA, MA, Ph.D. Degrees Granted 1972-73: 2 BA, 11 MA, 6 Ph.D. Majors:
102 g, 35 MA, 67 Ph.D., 80 Graduate in Residence, 12 u.

The Department aims in the professional training of its students to combine a foundation in one or more languages of the Pacific Basin -- including its Asian and American peri-meters -- with an involvement in modern linguistic theory as it develops. Speakers of languages from throughout the Basin are generally available to students, either on campus with its high proportion of foreign students, in cosmopolitan Honolulu, or through fieldwork. Major research projects in recent years have focused on the codification of languages of the Philippines, Micronesia, Melanesia, and Northwest America for various purposes including their learning by foreigners and their use in bilingual education; on the post-creole continuum in Hawaii; and on the development of speech in immigrant children. Spin-off from these projects infuses the program at every turn.
A phonetics laboratory and computer facilities support data analysis and storage. The University Library has special Asian, Hawaiian, and Pacific Collections, and the Department maintains a Reading Room containing key works. Students comprise a majority of the officers of the Linguistic Society of Hawaii, an active scientific and social organization. Prepublication drafts of student and faculty writings are disseminated in Working Papers in Linguistics to more than 250 institutions.

COURSE OFFERINGS

Introductory, 3; Phonology, 9; Theoretical Models, 12; Semantics & Logic, 1; Sociolinguis-tics, 9; Field Methods, 1; Psycholinguistics, 2; Math. & Comp. Linguistics, 3; Historical Linguistics, 5. Language Areas: Chamorro 1, Japanese 3, Slavic 1, Indo-Aryan 1, Proto-Oceanic 3, Thai 1, Palauan 1, Athapaskan 1, Guyanese Creole 1, Korean 2, Austronesian 2, Germanic 1, Hittite 1, Philippine 2, Polynesian 1. Other: Lexicography.

UNCOMMONLY-TAUGHT LANGUAGES

Bengali (6u, 2g)	Hawaiian (14u)	Korean (10u)	Sanskrit (4u, 5g)
Burmese (4u)	Hindi (6u)	Lao (4u)	Tagalog (10u, 4g)
Cambodian (6u, 4g)	Ilokano (4u)	Marathi (2u)	Tamil (4u)
	Indonesian (5u)	Pali (4u)	Thai (8u)
Cantonese (4u)	Japanese (48u, 12g)	Prakrit (2u)	Vietnamese (16u, 6g)

STAFF

Byron W. Bender (Ph.D., Indiana, 1963; Prof) Phonology, general linguistics, Micronesian languages.
Derek Bickerton (MA, Cambridge, 1950; Assoc Prof) Language variation, pidgins and creoles; language and literature.
Iovanna D. Condax (Ph.D., 1973; Princeton; Asst Prof) Experimental phonetics, phonology; English and Chinese linguistics.
Samuel H. Elbert (Ph.D., Indiana, 1950; Emeritus Prof) Comparative and descrip-tive linguistics; Hawaiian, other Polynesian and Micronesian languages.

Gordon H. Fairbanks (Ph.D., Wisconsin, 1947; Prof) Historical and comparative
    linguistics; Indo-European, especially Indo-Aryan, Slavic and Germanic.
Michael L. Forman (Ph.D., Cornell, 1972; Assoc Prof) General linguistics, lin-
    guistic anthropology, creoles and sociolinguistics.
George W. Grace (Ph.D., Columbia, 1958; Prof) Historical linguistics, Austronesian,
    especially Melanesian linguistics, ethnolinguistics.
Irwin Howard (Ph.D., M.I.T., 1972; Assoc Prof) Theoretical linguistics, phonology,
    syntax.
Robert W. Hsu (Ph.D., California, Berkeley, 1969; Asst Prof) Phonology, computer
    techniques, programming languages.
Roderick A. Jacobs (Ph.D., California, San Diego, 1972; Prof) Syntax and syntactic
    change, Germanic, English.
Lewis S. Josephs (Ph.D., Harvard, 1972; Asst Prof) Descriptive and theoretical
    linguistics, Japanese and Korean.
P. Gregory Lee (Ph.D., Ohio State, 1970; Asst Prof) Theoretical linguistics, phon-
    ology, syntax (1/2 time).
Patricia A. Lee (Ph.D., Ohio State, 1974; Asst Prof) Generative syntax and seman-
    tics, natural logic and the philosophy of language (1/2 time).
Fang-Kuei Li (Ph.D., Chicago, 1928, D. Litt., Michigan, 1972; Emeritus Prof)
    Chinese and Tai linguistics, other Sino-Tibetan languages, North American
    Indian linguistics.
Anatole V. Lyovin (Ph.D., California, Berkeley, 1972; Assoc Prof) Generative
    phonology, Chinese dialectology, Sino-Tibetan.
Samuel E. Martin (Ph.D., Yale, 1950; Visiting Prof) Japanese and Korean linguistics.
Howard P. McKaughan (Ph.D., Cornell, 1957; Prof) Descriptive and theoretical lin-
    guistics, Philippine and Papuan languages.
Ann M. Peters (Ph.D., Wisconsin, 1966; Asst Researcher) Children's speech, African
    languages, mathematical and computational linguistics.
Andrew K. Pawley (Ph.D., Auckland, New Zealand, 1966: Assoc Prof) Fijian, Polyne-
    sian and New Guinea linguistics, conversation.
Lawrence A. Reid (Ph.D., Hawaii, 1966; Assoc Researcher) Philippine linguistics,
    aboriginal languages of Formosa, lexicography.
Albert J. Schütz (Ph.D., Cornell, 1962; Prof) Descriptive linguistics, field methods,
    lexicography.
Stanley Starosta (Ph.D., Wisconsin, 1967: Assoc Prof) Theoretical linguistics,
    Asian and Pacific languages.
Laurence C. Thompson (Ph.D., Yale, 1954; Prof) Descriptive and comparative lin-
    guistics, field methods, North American Indian linguistics.
Donald M. Topping (Ph.D., Michigan State, 1963; Prof) Descriptive and applied lin-
    guistics; Philippine and Micronesian languages.
Stanley M. Tsuzaki (Ph.D., Michigan, 1963; Assoc Prof) Descriptive and applied
    linguistics; variation in language.
Jack H. Ward (Ph.D., Cornell, 1973; Asst Prof) Descriptive and comparative lin-
    guistics, Hawaiian and other Polynesian and Indonesian languages.

Linguists in other Departments and Schools

Evangelos Afendras (Ph.D., Johns Hopkins, 1968; Asst Prof) Bilingualism, language
    planning.
David E. Ashworth (Ph.D., Cornell, 1973; Asst Prof) Ryukyuan dialects, dialectology,
    sociology of the Japanese languages.
Charles Blatchford (Ph.D., Columbia, 1970; Asst Prof) Methods in teaching English as
    a second language, teacher training.
Verner Bickley (Ph.D., London, 1966; Director, Culture Learning Inst., East-West
    Center) Language attitudes, sociolinguistic problems in English language in-
    struction, historical perspectives in the sociology of language.
Robert Cheng (Ph.D., Indiana, 1966; Assoc Prof) Chinese linguistics, Japanese
    linguistics, language contact.
Ruth Crymes (Ph.D., Columbia, 1965; Prof) English Syntax, English as a second
    language--materials, methods, teacher training.
Richard Day (Ph.D., Hawaii, 1972; Asst Prof) Sociolinguistics, variation theory,
    language and education.
John DeFrancis (Ph.D., Columbia, 1948; Prof) Chinese language.
Gerald Dykstra (Ph.D., Michigan, 1955; Prof) Educational communications, dyadic
    grammar.

Robert Gibson (MA, Hawaii, 1968; Inst, ESL) ESL, bilingual education, Palauan.
Roger Hadlich (Ph.D., Michigan, 1961; Prof) Spanish structural, historical, dia-
    lectological, and applied linguistics; Comparative Romance (3/4 time).
Emily Hawkins (MA, Hawaii, 1969; Lecturer) Phonology and syntax of Hawaiian,
    syntactic change, Eastern Polynesian linguistics (1/2 time).
Masanori Higa (Ed.D., Harvard, 1962; Prof) Psycholinguistics, sociolinguistics.
Hsin-I Hsieh (Ph.D., California, Berkeley, 1971; Asst Prof) Chinese linguistics,
    psycholinguistics, historical linguistics.
Kenneth Jackson (Ed.D., Columbia, 1967; Assoc Prof) Interference, error analysis,
    reading.
Leon Jakobovits (Ph.D., McGill, 1962; Prof) Psycholinguistics, ethnosemantics,
    transactional engineering.
Everett Kleinjans (Ph.D., Michigan, 1958; Chancellor, East-West Center) Japanese
    language and culture, contrastive linguistics and cross-cultural comparisons.
Robert Krohn (Ph.D.,Michigan, 1969; Assoc Prof) English phonology, ESL.
Yutaka Kusanagi (Ph.D., Georgetown, 1970; Asst Prof) Japanese linguistics, history
    of Japanese, mathematical linguistics.
Mark Lester (Ph.D., California, Berkeley, 1964; Assoc Researcher, Culture Learning
    Inst., East-West Center) English, applied linguistics, mathematical linguistics.
Ying-che Li (Ph.D., Michigan, 1970; Assoc Prof) Semantics and syntax, psycho-
    linguistics, language acquisition, Chinese syntax and dialects.
Agnes Niyekawa-Howard (Ph.D., New York, 1960; Prof) Psycholinguistics, bilingualism,
    language education.
Tae-Yong Pak (Ph.D., Bowling Green State, 1969; Asst Prof) Mathematical linguistics,
    philosophy of language, logic.
Teresita Ramos (Ph.D., Hawaii, 1972; Asst Prof) Philippine linguistics, language
    teaching, bilingualism.
Kenneth Rehg (Ph.D., Hawaii, 1974; Asst Researcher, Pacific and Asian Linguistic
    Inst.) Micronesian linguistics, Ponapean, language teaching.
Ronald Scollon (Ph.D., Hawaii, 1974; Asst Prof) First language acquisition,
    Athapaskan-Kutchin.
Richard Seymour (Ph.D., Pennsylvania, 1956; Prof) Germanic linguistics.
Yao Shen (Ed.D., Michigan, 1944; Prof) Linguistics and literature, English and
    Mandarin.
Ho-min Sohn (Ph.D., Hawaii, 1969; Asst Prof) Korean, Korean-Japanese comparative
    linguistics, Ulthian and Woleaian (Micronesia).
Danny Steinberg (Ph.D., Hawaii, 1966; Assoc Prof) Psycholinguistics, language
    acquisition.
Hiroshi Sugita (MA, International Christian, 1966; Jr Researcher, Pacific and
    Asian Linguistic Inst.) Micronesian linguistics, Trukese, Japanese.

Support Available

Several teaching and research fellowships are awarded each year, and teaching
assistantships are sometimes available in related departments for students who
follow double degree programs. Assistantships provide free tuition and a stipend of
at least $3,700. A few tuition waivers are also available. All students are considered
for support on the basis of their original application and subsequent performance in
the program. Each year a few students are also supported by the East-West Center, especially doctoral students with sociolinguistic, psycholinguistic, or applied emphases
in their programs. Every effort is made to help students find employment on campus
or in Honolulu. Work-study programs are available for students who qualify -- inquiries
should be made to Financial Aids Office, 2444 Dole Street.

Academic Calendar 1974-1975

Fall Semester: September 3-December 21, 1974; Spring Semester: January 20-May 15, 1975;
Summer Session: First: May 27-July 3, 1975, Second: July 7-August 15, 1975. Deadline:
March 1 for Fall Semester, September 1 for Spring Semester.

DESCRIPTIVE MATERIAL: Write: Chairman, Graduate Field of Study, Department of
                         Linguistics, 1890 East-West Road, University of Hawaii,
                         Honolulu, Hawaii 96822.

Linguistics Concentration Committee
Betty Heard, Chairman
Degrees: BA. Degrees Granted 1972-73: 1 BA. Majors: 8 u.

Hilo College is able to support the only undergraduate linguistics major in the University of Hawaii system by relying on qualified faculty whose original commitment was
to other disciplines. This fact accounts for the program's emphasis on applied and
hyphenated linguistics. That is, part of the linguistics faculty is primarily respon-
sible for language instruction and they are heavily oriented toward applications of
linguistic theory; another part is drawn from the social sciences and are thus strongly
concerned with ethno-, socio-, and psycholinguistics. Basic linguistics courses are
offered by various members of the Committee, depending on their specific interests and
competence. The greatest general strength lies in the training of potential language
instructors.

COURSE OFFERINGS

Introductory, 3; Phonology, 5; Theoretical Models, 1; Semantics & Logic, 1; Sociolinguistics, 2; Dialectology, 1; Psycholinguistics, 1; Historical Linguistics, 1; Language
Pedagogy, 1. Language Areas: Japanese 1.

UNCOMMONLY-TAUGHT LANGUAGES

Hawaiian (8u)   Japanese (15u)   Portuguese (2u)

STAFF

Betty Ruth Heard (Ph.D., Louisiana State University, 1968; Assoc Prof) Phonology,
     dialectology.
Richard W. Howell (Ph.D., University of California, Berkeley, 1967; Assoc Prof)
     Sociolinguistics, Ethnolinguistics, Psycholinguistics.
Tadashi Kimura (MA, University of Hawaii, 1971; Acting Asst Prof) Japanese, Ap-
     plications of Linguistics to language teaching.
Michael H. McRae (Ph.D., University of Wisconsin, 1974; Asst Prof) History of
     English, Applied linguistics, Anglo-Saxon.
Fred Kalanianoeo Meinecke (AB, University of California, Berkeley, 1960; Acting Asst
     Prof) Hawaiian, Comparative and historical Linguistics, Ethnolinguistics.
Tazuko Ajiro Monane (Ph.D., Georgetown University, 1971) Japanese, Applications
     of linguistics to language teaching.

Linguists in other Departments and Schools

Paul W. Dixon (Ph.D., University of Hawaii, 1966; Prof) Verbal learning and psycho-
     linguistics.
Iva R. Goldman (MA, Northwestern University, 1960; Asst Prof) Semantics.
Leila L. Kanno (Ph.D., University of Missouri, 1971; Assoc Prof) Speech pathology
     and audiology.
Frank G. Nelson (Ph.D., University of California, Berkeley, 1937; Prof) History
     of English, Philology.

Academic Calendar 1974-1975

Fall Semester: 19 August 74; Spring Semester: 6 January 1975. Deadline: 1 May, for
Fall Semester (undergraduate only); 1 November, for Spring Semester (undergradiduate
only).

DESCRIPTIVE MATERIAL: Write: Mr. Bruce Bikle, Admissions Officer, University of
                        Hawaii at Hilo, P.P. Box 1357, Hilo, Hawaii 96720.

Comparative Literature & Languages Department
Frank S. Lambasa, Chairman
Degrees: A minor leading to BA & MA.

The undergraduate program provides a number of courses in linguistics that can be taken
as a minor in combination with a major in other fields, for ex. English, speech, psychology etc.

For the time being the graduate program is incomplete, offering only occasional seminars in linguistics with varying topics depending on the student's interests and needs.

COURSE OFFERINGS

Introductory, 2; Dialectology, 1; Math. & Comp. Linguistics, 2; Historical Linguistics,
1. Other Departments: Phonology, 1; Theoretical Models, 2; Sociolinguistics, 1.

UNCOMMONLY-TAUGHT LANGUAGES

Chinese   Hebrew   Japanese   Swahili
  (2-6 sem.)

STAFF

Vera S. Killian (Ph.D., Columbia U., 1968; Asst Prof) Historical linguistics, theoretical linguistics.
David I. Knee (Ph.D., MIT, 1962; Assoc Prof) Abstract algebra, mathematical linguistics.

Support Available

Some scholarships available. Loans are arranged through the Financial Aid office.

Academic Calendar 1974-1975

Fall Semester: September 12, 1974; Spring Semester: January 29, 1975; Summer Session:
2 summer sessions.

DESCRIPTIVE MATERIAL: Write: Registrar's Office, Hofstra University, 1000 Fulton
                       Avenue, Hempstead, New York 11550.

UNIVERSITY OF HOUSTON   Houston, Texas 77004   Tel. (713) 749-3431

Interdepartmental Committee on Linguistics
Thomas M. Woodell, Chairman
Degrees: BA and MA in English, both with a concentration in linguistics.

The Interdepartmental Committee on Linguistics coordinates a wide range of course offerings in linguistics from among the various departments of the University. While no
degree program in linguistics is currently available, the English Department offers
a concentration in linguistics on both the bachelor's and master's levels. Such concentrations permit the student to take half the work required for a degree in English
in linguistics and related fields. Whether the student is working at the graduate or
undergraduate level, the program has a requirement of core courses that provides broad
insight into the scientific study of language. After completion of such core courses,
the student may choose specialization in applied or theoretical fields. As with the
other courses of study offered by the English Department, the concentration in linguistics offers the option of a thesis or non-thesis program.

The facilities include the availability of coursework, research arrangements, and
clinical experience with Rice University, the Baylor College of Medicine, The

University of Texas Graduate School of Biomedical Sciences, and The University of Texas School of Public Health.

COURSE OFFERINGS

Introductory, 1; Phonology, 4; Theoretical Models, 1; Semantics & Logic, 1; Sociolinguistics, 2; Psycholinguistics, 5; Neurolinguistics, 2; Historical Linguistics, 2; History of Linguistics, 1; Language Pedagogy, 2. Language Areas: OE 1, French 3, German 2, Spanish 4.

UNCOMMONLY-TAUGHT LANGUAGES

Czech (4u)   Hebrew (4u)   Swahili (4u)

STAFF

Walter P. Allen (Ed.D., Columbia, 1948; Assoc Prof) ESL, General linguistics.
Peter Judson Gingiss (Ph.D., Northwestern University, 1973; Asst Prof) Sociolinguistics, African languages.
Hilda Jaffe (Ph.D., Michigan State University, 1966; Asst Prof) Historical linguistics, American Dialects.
Donald W. Lee (Ph.D., Columbia University, 1948; Prof) Old English, Historical linguistics, Lexicography.
Jeannette P. Morgan (MA, University of Houston, 1963; Instr) Teaching of Freshman Composition, Methods of Teaching English, General linguistics.
H. Joyce Merrill Valdes (Ph.D., University of Texas, 1961; Dir. Program in English for International Students) ESL, TESL, Bilingual Education.
Thomas M. Woodell (Ph.D., Florida State University, 1968; Assoc Prof) General linguistics, language maintenance, language acquisitions.

Linguists in Other Departments and Schools

Elizabeth Brandon (Ph.D., Laval, 1955; Prof) French phonetics.
Karl J. Reinhardt (Ph.D., Texas, 1969; Assoc Prof) Grammar of Portuguese, synchronic and diachronic structure of Spanish.
James B. Rhyne (Ph.D., Texas, 1974; Instr) Computational linguistics (1/4 time).
Carl L. Thompson (Ph.D., Florida, 1965; Assoc Prof) Speech perception.
Harry H. Walsh (Ph.D., North Carolina, 1970; Asst Prof) Phonology, Historical linguistics.

Support Available

Teaching fellowships are available through the Department of English. The usual rate is $300/mo. for nine months; summer support is on an "as available" basis. For application forms write the Director of Graduate Studies in English.

Academic Calendar 1974-1975

Fall Semester: 3 Sep - 20 Dec; Spring Semester: 20 Jan - 17 May; Summer Session: I: 2 June - 8 July; II: 10 July - 16 August. Deadline: for Fall: 10 July (24 July); for Spring: 3 Dec (18 Dec); for Summer I: 9 April (7 May); for Summer II: 11 June (18 June). International students should submit application and credentials about one month in advance of the above dates.

DESCRIPTIVE MATERIAL: Write: Office of the Registrar, University of Houston, Houston, Texas 77004.

HOWARD UNIVERSITY Washington, D.C. 20059   Tel. (202) 636-6711

Speech Department
Lyndry Niles, Chairman
Degrees: MA, Ph.D. Majors: 4g. In Residence: 4g.

The general orientation of this new program is geared toward the application of lin-
quistic data and theory to the resolution of applied linguistic issues and problems
in urban populations, especially as they relate to cultural and racial minorities.

COURSE OFFERINGS

Introductory, 2; Phonology, 3; Theoretical Models, 1; Semantics & Logic, 1; Sociolinguistics, 2; Field Methods, 1; Psycholinguistics, 3; Language Pedagogy, 1.

UNCOMMONLY-TAUGHT LANGUAGES

Amharic	Hausa	Swahili	Yoruba
Arabic	Lingala	Tswana	Zulu
Berber	Sotho	Twi	

STAFF

Benjamin Cooke (M.A., Chicago State, 1970) Sociolinguistics (1/4 time).
Orlando Taylor (Ph.D., Michigan, 1966; Prof) Psycholinguistics, Language Acquisition,
    Sociolinguistics.
David Woods (Ph.D., Georgetown, 1972; Assoc Prof) Theoretical Linguistics, Phonology,
    Psycholinguistics.

Linguists in Other Departments or Schools

Joseph Applegate (Ph.D., Pennsylvania; Prof) African Linguistics, Theoretical Lin-
    guistics.
Larry Hall (M.A., Georgetown) German Linguistics.
David Korn (Ph.D., Georgetown; Assoc Prof) German Linguistics.
Joseph Lelis (Ph.D., Harvard; Assoc Prof) English Linguistics, History of English.
Cesar Oro (Ph.D., Maryland; Asst Prof) Spanish Linguistics.
Alberto Rey (Ph.D., Georgetown, 1974; Asst Prof) Spanish Linguistics, Sociolinguistics.
Rosanne Weil-Malherbe (Ph.D., Maryland) French Linguistics.
Henry Zalucky (M.A., Illinois) Slavic Linguistics.

Academic Calendar 1974-1975

Fall Semester: August 25; Spring Semester: January 13; Summer Session: May 20.

DESCRIPTIVE MATERIAL: Write: Prof. Lyndry Niles, Dept. of Speech, Howard University,
                       Washington, D. C. 20059.

ILLINOIS INSTITUTE OF TECHNOLOGY Chicago, Illinois 60616   Tel. (321) 225-9600

Linguistics Division, Humanities Department
A. L. Davis, Chairman
Degrees: MS, Ph.D. Degrees Granted 1972-73: 2 MS, 2 Ph.D. Majors: 26g.

The Division of Linguistics, Humanities Department of the Illinois Institute of
Technology does not adhere to any one particular school of practice. All theories,
all fundamental premises, all methodologies are open to our inquiry and research.
The interests of the faculty are Biolinguistics, Theories of language and mind,
Structural and generative dialectology, phonologies of English, Methodology of
Language Teaching, British Dialects, Acoustic Phonetics, Studies in Morphophonemics,
Textforming Strategies.

66

The Center for American English, operated by the Division, services courses in English for foreign undergraduates and graduates of the campus as a whole.

Current research involves evolutionary explanations of language, models of the concept (rule of language), studies in English phonologies.

Program in MS Degree: 2 semesters or 32 hrs.

Program in PhD Degree: 3 years beyond the MS or 96 hrs.

A degree is granted in linguistics, with an area of concentration in theoretical or applied matters.

COURSE OFFERINGS

Phonology, 4; Theoretical Models, 3; Sociolinguistics, 1; Dialectology, 2; Psycholinguistics, 1; Historical Linguistics, 2; History of Linguistics, 1; Linguistics & Literature, 1; Language Pedagogy, 1. Language Areas: Igbo, Kondowatakai, Maka.

STAFF

A.L. Davis (Ph.D., University of Michigan; Prof) Structural Dialectology, Study in Social Dialects, English Linguistics.

W. Abler (Ph.D., University of Pennsylvania; Prof) Biolinguistics, Acoustic Phonetics, Evolutionary Theories of Language.

M.J.V. Blanton (Ph.D., Illinois Institute of Technology, 1974; Prof) Phonemic Descriptions, History of Linguistics, Studies in Morphological Description.

Support Available

Tuition Awards; Research Assistantships; Teaching Assistantships; Recipients of a Research or Teaching Assistantship may pursue only 12 credit hours of courses per semester.

Academic Calendar 1974-1975

Fall Semester: September 14 - December 20; Spring Semester: January 14 - May 2. Deadline: July 29/Dec. 10.

DESCRIPTIVE MATERIAL: Write: Graduate School Office, Illinois Institute of Technology, Chicago, Illinois 60616.

UNIVERSITY OF ILLINOIS AT CHICAGO CIRCLE Chicago, Illinois 60680 Tel. (312) 996-5334

Linguistics Department
Andrew Schiller, Department Head
Degrees: MA; MA in Applied Linguistics; Specialization in TESOL. Majors: 40 g, 40 MA, 19 Grad. in Residence.

The UICC Department of Linguistics was formed in the summer of 1973 and offers at present an MA in Theoretical Linguistics, an MA in Applied Linguistics, and an MA in Applied Linguistics with Specialization in TESOL. With the exception of the TESOL program, which is somewhat more restrictive, the curricula are highly flexible. Work in the Department of Linguistics can be combined with offerings in any relevant departments. Among the special facilities of the program are the PLATO computer network and the phonetics laboratory.

COURSE OFFERINGS

Introductory, 7; Phonology, 3; Theoretical Models, 4; Semantics & Logic, 1; Sociolinguistics, 2; Dialectology, 1; Field Methods, 1; Psycholinguistics, 3; Historical Linguistics, 2; History of Linguistics, 1; Linguistics & Literature, 1; Language Pedagogy, 3, Applied Ling., 2.

UNCOMMONLY-TAUGHT LANGUAGES

Arabic (u 3q)	Hebrew	Lithuanian	Serbo-Croatian
Chinese (u 6q)	(u 22q)	(u 11q, g 2q)	(u 6q)
			Swahili (u 6q)

STAFF

Michael A. K. Halliday (Ph.D., Cambridge U.; Prof) Systematic grammar, language acquisition, sociolinguistics.

Falk S. Johnson (Ph.D., U. of Chicago; Prof) Transformational English Grammar, application of linguistics to composition and literature.

Adam Makkai (Ph.D., Yale U.; Prof) Stratificational theory, idiomaticity, Hungarian linguistics.

Valerie Becker Makkai (Ph.D., Yale U.; Assoc Prof) Phonological theory, descriptive methodology, Arabic linguistics.

Janine K. Reklaitis (Ph.D., Stanford U.; Asst Prof) Comparative linguistics, Sanskrit, Baltic linguistics.

Andrew Schiller (Ph.D., U. of Iowa; Prof) Applied linguistics, transformational grammar, stylistics.

Edward J. Stone (Ph.D., U. of California, Berkeley; Asst Prof) Germanic linguistics, German structure.

Dale E. Woolley (Ph.D., U. of Illinois at Urbana-Champaign; Asst Prof) Phonology, acoustic and articulatory phonetics.

Linguists in other Departments and Schools

Laura Bohannan (Ph.D., Oxford U.; Prof) Language and culture.

Elizabeth A. Brandt (Ph.D., Southern Methodist U.; Asst Prof) Amerindian languages, ethnolinguistics.

Brian Dutton (Ph.D., U. of London; Prof) Correctional grammar, applied linguistics.

Paul Hockings (Ph.D., U. of California at Berkeley; Assoc Prof) Dravidian languages, folklore analysis.

Robert J. Kispert (Ph.D., Harvard U.; Assoc Prof) Indo-Eurpoean philology, Old English.

Thomas M. Kochman (Ph.D., New York U.; Assoc Prof) Sociolinguistics, black communication, cross-cultural contacts.

Katherine Loesch (Ph.D., Northwestern U.; Assoc Prof) Linguistics and poetics.

Jack Prost (Ph.D., U. of Chicago; Assoc Prof) Nonverbal communication and mathematical models of interaction networks.

Sheldon Rosenberg (Ph.D., U. of Minnesota; Prof) Experimental psycholinguistics.

Barbara Wood (Ph.D., U. of Wisconsin; Assoc Prof) Developmental psycholinguistics and communication acquisition.

Support Available

Tuition and Fee Waiver - Applications available through department - deadline date - August 2; University Fellowships - Applications available through Graduate College - deadline date - July 8; NSF Graduate Fellowships - Students apply directly to the National Science Foundation - deadline date - October 15; Minority Graduate Fellowships - Applications available through department - deadline date - March 28.

Academic Calendar 1974-1975

Fall Quarter: Sept. 23 - Dec. 6; Winter Quarter: Jan. 6 - Mar. 21; Spring Quarter: Mar. 31 - Je. 13; Summer Quarter: Je. 23 - Sep. 5.

DESCRIPTIVE MATERIAL: Write: Linguistics Department, P. O. Box 4348, Chicago, Illinois 60680.

Department of Linguistics
Braj B Kachru, Chairman
Degrees: MA, Ph.D.   Degrees Granted 1972-73: 12 MA, 6 Ph.D.   Majors: 66 g; 44 MA,
      22 Ph.D., 62 Grad. in Residence.

The Department of Linguistics has a strong theoretical linguistics program especially
in syntax and phonology. In recent years we have also developed a full spectrum of
offerings in psycholinguistics, sociolinguistics, applied linguistics, experimental
phonetics, mathematical and computational linguistics. In addition, the Department
teaches and administers the following non-western languages: Arabic, Hindi, Modern and
Classical Hebrew, Hindi, Kashmiri, Swahili and Yoruba. Research is conducted in all
of these languages. The Department also has a phonetics laboratory where students are
able to work on projects in instrumental phonetics. The faculty represents practically
all of the contemporary areas of linguistics and encourages students to develop sub-spec-
ialities in all those areas where the linguistic sciences are relevant. In addition,
the University supports several centers: Center for Asian Studies - Dir. R. B. Crawford;
Center for Latin American And Caribbean Studies -Dir. M. H. Forster; Slavic Languages
and Literatures - Head, C. L. Dawson; Russian and East European Center - Dir. R. T.
Fisher; Unit for Foreign Languages Study and Research - Dir. B. H. Mainous.

COURSE OFFERINGS

Introductory, 3; Phonology, 8; Theoretical Models, 5; Semantics & Logic, 2; Sociolinguistics, 2; Psycholinguistics, 3; Math. & Comp. Linguistics, 2; Historical linguistics,
4; History of Linguistics, 1; Linguistics & Literature, 1; Language Pedagogy, 3; Intro
to Applied Ling., 1. Language Areas: African 2, Non-Western ling. 1, Greek & Latin
1, French 1, Far Eastern 1, Romance Ling. 2, Gmc. 1, Slavic 1, Skt. 2.

UNCOMMONLY-TAUGHT LANGUAGES

Arabic	Class. Greek	Japanese	Old Church
Burmese	Mod. Greek	Kashmiri	Slavonic
Chinese	Gothic	Korean	Old Spanish
Mid. English	Class. Hebrew	Old Norse	Swahili
Old English	Mod. Hebrew	Persian	Thai
Old French	Hindi	Polish	Urdu
Mid. High German	Hittite	Sanskrit	Ukrainian
Old High German	Indonesian	Serbo-Croatian	Yoruba

STAFF

E. Georges Bokamba (Ph.D., U. of Indiana, 1974; Visiting Lecturer) African Lin-
    guistics.
Chin-chuan Cheng (Ph.D., U. of Illinois, 1968; Assoc Prof) Computational Linguistics,
    Chinese linguistics, phonology.
Peter Cole (Ph.D., U. of Illinois, 1973; Asst Prof) Syntax, semantics, Hebrew.
Georgia Green (Ph.D., U. of Chicago, 1971; Assoc Prof) Syntax, semantics.
Hans Henrich Hock (Ph.D., Yale, 1971; Assoc Prof) Historical linguistics.
Braj B. Kachru (Ph.D., Edingurgh U., 1961; Prof) General linguistics, sociolin-
    guistics.
Yamuna Kachru (Ph.D., U. of London, 1965; Prof) General linguistics, Hindi lin-
    guistics (60%).
Henry Kahane (Ph.D., U. of Berlin, 1930; Prof) Romance linguistics, historical
    linguistics (50%).
Michael Kenstowicz (Ph.D., U. of Illinois, 1971; Assoc Prof).
Chin-W Kim (Ph.D., U. of California, 1966; Prof) Phonetics, phonology, African and
    Korean linguistics.
Charles Kisseberth (Ph.D., U. of Illinois, 1969; Prof) Phonology, general linguistics.
Howard Maclay (Ph.D., U. of New Mexico, 1956; Prof) Psycholinguistics (1/3 time).
Jerry Morgan (Ph.D., U. of Chicago, 1973; Asst Prof) Syntax, Semantics, Balkan
    languages.
Margie O'Bryan (Ph.D., U. of Illinois, 1973; Visiting Lecturer) Indo-European
    linguistics, historical linguistics (50%).

David L. Peterson (Ph.D., Yale U., 1972; Asst Prof) Classical Hebrew (33% time).
G. L. Tikku (Ph.D., U. of Tehran, 1956; Prof) Comparative Literature and Persian
   Language (40% Time).

Linguists in other Departments and Schools

J. H. D. Allen (Prof) Romance linguistics.
Elmer Antonsen (Prof) Germanic linguistics.
Katharine Aston (Prof) English, TESL.
Lawrence Bouton (Asst Prof) TESL, Applied linguistics.
Joseph Casagrande (Prof) Anthropology.
Clayton L. Dawson (Prof) Slavic linguistics.
Wayne B. Dickerson (Asst Prof) Sociolinguistics, TESL.
Rasio Dunatov (Assoc Prof) Russian linguistics.
Frank Gladney (Assoc Prof) Russian linguistics.
Frederick Jenkins (Assoc Prof) French linguistics.
F. K. Lehman (Prof) Anthropological linguistics.
Seiichi Makino (Assoc Prof) Japanese linguistics.
James W. Marchand (Prof) Germanic linguistics.
Charles Osgood (Prof) Psycholinguistics.
Irmengard Rauch (Prof) Germanic linguistics.
Mario Satarelli (Assoc Prof) Romance linguistics.
Dieter Wanner (Asst Prof) Romance linguistics.
Willard Zemlin (Assoc Prof) Speech, experimental phonetics.

Support Available

University Fellowships, $2500 for nine-month academic year, plus $500 for a summer session,
plis tuition and fee waiver of Approx. $2000. Tuition and Fee Waivers. Teaching and
Research Assistantships. National Defense Foreign Language Fellowships. Deadline for
application for financial aid: February 15, 1975.

Academic Calendar 1974-1975

Fall Semester: August 21, 1974 - December 21, 1974; Spring Semester: January 15, 1975
- May 17, 1975; Summer Session: June 9, 1975 - August 2, 1975. Deadline: June, 1975
for August 1975 admission.

DESCRIPTIVE MATERIAL: Write: Department of Linguistics, 4088 Foreign Languages
                       Building, University of Illinois, Urbana, Illinois 61801.

INDIANA STATE UNIVERSITY   Terre Haute, Indiana 47809   Tel. (812) 232-6311, x2908

Department of English and Journalism
Committee for Linguistics and Lexicography
Edward Gates, Chairman
Degrees: BA with minor in linguistics

An undergraduate minor in linguistics is administered by a committee of the Department
of English and Journalism which includes members from other departments offering courses
in the program. The minor is designed especially to encourage students majoring in
such fields as English, foreign languages, and anthropology to obtain an objective and
systematic understanding of language. Beyond two core courses, students can select
from offerings in nine departments those appropriate to their needs and interests.
   Graduate courses relating to linguistics are offered by several departments. The
Department of English and Journalism is developing studies in lexicology and lexicography
on the master's level. These are designed for professional preparation in lexicographic
research, dictionary making, or classroom and library use of dictionaries.

Facilities include extensive library holdings in 16th century and later dictionaries significant for the study of the history of lexicography. Students of dictionary making may participate in one or more ongoing dictionary projects.

COURSE OFFERINGS

Introductory, 1; Phonology, 2; Theoretical Models, 3; Semantics & Logic, 2; Sociolinguistics, 2; Psycholinguistics, 7; Historical Linguistics, 1; Language Pedagogy, 1. Language Areas: French 1, Latin 2. Other: Intro to Word Study, The Dictionary: Form & Function, Evolution of Dictionaries.

STAFF

Marvin Carmony (Ph.D., Indiana U.; Prof) Dialectology and English linguistics (1/3 time).
J. Edward Gates (Ph.D., Hartford Seminary Foundation; Assoc Prof) Lexicology and Lexicography (2/3 time).
Berta Lee (Ph.D., U. of Nevada; Assoc Prof) Historical and English linguistics (2/3 time).
Glen Pound (Ph.D., Indiana U.; Assoc Prof) General linguistics (2/3 time).

Linguists in other Departments and Schools

Wayne Aller (Ph.D., U. of Washington; Prof) Psycholinguistics (1/3 time).
Ruth Grun (Doctor of Philosophy and Letters, U. of Marburg; Assoc Prof) Germanic and Romance linguistics (1/3 time).
Frank Nuessel (Ph.D., U. of Illinois; Asst Prof) Linguistic theory (1/3 time).
Raymond Quist (Ph.D., U. of Minnesota; Assoc Prof) Speech Pathology and Verbal Learning (1/3 time).
Herbert Weinberg (Ph.D., U. of Wisconsin; Assoc Prof) Historical and Spanish linguistics (1/3 time).

Support Available

The Department of English and Journalism regularly offers a limited number of graduate assistantships and graduate fellowships.

Academic Calendar 1974-1975

Fall Semester: August 29 - December 21, 1974; Spring Semester: January 9 - May 11, 1975; Summer Session: 1st. summer: June 9 - July 11, 1975; 2nd. summer: July 14 -August 15, 1975. Indiana State University also has an "intersession" which will begin on May 19 and end on June 6, 1975. Deadline: Graduate: One month prior to expected enrollment (for a degree-seeking individual).

DESCRIPTIVE MATERIAL: Write: Dr. J. Edward Gates (Parsons Hall 245), Department of English and Journalism, Indiana State University, Terre Haute, Indiana 47809.

INDIANA UNIVERSITY Bloomington, Indiana 47401   Tel. (812) 337-6457

Linguistics Department
F.W. Householder, Chairman
Degrees: BA, MA, Ph.D. Degrees Granted 1972-73: 8 MA, 12 Ph.D. Majors: 77g.
     In Residence: 60g, 20u.

The Undergraduate Program in Linguistics is designed to introduce students to methods of analysis and comparison of languages. Students who expect to be scholars and

teachers of foreign languages, English, anthropology, folkore, library science, literature, psychology, or philosophy will find a background in linguistics invaluable. The
core of the graduate program deals with the theory of language and concentrates on phonology, syntax, and historical-comparative linguistics. The department has close ties
with several other departments and offices in related fields, making possible the study
of a wide spectrum of specialized subjects, such as African languages and studies,
anthropological linguistics, psycholinguistics, etc.

The department maintains a phonetics laboratory which includes an adequate store
of equipment; the linguistics library contains up-to-date research materials. A complete
collection of volumes on linguistics and related areas is available and is supplemented
by books on file in the graduate library of Indiana University. The University also
has the Research Center for the Language Sciences which sponsors research, conferences,
visiting lecturers, and maintains an extensive publications program.

COURSE OFFERINGS

Introductory, 5; Phonology, 6; Theoretical Models, 9; Semantics & Logic, 1; Sociolinguistics, 3; Field Methods, 1; Math. & Comp Linguistics, 1; Historical Linguistics, 2; History of Linguistics, 1; Linguistics & Literature, 1; Language
Pedagogy, 2. Applied Lx. Lx. & Adjacent Arts & Sciences.

UNCOMMONLY-TAUGHT LANGUAGES

Akkadian	Finnish	Old Irish (g1)	Sanskrit
Arabic	Georgian	Japanese	Old Church Slavic
Aramaic	Old High German	Korean	Serbo-Croatian
Chinese	Mid. High German	Mandingo (1 yr)	Swahili (g6 u6)
Chuvash	Greek	Mongolian (g4 u4)	Tibetan
Czech	Haitian Creole	Class. Mongolian	Old Turkic
Danish	Hausa (g6 u6)	(g4 u4)	Turkish
Dutch	Hungarian	Persian	Ukrainian
Mid. English (g1)	Hebrew	Polish	Uzbek
Old English (g1)	Old Icelandic	Quechua	
Estonian	Mid. Irish (g1)	Romanian	

STAFF

Charles S. Bird (Ph.D., U.C.L.A.; Prof) Theoretical Linguistics, Syntax, African
Languages.
Daniel Dinnsen (Ph.D., U. of Texas; Prof) Phonology.
F. Roger Higgens (Ph.D., Massachusetts Institute of Technology; Asst Prof)
Historical Linguistics, Bilingualism.
Carleton T. Hodge (Ph.D., U. of Pennsylvania; Prof) Historical Linguistics, San-
skrit, Egyptian.
F. W. Householder (Ph.D., Columbia U.; Prof) Syntax, Historical Linguistics,
Sanskrit.
John Kimball (Ph.D., Massachusetts Institute of Technology; Prof) Theoretical and
Mathematical Linguistics, Syntax.
Andreas Koutsoudas (Ph.D., U. of Michigan; Prof) Theoretical Linguistics, Syntax.
LaRaw Maran (Ph.D., U. of Illinois; Asst Prof) Theoretical Linguistics and Syntax.
Linda Norman (Ph.D. cand., U. of Minnesota; Lecturer) Theoretical Linguistics
and Syntax.
Alo Raun (Ph.D., U. of Tartu; Prof) Lexicology, Uralic and Altaic Languages.
Thomas A. Sebeok (Ph.D., Princeton U.; Prof) Semiotics and Zoosemiotics.
Albert Valdman (Ph.D., Cornell U., Prof) French Linguistics, Applied Linguistics,
Bilingualism.
Charles F. Voegelin (Ph.D., U. of California; Prof) Anthropological Linguistics.

Linguists in other Departments or Schools

Education: Professor M. Semmel
English: Professors K. Huntsman, O. Thomas.
French: Professor M. Mazzola
Germanics: Professors F. Bana, Magnuson, N. Shetter, H. Vater
Near Eastern Languages and Literatures: Professor Alani

Philosophy: Professors Castaneda,Tienson
Psychology: Professors Peterson, Pisonit
Slavics: Professors F. Oinas, C. von Schooneveld
Sociology: Professors A. Grimshaw, H. Mehan
Spanish: Professor M. Goldin
Speech and Hearing: Professor R. Naremore, Schultz
Urban and Overseas English: Professors H. Gradman, M. Imhoof

Support Available

Undergraduate students interested in obtaining information concerning scholarships as
well as other types of financial aid should contact the Office of Scholarships and Financial Aids. Graduate students may obtain information concerning loans and part-time
employment through the Office of Scholarships and Financial Aids. Other types that
the graduate student may write to the Department about are : Associate Instructorships,
Ford Foundation Fellowshps, NDEA's, NSF's, IIE, AID.

Academic Calendar 1974-1975

Fall Semester: August 26-December 14; Winter Quarter: not applicable; Spring Semester:
January 13-May 3; Summer Session: First Summer Session: May 13-June 19; 2nd SS: June
23-Aug. 15. Indiana University also offers five Intensive (two-week) Summer Sessions:
May 13 - May 29; June 7 - June 21; June 23 - July 10; July 14 - July 29; July 30 - Aug
15. Deadline: Applications for admissions are accepted through July for entrance the
following fall semester. Undergraduate: December 1 for 2nd semester, April 15 for summer
sessions, and July 1 for first semester.

DESCRIPTIVE MATERIAL: Write: Linguistics Dept or for undergraduates: Admissions,
                        Lindley Hall 401B, Student Services 011, Bloomington,
                        Bloomington, Bloomington, IN. 47401

INTER AMERICAN UNIVERSITY   San German, Puerto Rico 00753   Tel. (809) 892-1095

Department of English & Linguistics
Robert L. Muckley, Chairman
Degrees: BA in TESL. In Residence: 140u.

The Department of English and Linguistics carries out two major functions at Inter
American University. First, as a service department, it provides courses in language
skills in fulfillment of basic university requirements, and second, it offers a major
in teaching English as a second language and a major in English literature. The
second function involves the major offerings. One of these, in English as a Second
Language, is designed to prepare teachers of English as a Second Language for the Puerto
Rican Public School System, and includes all courses considered necessary for exercising
this specialty. For example, in Introduction to Linguistics, the student is introduced
to basic linguistic concepts. In another course, the structure of the English language
is analyzed. The literature courses required for this major enable the student to know
something of the culture of the English-speaking peoples, and there is a methodology
course in teaching English as a second language which is usually combined with the
practice teaching course offered by the Department of Teacher Education. This department
also offers a number of other courses in education enabling the student to become a
certified teacher within the Puerto Rican Public School System and we urge our majors
to take these courses.
    Most of our students plan to teach in Puerto Rico, but we also keep up with oppor-
tunities elsewhere. For example, our department maintains close relations with recruit-
ing officials for the large cities along the Eastern Coast which have developed bilingual
education programs in need of Puerto Rican teachers.

COURSE OFFERINGS

Introductory, 1; Phonology, 1; Theoretical Models, 1; Psycholinguistics 1; Language Pedagogy, 1.

STAFF

Carmen Chevalier, Literature, English as a 2nd Language.
Herbert O. Christian, English as a 2nd Language.
Eileen Cortes, English as a 2nd Language, Literature.
Harold Elphick, Literature and Composition.
Zulma Figueroa, English as a 2nd Language.
Avelino Guzman, English as a 2nd Language.
Paul Livoti, English as a 2nd Language, Linguistics.
Joseph O'Neill, Literature.
Robert L. Muckley, ESL, Linguistics.
Julia Quinones, English as a 2nd Language.
Aurora, Rodriguez, English as a 2nd Language, Linguistics.
Dan Sweeney, English as a 2nd Language, Literature.
Ann Travis, French, Linguistics, Eng. as a 2nd Language.
Eduardo Vargas, Spanish as a 2nd Language.
Jeanette Velez, English as a Second Language.

Academic Calendar 1974-1975

Fall Semester: Aug 15 -Dec 15; Spring Semester: Jan 15 - May 15; Summer Session: I~June; II-July.

DESCRIPTIVE MATERIAL: Write: Luis Acosta, Admissions, Inter Amer. Univ., San German, P.R. 00753.

IOWA STATE UNIVERSITY   Ames, Iowa 50010   Tel. (515) 294-2180

English Department
Donald R. Benson, Chairman
Degrees: Minor in linguistics, graduate and undergraduate, for majors in any discipline.

Iowa State University offers an English for Speakers of Other Languages Institute each summer. Courses in linguistics are taught in several different departments, both graduate and undergraduate levels. Undergraduate students may elect a minor in linguistics as supporting work for any major. Graduate students may include work in linguistics in the same way. The University does not offer a major in linguistics alone.

COURSE OFFERINGS

Introductory, 1g 1u; Phonology, 1u; Theoretical Models, 1g 1u; Semantics & Logic, 1g; Sociolinguistics, 2g 3u; Dialectology, 1g; Psycholinguistics, 1g 2u; Historical Linguistics, 1g 1u; Linguistics & Literature, 1g; Language Pedagogy, 2g 1u. Language Areas: Romance 3.

UNCOMMONLY-TAUGHT LANGUAGES

Hausa (u 3q)   Swahili (u 3q)   Twi (u 3q)   Yoruba (u 3q)
Ibo (u 3q)

STAFF

Wayne Bartz (Ph.D., Purdue, 1963; Prof) Psycholinguistics.
Ray D. Dearin (Ph.D., Illinois, 1970; Assoc Prof) Rhetoric, General Semantics.
Aubrey E. Galyon (Ph.D., Iowa, 1970; Assoc Prof) General Linguistics, Historical
   Linguistics.
Quentin G. Johnson (Ph.D., Oregon, 1967; Prof) Historical Linguistics, Middle
   Scots, English Dialects.
Motoko Lee (Ph.D., Iowa State, 1969; Visiting Lecturer) Sociolinguistics.
Barbara Matthies (MA, Ohio, 1967; Asst Prof) EFL/TESOL.
Rajendra Singh (Ph.D., Brown, 1972; Asst Prof) Syntax, Scientific English.
Clyde Thogmartin (Ph.D., Michigan, 1970; Assoc Prof) Romance Linguistics, French
   in North America.
Charles W. Twyford (MS Ed., Indiana 1970; Instr) EFL, Introductory Linguistics.
Fred Vallier (MA, U. of Pacific, 1961; Asst Prof) Speech Disorders.
Dennis M. Warren (Ph.D., Indiana, 1973; Asst Prof) Language and Culture, African
   Studies.
Gilbert C. Youmans (BS, Wisconsin, 1965; Cand. Ph.D., Wisconsin; Instr) Language
   and Style, Stylistics.

Support Available

Inquiries about teaching assistantships should be directed to the departments of English,
Psychology, Sociology, or Anthropology.

Academic Calendar 1974-1975

Fall Quarter: September 3, 1974; Winter Quarter: December 2, 1974; Spring Quarter: March
10, 1974; Summer Sessions: June 2, 1975 & July 9, 1975. Deadline: Qualified persons
are admitted right up to beginning of each quarter, but one month lead time recommended.
Transcripts from former schools required.

DESCRIPTIVE MATERIAL: Write: Admissions Office, 9 Bearshear Hall, Iowa State
                        University, Ames, Iowa 50010.

UNIVERSITY OF IOWA   Iowa City, Iowa 52240   Tel. (319) 353-3621

Department of Linguistics
Robert Howren, Chairman
Degrees: BA, MA in Linguistics; Ph.D in Linguistics with concentration in English;
          Ph.D in Cultural Anthropology and Linguistics

COURSE OFFERINGS

Introductory, 2; Phonology, 3; Theoretical Models, 1; Semantics & Logic, 1; Sociolinguistics, 2; Dialectology, 1; Field Methods, 1; Psycholinguistics, 2; Math. & Comp.
Linguistics, 1; Historical Linguistics, 1; History of Linguistics, 1; Linguistics
and Literature, 1; Language Pedagogy, 2; Applied Linguistics, 1; Language Areas:
German, Russian, English.

UNCOMMONLY-TAUGHT LANGUAGES

Chinese	Old High German	Old Norse	Old Spanish
Old English	Gothic	Portuguese	
Middle High German	Japanese	Old Saxon	

STAFF

David Hacker (PhD, Iowa; Asst Prof) Syntactic Theory.
Robert Howren (PhD, Indiana; Prof) Phonological Theory, Athabaskan.
Larry W. Martin (PhD, Texas; Asst Prof) Syntactic Theory.
John C. McLaughlin (PhD, Indiana; Prof) History of English.
Catherine Ringen (PhD, Minnesota, Asst Prof) Phonological Theory, Syntactic Theory.
Robert Wachal (PhD, Wisconsin, Asst Prof) Computational Linguistics, Psycholinguistics.

Linguists in Other Departments or Schools

Richard Blasedell (Asst Prof) Speech Pathology, Psycholinguistics.
John W. Bowers (Assoc Prof) Speech, Rhetoric.
James F. Curtis (Prof) Speech Pathology, Phonetics.
Thomas Douglass (Asst Prof) Romance Linguistics.
Cynthia Gardiner (Asst Prof) Classics, Comparative Indo-European.
Edwin Kozlowski (Asst Prof) Anthropological Linguistics.
Richard Runge (Asst Prof) Germanic Linguistics.
Richard Teschner (Asst Prof) Bilingualism, Lexicography.
Ho Ting (Asst Prof) Chinese.

DESCRIPTIVE MATERIAL: Write: Department of Linguistics, University of Iowa,
Iowa City, Iowa 52240.

UNIVERSITY OF KANSAS   Lawrence, Kansas 66045   Tel. (913) 864-3450

Department of Linguistics
David A. Dineen, Chairman
Degrees: BA, MA, Ph.D., M.Phil. Degrees Granted 1972-73: 9 BA, 6 MA, 1 Ph.D.
        Majors: 48 g. In Residence: 43 g, 23 u.

The Linguistics Department at the University of Kansas offers the Ph.D. as well as an
MA in General Linguistics and an MA in Applied Linguistics. Although a small department,
with little depth in numbers of faculty in any specialty, we do have particular strength
in Phonetics, Applied Linguistics, Computational Linguistics and Romance Linguistics.
Interest is high in American Indian Languages and we are especially fortunate in being
located in the same city as Haskell Indian Junior College, with speakers of many Native
American languages. Cooperation with other departments isexcellent and accounts for
research specialties in Language Acquisition, Language Teaching, and others. We insist
on and feel we have succeeded in maintaining a strong core curriculum, allowing students
to develop their own specialties with the aid of our very willing and flexible faculty.

COURSE OFFERINGS

Introductory, 4; Phonology, 7; Theoretical Models, 6; Semantics & Logic, 1; Sociolin-
guistics,2; Field Methods, 1; Applied Linguistics, 1; Psycholinguistics, 2; Math. &
Comp. Linguistics, 2; Historical Linguistics, 2; History of Linguistics, 1; Linguistics
& Literature, 2; Language Pedagogy, 2. Language Areas: Israeli Hebrew 4, Sanskrit 2,
Pidgin 1, N. Amerindian 1, German 1, Yuman Lgs. 1, Lakota 1.

UNCOMMONLY-TAUGHT LANGUAGES

Arabic (4g, 4u)   Hebrew (4g, 4u)

STAFF

David A. Dineen (Ph.D., Harvard, 1963; Prof) Comparative Romance, Computational
    Linguistics (7/10 time).

Edward Erazmus (Ph.D., Michigan, 1962; Prof) Teaching English as a Second Language (1/2 time).
Frances Ingemann (Ph.D., Indiana, 1956; Prof) New Guinea Languages, Acoustic Phonetics, Teaching English as a Second Language.
Choon-Kyu Oh (Ph.D., Hawaii, 1971; Asst Prof) Generative Syntax and Semantics.
W. Keith Percival (Ph.D., Yale, 1964; Prof) History of Linguistics.
Robert Rankin (Ph.D., Chicago, 1972; Asst Prof) Comparative Romance, Generative Phonology.
Sally Y. Sedelow (Ph.D., Bryn Mawr, 1960; Prof) Computational Linguistics (1/2 time).
Akira Yamamoto (Ph.D., Indiana, 1973; Asst Prof) Anthropological and Ethnolinguistics (1/2 time).

Linguists in other Departments or Schools

Melissa Bowerman (Ph.D., Harvard, 1970; Adjunct Asst Prof) Acquisition of Language in Children.
O. Dean Gregory (Ph.D., Columbia, 1966; Asst Prof) Teaching English as a Second Language.
James Hartman (Ph.D., Michigan, 1966; Assoc Prof) Dialectology, Sociolinguistics.
Karl M. D. Rosen (Ph.D., Yale, 1960; Assoc Prof) Classical Languages, Indo-European Comparative Grammar.
Kenneth Ruder (Ph.D., Florida, 1969; Adjunct Assoc Prof) Acoustic Phonetics.
George Wedge (Ph.D., Minnesota, 1967; Assoc Prof) English Language, Medieval Latin, Sociolinguistics.

Support Available

Teaching and Research Assistantships in Linguistics Department; Teaching Assistant-ships (Teaching English to Foreign Students) at Intensive English Center. Foreign Students Scholarships through the Institute of International Education; Graduate Honors Fellowships for highly qualified students, through Linguistics Department.

DESCRIPTIVE MATERIAL: Write: David A. Dinneen, Chairman, Department of Linguistics, University of Kansas, Lawrence, Kansas 66045.

KANSAS STATE UNIVERSITY Manhattan, Kansas 66506   Tel. (913) 532-6880

Interdepartmental Linguistics
James L. Armagost, Chairman
Degrees: BA, MA. Majors: 5g. In Residence: 4g, 3u.

The interdepartmental linguistics program is coordinated by the departments of English, Modern Languages, and Speech. All students take essentially the same sequence of core courses emphasizing modern theoretical linguistics, in particular the linguistics of the Chomskyan revolution. Non-core courses are offered by several departments and stu-dents are urged to pursue as many of these as possible so as to avoid an overly narrow view of linguistics. These courses provide study in various interest areas (such as anthropological linguistics, psycholinguistics, second language teaching, etc.) and may serve as the subject of the Master's thesis or research report.
     Facilities include the Speech and Hearing Clinic, the South Asia Center, and the Minorities Resource and Research Center.

COURSE OFFERINGS

Introductory, 2; Phonology, 3; Theoretical Models, 1; Language Pedagogy, 1; Topics in Applied Lx., 1.

UNCOMMONLY-TAUGHT LANGUAGES

Hindi (2g, 2u)   Tamil (2g, 2u)   Urdu (5g, 5u)

STAFF

James L. Armagost (Ph.D., U. of Washington, 1973; Asst Prof) Linguistic Theory,
    Syntax, Phonology.
Peggy M. Null (MA, Kansas St. U., 1971; Temp. Inst) General Phonetics.
George C. Tunstall (Ph.D., Princeton, 1968; Asst Prof) Historical Linguistics,
    Language Typology.

Linguists in other Departments or Schools

William Burke (Ph.D., Northwestern, 1965; Assoc Prof) General Semantics.
Robert Grindell (Ph.D., U. of Arizona, 1972; Asst Prof) Modern English Grammar,
    History of English, ESL.
William Hankley (Ph.D., Ohio St. U., 1967; Assoc Prof) Programming Languages.
Richard Harris (Ph.D., Illinois, 1974; Asst Prof) Psycholinguistics.
Thomas Longhurst (Ph.D., U. of Minnesota, 1970; Asst Prof) Psycholinguistics.
Carol Miller (Ph.D., Washington U., 1963; Asst Prof) History of German.
Harriet Ottenheimer (Ph.D., Tulane U., 1973; Asst Prof) Linguistic Anthropology
    (1/2 time).
Harry Rainbolt (Ph.D., Indiana, 1965; Assoc Prof) Experimental Phonetics.
Richard Scheer (Ph.D., U. of Nebraska, 1958; Assoc Prof) Language and Philosophy.
Virgil Wallentine (Ph.D., Iowa St. U., 1972; Asst Prof) Semantics of Programming
    Languages.

Support Available

A limited number of graduate teaching assistantships are available, normally as half-
time, nine-month appointments. Applications are due by 15 March for the following year.
The Graduate School has funds for in-residence foreign students who have shown high
academic achievement. Applications are initiated by the departments concerned. Funds
are for the final stages of degree requirements.

Academic Calendar 1974-1975

Fall Semester: 22 August - 23 December; Spring Semester: 13 January - 19 May; Summer
Session: 9 June - 1 August. Deadline: 15 June.

DESCRIPTIVE MATERIAL: Write: James L. Armagost, Interdepartmental Linguistics,
                        Kansas State University, Manhattan, Kansas 66506.

HERBERT H. LEHMAN COLLEGE OF THE CITY UNIVERSITY OF NEW YORK
Bronx, New York 10468   Tel. (212) 960-8400)

Interdepartmental Program in Linguistics
Arthur J. Bronstein, Coordinator IDL Program
Degrees: BA.

The Interdisciplinary Linguistics Program offers courses to prepare students: (1) for
graduate study in theoretical and applied linguistics; and (2) for careers in linguistics
research; the teaching of linguistics; applied linguistics, such as lexicography and
the teaching of English as a second language. Cooperating departments participating
in the IDL Program are: Math, Speech, English, Philosophy, Anthropology, and Sociology.

COURSE OFFERINGS

Introductory, 3; Phonology, 4; Theoretical Models, 1; Semantics & Logic, 5; Sociolinguistics, 3; Dialectology, 1; Psycholinguistics, 3; Math. & Comp. Linguistics, 1; Historical Linguistics, 2; Language Pedagogy, 1.

UNCOMMONLY-TAUGHT LANGUAGES

Elem. Chinese (u) Elem. Swahili (u) Swahili Lit. (u) Intermed. Yoruba
Intermed. Chinese Intermed. Swahili   (u)
  (u)   (u)

STAFF

Joseph Aurbach (Ph.D., U. of Southern California, 1970; Asst Prof) Phonetics, Phonology, Sociolinguistics.
Walter Blanco (Ph.D., Harvard University; Asst Prof).
Arthur J. Bronstein (Ph.D., New York U., 1949; Prof).
Daniel Ronnie Cohen (MA, Columbia, 1972; Adjunct Lecturer) Semitics, Grammar.
Michael F. Dorman (Ph.D., U. of Connecticut, 1971; Asst Prof) Speech Perception, Language Development.
Elizabeth W. Ferentz (Ph.D., Syracuse University; Asst Prof).
Helen Fleshler (Ph.D., Penn. State U., 1969; Asst Prof) General Semantics & Cultural Communications.
Erica C. Garcia (Ph.D., Columbia, 1964; Assoc Prof) History of English, Spanish Linguistics, Experimental Phonology.
Joseph A. Ilardo (Ph.D., U. Illinois, 1968; Asst Prof) Communication Theory & Semantics.
Norman Isaacson (Ph.D., NYU, 1968; Asst Prof) Semantics, Thought & Language.
Dale K. Kitzgerald (MA, U. of Calif., Berkeley, 1971; Ph.D. to be given Fall, 1974) Sociolinguistics.
Jack Kligerman (Ph.D., U. of Calif., Berkeley; Asst Prof) Stylistics, Structure of Modern English, History of the English Lang.
Lois R. Kuznets (Ph.D., Indiana U., 1973; Asst Prof) History of the English Lang.
Victoria Markstein (MA, NYC, 1968; MA, Pratt Institute, 1969; Lecturer) Computer Linguistics.
Richard L. Mendelsohn (BA, Cornell U.; Lecturer).
Geoffrey Nunberg (MA, U. of Pa., 1972; Lecturer) (part-time).
Leonard Presby (MS, Columbia U.; Adjunct Lecturer) Studied Pattern Information on a Computer.
Lawrence J. Raphael (Ph.D., City U. of NY, 1970; Asst Prof) Speech & Language Physiology, Acoustic Phonetics.
Harold Shulman (Ph.D., New York U., 1958; Asst Prof) Computer Programming.
Luther Sies (Ed.D., George Washington U.; Asst Prof).
Cj Stevens (Ph.D., Louisiana State University; Prof).
Lynda Weiner (MA, Hunter College of the CUNY, 1967; Lecturer) Developmental Psycholinguistics (and related Language Disorders).

Support Available

Counseling available in the office of the Dean of Students.

Academic Calendar 1974-1975

Fall Semester: September - January; Spring Semester: February - June.

DESCRIPTIVE MATERIAL: Write: Registrar, Herbert H. Lehman College of the City University of New York, Bedford Park Blvd. West, Bronx, New York 10468.

Linguistics Steering Committee
Richard C. Clark, Chairman
Degrees: BA. Degrees Granted 1972-73: 4 BA. Majors: 6g. In Residence: 20u.

The goal of the interdepartmental major concentration in linguistics is to enable the
student to gain a broad knowedge of the phenomenon of language and its relation to other
disciplines, to acquire the methods and techniques used in studying it, and to bring
his knowledge of theory and methodology to bear on various practical problems such as
the teaching of reading, remedial reading, bi-lingual education, foreign language pedagogy and anthropology field work. The concentration thus includes work in three main
areas: 1. Linguistic theory and methodology; 2. Familiarity with languages other than
one's own; 3. The culture or civilization out of which language grows and the relation
of language to cultural and ethnic values.

COURSE OFFERINGS

Introductory, 1; Phonology, 1; Theoretical Models, 1; Semantics & Logic, 1; Sociolinguistics, 2; Psycholinguistics, 1; Historical Linguistics, 3; Language Pedagogy, 1.

STAFF

Richard C. Clark (Ph.D., University of Pennsylvania, 1954; Prof) German.
Charles R. Johnson (MA, George Peabody College, 1958; Inst) French.
Walter D. Mink (Ph.D., University of Minnesota, 1957; Prof) Psychology.
Jeffrey E. Nash (Ph.D., Washington State University, 1971; Asst Prof) Sociology.
Karl C. Sandberg (Ph.D., University of Wisconsin, 1960; Prof) French.
James P. Spradley (Ph.D., University of Washington, 1967; Prof) Anthropology.
Donald B. Steinmetz (Ph.D., University of Minnesota, 1973; Assoc Prof) Foreign
     Languages.
Glen M. Wilson (Ph.D., Ohio State University, 1957; Prof) Speech Communication
     and Dramatic Atrs.

Support Available

All those normally available to students at Macalester College.

Academic Calendar 1975-1975

Fall Semester: Sept. 3 - December 15; Interim--- January; Spring Semester:
February - May 13; Summer Session: June and July. Deadline: as applicable to all
students.

DESCRIPTIVE MATERIAL: Write; Admissions Office, 77 Macalester, St. Paul, Minn.
                 55105.

MARION COLLEGE   Marion, Indiana 46952   Tel. (317) 674-6901, x335,336

Language-Linguistics Department
Russell E. Cooper, Coordinator
Degrees: BA.

Program is integrated with foreign languages (three modern, plus Greek and Hebrew) and
with English. Linguistics courses are part of the Division of Modern Languages and
Literature. Most of our emphasis is liberal arts general education courses for all
students and special linguistics cognate areas and minors for Spanish or English majors.
However, linguistics concentrations are also used with Anthropology and with various
Church ministries programs. Spanish-Linguistics majors travel to Mexico during a short
January term. We do not actively seek Linguistics majors except under special circum-
stances when the student has unusual competence in 2 or more languages as an entering

student, but prefer to develop strong linguistics minors to complement foreign language majors, English majors, etc.

COURSE OFFERINGS

Introductory, 4; Phonology, 2; Theoretical Models, 1; Sociolinguistics, 1; Applied Lx., 1; Historical Linguistics, 2; Linguistics & Literature, 1.

UNCOMMONLY-TAUGHT LANGUAGES

Hebrew (4u)   Mandarin

STAFF

Russell E. Cooper (AB, Marion College; Cand. Ph.D., Hawaii; Asst Prof) General Ling., Melanesian Languages of Papua, Suau.
Marjorie Elder (Ph.D., Chicago, 1965) English, English-linguistics.
Owen Snyder (MA, InterAmerican U., 1968) Spanish.

Linguists in other Departments or Schools

Thomas Brown (MA, San Fernando State College) Anthropology.
David L. Thompson (Ph.D., John Hopkins U.) Hebrew Syntax, Greek.

Support Available

None except undergraduate laboratory assistantships, usually for native speaker assistants in Spanish, etc., or teaching assistants in E.F.L. program. Covers up to cost of tuition and fees.

Academic Calendar 1974-1975

Fall Quarter: September 5 - December 18; Winter Quarter: January 6 - January 24; Spring Quarter: February 29 - May 21; Summer Sessions: June 2-20; June 23 - July 11; July 14 - August 1. Deadline: by 2 weeks before registration.

DESCRIPTIVE MATERIAL: Write: Russell E. Cooper, Marion College, Marion, Indiana 46952.

MARY WASHINGTON COLLEGE Fredericksburg, Virginia 22401   Tel. (703) 373-7250

Linguistics Program
A. Stephen Disraeli, Director
Degrees: BA. Degrees Granted 1972-73: 0 BA. In Residence: 3u.

Courses in linguistics may serve as the core for interdisciplinary majors in human growth and development; stylistics; theoretical, psycho-, socio-, anthropological and applied linguistics, and they contribute to several departmental major programs including psychology, sociology, English, speech pathology and audiology. Undergraduates in an interdisciplinary program in linguistics are required to explore an area in linguistics under the guidance of a tutor by taking up to 12 hours of independent study.

The library maintains a good collection of the contemporary works especially in the area of psycho- and theoretical linguistics.

COURSE OFFERINGS

Introductory, 1; Phonology, 1; Sociolinguistics, 2; Field Methods, 1; Psycholinguistics, 1; Historical Linguistics, 1; Language Pedagogy, 1.

UNCOMMONLY-TAUGHT LANGUAGES

Japanese (u4)   Mod. Greek (u4)

STAFF

A. Stephen Disraeli (MA, Indiana, 1960; Asst Prof) Theoretical linguistics, socio-
    linguistics, anthropological linguistics.

Linguists in Other Departments or Schools

Marilyn Bresler (Ph.D., U. of Mass., 1974; Asst Prof) Psycholinguistics.
Lydia S. Mann (Diploma, Institute Phonetique, 1972; Asst Instr) French phonology.
John C. Manolis (M.A., Florida State, 1969; Asst Prof) French, Greek.
Taketo Ohtani (MA, Scarritt College, 1968; Instr) Japanese.
Paul C. Slayton, Jr. (D.Ed., Virginia, 1969; Assoc Prof) Applied linguistics.
Paul M. Zisman (Ph.D., Catholic, 1974; Asst Prof) Teaching of foreign languages.

Academic Calendar 1974-1975

Fall Semester: August 23-December 14; Spring Semester: January 13- May 13.

DESCRIPTIVE MATERIAL: Write: Director of Admissions, Mary Washington College,
                       Fredericksburg, Virginia 22401.

UNIVERSITY OF MARYLAND   College Park, Maryland 20742   Tel. (301) 454-5223

Linguistics Program
William Orr Dingwall, Chairman
Degrees: BA in linguistics; MA, Ph.D. in Anthropology, Psychology, Speech and
         Hearing with minor in linguistics.

The U. of Maryland is currently in the process of instituting a broadly interdisciplinary,
degree-granting undergraduate program. It will provide basic core courses, courses
in scientific method, theoretical, experimental and applied courses linking linguistics
with anthropology, psychology, hearing and speech science, computer science, and neurology.
Institutes etc.: Center for Language and Cognition (with Psychology Dept.), Computer
Science Center, Institute for Child Development (within Education).

COURSE OFFERINGS

Introductory, 1; Phonology, 2; Theoretical Models, 1; Semantics & Logic, 1; Sociolinguistics, 1; Psycholinguistics, 2; Neurolinguistics, 1; Math. & Comp. Linguistics, 4; Historical Linguistics, 1; History of Linguistics, 1.

UNCOMMONLY-TAUGHT LANGUAGES

Greek (u)   Latin (u)   Sanskrit   Swahili (u)
Japanese (u)   Mandarin (u)

STAFF

William Orr Dingwall (Ph.D., Georgetown U., 1964; Assoc Prof) Experimental and
    Developmental Psycholinguistics, Neurolinguistics, Syntax.
James Lawrence Fidelholtz (Ph.D., M.I.T., 1974) Generative Phonology, American
    Indian Linguistics, Mathematical Linguistics.

Linguists in other Departments or Schools

D. Baker (Assoc Prof) Experimental Phonetics, Pre-linguistic Vocalization.
James Celarier (Assoc Prof) Logic and Linguistics, Gen. Semantics, Montague's
    Theory of Language.
Tsung Chin (Asst Prof) Structure of Chinese.
H. Edmunson (Prof) Mathematical and Comp. Linguistics.
John Eliot (Assoc Prof) Language Acquisition, Piagetian Psychology.
David Horton (Prof) Sentence Processing, Verbal Behavior.
James Martin (Prof) Experimental Phonetics, Rhythmic Structure in Speech.
Earnest Migliazza (Asst Prof) Anthropological Linguistics, Field Methods, American
    Indian Linguistics.
Mary Miller (Assoc Prof) Structure of English, Tagmemics, Sociolinguistics.
Charles Rieger (Asst Prof) Semantic Processing, Memory, Question-answering Systems.

Support Available

Available only through the Center for Language and Cognition within the Psychology Dept.

Academic Calendar 1974-1975

Fall Semester: August-December; Winter/Spring Semester: January-May.

DESCRIPTIVE MATERIAL: U. of Maryland, Catalog Mailing, 4910 Calvert Road, College
                      Park, Maryland 20742.

UNIVERSITY OF MASSACHUSETTS AT AMHERST   Amherst, Massachusetts 01002
Tel. (413) 545-0885

Department of Linguistics
Samuel Jay Keyser, Chairman
Degrees: MA, Ph.D. Majors: 29g. In Residence: 25g.

Work in the department of linguistics is carried out almost entirely within the framework
of generative (transformational) grammar. The primary goal of the graduate program
is to train a small number of first-rate theoretical linguists who will, in most cases,
become teachers at the college or university level. The faculty of the department is
small and likely to remain small; hence, and because of our commitment to theoretical
linguistics, there is heavy emphasis upon the core areas of syntax, semantics, phonology,
and historical linguistics. The first task of the incoming student is to develop a
working knowledge of research methods in those areas to the point of being able to do
original research of her own as well as to critically evaluate the research of others.
Other areas offered in the department include psycholinguistics, sociolinguistics, mathematical linguistics, linguistics and literature, and the structure of various languages
and language families. During 73-74 a two-semester sequence was arranged in conjunction
with the Asian Studies Program: Beginning Japanese the first semester, Structure of
Japanese the second semester. Similar sequences for other languages may be arranged
in the future if student and faculty interest is sufficient, and there are occasional
structure courses in African and American Indian languages for which no background in
the language is assumed. Students are encouraged to work in depth in languages other
than English and to make crucial use of that work in their study of theoretical problems,
since advances in linguistic theory depend heavily on the discovery of universal properties of human languages, and since strength in language areas can be very helpful in
the job market.

COURSE OFFERINGS

Phonology, 5; Theoretical Models, 8; Semantics & Logic, 3; Dialectology, 1; Psycholinguistics, 2; Math. & Comp. Linguistics, 1; Historical Linguistics, 2; Linguistics & Literature,

1. Language Areas: Structure of Unfamiliar Lg., African Lg. 1, Amerindian 1, IE Lg.
1, Malayo-Polynesian 1, Finno-Ugric 1, Near Eastern 1, Oriental 1, SEAsian 1, NonIE
1.

UNCOMMONLY-TAUGHT LANGUAGES

Akkadian	Dutch	Italian	Old Saxon
Armenian	Gothic	Japanese	Old Church
Arabic	Greek	Old Norse	Slavonic
Chinese	Hebrew	Persian	Swahili
Danish	Old Icelandic	Portuguese	Swedish
			Turkish

STAFF

Adrian Akmajian (Ph.D., MIT, 1970; Assoc Prof) Theoretical Syntax, Navajo, Japanese.
Emmon Bach (Ph.D., U. of Chicago, 1959; Prof) Syntactic Theory, Universals,
    Wakashan Linguistics (1/2 time).
Joan Bresnan (Ph.D., MIT, 1972; Asst Prof) English Syntax, Grammatical Theory.
Richard A. Demers (Ph.D., U. of Washington, 1968; Assoc Prof) Phonology, Diachronic
    Linguistics, American Indian Languages.
Donald C. Freeman (Ph.D., U. of Connecticut, 1965; Prof) Stylistics, Literary
    Theory, English Language Teaching.
Frank W. Heny (Ph.D., UCLA, 1970; Assoc Prof) African Languages, Phonology, Se-
    mantics.
Samuel Jay Keyser (Ph.D., Yale, 1962; Prof) History & Structure of English,
    Phonology, Literary Theory.
Barbara Hall Partee (Ph.D., MIT, 1965; Prof) Semantics, Syntax, Philosophy of
    Language.
Tom Roeper (Ph.D., Harvard, 1973; Asst Prof) Psycholinguistics, Language Acquisi-
    tion, Sociolinguistics.
Lisa Selkirk (Ph.D., MIT, 1972; Asst Prof) Phonology and its Interaction with
    Syntax.

Linguists in other Departments or Schools

Michael Arbib (Ph.D., MIT; Prof) Computer and Information Science, Psychology.
James E. Cathey (Ph.D., U. of Washington; Asst Prof) Germanic Languages.
Charles Clifton (Ph.D., U. of Minnesota; Assoc Prof) Psychology.
Edmund L. Gettier III (Ph.D., Cornell U.; Prof) Philosophy.
Chisato Kitagawa (Ph.D., U. of Michigan; Asst Prof) Japanese.
Terry Parsons (Ph.D., Stanford U.; Assoc Prof) Philosophy.
Carroll E. Reed (Ph.D., Brown U.; Prof) Germanic Languages.
Robert A. Rothstein (Ph.D., Harvard U.; Assoc Prof) Slavic Languages.
Zdenek Salzmann (Ph.D., Indiana U.; Assoc Prof) Anthropology.
Shou-Hsin Teng (Ph.D., U. of California at Berkeley; Asst Prof) Chinese.
Ian B. Thomas (Ph.D., U. of Illinois; Assoc Prof) Electrical Engineering and Speech.

Support Available

(All of these subject to change) 2 Assistantships in TEFL, $3600-$3800; 2-3 Teaching
Assistantships in Linguistics, $3600; 3-5 Teaching Assistantships in Rhetoric, $3600;
University Fellowships (university-wide competition), $2800/year for 2 years; Research
Assistantships on Faculty Grants, variable amounts. Application deadlines: February 1.

Academic Calendar 1974-1975

Fall Quarter: September 1 - December 20; Winter Quarter: January interim (no official
courses); Spring Quarter: February 1 - May 20. Deadline: March 1.

DESCRIPTIVE MATERIAL: Write: Barbara H. Partee, Graduate Advisor, Linguistics
                      Department, University of Massachusetts, Amherst, Massa-
                      chusetts 01002.

Linguistics Program
Department of Foreign Literatures & Linguistics
Morris Halle, Chairman
Degrees: Ph.D. Degrees Granted 1972-73: 6 Ph.D.   Majors: 35g; 35 Ph.D.   In
          Residence: 35g.

A special feature of the program is the active role that graduate students play in the
research. It is our belief that graduate education gains immeasurably in significance
if students are made to work on real problems almost from the very beginnings of their
career in graduate school. We are fortunate that at this point in the evolution of linguistics as a science, it is possible to achieve some facility with linguistic techniques
rather rapidly, so that students in their second year in graduate school are often in
a position to obtain results that are of sufficient interest to be reported in the professional journals, or at meetings of professional societies. Consequently, our academic
program is so organized as to encourage students to participate actively in the ongoing
research of the group.
   We do not have any departmental publications, but work of members of the group is
often published in the Quarterly Progress Report of MIT's Research Laboratory of Elec-
tronics (with which we are affiliated).
   Faculty members from this department teach at the LSA's Summer Institutes, but the
summer program here is one of independent study (there are no summer courses offered).

COURSE OFFERINGS

Phonology, 5; Theoretical Models, 11; Semantics & Logic, 2; Psycholinguistics, 1; Math.
& Comp. Linguistics, 1; Historical Linguistics, 2; History of Linguistics, 2; Linguistics
& Literature, 5. Language Areas: Romance 1, Russian 1, German 1.

UNCOMMONLY-TAUGHT LANGUAGES

None; we have a cross-enrollment agreement with Harvard. Our students take "uncommon"
languages at Harvard.

STAFF

Noam Chomsky (Ph.D., U. of Pennsylvania, 1955; Prof) Syntax, Semantics.
Kenneth Hale (Ph.D., Indiana, 1959; Prof) Syntax, American-Indian Languages.
Morris Halle (Ph.D., Harvard, 1955; Prof) Phonology, Metrics, Phonetics.
James W. Harris (Ph.D., M.I.T., 1967) Spanish Phonology, Literature.
Paul Kiparsky (Ph.D., M.I.T., 1965; Prof) Phonology, Metrics, Poetics.
David Perlmutter (Ph.D., M.I.T., 1968; Assoc Prof) Syntax.
John R. Ross (Ph.D., M.I.T., 1967; Prof) Syntax.

Linguists in other Departments or Schools

Sylvain Bromberger (Ph.D., Harvard, 1956) Philosophy of Language.
Jerry A. Fodor (Ph.D., Princeton, 1960; Prof) Psychology, Psycholinguistics.
Merrill F. Garrett (Ph.D., U. of Illinois, 1965; Assoc Prof) Psychology and Psycho-
   linguistics.
Wayne A. O'Neil (Ph.D., U. of Wisconsin, 1960; Prof) Old English, History of English.

Support Available

We have a limited number of traineeships and assistantships available from NIH and NIMH
funds. These funds are subject to change from year to year so we cannot give definite
information on stipends, number of awards, etc. There is no special application procedure or deadline. Financial aid application is part of the regular graduate school
application (due January 15).

Academic Calendar 1974-1975

Fall Semester: September 9 - mid December; Winter Quarter: Independent Activities Period,
January; Spring Semester: First week of February - end of May; Summer Session: June
- mid August. Deadline: January 15.

<u>DESCRIPTIVE MATERIAL</u>: Write: Linguistics, Rm. 20C-128, Massachusetts Institute of Technology, Cambridge, Massachusetts 02139.

MIAMI UNIVERSITY Oxford, Ohio 45056   Tel. (513) 529-2227

Department of English
Linguistics Committee
Andrew Kerek, Chairman
Degrees: BA, AB, BS, MA, MAT in English with Linguistics Emphasis. Degrees Granted
       1972-73: 8 BA, 3 MA. Majors: 5g; 5 MA. In Residence: 15u.

The undergraduate and graduate programs in English with Linguistics Concentration combine (about half and half) courses in general and English linguistics with courses in
literature.
   The new undergraduate interdisciplinary program in linguistics, offered under the
auspices of the Department of English and involving course work in ten other departments,
stresses a multi-disciplinary approach to the study of language. The student is offered
an intensive five-course introduction to the discipline of scientific language study,
to be followed by cognate courses in which language is approached through the distinct
scientific criteria and characteristic methodologies of a number of related disciplines.
The program attempts to combine a modern theoretical orientation with socio-cultural
relevance and practical applicability.

<u>COURSE OFFERINGS</u>

Introductory, 1; Phonology, 1; Theoretical Models, 2; Semantics & Logic, 1; Sociolinguistics, 2; Psycholinguistics, 2; Historical Linguistics, 2; Linguistics & Literature,
1; Language Pedagogy, 2; Seminar in Applied Linguistics, 1. Language Areas: Spanish
3, German 2.

<u>UNCOMMONLY-TAUGHT LANGUAGES</u>

Mod. Chinese (u6)   Hebrew (u6)   Japanese (u6)

<u>STAFF</u>

Helene R. Fuller (MA, Columbia T.C., 1955; Asst Prof) TEFL (1/2 time).
Andrew Kerek (Ph.D., Indiana, 1968; Assoc Prof) Phonology, Language Variation, Hungarian.
Max Morenberg (Ph.D., Florida State, 1972; Asst Prof) Generative Grammar, Child
   Language, Stylistics.
Claire J. Raeth (Ph.D., Northwestern, 1952; Assoc Prof) English Language (1/4
   time).
Theodore Williams (AM, Western Reserve, 1951; Senior Instr) English Language (1/4 time).

<u>Linguists in other Departments or Schools</u>

Lawrence Baldwin (Ph.D., Harvard, 1972; Asst Prof) Psychology of Language (1/3 time)
Jean Cazajou (MA, Yale, 1971; Inst) French Structuralism (1/4 time).
Daniel Franzblau (Ph.D., Miami, 1972; Asst Prof) French and Russian Linguistics,
   Foreign Language Pedagogy.
Harvey L. Grandstaff (Ph.D., Cincinnati, 1974; Asst Prof) Speech Pathology.
J. Keith Jensen (Ph.D., Iowa, 1973; Asst Prof) Communication Theory (1/4 time).
Kenneth B. Kane (MA, Penn State, 1969; Instr) French Linguistics, Psycholinguistics
   (1/3 time).
Robert N. Phillips (Ph.D., Wisconsin, 1967; Assoc Prof) Spanish Linguistics (1/2 time).
Raymond M. White (Ph.D., Colorado, 1967; Assoc Prof) Social Psychology, Psychology
   of Language (1/3 time).
Hugh T. Wilder (Ph.D., Western Ontario, 1973; Asst Prof) Philosophy of Language
   (1/2 time).

Nathaniel Wing (Ph.D., Columbia, 1968; Assoc Prof) French Semiotics (1/4 time).
Daniel E. Wozniak (Ph.D., Michigan State, 1963; Assoc Prof) Sociology of Language
    (1/4 time).

Support Available

Teaching assistantships available in English with Linguistics Concentration.
Write to: Director, Graduate Program, Department of English, Miami University, Oxford,
Ohio 45056.

Academic Calendar 1974-1975

Fall Quarter: September 25 - December 13; Winger Quarter: January 3 - March 14; Spring
Quarter: March 24 - June 6; Summer Quarter: June 16 - August 22. Deadline: One month
prior to entrance (graduate), March 1 (undergraduate).

DESCRIPTIVE MATERIAL: Write: The Office of Admission, Grey Gables (undergraduate),
    The Graduate School, Roudebush Hall (graduate), Miami Uni-
    versity, Oxford, Ohio 45056.

UNIVERSITY OF MICHIGAN Ann Arbor, Michigan 48104   Tel. (313) 764-0353

Department of Linguistics
William J. Gedney, Chairman [Kenneth Pike as of July 1975]
Degrees: BA, MA, Phd. Degrees Granted 1972-73: 25 BA, 24 MA, 12 Ph.D. Majors:
    170 g. In Residence: 40u.

The program has for many years been mainly a graduate one, with increasing attention
in recent years to an undergraduate program in linguistics, which includes many courses
designed for majors in other fields, such as anthropology, sociology, speech, and education; some are offered jointly. One of our chief aims is variety in theoretical points
of view in faculty and course offerings.
    The Department also offers instruction in languages (e.g., South and Southeast Asian
languages) which do not fall within the domain of any of the language departments.
Many of our students utilize the facilities of such related units as the Phonetics Laboratory, the Language Laboratory, the English Language Institute, and various area centers.
    Each summer we offer four or five courses in the first half-term (May-June) and four
or five also in the second half-term (July-August). From time to time the Linguistic
Institute of the Linguistic Society of America has been hosted by this University, most
recently in 1965, 1967, and 1973.
    UMPIL (University of Michigan Papers in Linguistics) is published at irregular inter-
vals by a departmental student-faculty committee.

COURSE OFFERINGS

Introductory, 3; Phonology, 4; Theoretical Models, 11; Semantics & Logic, 5; Sociolinguistics, 10; Dialectology, 2; Field Methods, 2; Psycholinguistics, 2; Historical Linguistics, 4; History of Linguistics, 1; Linguistics & Literature, 4; Language Pedagogy,
4. Language Areas: Hungarian 1, Lithuanian 1, Yiddish 2, Ojibwa 1, Thai 4, Indonesian
2, Hindi-Urdu 7, Marathi 2, Sanskrit 4, Buddhism 1, Burmese 1, S.E. Asian 3, Amerindian
Lgs. 1, Pali & Prakrit 1, Caucasian 1, Javanese 1, Malayo-Polynesian 1.

UNCOMMONLY-TAUGHT LANGUAGES

Arabic	Old High German	Marathi	Sanskrit
Berber	Mid. High German	Norwegian	Old Saxon
Burmese	Hebrew	Ojibwa	Serbo-Croatian
Chinese	Hindi-Urdu	Pali	Old Church
Czech	Hungarian	Persian	Slavic
Dutch	Indonesian	Old Persian	Thai
Old English	Japanese	Polish	Turkish
Mid. English	Kurdish	Portuguese	Ukrainian
Gaelic	Lithuanian	Prakrit	Yiddish

STAFF

Alton L. Becker (Ph.D., U. of Michigan, 1967; Prof) Southeast Asian lags., Linguistics.

Ann H. Borkin (Ph.D., U. of Michigan, 1974; Asst Prof) Syntax and Semantics.

H. Douglas Brown (Ph.D., U.C.L.A., 1970; Asst Prof) Applied Linguistics, Teaching English as a Second Language, Language Acquisition.

Robbins Burling (Ph.D., Harvard, 1958; Prof) Anthropology, Sociolinguistics.

John C. Catford (Diplome de phonetique generale 1938, Universities of Paris and London; Prof) Phonetics, Caucasic Languages.

Madhav M. Deshpande (Ph.D., U. of Pennsylvania, 1972; Asst Prof) Indic Languages.

Penelope Eckert (MA, Columbia University, 1969; Lecturer) Anthropology, Socio-linguistics.

Peter Fodale (Ph.D., U. of Michigan, 1964; Assoc Prof) Syntax, Sociolinguistics, TEFL.

William J. Gedney (Ph.D., Yale, 1947; Prof) Thai Languages.

Kenneth C. Hill (Ph.D., U.C.L.A., 1967; Assoc Prof) Phonology, Amerindian Languages.

Peter E. Hook (Ph.D., U. of Pennsylvania, 1973; Asst Prof) Indic Languages, Linguistics, and Literature.

Deborah Keller-Cohen (Ph.D., S.U.N.Y.A.B., 1974; Asst Prof) First and Second Language Acquistion, Applied Linguistics.

John M. Lawler (Ph.D., U. of Michigan, 1973; Asst Prof) Syntax and Semantics.

Thomas Markey (Ph.D., U. of Uppsala; Asst Prof) Germanic Linguistics.

Herbert H. Paper (Ph.D., U. of Chicago, 1951; Prof) General Linguistics, Iranian Linguistics.

Kenneth L. Pike (Ph.D., U. of Michigan, 1942; Prof) Phonetics, Phonology, Tagmemics.

Charles R. Pyle (Ph.D., U. of Illinois, 1971; Asst Prof) Phonology.

Gene Schramm (Ph.D., Dropsie College, 1956; Prof) Semitic Linguistics.

Harvey M. Taylor (Ph.D., U. of Hawaii, 1971; Asst Prof) TEFL, Language Acquisition, Japanese Linguistics.

Ronald Wardhaugh (Ph.D., U. of Alberta, 1965; Prof) Applied Linguistics, TEFL.

Linguists in other Departments or Schools

Ernest T. Abdel-Massih (Assoc Prof) Near East.

Richard W. Bailey (Assoc Prof) English.

G. Lee Bowie (Asst Prof) Philosophy.

George G. Cameron (Prof) Near East.

H. Don Cameron (Assoc Prof) Classics.

Vern Carroll (Assoc Prof) Anthropology.

Edna Coffin (Asst Prof) Near East.

James E. Dew (Assoc Prof) Far East.

James W. Downer (Prof) English.

James O. Ferrell (Prof) Slavic.

Russell A. Fraser (Prof) English.

Joyce B. Friedman (Prof) Communication Sciences.

Michio P. Hagiwara (Assoc Prof) Romance.

Satendra Khanna (Asst Prof) English.

Lawrence B. Kiddle (Prof) Romance.

Harold V. King (Prof) English.

Glenn Knudsig (Asst Prof) Classics.

Frank M. Koen (Assoc Prof) Psychology.

Sherman M. Kuhn (Prof) English.

Robert L. Kyes (Prof) Germanic.

Clifford S. Leonard (Assoc Prof) Romance.

Margaret Lourie (Asst Prof) English.
Dorothy Mack (Asst Prof) Humanities.
Melvin Manis (Prof) Psychology.
Ladislav Matejka (Prof) Slavic.
Ernest N. McCarus (Prof) Near East.
Naomi McGloin (Lecturer) Far East.
Frances McSparran (Asst Prof) English.
Raleigh Morgan (Prof) Romance.
Susumu Nagara (Assoc Prof) Far East.
Ernst Pulgram (Prof) Romance.
Raji Rammuny (Assoc Prof) Near East.
John Reidy (Prof) English.
Klaus F. Riegel (Prof) English.
Jay L. Robinson (Prof) English.
Donald B. Sands (Prof) English.
Gerda M. Seligson (Prof) Classics.
Stephen P. Stich (Assoc Prof) Philosophy.
Waldo Sweet (Prof) Classics.
Bernard Van't Hul (Assoc Prof) English.
Gernot Windfuhr (Prof) Near East.
David L. Wolfe (Assoc Prof) Romance.
Richard E. Young (Prof) Humanities.

Support Available

Fellowships in varying amounts and teaching assistantships are awarded each year by
a departmental committee. These are usually not awarded to first-year students. Application deadline is February 1.

Academic Calendar 1974-1975

Fall Semester: September 6 - December 21; Winter Semester: January 9 - May 2;
Spring Semester: May 7 - June 28; Summer Semester: July 2 - August 23. Deadline: June
1 absolute deadline.

DESCRIPTIVE MATERIAL: Write: Admissions Secretary, Department of Linguistics -
University of Michigan, 1076 Frieze, Ann Arbor, Michigan 48104.

MICHIGAN STATE UNIVERSITY East Lansing, Michigan 48824   Tel. (517) 353-0740

Linguistics & Oriental & African Languages
James Wang, Dept. Chairman
Degrees: BA, MA, Ph.D. Degrees Granted 1972-73: 19 MA, 3 Ph.D. Majors: 22g.
        In Residence: 12u, 1 Special.

Linguistic degree programs in this department emphasize a multiple approach to linguistic
theory while also stressing the application of theory to linguistic data.
    The undergraduate program contains a core of required courses in linguistic theory
and analysis, which are combined with advanced courses in foreign language to comprise
the total program. The student is encouraged to pursue cognate sequences in a wide
variety of related fields.
    On the Master's Degree level, two alternate degree programs are offered. One program
requires the completion and successful defense of a thesis, and emphasizes linguistic
theory. Every student in this program must study at least two of the linguistic theories
regularly taught in the department: stratificational, tagmemic, and transformational.
    The alternate Master's program requires a written examination instead of a thesis,
and emphasizes applied linguistics. Basic courses in theory and analysis are required.
The remainder of the student's program and written examination are planned by an individual guidance committee.

Admission to the doctoral program requires the equivalent of our Master's with thesis and a demonstrated ability for independent study. Course work on this level is aimed at preparing the student for a four-part Comprehensive Examination.

COURSE OFFERINGS

Introductory, 4; Phonology, 3; Theoretical Models, 2; Semantics & Logic, 1; Field Methods, 1; Historical Linguistics, 2; History of Linguistics, 1; Language Pedagogy, 1. Language Areas: African Languages 1. Other Departments: Introductory, 2; Phonology, 3; Theoretical Models, 2; Semantics & Logic, 5; Sociolinguistics, 1; Dialectology, 1; Psycholinguistics, 7; Historical Linguistics, 3; Language Pedagogy, 2. Language Areas: OE, ME, French 3, Spanish 3.

UNCOMMONLY-TAUGHT LANGUAGES

Chinese	Ibo (u & g 12q)	Pidgin	Swahili
(u & g 21q)	Japanese	(u & g 12q)	(u & g 12q)
Hausa (u & g 12q)	(u 10q, g)	Sanskrit	Yoruba (u & g 12q)

STAFF

Ruth M. Brend (Ph.D., U. of Michigan; Assoc Prof) Tagmemics.
Rachel M. Costa (Ph.D., U. of Michigan; Visiting Asst Prof) Generative Semantics and Comparative Indo-European Linguistics.
John B. Eulenberg (Ph.D., U. of California, San Diego; Asst Prof) Computational and Mathematical Linguistics.
Julia S. Falk (Ph.D., U. of Washington; Assoc Prof) Transformational Grammar, Child Language Acquisition.
David G. Lockwood (Ph.D., U. of Michigan; Assoc Prof) Stratificational, Slavic Linguistics.
Alfred E. Opubor (Ph.D., Michigan State U.; Asst Prof) African Languages and Literature.
Irvine Richardson (Ph.D., U. of London; Prof) African Languages.
John T. Ritter (BS, Michigan State U.; Asst Prof) Generative Phonology.
Seok C. Song (Ph.D., Indiana U.; Assoc Prof) Transformational Grammar, Japanese and Korean Linguistics.
James P. Wang (MA, Cornell U.; Assoc Prof and Chairman) Chinese Language and Linguistics.
Meyer L. Wolf (Ph.D., Columbia U.; Asst Prof) Dialectology.

Linguists in other Departments or Schools

Abram Barch (Ph.D.; Prof) Psychology.
Ralph Barrett (Ph.D.) Director, English Language Center.
Daniel Beasley (Ph.D.; Assoc Prof) Audiology and Speech Sciences.
Dean Detrich (Ph.D.; Asst Prof) Romance Languages.
David Dwyer (Ph.D.; Asst Prof) Anthropology.
Ann Harrison (Ph.D.; Prof) Romance Languages.
Thomas Juntune (Ph.D.; Assoc Prof) German and Russian.
Paul Munsell (Ph.D.; Asst Prof) Assistant Director, English Language Center.
Gary Olson (Ph.D.; Asst Prof) Psychology.
Morteza Rahimi (Ph.D.; Assoc Prof) Computer Science.
Lee Shulman (Ph.D.; Prof) Educational Psychology.
James Stalker (Ph.D.; Asst Prof) English.

Support Available

Graduate teaching assistantships and Graduate Office Fellowships available. Stipend ranges from $3,200 to $3,600 per academic year. Application deadline is April 15, 1975.

Academic Calendar 1974-1975

Fall Quarter: September 26 - December 13; Winter Quarter: January 6 - March 14; Spring Quarter: March 26 - June 6; Summer Quarter: June 18 - August 29. Deadline: April 1, 1974.

DESCRIPTIVE MATERIAL: Write: Office of Admissions and Scholarships, 250 Administration Bldg., Michigan State University, East Lansing,
Michigan 48824.

UNIVERSITY OF MINNESOTA Minneapolis, Minnesota 55455   Tel. (612) 373-5769

Department of Linguistics
Bruce T. Downing, Chairman
Degrees: BA, MA, Ph.D., MA in English as a Second Language. Degrees Granted 1972-
1973: 8 BA, 2 MA, 3 Ph.D., 6 MA ESL. Majors: 23g. In Residence: 20g, 37u,
31 MA ESL.

The Department of Linguistics at the University of Minnesota offers the BA, MA, and
Ph.D. in Linguistics, and the MA in English as a Second Language. Extensive opportunities are available for study and research in phonology, syntax, semantics, historical
linguistics, phonetics, mathematical linguistics, and foundations of linguistics, as
well as in such applied areas as application of linguistics to language teaching, contrastive analysis, first and second language acquisition, sociolinguistics, and computational linguistics. There are also numerous interdisciplinary opportunities available
in cooperation with other academic units such as the Department of Philosophy, the various language departments, the Minnesota Center for the Philosophy of Science, the Institute of Child Development, the Center for Research in Human Learning, and the Center
for the Advanced Study of Language, Style, and Literary Theory. Work by both students
and faculty appears in MINNESOTA WORKING PAPERS IN LINGUISTICS AND PHILOSOPHY OF LANGUAGE,
published jointly with the Department of Philosophy.
   The theoretical interests of the Department are focused on generative grammar, with
a strong emphasis on foundations of linguistics and on the philosophical and empirical
issues underlying significant recent developments in linguistic theory. Students receive
a thorough grounding in standard theories and approaches, but are expected to think
independently and innovatively in their own research and to be rigorously objective
in the formulation and critical evaluation of all linguistic hypotheses. Contact between
students and faculty is close and informal, affording opportunities for personal attention, guidance, and active participation in ongoing research that are frequently absent
in larger departments.

COURSE OFFERINGS

Introductory, 3; Phonology, 6; Theoretical Models, 6; Semantics & Logic, 3; Sociolinguistics, 1; Field Methods, 1; Psycholinguistics, 2; Math. & Comp. Linguistics, 1; Historical
Linguistics, 4; History of Linguistics, 1; Language Pedagogy, 2. Other Departments:
Phonology, 1; Theoretical Models, 2; Semantics & Logic, 1; Sociolinguistics, 1; Dialectology, 1; Psycholinguistics, 4; Neurolinguistics, 1; Math. & Comp. Linguistics, 2;
Historical Linguistics, 1; Language Pedagogy, 1. Language Areas: Classics 1, Greek
2, Latin 2, Chinese 2, Hindi 1, Spanish 3, Japanese 1, OE 1, ME 1, French 1, Italian
2, Vedic 1, Romance 1, German 3, Arabic 2, Semitic 2, Finnish 1, Scandinavian 2, Russian
2.

UNCOMMONLY-TAUGHT LANGUAGES

Akkadian (g3)
Arabic (g10, u9)
Aramaic (g2)
Bengali (g12, u6)
Chinese (g17, u10)
Dakota (u5)
Danish (u9)
Dutch (u5)
Mid. English (g5)
Old English (g3)
Ancient Egyptian (g3, u3)
Finnish (u9)

Old French (g7, u1)
Mid. High German (g7, u1)
Old High German (g3)
Gothic (g1)
Mod. Greek (u4)
Hebrew (u22)
Hindi (g12, u6)
Mod. Icelandic (g2)

Japanese (g13, u11)
Marathi (g12, u6)
Old Norse (g2)
Norwegian (u9)
Ojibwa (Chippewa) (u5)
Oscan-Umbrian (g1)
Persian (g6, u6)
Old Persian (g1)
Old Provencal (g2)

Polish (g1, u8)
Portuguese (g10, u9)
Sanskrit (g11, u3)
Old Saxon (g1)
Serbo-Croatian (u6)
Sumerian (g1)
Swahili (u5)
Swedish (u9)
Syriac (g1)
Turkish (u3)
Urdu (g6, u3)
Yiddish (u3)

STAFF

Bruce T. Downing (Ph.D., Texas, 1970; Assoc Prof) Syntax, Linguistic Theory.
Kathleen Houlihan (Ph.D. pending, Texas, 1974; Inst) Phonetics, Phonology.
Larry G. Hutchinson (Ph.D., Indiana, 1969; Assoc Prof) Syntax, Semantics, Mathematical Linguistics.
Michael B. Kac (Ph.D., UCLA, 1972; Asst Prof) Syntax, Semantics, Sociolinguistics.
Rocky V. Miranda (Ph.D., Cornell, 1971; Asst Prof) Historical Linguistics, Indo-European, South Asian Linguistics.
Jean D. Petersen (Ph.D. pending, Stanford, 1974; Inst) Phonetics, English as a Second Language.
Betty Wallace Robinett (Ph.D., Michigan, 1951; Prof) Applied and English Linguistics, English as a Second Language.
Gerald A. Sanders (Ph.D., Indiana, 1967; Assoc Prof) Syntax, Phonology, Semantics.
Amy L. Sheldon (Ph.D., Texas, 1972; Asst Prof) Psycholinguistics, Syntax, English as a Second Language.

Linguists in other Departments or Schools

Harold B. Allen (emeritus) English, Dialectology.
M.A.R. Barker, Urdu, Baluchi, Brahui.
Patricia S. Broen, Communication Disorders.
Adele Donchenko, Russian.
Timothy Dunnigan, Dakota, Ojibwe.
Larry M. Grimes, Spanish.
Nils Hasselmo, Scandinavian Languages.
James J. Jenkins, Psychology.
Indira Y. Junghare, Sanskrit, Marathi, Hindi.
Owen R. Loveless, Japanese, Okinawan.
Andrew Macleish, English.
Lawrence C. Mantini, French.
Michael P. Maratsos, Child Development.
H.E. Mason, Philosophy.
J. Lawrence Mitchell, English.
Ricardo A. Narvaez, Spanish.
Michael Root, Philosophy.
Charles E. Speaks, Communication Disorders.
Paul Staneslow, Hindi.
Martin Steinmann, English.
Donald C. Swanson, Classical Philology.
John Wallace, Philosophy.
Stephen S. Wang, Chinese, Tibetan, Thai.
Cecil Wood, Germanic Languages.

Support Available

Graduate School Fellowships (approx. $3000 plus tuition); Teaching Assistantships ($1917 plus in-state tuition status); Research Assistantships ($1863 plus in-state tuition status). Applications for support, available from the Graduate School, are due by February 15.

UNIVERSITY OF MINNESOTA (Continued)

Academic Calendar 1974-1975

Fall Quarter: September 23; Winter Quarter: January 6; Spring Quarter: April 1; Summer Quarter: June 17. Deadline: Four weeks prior to opening of quarter or summer session.

DESCRIPTIVE MATERIAL: Write: Graduate School (graduate), 322 Johnston Hall,
              Office of Admissions (undergraduate), 6 Morrill Hall,
              University of Minnesota, Minneapolis, Minnesota 55455.

UNIVERSITY OF MINNESOTA, DULUTH   Duluth, Minnesota 55812   Tel. (218) 726-8235

Linguistics Program
Edith J. Hols, Coordinator
Degrees: B.A. with minor in linguistics.

COURSE OFFERINGS

Introductory, 3; Phonology, 1; Sociolinguistics, 2; Psycholinguistics, 1; Historical Linguistics, 1; Language Pedagogy, 3. Other Departments: Semantics & Logic, 2; Psycholinguistics, 5; Linguistics & Literature, 2. Language Areas: Chippewa 1, Spanish 1.

UNCOMMONLY-TAUGHT LANGUAGES

Chippewa

STAFF

Henry J. Ehlers (Ph.D., U. of Pittsburgh, 1941; Prof) Education: Language Problems
    of Minority groups; and Logic: The Logical Structures in Language.
John T. Hatten (Ph.D., U. of Wisconsin, 1965; Assoc Prof) Communication Disorders.
Linda R. Hilsen (MA, U. of Minnesota; Inst) ESL and TESL.
Edith J. Hols (Ph.D., U. of Iowa, 1970; Assoc Prof) Grammar, TESL, Stylistics.
Jackson Huntley (Ph.D., Michigan State U., 1969; Assoc Prof) Interpersonal Com-
    munication.
Klaus Jankofsky (Dr. Phil., Universitat des Saarlandes, Germany, 1969; Assoc
    Prof) Historical Linguistics, esp. English and French.
Michael L. Kamil (Ph.D., U. of Wisconsin, 1969; Asst Prof) Psycholinguistics.
Bernard J. Langr (Ph.D., U. of Minnesota, 1973; Asst Prof) Linguistics Applied
    to Teaching and Learning Spanish.
Robert F. Pierce (Ph.D., U. of Wisconsin, 1953; Prof) Phonetics.
Timothy Roufs (Ph.D., U. of Minnesota, 1970; Asst Prof) Language and Culture.
Sandra J. Woolum (Ph.D., Michigan State U.; Asst Prof) Psycholinguistics.

Academic Calendar 1974-1975

Fall Quarter: September 29 - December 18; Winter Quarter: January 5 - March 20; Spring Quarter: March 29 - June 12; Summer Sessions: June 15 to July 16; July 20 to August 20.

DESCRIPTIVE MATERIAL: Write: Edith Hols, Coordinator of Linguistics Program,
              Humanities 425, UMD, Duluth, Minnesota 55812.

Linguistics Area Program
Donald M. Lance, Chairman
Degrees: BA, MA in Linguistics, Ph.D. in Anthropological Linguistics. Degrees
          Granted 1972-73: 4 BA, 4 MA. In Residence: 7g, 5u.

The Linguistics Area Program is a non-budgeted, degree-offering unit of the College
of Arts and Science, and is administered by the Linguistics Committee. The BA and MA
degree programs consist of a set of core courses in linguistic theory, plus at least
four cross-listed courses in other departments of the College. Supporting work may
be taken in a number of disciplines, so as to develop an emphasis in a particular language (or languages), anthropology, sociology, education, English, or any other academic
field of particular interest to the student. The MA thesis is optional.
    Facilities and programs of interest to linguistics students and faculty include the
Center for Research in Social Behavior, Speech and Hearing Clinic, South Asia Program,
Honors College, General Studies Program.

COURSE OFFERINGS

Introductory, 2; Phonology, 5; Theoretical Models, 2; Semantics & Logic, 1; Sociolinguistics, 4; Dialectology, 1; Field Methods, 1; Psycholinguistics, 3; Historical Linguistics,
2; Language Pedagogy, 1. Language Areas: OE 1, French 3, Spanish 3, German 2, Russian 2.

UNCOMMONLY-TAUGHT LANGUAGES

Hindi (u4)   Sanskrit (u4)

STAFF

Louanna Furbee-Losee (Ph.D., U. of Chicago, 1974; Asst Prof) Anthropological
    Linguistics, Historical Linguistics, Mayan Studies.
Daniel E. Gulstad (Ph.D., U. of Illinois, 1969; Assoc Prof) Theoretical Linguistics,
    Romance Linguistics.
John M. Howie (Ph.D., Indiana U., 1970; Asst Prof) Theoretical Linguistics, French
    Linguistics.

Linguists in other Departments or Schools

James D. Amerman (Ph.D., U. of Illinois, 1970; Asst Prof) Acoustic and Physio-
    logical Phonetics.
Ruth H. Firestone (Ph.D., U. of Colorado, 1972; Asst Prof) Germanic Linguistics.
Daniel Greenblatt (Ph.D., U. of Michigan, 1974; Asst Prof) English Linguistics,
    Computational Linguistics.
Ben F. Honeycutt (Ph.D., Ohio State U., 1969; Assoc Prof) Romance Linguistics.
Winifred B. Horner (MA, U. of Missouri, 1960; Inst) English Linguistics, Rhetoric.
Donald M. Lance (Ph.D., U. of Texas-Austin, 1968; Assoc Prof) English Linguistics,
    TESL.
Eugene N. Lane (Ph.D., Yale, 1962; Assoc Prof) Greek, Classics.
Dena Lieberman (Ph.D., U. of Wisconsin, 1974; Asst Prof) Anthropological Lin-
    guistics, Sociolinguistics.
Linnea Lilja (Ph.D., U. of Minnesota, 1969; Assoc Prof) Linguistics and Elementary
    Education.
Marjorie M. Marlin (Ph.D., U. of Illinois, 1967; Assoc Prof) Psycholinguistics.
Ben F. Nelms (Ph.D., U. of Iowa, 1967; Assoc Prof) Linguistics and Secondary
    Education.
George B. Pace (Ph.D., U. of Virginia, 1942; Prof) English Linguistics.
Olga C. Shopay-Morton (Ph.D., Ohio State U., 1971; Asst Prof) Slavic Linguistics.
Thelma Trombly (Ph.D., U. of Missouri, 1958; Prof) Child Language Acquisition.

Academic Calendar 1974-1975

Fall Semester: August 22 - December 19; Winter Semester: January 9 - May 10;
Summer Session: June 9 - August 1. Deadline: 4 weeks prior to registration.

UNIVERSITY OF MISSOURI - COLUMBIA (Continued)

DESCRIPTIVE MATERIAL: Write: Office of Admissions, 130 Jesse Hall, University of
Missouri, Columbia, Missouri 65201.

UNIVERSITY OF MONTANA Missoula, Montana 59801   Tel. (406) 243-4751

Program in Linguistics
Robert B. Hausmann, Chairman
Degrees: Interdisciplinary BA/MA with a concentration in linguistics. Degrees
        Granted 1972-73: 1 MA. In Residence: 1g, 3u.

The program in linguistics is offered through the cooperation of the departments represented on the Linguistics Committee. There is a set of core courses on linguistic theory
and method which attempt to teach a scientific approach to the study of language. The
core courses are supplemented by courses oriented to majors in other programs.
    Almost all students, at the present time, work towards majors in other fields. The
number of faculty who are fully trained linguists is so small and the job market for
BAs in linguistics is so poor that we feel we can best serve the student by requiring
him to major in a related field. The MA program is interdisciplinary (at least three
fields including linguistics) and requires a thesis. Graduate training is directed
toward linguistic theory and field methods, the strengths of our faculty.

COURSE OFFERINGS

Introductory, 2; Phonology, 2; Theoretical Models, 3; Semantics & Logic, 1; Sociolinguistics, 1; Dialectology, 1; Field Methods, 1; Psycholinguistics, 1; Historical Linguistics, 2; Language Pedagogy, 1. Language Areas: Salishan 1, Romance 1, German 1.

UNCOMMONLY-TAUGHT LANGUAGES

Chinese

STAFF

Anthony Beltramo (Ph.D., Stanford, 1973) Applied Linguistics, Spanish-American
    Linguistics (1/4 time).
Merrel D. Clubb, Jr. (Ph.D., Michigan, 1953; Prof) TEFEL, English Linguistics (1/4 time).
Robert B. Hausmann (Ph.D., Wisconsin, 1972; Asst Prof) Generative Syntax, Varia-
    tion Theory, English Linguistics (2/3 time).
Anthony Mattina (Ph.D., Hawaii, 1973; Asst Prof) Amerindian-Salishan, Anthropo-
    logical, Historical (2/3 time).
O. W. Rolfe (Ph.D., Stanford, 1968; Assoc Prof) Pedagogy, French (1/4 time).

Support Available

Work-Study Programs, Loans, scholarships and prizes are available. Contact
Financial Aids Office, Lodge 101.

Academic Calendar 1974-1975

Fall Quarter: September - December; Winter Quarter: January - March; Spring Quarter:
March - June; Summer Quarter: June - August. Deadline: September 1 for admission to
Fall quarter; one month prior to first day of registration for Winter & Spring quarters.

DESCRIPTIVE MATERIAL: Write: Program in Linguistics, University of Montana,
                       Missoula, Montana 59801.

Linguistics Department
Robert L. Miller, Chairman
Degrees: BA. Degrees Granted 1973-74: 2 BA. In Residence: 16u.

Montclair State College has the only undergraduate program in Linguistics in New Jersey. It is sufficiently well staffed to accommodate a range of required and elective courses each semester.
   Swahili is available at elementary and intermediate levels.
   A concentration in ESOL leads to certification in English with a strong component of linguistics courses.
   Our first majors were graduated in '74; we anticipate growth.

COURSE OFFERINGS

Introductory, 1; Phonology, 1; Theoretical Models, 3; Sociolinguistics, 4; Psycholinguistics, 1; Historical Linguistics, 1; Language Pedagogy, 2.

UNCOMMONLY-TAUGHT LANGUAGES

Swahili (ul2)

STAFF

Alice F. Freed (ABD, U. of Pennsylvania; Asst Prof) ESOL, Transformational Grammar, Structure of English.
Mathilda S. Knecht (MA, Columbia U.; Assoc Prof) Applied Linguistics, Romance Linguistics.
Robert L. Miller (Ph.D., Michigan; Prof) Linguistic Theory.
Ngari N. Ngunjiri (ABD, St. John's U.; Inst) Swahili (1/2 time).
Milton S. Seegmiller (Ph.D., New York U.; Asst Prof) Phonological Theory, History of English, Russian Linguistics.
Janet Susi (MA, Middlebury; Assoc Prof) ESOL, Contrastive Linguistics (1/4 time).

Linguists in other Departments or Schools

David Kelley, Classics.
Harriet Klein, Anthropology.
Jerold Schwarz, Psychology.

Support Available

N.J. State Scholarships; Work-Study Programs; small departmental scholarships and loans are available. Contact Director of Financial Aids.

DESCRIPTIVE MATERIAL: Write: Office of the Registrar, Montclair State College,
                       Upper Montclair, New Jersey 07043.

Division of Languages and Literature
Dr. Robert Charles, Chairman
Degrees: MA under English; BA English: Linguistics. Degrees Granted 1972-73:
         11 BA, 14 MA. Majors: 25g. In Residence: 8g, 11u.

Linguistics courses at Morehead are offered through the Division of Languages and Literature, with each course being given an "English" number and description. Six courses are required as a minimum for Linguistics emphasis for the BA in English.

The MA in English: Linguistics required eighteen semester hours as a minimum, with other courses suggested in mathematics or psychology.

There is also the MA in Education, with emphasis in Linguistics. At least fifteen semester hours of Linguistics are required for that program.

Further, there are required from six to nine semester hours for the MA in Education: Emphasis in Reading.

During each summer session two institutes are offered in Linguistics. Two courses in Linguistics are offered in each Institute. The institutes have been carried on for the past nine (9) years.

There is also the Bulletin of Applied Linguistics now in its ninth year. There are thirty-six issues -- each of three pages -- published during each academic year.

COURSE OFFERINGS

Phonology, 1g; Theoretical Models, 2g 2u; Semantics & Logic, 2g 1u; Sociolinguistics, 3g 2u; Dialectology, 1g; Psycholinguistics, 2g 1u; Linguistics & Literature, 3g 2u; Language Pedagogy, 1g 1u.

STAFF

Lewis Barnes (Ph.D., Ottawa, Lon 1952, 1968) Programmed Learning and Writing, Psycholinguistics, Phonology.

Ruth Barnes (Ph.D., California, Lon 1968) Linguistics Composition, English Syntax, Sociolinguistics.

Marc Glasser (Ph.D., Indiana) Structure of English (1/3 time).

Charles Pelfrey (Ph.D., Kentucky, 1960, Michigan post-doctoral) Linguistics Composition, Linguistics Grammar, Semantics (1/3 time).

M. K. Thomas (Ph.D., Oklahoma, 1961) History of the Language (part time).

Support Available

Up to two graduate assistantships: $2300, to follow the MA in English: Linguistics; application by November or March.

Academic Calendar 1974-1975

Fall Semester: Deadline August 1; Spring Semester: Deadline December 1; Summer Session: April 25.

DESCRIPTIVE MATERIAL: Write: Registrar, Morehead State University, Morehead, Kentucky 40351.

NASHVILLE UNIVERSITY CENTER COUNCIL Nashville, Tennessee 37203   Tel. (615) 322-7311

Inter-institutional Committee on Linguistics
Walburga von Raffler Engel, Chairman
Degrees: NUC offers no degrees. Participating schools offer B.A., M.A., Ph.D,
          mostly as a minor.

The Nashville University Center is a cooperative enterprise among Fisk University, Meharry Medical College, George Peabody College for Teachers, Scarritt College for Christian Workers, and Vanderbilt University. One of its functions is to draw together people from the member institutions in order to create a "critical mass" of expertise and resources which would not otherwise exist. In the case of linguistics, a committee was formed five years ago to draw together resources. The study of linguistics in the University Center gains its unique strength from the contribu- tions of five quite different institutions. Vanderbilt's College of Arts and Sciences emphasizes the liberal arts and basic research. In addition, the Bill Wilkerson

Speech and Hearing Center offers extensive laboratory equipment for research in phonetics. Peabody specializes in teacher education and related fields and includes the John F. Kennedy Center for Research on Education and Human Development which offers its research facilities for clinical applications of linguistics. Scarritt has a concern for practical applications of linguistics for work in developing countries. Fisk makes its unique contribution in the area of Black English, and Meharry is involved in language and personality.

COURSE OFFERINGS

Introductory, 5; Phonology, 3; Theoretical Models, 5; Semantics & Logic, 3; Sociolinguistics, 2; Field Methods, 2; Psycholinguistics, 5; Math. & Comp. Linguistics, 6; Historical Linguistics, 1; Language Pedagogy, 2. Language Areas: French 3, German 4, Greek 1, Hebrew 3, Italian 1, Latin 1, Portuguese 3, Russian 2, Comp. Slavic 1, Spanish 6.

STAFF

J. Richard Andrews (Ph.D.) American Indian Languages.
John H. Cheek (Ph.D.) Russian Linguistics, Chinese Linguistics.
Robert Coleman (Ph.D.) Speech & Hearing Sciences, Experimental Phonetics, Acoustics.
James L. Crenshaw (Ph.D.) Biblical Languages & Linguistics.
Larry S. Crist (Ph.D.) French Linguistics.
Adaihudma Rosaline Ekeleme (MA) African Linguistics.
James E. Engel (Ph.D.) German Linguistics.
Jeffrey J. Franks (Ph.D.) Psycholinguistics.
Antonina Filonov Gove (Ph.D.) Russian Linguistics, Stylistics.
Robert G. Hackenberg (Ph.D.) Spanish Linguistics, Applied Linguistics.
Patrick D. Krolak (D.Sc.) Linguistics & the Computer.
Russell Love (Ph.D.) Speech & Language Development, Neuro-linguistics.
Teresa Ann McAllister (MA) General Linguistics, Children's Language.
Vivian C. Morter (MA) Teaching English as a Foreign Language.
Penelope B. Odum (Ph.D.) Psycho-linguistics, Language of the Deaf.
Rupert E. Palmer, Jr. (Ph.D.) English Linguistics.
Daniel M. Patte (Ph.D.) Semiotics.
John F. Post (Ph.D.) Symbolic Logic.
Richard A. Pride (Ph.D.) Linguistics & Politics.
Lawrence T. Ratner (Ph.D.) Mathematical Linguistics.
Ronald Spores (Ph.D.) Anthropology.
Earl W. Thomas (Ph.D.) Portuguese Languages & Linguistics.
Jeffrey S. Tlumak (Ph.D.) Philosophy of Language.
Walburga von Raffler Engel (Ph.D.) General Linguistics, Language Acquisition, Sociolinguistics.

DESCRIPTIVE MATERIAL: Write: Walburga von Raffler Engel, Inter-institutional Committee on Linguistics, Nashville University Center, Box 26, Vanderbilt University, Nashville, Tennessee 37203.

UNIVERSITY OF NEBRASKA   Lincoln, Nebraska 68508   Tel. (402) 472-7211

Interdisciplinary Linguistics Program
James Gibson, Chairman
Degrees: B.A. in Linguistics; M.A., Ph.D. with emphasis on Linguistics.

COURSE OFFERINGS

Introductory, 2; Phonology, 3; Theoretical Models, 2; Semantics & Logic, 1; Dialectology, 1; Historical Linguistics, 2; Linguistics & Literature, 1; Applied Linguistics, 1; Language Areas: English, French, German, Greek, Latin, Spanish.

UNCOMMONLY-TAUGHT LANGUAGES

Old English	Old High German	Old Icelandic
Middle English	Middle High German	Modern Icelandic
Old French	Gothic	Old Spanish

STAFF

Dudley Bailey (Prof) Historical Linguistics, Structural Grammar, Rhetoric.
Edward F. Becker (Asst Prof) Philosophy of Language.
John A. Boyd (Asst Prof) Speech.
Harry J. Crockett (Prof) Sociolinguistics.
William B. Gibbon (Prof) Modern Languages.
Robert Haller (Prof) Rhetoric and Linguistics.
Dieter Karch (Assoc Prof) Historical Linguistics.
Thomas Klammer (Assoc Prof) English Linguistics.
Valdis Lejneiks (Prof) Stratificational Theory.
David Levine (Prof) Psycholinguistics.
William J. Long (Assoc Prof) Reading.
Paul Olson (Prof) Rhetoric and Reading.
Lawrence Poston (Prof) Dialectology.
Royce Ronning (Prof) Reading and Linguistics.
E. Hugh Rudorf (Assoc Prof) Reading, Sociolinguistics.
Bruce Sales (Asst Prof) Psycholinguistics.
Charles W. Sayward (Assoc Prof) Philosophy and Linguistics.
Paul Schach (Prof) Historical Linguistics.
Hassan Sharifi (Asst Prof) English Linguistics.
Harry Shelley (Prof) Psycholinguistics.
William Shrum (Asst Prof) Phonetics.
Sheldon Stick (Asst Prof) Speech Pathology.
Leslie Whipp (Assoc Prof) Rhetoric.

DESCRIPTIVE MATERIAL: Write: Professor James Gibson, Anthropology Department, University of Nebraska, Loncoln, Nebraska 68508.

UNIVERSITY OF NEVADA—RENO   Reno, Nevada 89507   Tel. (702) 784-6689

English Department
R. D. Harvey, Chairman
Degrees: BA in English with concentration in Language and Linguistics.

An option in Language and Linguistics is offered for the BA in English. This requires a set of courses in general and English linguistics, with a choice of related subjects such as foreign languages, anthropology, philosophy, and speech.
    Other programs include a Basque Studies Program, offering a Basque Studies Summer Session in Europe.
    Facilities include library holdings in Basque and American Indian languages; and the Western Studies Center of the Desert Research Institute.

COURSE OFFERINGS

Introductory, 1; Phonology, 1; Theoretical Models, 2; Sociolinguistics, 1; Dialectology, 1; Psycholinguistics, 1; Historical Linguistics, 2; Language Pedagogy, 1; Applied English Linguistics, 1. Language Areas: Amerindian 1, Basque 1, French 1, German 2, Near East 1, Spanish 1.

UNCOMMONLY-TAUGHT LANGUAGES

Basque (u2)	Old English (g2, u2)	Mid. English (g2, u1)	Old Norse (g1)
			Portuguese (u4)

STAFF

Phillip C. Boardman (Ph.D., Washington, 1974; Asst Prof) Old and Middle English.
Robert E. Diamond (Ph.D., Harvard, 1954; Prof) Old and Middle English.
Robert M. Gorrell (Ph.D., Cornell, 1936; Prof) Rhetoric.
Nancy Hooper (Ph.D., Nevada, 1972; Asst Prof) Old English, TEFL.
William H. Jacobsen, Jr. (Ph.D., California at Berkeley, 1964; Prof) General
    Linguistics, Amerindian Languages.
Charlton G. Laird (Ph.D., Stanford, 1940; Prof Emeritus) Linguistics, Old and
    Middle English.
Robert W. Merrill (Ph.D., Chicago, 1971; Asst Prof) English Linguistics.
H. Jennings Woods (Ph.D., Florida, 1952; Assoc Prof) Linguistics, TEFL.

Linguists in other Departments or Schools

Jon Bilbao (MA, Columbia, 1939; Basque Studies Bibliographer) Basque.
Catherine S. Fowler (Ph.D., Pittsburgh, 1972; Asst Prof) Anthropological Linguistics.
R. Allen Gardner (Ph.D., Northwestern, 1954; Prof) Psycholinguistics.
Edward A. Kennard (Ph.D., Columbia, 1936; Adjunct Prof) Anthropological linguistics,
    Amerindian Languages, Hopi.
Sven S. Liljeblad (Ph.D., Lund, 1927; Adjunct Prof) Anthropological Linguistics,
    Amerindian Languages, Numic.
Frank S. Lucash (Ph.D., Southern Illinois, 1970; Asst Prof) Philosophy of Language.
J. Nelson Rojas (Ph.D., Washington, 1971; Asst Prof).
Curtis E. Weiss (Ph.D., Missouri, 1968; Assoc Prof) Phonetics.

Support Available

Graduate Teaching Fellowships.

Academic Calendar 1974-1975

Fall Semester: September 3 - December 20; Spring Semester: January 20 - May 14; Summer
Session: June 28 - August 15. Deadline: July 15.

DESCRIPTIVE MATERIAL: Write: Admissions and Records, University of Nevada, Reno,
                       Nevada 89507.

UNIVERSITY OF NEW HAMPSHIRE Durham, New Hampshire 03824   Tel. (603) 862-1313

Interdepartmental Committee for Linguistics
Karl Diller, Chairman
Degrees: BA, MA in English Language and Linguistics. Degrees Granted 1973-74:
        2 MA. Majors: 6g.

Undergraduates choose at least eight of the 32 linguistics courses offered by eight
departments. They must have at least one course in each of four specified core areas:
General Linguistics, Phonology, Syntax and Semantics, and Historical and Comparative
Linguistics. Specialized independent study courses are available for upperclassmen.
Double majors are encouraged. The language departments offer programs of study abroad.
Students must study two languages from different language families or sub-families.
    The MA degree in English language and linguistics requires eight four credit courses
including a four credit research paper and two graduate seminars. Reading knowledge

of one foreign language is required. Specialties include applied lingistics (teaching English as a Second Language) and the history of the English language, but students may do their research in any aspect of English language or linguistics. Students may take up to two courses outside the English department. Graduate courses in psycholinguistics are offered through the Psychology Department. Linguists in other departments offer specialized independent study courses.

COURSE OFFERINGS

Introductory, 1; Phonology, 2; Theoretical Models, 2; Semantics & Logic, 5; Sociolinguistics, 1; Psycholinguistics, 7; Historical Linguistics, 3; Applied Linguistics, 1.

UNCOMMONLY-TAUGHT LANGUAGES

Dutch (u2)	Old Frisian	Old High German	Hittite
Old English	Mid. High German	Gothic	Japanese (u4)
			Sanskrit

STAFF

Thomas A. Carnicelli (Ph.D., Harvard, 1966; Assoc Prof) History of the English
  Language.
Robert M. Davis (Ph.D., Wisconsin, 1972; Asst Prof) French, Romance Linguistics.
Karl C. Diller (Ph.D., Harvard, 1967; Assoc Prof) Applied Linguistics, English
  Phonology and Syntax.
R. Valentine Dusek (Ph.D., Texas, 1972, Asst Prof) Philosophy of Language.
Marron C. Fort (Ph.D., U. Pennsylvania, 1965; Assoc Prof) Comparative Germanic,
  Bilingualism.
Rand B. Foster (MA, U. Arizona, 1969; Inst) Anthropological Linguistics, Amerindian,
  Transformational Syntax.
Anthony S. Giles (Ph.D., Syracuse, 1970; Asst Prof) Communications Disorders,
  Language Acquisition, Phonetics.
Lewis C. Goffe (Ph.D., Boston University, 1961; Assoc Prof) Secondary School
  English, English Grammar.
Lois S. Grossman (Ph.D., Rutgers, 1972, Asst Prof) Romance Linguistics, Indo-
  European.
Warren H. Held, Jr. (Ph.D., Yale, 1955, Prof) Indo-European, Comparative and
  Historical Linguistics.
Annette Kolodny (Ph.D., U. Cal. Berkeley, 1969; Asst Prof) Stylistics, Psycho-
  linguistics, Feminist linguistics.
John E. Limber (Ph.D., Illinois, 1968; Asst Prof) Psycholinguistics, Language
  Acquisition.
Neil B. Lubow (Ph.D., UCLA, 1974; Asst Prof) Philosophy of Language.
John C. Rouban (PH.D., Wisconsin, 1965; Assoc Prof) Greek, Historical and Compa-
  rative Linguistics.
Philip J. Sabatelli (Ph.D., Temple, 1970; Asst Prof) General Semantics.
James L. Sherman (Ph.D., Michigan, 1969; Asst Prof) Germanic Linguistics, Phonology,
  Historical and Comparative Linguistics.
Duane H. Whittier (Ph.D., Illinois, 1961; Assoc Prof) Philosophy of Language.

Support Available

MA program: teaching assistantships for freshman composition; tuition scholarships.

Academic Calendar 1974-1975

Fall Semester: Sept 3 - Dec 21; Spring Semester: Jan 27 - May 30.

DESCRIPTIVE MATERIAL: Write: Admissions Office, Thompson Hall, Univ. of New
                      Hampshire, Durham, N.H. 03824.

UNIVERSITY OF NEW MEXICO   Albuquerque, New Mexico 87131   Tel. (505) 277-5843

Linguistics Department
John W. Oller, Jr., Chairman
Degrees: BA in linguistics. M.A., Ph.D. with emphasis in linguistics.

The Department of Linguistics at the University of New Mexico offers a program of undergraduate and graduate level courses. While the Department of Linguistics does not control any graduate degree programs, it acts in an advisory capacity as a coordinator
for students who are interested in emphasizing linguistics at the MA or PhD levels.
The primary focus of the department is on theoretical inquiry which is relevant to the
practical concerns of applied linguistics, psycholinguistics, sociolinguistics, Amerindian linguistics, and related fields.

COURSE OFFERINGS

Introductory, 3; Phonology, 3; Theoretical Models, 3; Sociolinguistics, 5; Field Methods,
1; Psycholinguistics, 1; Math. & Comp. Linguistics, 1; Historical Linguistics, 1; History
of Linguistics, 1; Language Pedagogy, 1.

UNCOMMONLY-TAUGHT LANGUAGES

Navajo   Quechua

STAFF

Garland Bills (Ph.D., Texas at Austin, 1969; Asst Prof) Syntax, Spanish Linguistics,
    Quechua Linguistics.
Dean Brodkey (Ed.D., UCLA, 1969; Asst Prof) Teaching English as a Second Language,
    Educational Linguistics.
Fred Chreist (Ph.D., Northwestern; Prof) Phonetics.
Vera John-Steiner (Ph.D., Chicago, 1956; Assoc Prof) Psycholinguistics, Semantics,
    Bilingual Education.
William Morgan, Navajo Linguistics.
John Oller (Ph.D., Rochester, 1969; Assoc Prof) Pragmatics, Theoretical Linguistics,
    Applied Linguistics.
Bruce Rigsby (Ph.D., Oregon, 1965; Assoc Prof) Phonology, Grammar, Anthropological
    Linguistics.
Bernard Spolsky (Ph.D., Montreal, 1966; Prof) Sociolinguistics, Applied Linguistics,
    History of Linguistics.
Susan Steele (Ph.D., UC at San Diego, 1973; Asst Prof) Historical and Comparative
    Linguistics, Universal Grammar, Phonology.
Robert White (Ph.D., Arizona; Assoc Prof) Teaching English as a Second Language,
    Educational Linguistics, Reading.
Robert Young, Navajo Linguistics.
Rodney Young (Ph.D., U. of New Mexico, 1971; Asst Prof) Phonology, Grammar, Edu-
    cational linguistics.
Miles Zintz (Ph.D., Iowa, 1949; Prof) Phonetics.

Linguists in Other Departments or Schools

Jean Civikly, Sociolinguistics.
Carole Conrad, Psycholinguistics.
Nancy Martin, Formal Language Theory.
Charlene McDermott, Logic and Grammar.
William Ryan, Phonetics.
John Ullrich, Formal Language Theory.

Support Available

Two assistantships in the Department of Linguistics and about fourteen through the
English Tutorial Program.

Academic Calendar 1974-1975

Fall Semester: August 21; Spring Semester: January 15; Summer Session: June 6.
Deadline: Graduate: July 1; Undergraduate: June 1.

DESCRIPTIVE MATERIAL: Write: John W. Oller, Jr., Chairman, Department of Linguistics, University of New Mexico, Albuquerque, New Mexico 87131.

NEW YORK UNIVERSITY New York, New York 10003   Tel. (212) 598-7664

Department of Linguistics
Professor Lewis Levine, Chairman
Degrees: BA, MA, Ph.D. Degrees Granted 1972-73: 5 BA, 8 MA, 2 Ph.D. Majors: 65g.
       In Residence: 23g, 12u.

The undergraduate program for majors is broad; however, with independent study, available graduate courses and work in other departments, majors wishing to go beyond undergraduate degree requirements may specialize in, e.g., syntax, mathematical linguistics, Indo-European, sociolinguistics.
     An undergraduate concentration in linguistics is not required for graduate admission. The regular graduate program, leading to the MA and Ph.D. degrees, provides fundamental and advanced training in contemporary syntactic theory, phonological theory, historical linguistics, sociolinguistics and aspects of the philosophy of science relevant to the recent history of linguistics. Dissertations, recently completed or actively in progress, have been on topics in syntactic theory, sociolinguistics and dialectology, and Germanic historical linguistics. Work in computational linguistics, applied linguistics, and work in connection with the psychology department, are also possible.
     The special summer MA program, "Language in Action," offers approaches to applied linguistics and offers work in general linguistics for those in other professions who wish to explore the relevance of linguistics to their own work. Facilities include an extensive collection in a newly-completed open-stack library, a small phonology laboratory and the N.Y.U. String Project.

COURSE OFFERINGS

Introductory, 3g 1u; Phonology, 2g 1u; Theoretical Models, 7g 4u; Sociolinguistics, 1g 1u; Psycholinguistics, 1g; Math. & Comp. Linguistics, 2g; Historical Linguistics, 2g 2u; History of Linguistics, 1g. Language Areas: Sanskrit 1, Indo-Iranian 1, Celtic 1. Other Departments: Phonology, 1; Theoretical Models, 1; Semantics & Logic, 1; Psycholinguistics, 4; Historical Linguistics, 2. Language Areas: Semitic 1.

UNCOMMONLY-TAUGHT LANGUAGES

Akkadian (g6)	Chinese (u8)	Persian (g6, u4)	Sumerian (g6)
Arabic (g7, u4)	Hebrew (g8, u6)	Sanskrit (g2)	Turkish (g2, u4)
Aramaic (g2)	Japanese (u4, 2 intens.)	N.W. Semitic (g1)	Ugaritic (g2)

STAFF

John R. Costello (Ph.D., N.Y.U., 1968; Assoc Prof) Comparative-historical Linguistics, Germanics.
Ray C. Dougherty (Ph.D., M.I.T., 1968; Assoc Prof) Syntax, Transformational Theory.
Robert A. Fowkes (Ph.D., Columbia, 1947; Prof) Comparative-historical Linguistics.
Michael Helke (Ph.D., M.I.T., 1970; Asst Prof) Syntax, Transformational Theory, Language Acquisition.
Lewis Levine (Ph.D., Columbia, 1959; Prof) Sociolinguistics.
Naomi Sager (Ph.D., Pennsylvania, 1967; Adjunct Assoc Prof) Computational Linguistics.

Linguists in other Departments or Schools

Martin D. Braine (Ph.D., N.Y.U., 1957; Prof) Psychology of Language.
Murray Glanzer (Ph.D., Michigan, 1952; Prof) Psychology of Language.

Allan F. Hubbell (Ph.D., Columbia, 1948; Prof) English Language History and
    Dialects, Phonetics.
Sumner A. Ives (Ph.D., Texas, 1950; Prof) English Language History and Dialects.

Support Available

Assistantships as research funds permit; scholarships and fellowships in varying amounts,
depending upon merit and need, awarded competitively. (In 1973-74, 14 of 23 full-time
graduate students received financial aid of one of the three kinds just mentioned.
A number of part-time students received tuition remission as a benefit of University
employment). Application for assistantship, scholarship or fellowship made by appropriate use of combined admission and financial aid form; deadline January 15.

Academic Calendar 1974-1975

Fall Semester: September 19 - January 24; Spring Semester: February 3 - May 30; Summer
Session: June 10 - July 19, July 22 - August 30; June 4 registration for 1st summer
session, July 16 registration for 2nd summer session. Special Summer Program in Linguistics: first session - July 2 - July 25; second session - July 30 - August 22.
Deadlines: January 15 for admission and financial aid consideration for Fall 1975; May
15 for admission without financial aid for the summer 1975; July 1 for admission without
financial aid for the Fall 1975.

DESCRIPTIVE MATERIAL: Write: Lewis Levine, Chairman, Department of Linguistics,
                        807 Rufus D. Smith Hall, 25 Waverly Place, New York Uni-
                        versity, New York, New York 10003.

STATE UNIVERSITY OF NEW YORK AT BINGHAMTON   Binghamton, New York 13901
Tel. (607) 798-2641

Linguistics Program
Paul J. Hopper, Chairman
Degrees: BA. Degrees Granted 1972-73: 10 BA. In Residence: 30u.

The Linguistics Program at SUNY-Binghamton aims at providing a general survey of
the field at the undergraduate level, without any special emphasis. Students begin
with introductory courses in general linguistics (nature of language, elementary linguistic structures), and proceed to more advanced work in linguistic theory (syntax,
phonology) and sub-disciplines such as sociolinguistics, psycholinguistics, and historical linguistics. The Program also cooperates with other departments offering a linguistic specialty, such as English and Anthropology. It is possible to offer a double major
in linguistics and some other field; typical co-majors are in Arabic, Anthropology,
French, etc. The State University of New York system, which includes about 60 campuses,
cooperates in producing the SUNY Working Papers in Linguistics.

COURSE OFFERINGS

Introductory, 2; Phonology, 1; Theoretical Models, 2; Semantics & Logic, 1; Sociolinguistics, 2; Field Methods, 1; Psycholinguistics, 3; Neurolinguistics, 1; Historical
Linguistics, 3; Language Pedagogy, 2. Language Areas: German 2, Romance 1, Arabic 1.

UNCOMMONLY-TAUGHT LANGUAGES

Amharic (2u)	Hebrew (8u)	Persian (2u)	Serbo-Croatian (2u)
Arabic (8u)	Hungarian (2u)	Polish (2u)	Swahili (2u)
Chinese (4u)	Japanese (4u)	Portuguese (2u)	Swedish (2u)
Mod. Greek (2u)	Malay (2u)	Sanskrit (2u)	Yiddish (2u)

STAFF

Donald Forman (Ph.D., U. of California at San Diego, 1974; Inst) Conversational
Analysis, Sociolinguistics, Syntactic Theory.
Paul J. Hopper (Ph.D., U. of Texas, 1967; Assoc Prof) Historical Linguistics,
Germanic, Indonesian.
William J. Snyder (Ph.D., Tübingen, 1964; Prof) Indo-European, Sanskrit, Germanic.

Linguists in other Departments or Schools

Richard Boswell (Ph.D., Yale U., 1968; Asst Prof) Applied Linguistics, French.
Ronald Feldstein (Ph.D., Princeton U., 1972; Asst Prof) Comparative Slavic,
Phenology.
Saul Levin (Ph.D., U. of Chicago, 1949; Prof) Indo-European, Semitic.
Richard McLain (Ph.D., U. of California at Berkeley, 1972; Asst Prof) Philosophy
of Language, Literary Linguistics.
Wilhelm Nicolaisen (Ph.D., Tübingen, 1955; Prof) Onomastics, History of English.
Thomas Plum (Ph.D., U. ofMichigan, 1972) Computational Linguistics.
H. Stephen Straight (Ph.D., U. of Chicago, 1972) Psycholinguistics, Mayan.

DESCRIPTIVE MATERIAL: Write: Linguistics Program, State University of New York
at Binghamton, Binghamton, New York 13901.

STATE UNIVERSITY OF NEW YORK AT BUFFALO   Buffalo, New York 14214

Tel. (716) 831-5031

Department of Linguistics
Paul L. Garvin, Chairman
Degrees: BA, MA, Ph.D. Degrees Granted 1972-73: 4 BA, 9MA, 2 Ph.D. Majors: 71g.
In Residence: 55g, 31u.

The Linguistics Department at SUNY/Buffalo provides graduate students with a kind of
education which is relatively uncommon today.
On the basis of an excellent grounding in contemporary theories of phonology, syntax and semantics, students can either pursue work in these core areas, or continue
with a full course of study in the sociological, psychological and ethnological aspects
of language and its use.
Graduate students develop their own programs with the help of a tudor, whom they
choose. Their examinations for the MA and Ph.D. are tailored to their programs and
special interests by the three of more faculty members whom they have chosen to be on
their degree committees.
The governance of the Department is democratic. For each faculty member there is
one elected student representative on the Executive Council. Student representatives
have the same voting privileges as faculty on all matters brought before the Council.

COURSE OFFERINGS

Introductory, 1g 2u; Phonology, 3g 1u; Theoretical Models, 7g 2u; Semantics & Logic,
4g 1u; Sociolinguistics, 5g 5u; Dialectology, 1g; Field Methods 1g 1u; Applied Lx., 1g;
Psycholinguistics, 5g; Historical Linguistics 2g; Language Pedagogy, 1g. Language Areas:
The Caribbean 1g, Afro-American 1g. Other: Lexicology 1g.

STAFF

Mervyn C. Alleyne (Ph.D., Université de Strasbourg, 1959; Assoc Prof) Sociolinguistics, Historical Linguistics, Applied Linguistics.
Paul L. Garvin (Ph.D., Indiana U., 1947; Prof) Discovery Procedure, Functional Linguistic Theory, The Use of Linguistics in Dealing with Language Problems.

David G. Hays (Ph.D., Harvard U., 1953; Prof) The Social Sciences, Cross-cultural
  Linguistics, Cognition and Language.
Joan B. Hooper (Ph.D., U. of California, Los Angeles, 1973; Asst Prof) Generative
  Phonology, Historical Linguistics.
Madeleine Mathiot (Ph.D., Catholic U., 1966; Prof) Empirical Semantics, Ethno-
  linguistics, Lexicology.
George W. Williams (Ph.D., Massachusetts Institute of Technology, 1971; Asst
  Prof) Transformational Theories of Syntax and Semantics, The Syntax of Germanic
  Languages.
Wolfgang Wölck, (Ph.D., U. of Frankfurt, 1963; Assoc Prof) Dialectology, Bilingualism,
  Language Attitudes.

Linguists in other Departments or Schools

Peter Boyd-Bowman (Ph.D., Harvard U.; Prof) Hispanic and Romance Languages.
John P. Corcoran (Ph.D., Johns Hopkins U.; Assoc Prof) Philosophy of Linguistics,
  Philosophy of Mathematics.
Eugenio Donato (Ph.D., Johns Hopkins U.; Assoc Prof) Critical Theory, Philosophy,
  Structuralism.
Thomas J. Edwards (Ph.D., Temple U.; Assoc Prof) Reading, Study Skills.
Michael P. Farrell (Ph.D., Yale U.; Asst Prof) Small Groups, Social Psychology.
Nicholas Findler (Ph.D., U. of Budapest; Prof) Artificial Intelligence, Symbol
  Manipulating Languages, Simulation.
Charles Frantz (Ph.D., U. of Chicago; Prof) Social and Political Systems, Pluralism,
  Stratification.
G. Lee Fullerton (Ph.D., U. of Michigan; Asst Prof) German and Germanic Linguistics.
Newton Garver (Ph.D., Cornell U.; Prof) Epistemology, Moral Philosophy, Logic and
  Philosophy of Language.
Jorge Guitart (Ph.D., Georgetown U.; Asst Prof) Hispanic Linguistics.
William S. Hamilton, Jr. (Ph.D., Yale U.; Asst Prof) Russian and Slavic Linguistics.
Mac S. Hammond (Ph.D., Harvard U.; Prof) Modern Poetry, Literature and Linguistics,
  Creative Writing).
Byron J. Koekkoek (Ph.D., U. of Vienna; Prof) German and Germanic Linguistics.
Robert E. McGlone (Ph.D., U. of Iowa; Assoc Prof) Speech Science.
Raoul Naroll (Ph.D., U. of California, Los Angeles; Prof) European Peasantry and
  Urbanization, Cross Cultural Methodology, Cross Historical Studies.
Anthony Papalia (Ed.D., State University of New York at Buffalo: Asst Prof)
  Psycholinguistics, Sociolinguistics, Classroom Interaction Analysis.
Erwin M. Segal (Ph.D., U. of Minnesota; Assoc Prof) Psycholinguistics, Theoretical
  Psychology.
Arthur L. Smith (Ph.D., U. of California, Los Angeles; Prof) Rhetorical Theory,
  Cross-cultural Communication.

Support Available

University Teaching Assistantship - 6 - $2,617 annual stipend; Graduate School -Graduate
Assistantship - 2 - $3,000 annual stipend. Application deadline: February 15th.

Academic Calendar 1974-1975

Fall Semester: September 3 - December 21; Spring Semester: January 14 - May 16.

DESCRIPTIVE MATERIAL: Write: Department of Linguistics, 308 Hayes Hall SUNYAB,
                       3435 Main Street, Buffalo, New York 14214.

Linguistics Program
Carol J. Raman, Coordinator
Degrees: BA. Degrees Granted 1972-73: 6 BA. In Residence: 25u.

Linguistics at Oswego is an interdepartmental program administered by a coordinator.
The Coordinator and delegates from Anthropology, Sociology, Communications Studies,
Computer Science, English, Education, Foreign Studies, Philosophy, Psychology, and
Reading compose the Linguistics Committee. The Coordinator, a full-time linguist, offers
basic courses in linguistics and advises majors.
  In addition to the BA in linguistics, undergraduates in elementary education may
opt for linguistics as their academic specialty. It is also possible for students to
have a double major in linguistics and a related field. Courses offered at the graduate
level focus on introducing nonspecialists to linguistic principals which they, as
specialists in other areas, can apply. Many teachers come to Oswego to fulfill the
state requirement of 30 hours beyond the bachelor's degree for permanent certification.
  Facilities include a strong language department and professional studies division.
The Reading Center holds a summer clinic and there is an International Summer Session
for students from abroad. The college is located on Lake Ontario in upstate New York.
Administratively, it forms part of the State University of New York, and is basically
an undergraduate liberal arts school, with graduate programs primarily in education.

COURSE OFFERINGS

Introductory, 1; Phonology, 1; Theoretical Models, 1; Sociolinguistics, 1; Field Methods,
1; History of Linguistics, 1. Other Departments: Theoretical Models, 1; Oemantics &
Logic, 3; Sociolinguistics, 1; Dialectology, 1; Psycholinguistics, 3; Math. & Comp.
Linguistics, 1; Historical Linguistics, 1; Language Pedagogy, 1. Language Areas: French
2, German 1.

UNCOMMONLY-TAUGHT LANGUAGES

Polish

STAFF

Carol J. Raman (Ph.D., U. of Texas, 1973; Asst Prof) Historical Syntax.

Linguists in other Departments or Schools

Klaus Burkhardt (MA, Middlebury College; Asst Prof) German Language.
Robert Canfield (Ed.D., Syracuse U.; Prof) Reading (1/8 time).
Robert D. Carnes (Ph.D., Duke, 1965; Assoc Prof) Logic and Philosophy of Language
   (1/4 time).
John C. Fisher (Ed.D., Harvard, 1962; Prof) TESOL (1/8 time).
Charles D. Laughlin, Jr. (Ph.D., U. of Oregon, 1972; Asst Prof) Anthropology,
   Neurolinguistics (1/4 time).
J. Edward McEvoy (Ph.D., U. of Southern California; Prof) Communications (1/8 time).
Marcia Moore (MA, U. of Conn., 1968; Asst Prof) Speech Therapy (1/8 time).
Patrick Sullivan (Ph.D., U. of Oregon, 1970; Asst Prof) French Language.
Oebele VanDyk (Ph.D., Amsterdam; Assoc Prof) Computer Science (1/8 time).
Howard Walker (Ph.D., Penn. State; Asst Prof) Psycholinguistics (1/8 time).

Support Available

Aid for students who qualify for work study; Regents scholarships.

Academic Calendar 1974-1975

Fall Semester: August 24 - December 21; Spring Semester: January 11 - May 16;
Summer Session: late May.

DESCRIPTIVE MATERIAL: Write: Registrar, Culkin Hall, SUC- Oswego, Oswego, New
                       York 13126.

Program in Linguistics
Beatrice L. Hall, Chairman
Degrees: BA. Degrees Granted 1972-73: 12 BA. In Residence: 35u.

Stony Brook at present offers an undergraduate major in Linguistics. The aim of this program is to provide the student with a firm grounding in the central aspects of modern theoretical linguistics, syntax, semantics, phonetics and phonology, and an acquaintance with related areas, including especially sociolinguistics, TESL, and psycholinguistics.

COURSE OFFERINGS

Introductory, 1; Phonology, 3; Theoretical Models, 4; Semantics & Logic, 1; Sociolinguistics, 5; Field Methods, 1; Psycholinguistics, 2; Neurolinguistics, 1; Math. & Comp Linguistics, 1; Historial Linguistics, 4; History of Linguistics, 2; Language Pedagogy, 1. Language Areas: Semitic.

UNCOMMONLY-TAUGHT LANGUAGES

Bulgarian (u2)	Gothic (g1)	Macedonian (u2)	Slovak (u2)
Chinese (u6)	Mod. Hebrew	Polish (u4)	Slovenian (u2)
Czech (u2)	(u6)	Portuguese (u2)	Swedish (u4)
Danish (u2)	Class. Hebrew	Old Russian (u1)	Tibetan (u2)
Mid. High German	(u1)	Sanskrit (u2)	Ukrainian (u2)
(g1)	Hungarian (u2)	Serbo-Croatian (u2)	Yiddish (u4)
Old High German	Icelandic (u2)	Old Church Slavonic	
(1g)		(u2)	

STAFF

Frank Anshen (Ph.D., NYU, 1968; Asst Prof) Sociolinguistics, Variation Theory, Syntax.
Mark Aronoff (Ph.D., M.I.T., 1974, Asst Prof) Phonlogy and Morphology, Word-Formation, North-West Semitic Languages.
Susan Chanover (M.A., NYU, 1968; Lecturer) Methods of TESL.
Alice Davison (Ph.D., Chicago, 1972; Asst Prof) Syntactic theory, Speech Acts and Pragmatics, Indic Languages.
Beatrice L. Hall (Ph.D., N.Y. U., 1963; Asst Prof) Syntactic Theory; Indo-European syntax, Afro-Caribbean Creoles.

Linguists in other Departments or Schools

Samuel Berr (Ph.D, NYU, Assoc Prof) Historical and Comparative Germanic, Yiddish.
Aaron Carton (Ph.D., Harvard; Prof) Educational Psycholinguistics.
Stanley Regelson (Ph.D., Columbia, Asst Prof) Indic Studies.
Ferdinand Ruplin (Ph.D., Univ. of Minnesota, Assoc Prof) Historical German.
Sally Springer (Ph.D., Stanford Univ.) Psycholinguistics, speech perception.
Roger W. Schvanveldt (Ph.D., Asst. Prof; Univ. of Wisconsin) Psycholinguistics.

Academic Calendar 1974-1975

Fall Semester: Sept. 3 - Dec.16; Spring Semester: Jan. 13 - May 9; Summer Session: I: May 20 - June 27 II: July 8 - Aug. 15.

DESCRIPTIVE MATERIAL: Write: Admissions Office, SUNY Stony Brook, Stony Brook LI, NY 11794.

Linguistics & Non-Western Languages
Julio Cortés, Acting Chairman
Degrees: BA, MA, Ph.D. Degrees Granted 1972-73: 2 BA, 4 MA, 2 Ph.D. Majors: 25g.
   In Residence: 25g, 3u.

The Department of Linguistics offers courses leading to degrees either in historical
or general linguistics.
   The Department of Linguistics offers the AB, MA, and Ph.D. degrees with specialization either in historical or in general linguistics. Also, students are encouraged
to specialize in at least one subfield. Historical students may do intensive work in
Germanic or Romance Linguistics. Students in General Linguistics may in addition to
syntax and phonology do special work in sociolinguistics within the department, psycholinguistics in cooperation with the psychology department, philosophy of language or
semantics in cooperation with the department of philosophy and computational linguistics
in cooperation with the department of Computer Sciences. Some students have shown
interest in applied linguistics and have been encouraged to pursue their interests.

COURSE OFFERINGS

Introductory, 5; Phonology, 4; Theoretical Models, 7; Semantics & Logic, 3; Sociolinguistics, 3; Dialectology, 1; Field Methods, 1; Math. & Comp. Linguistics, 2; Historical
Linguistics, 3; History of Linguistics, 1. Language Areas: Hittite 1, Greek 1, Sanskrit
3, Comp. Gk. & Latin 1, Comp. African 4, OHG 1, ONorse 1, Hebrew 3, Arabic 2, Irish
2, Chinese 5, Japanese 1, Swahili 2, Hausa 1, Latin & Italic 1, Comp. Gmc. 1.

UNCOMMONLY-TAUGHT LANGUAGES

Arabic (g6 u6)	Mod. Greek (g2	Class. Hebrew (g2)	Japanese (g2 u2)
Celtic (g1 u1)	u2)	Hebrew (u4)	Sanskrit (g3 u3)
Chinese (g6 u6)	Hausa (g2 u2)	Hittite (g1 u1)	Swahili (g4 u4)

STAFF

Julio Cortés (Ph.D., Madrid, 1965; Assoc Prof) Arabic Language (1/2 time).
Robert C. Hollow (Ph.D., Berkeley, 1970; Asst Prof) Phonology.
Stephanie Jamison (Ph.D. in progress; Inst) Indo-European Linguistics.
Bruce C. Johnson (Ph.D., Northwestern, 1973; Asst Prof) African Linguistics,
   Sociolinguistics.
Robert D. Rodman (Ph.D., UCLA, 1973; Asst Prof) Syntax.
Jerome P. Seaton (Ph.D., Indiana, 1968; Assoc Prof) Chinese Language, Literature
   in Translation.
Maria Tsiapera (Ph.D., Texas, 1963; Prof) Historical Linguistics, Dialectology.

Linguists in other Departments or Schools

Gerald Berrent (Ph.D., North Carolina, 1973; Visiting Prof) Slavics.
John B. Carroll (Ph.D., Minnesota, 1941; Kenan Prof) Psychology.
Larry Feinberg (Ph.D., Harvard, 1969; Asst Prof) Russian Literature.
H. Phelps Gates (Ph.D., Princeton, 1971; Assoc Prof) Classics and Linguistics.
Alice Gordon (Ph.D., Stanford, 1972; Asst Prof) Psychology.
Ross Hall (Ph.D., Princeton, 1970; Asst Prof) German, English.
Edward D. Montgomery, Jr. (Ph.D., North Carolina, 1968; Asst Prof) Romance Philology.
Donna Jo Napoli (Ph.D., Harvard, 1973; Inst) Italian (1/3 time).
Rita D. Nolan (Ph.D., Pennsylvania, 1965; Assoc Prof) Philosophy.
Lawrence A. Sharpe (Ph.D., North Carolina, 1956; Assoc Prof) Spanish, Portuguese.
Sidney Smith, Jr. (Ph.D., North Carolina, 1965; Assoc Prof) German.
Paul Ziff (Ph.D., Cornell, 1956; Prof) Philosophy.

Support Available

Financial support available for graduate students is offered in the form of University
fellowships; fellowships and other awards sponsored through federal, state, and private
grants; departmental assistantships and part-time instructorships; graduate aid scholarships; and student loans. Though some awards are restricted to first-year graduate
students, many are available for current students.

Academic Calendar 1974-1975

Fall Semester: August 26 - December 19; Spring Semester: January 8; Summer
Sessions: May 20 - June 30, July 1 - August 6. Deadline: Fall Semester - July 1;
Spring Semester - November 1. Last day for submitting application for most
graduate appointments - February 1. Last day for submitting application for admission to the First Term of the Summer Session - May 19. Last day for submitting
application for admission to the Second Term of the Summer Session - June 23.

DESCRIPTIVE MATERIAL: Write: The Graduate School, 1st Floor Steele Building,
The University of North Carolina, Chapel Hill, North
Carolina 27514.

NORTHEASTERN ILLINOIS UNIVERSITY Chicago, Illinois 60625   Tel. (312) 583-4050

Department of Linguistics
Joseph C. Beaver, Chairman
Degrees: BA, MA. Degrees Granted 1972-73: 36 BA, 9 MA.

The program is designed for the present or prospective high school or college English
teacher who, sensitive to what may be a wide "language gap" in his education, desires
to acquire a thorough groundwork in modern linguistic descriptions of language, and
of the English language in particular. This program is also designed for the general
student of linguistics, with or without plans to teach, who wishes to specialize in
English linguistics.

COURSE OFFERINGS

Introductory, 1; Phonology, 2; Theoretical Models, 5; Semantics & Logic, 3; Sociolin-
guistics, 2; Dialectology, 1; Field Methods, 1; Applied Lx., 3; Psycholinguistics, 4;
Math. & Comp. Linguistics, 2; Historical Linguistics, 11; History of Linguistics, 1;
Linguistics & Literature, 6; Language Pedagogy, 5. Language Areas: OE 1, ME 1. Other:
Lexicography 2, Writing Systems.

UNCOMMONLY-TAUGHT LANGUAGES

Arabic (g1)   Twi (g1)

STAFF

Joseph C. Beaver (Ph.D., New York U., 1952; Prof) Syntax, Linguistic Analysis of
Literature.
Gary Bevington (Ph.D., U. of Mass., 1970; Asst Prof) Syntax, Phonology.
Emily Ellison (MA, Wellesley College, 1944; Inst) Psycholinguistics.
Mary Ann Geissal (MA, Northeastern Illinois State College, 1966; Asst Prof) Syntax,
Linguistics for Classroom Teachers.
Eugene C. Grace (Ph.D., U. of Texas, 1970; Asst Prof) Indo-European, TESL.
Robert P. Illwitzer (Ph.D., Georgetown U., 1965; Assoc Prof) Phonology, TESL.
J. Peter Maher (Ph.D., Indiana U., 1965; Prof) Indo-European, Sociolinguistics.
Edward R. Maxwell (Ph.D., Northwestern U., 1973; Asst Prof) Semantics, Computational
Linguistics.
Audrey L. Reynolds (Ph.D., Northwestern U., 1969; Assoc Prof) Psycholinguistics,
History of English.
Don M. Seigel (MA, U. of Illinois, 1961; Assoc Prof) Dialectology, Sociolinguistics.

Support Available

Loan programs, student employment, some assistantships and fellowships are available. Call 583-4050, ex. 451.

Academic Calendar 1974-1975

Fall Quarter: September - December; Winter Quarter: January - April; Spring Quarter: April - August.

DESCRIPTIVE MATERIAL: Write: Director of Admissions, Northeastern Illinois U., Bryn Mawr at St. Louis Avenue, Chicago, Illinois 60625.

NORTHERN ARIZONA UNIVERSITY   Flagstaff, Arizona 86001   Tel. (602) 523-4521

Anthropology Department
William B. Griffen, Chairman
Degrees: BA, BS, MA Specialization within Anthropology. Degrees Granted 1972-73: 2 BA.

Area Studies Minor in Linguistics -- includes courses in Anthropology, Data Processing, Education, English, Mathematics, Languages, Philosophy and Logic, Psychology, and Sociology.
  For the past several years in the summer (1974 excepted) we have run under Dr. P. David Seaman a summer linguistic institute for advanced Senior High School Students. We hope to renew the institute as funding becomes available again.

COURSE OFFERINGS

Introductory, 1; Phonology, 1; Theoretical Models, 1; Sociolinguistics, 1; Historical Linguistics, 1.

UNCOMMONLY-TAUGHT LANGUAGES

Hopi (u2)   Navajo (u4)   Zuni (u2)

STAFF

P. David Seaman (PhD, Indiana University; Prof) General Linguistics, Social
    Linguistics.
Irvy W. Goossen (B.A., Northern Arizona University; Inst) Navajo Language.
Gina Harvey (PhD, The University of Rome, Italy; Assoc Prof) English.

NORTHERN ILLINOIS UNIVERSITY   DeKalb, Illinois 60115   Tel. (815) 753-0611

Interdepartmental Committee on Linguistics
Lev I. Soudek, Chairman
Degrees: BA in linguistics; MA and Ph.D. in English with concentration in Linguistics, MA in Anthropology with focus on Linguistics. Degrees Granted 1972-73: 2 MA. Majors: 5g.

The undergraduate concentration (Studies in Linguistics) provides an interdepartmental focus on general and applied linguistics, with a full range of courses offered through four departments.

The graduate program concentrates on work in English and linguistics on the MA and Ph.D. levels, and in anthropology and linguistics on the MA level. It includes core courses in linguistic theory, historical linguistics and English linguistics. Specialized offerings include dialectology (regional and social), semantics, structural and generative phonology, and applied linguistics.

Facilities include Speech and Hearing Clinic, Communication Disorders Center, Communication Skills Program, Center for Southeast Asian Studies, and language laboratories.

COURSE OFFERINGS

Introductory, g2 u2; Phonology, g3 u3; Theoretical Models g4 u3; Semantics & Logic, g2 u1; Sociolinguistics, g5 u3; Dialectology, g1; Field Methods, g1 u1; Psycholinguistics, g5 u3; Neurolinguistics, u1; Historical Linguistics, g2 u1; Language Pedagogy, g1 u1. Language Areas: French g1 u2, German g1 u2, Spanish g1 u2, OE g1, ME g1, Indonesian g1.

UNCOMMONLY-TAUGHT LANGUAGES

Arabic	Mod. Greek	Japanese	Swahili
Chinese	Hebrew	Malay	Thai
(Mandarin)	Indonesian	Portuguese	

STAFF

Cecil H. Brown (Ph.D., Tulane U., 1971; Asst Prof) Cognitive Anthropology, Structural Semantics, Language Philosophy.

Robert E. Callary (Ph.D., Louisiana State U., 1971; Asst Prof) English Linguistics, Dialectology, Social Dialects.

William R. Cantrall (Ph.D., U. of Illinois, 1969; Assoc Prof) Transformational Syntax, Generative Semantics, English Methods.

David W. Dellinger (Ph.D., Australian National U., 1969; Asst Prof) Descriptive Linguistics, Phonology, Tibeto-Burman Linguistics.

David H. deQueljoe (Ed.D., Columbia U., 1959; Assoc Prof) Applied Linguistics, Indonesian.

Michael W. Grady (Ph.D., Stanford U., 1969; Assoc Prof) English Linguistics, Semantics, Applied Linguistics.

Dolores A. Gunnerson (Ph.D., U. of Utah, 1971; Asst Prof) Anthropology, Language and Culture.

Bruce E. Irvin (Ph.D., Stanford U., 1970; Asst Prof) Experimental Phonetics, Acoustic Phonetics.

Benjamin Jegers (Ph.D., U. of Göttingen, 1949; Assoc Prof) Indo-European, Historical Linguistics.

Joseph L. LaBelle (Ph.D., U. of Wisconsin, 1971; Asst Prof) Language Acquisition, Language Pathologies.

J. D. Meacham (Ph.D., U. of Iowa, 1974; Asst Prof) Psycholinguistics, Language Acquisition, Communication Theory.

James R. Shawl (Ph.D., U. of Washington, 1968; Asst Prof) Spanish Phonology, Spanish Transformational Syntax.

Lev I. Soudek (Ph.D., Charles U., Prague, 1966; Prof) English Linguistics, Lexicology, TESOL.

George L. Trager (Ph.D., Columbia U., 1932; Prof) General Linguistics, Linguistic Theory, American Indian Languages.

Raymond D. Wilderman (Ph.D., State U. of Iowa, 1955; Assoc Prof) Psycholinguistics, Oral Language.

Support Available

Some state scholarships and grants are available. Teacher education scholarships are available. Apply before May 1 for following academic year.

Academic Calendar 1974-1975

Fall Semester: August 26 - December 28; Spring Semester: January 13 - May 10;
Summer Session: June 23 - August 15.

DESCRIPTIVE MATERIAL: Write: Admissions and Records (Undergraduate); Graduate
School (Graduate), Northern Illinois University, DeKalb,
Illinois 60115.

UNIVERSITY OF NORTHERN IOWA Cedar Falls, Iowa 50613   Tel. (319) 273-2821

Section for Linguistics and TEFL
Department of English Language and Literature
Charlene Eblen, Section Director
Degrees: BA, MA. Degrees Granted 1972-73: 3 MA. Majors: 7g. In Residence: 6g.

The Section for Linguistics and TEFL is a part of the Department of English Language
and Literature. The undergraduate program in English Linguistics provides a full curriculum for students interested in the study of language in general and of English in
particular. The major is intended as a prelude to advanced work in comparative literature, philosophy, formal languages, communications theory, psycholinguistics, cultural
anthropology, sociolinguistics, and linguistics proper. A series of cognate courses
in related fields emphasises the interdisciplinary aspect of this program and of a
second, combined program in English Language and a Foreign Language (French, German,
Spanish), consisting of a linguistics core and particular language emphases. The linguistics minor serves as a valuable adjunct to major programs in literature, foreign
languages, speech pathology, philosophy, psychology, sociology, and mathematics.
    The graduate program in English Linguistics consists of a core in linguistic theory
(T-Grammar, Generative Syntax and other grammatical models, Generative Phonology).
Students may then choose topics in Historical-Comparative Linguistics, Dialectology,
Psycholinguistics, Child Language Acquisition, Problems in English Grammar, and others
through a series of courses and seminars; students also have access to native informants
from overseas through the section's strong companion programs in Teaching English as
a Foreign Language (TEFL). The MA program is available on the thesis and non-thesis
option (department research paper required). Similar to the undergraduate program,
teaching and liberal arts programs with a strong grounding in linguistics are offered
in TEFL combined with a Foreign Language.

COURSE OFFERINGS

Introductory, 1; Phonology, 2; Theoretical Models, 4; Semantics & Logic, 1; Sociolinguistics, 1; Dialectology, 1; Historical Linguistics, 2; Language Pedagogy, 3.

UNCOMMONLY-TAUGHT LANGUAGES

Bulgarian	Mod. Greek	Norwegian	Swedish
Danish	Lithuanian	Sanskrit	

STAFF

Gordon B. Ford, Jr. (Ph.D., Harvard, 1965; Prof) Historical-Comparative, Indo-
    European, Dialectology.
Ralph M. Goodman (Ph.D., UCLA, 1970; Assoc Prof) English, Theoretical Linguistics,
    Psycholinguistics.
Adolf E. Hieke (M.Phil., Kansas, 1974; Asst Prof) Generative Syntax, Semantics,
    TEFL.
Valdon L. Johnson (MA, U. of No. Iowa, 1959; Asst Prof) English Historical Lin-
    guistics, Computational Linguistics.

Norman C. Stageberg (Ph.D., Wisconsin, 1946; Prof Emer.) English, Historical
    Linguistics.
George W. Tharp (MA, Purdue, 1963; Asst Prof) Generative Phonology, Amerindian
    Linguistics.

Linguists in other Departments or Schools

Roy Eblen (Ph.D., U. of Iowa, 1961) Acoustic Phonetics.
Michael Millar (MA, U. of Chicago, 1957) Logic, Automata Theory.
David Morgan (MA, Washington U., St. Louis, 1966) Philosophy, Logic and Language.
Samuel Nodarse (Ph.D., U. of Illinois, 1971) Spanish.
Michael Oates (Ph.D., Georgetown, 1970) French.
Karl Odwarka (Ph.D., U. of Michigan, 1973) German.
Timothy Rooney (MA, U. of South Florida, 1971) Psycholinguistics, Child Language
    Acquisition.

Support Available

Graduate Assistantships (limited).

Academic Calendar 1974-1975

Fall Semester: August 23 - December 20; Spring Semester: January 5 - May 15;
Summer Session: June 7 - August 2. Deadline: 6 weeks prior to semester start.

DESCRIPTIVE MATERIAL: Write: Office of Admissions, University of Northern Iowa,
                       Cedar Falls, Iowa 50613.

NORTHWESTERN UNIVERSITY Evanston, Illinois 60201   Tel. (312) 492-7020

Department of Linguistics
Richard A. Spears, Chairman
Degrees: BA, MA, Ph.D. Degrees Granted 1972-73: 2 BA, 2 MA, 3 Ph.D. Majors: 19g.
    In Residence: 12g, 11u.

COURSE OFFERINGS

Introductory, 4; Phonology, 4; Theoretical Models, 4; Semantics & Logic, 1; Sociolinguistics, 3; Dialectology, 1; Field Methods, 1; Applied Lx., 1; Psycholinguistics, 3;
Math. & Comp. Linguistics, 4; Historical Linguistics, 4; History of Linguistics, 1;
Linguistics & Literature, 2; Language Pedagogy, 2. Language Areas: Russian 2, Czech
1, Serbo-Croatian 1, African 1, OCS 1, Bantu 2, Slavic 1, West African 1. Other Departments: Phonology, 4; Theoretical Models, 2; Semantics & Logic, 5; Sociolinguistics,
5; Psycholinguistics, 3; Neurolinguistics, 1; Math. & Comp. Linguistics, 1; Historical
Linguistics, 1; Language Pedagogy, 3. Language Areas: OE 1, French 3, Spanish 2.

UNCOMMONLY-TAUGHT LANGUAGES

Akan (g6, u)	Arabic (u9)	Hausa (g1)	Krio (g6)
Amharic (g6, u)	Chinese (u9)	Hebrew (u9)	Mande (g6)
			Swahili (u9)

STAFF

Jack Berry (Ph.D., U. of London, 1952; Prof) Sociolinguistics, African Languages and
    Linguistics, Caribbean Linguistics.
Morris Goodman (Ph.D., Columbia U., 1961; Assoc Prof) Romance Creoles, Hausa.
Mary R. Haas (Ph.D., Yale U., 1935; Visiting Prof) Amerindian linguistics.

Marvin Kantor (Ph.D., U. of Michigan, 1966; Assoc Prof) Slavic Linguistics.
Gilbert Krulee (Ph.D., Massachusetts Institute of Technology, 1950; Prof) Psycho-
    linguistics, Computer Science.
Judith Levi (Ph.D., U. of Chicago, 1974; Asst Prof) Syntax and Semantics.
Rae Moses (Ph.D., U. of Texas, 1966; Asst Prof) Psycholinguistics, Child Language.
David Reed (Ph.D., U. of Michigan, 1949; Prof) English Linguistics, Dialectology.
Raoul Smith (Ph.D., Brown University, 1968; Assoc Prof) Computational Linguistics,
    Slavic Linguistics.
Richard Spears (Ph.D., Indiana University, 1965; Assoc Prof) African Linguistics,
    Acoustic Phonetics.
Klaus Wachsmann (Ph.D., U. of Fribourg, 1935; Prof) Verbal Art, Luganda.
Edwin Webber (Ph.D., U. of California, Berkeley, 1949; Prof) Spanish Linguistics.
Oswald Werner (Ph.D., Indiana U., 1963; Prof) Anthropological Linguistics, Ethno-
    linguistics.
Robert Wilkinson (Ph.D., U. of Illinois, 1971; Asst Prof) Generative Phonology.

Linguists in other Departments or Schools

Sidney Bergquist (Ph.D.; Assoc Prof) Reading.
Jan R. Carew (Prof) Caribbean Sociolinguistics.
Hilda Fisher (Ph.D.; Prof) Phonetics.
David Hill (Ph.D.; Assoc Prof) English Linguistics.
Roy Koenigsknecht (Ph.D.; Assoc Prof) Phonology.
Laura Lee (MA; Assoc Prof) Language Acquisition.
Richard Martin (Ph.D.; Prof) Philosophy of Language.
Bill Paden (Ph.D.; Assoc Prof) French Linguistics.

Support Available

Departmental Assistantships, University Fellowships and Scholarships, NDFL in African
Languages (anticipated), Assistantship in Program of Oriental and African Languages
(2010 Sheridan Road, Evanston, Illinois 60201). Stipends in Language Laboratories (Room
48B Kresge Hall, Evanston, Illinois 60201). Deadline: 1 February annually. 1974-1975
tuition $3150.00 stipends may range from $2300 to $2500. GRE scores required.

Academic Calendar 1974-1975

Fall Quarter: September 27; Winter Quarter: January 6; Spring Quarter: March 31; Summer
Quarter: June 23. Deadline: August 30 (March 1).

DESCRIPTIVE MATERIAL: Write: Chairman, Department of Linguistics, Northwestern
                      University, 2016 Sheridan Road, Evanston, Illinois 60201.

OAKLAND UNIVERSITY Rochester, Michigan 48013   Tel. (313) 377-2175

Department of Linguistics
William Schwab, Chairman
Degrees: BA. Degrees Granted 1972-73: 4 BA. Majors: 10g.

Oakland University currently provides a undergraduate major in linguistics and has
requested the State Board of Education to authorize the Department of Linguistics to
offer a secondary major in the field. The program, with its cross-disciplinary thrust,
is designed to serve students who desire a general education as well as those who may
be disposed to graduate work in linguistics and related fields. It provides
a broad, yet rigorous, course in the nature of language and human behavior and gives
a thorough comprehension of the instrument that uniquely distinguishes man from all
other living things. For students interested in careers in the teaching of language,
dialectology, and second-language teaching at the primary or secondary school level,

concentrations in linguistics are available together with a modified major in another department.

COURSE OFFERINGS

Introductory, 2; Phonology, 2; Theoretical Models, 2; Semantics & Logic, 2; Sociolinguistics, 1; Psycholinguistics, 1; Neurolinguistics, 2; Historical Linguistics, 1; Language Pedagogy, 1. Language Areas: French 1, German 1.

UNCOMMONLY-TAUGHT LANGUAGES

Chinese (u6)	Hindi-Urdu	Portuguese (u4)	Swahili (u4)
Hebrew (u4)	(u2)		

STAFF

Peter J. Binkert (Ph.D., U. of Michigan, 1970; Asst Prof) Linguistic Theory, Neurolinguistics, Indo-European Linguistics.
Daniel H. Fullmer (Ph.D., U. of Michigan, 1969; Asst Prof) English Language, Generative Phonology.
Gayle H. Partmann (Ph.D., Stanford U., 1973; Asst Prof) Anthropological Linguistics.
William Schwab (Ph.D., U. of Wisconsin, 1951; Prof) Grammar, Second-Language Teaching.

Linguists in other Departments or Schools

John W. Barthel (Ph.D., U. of Illinois, 1965; Assoc Prof) German Language, Applied Linguistics for Teachers of German, Historical and Comparative Linguistics.
Carlo Coppola (Ph.D., U. of Chicago, 1974; Asst Prof) Indo-Aryan Structure of Hindi, Urdu, Sanskrit.
Jack A. Cumbee (BS, Auburn U., 1960; Inst) Logic, Philosophy of Language, Linguistics.
Jerry M. Freeman (Ph.D., U. of Michigan, 1973; Asst Prof) Russian Language and Literature, Comparative Slavic Linguistics, Stylistics.
Donald C. Hildum (Ph.D., Harvard, 1960; Prof) Communication Theory, Semantics, Psycholinguistics.
Don R. Iodice (MA, Yale U., 1956; Assoc Prof) French Language and Literature, Applied Linguistics of French, Phonetics.

Academic Calendar 1974-1975

Fall Quarter: September 3 - December 18; Winter Quarter: January 6 - April 22; Spring Quarter: April 28 - June 21; Summer Quarter: June 24 - August 15.

DESCRIPTIVE MATERIAL: Write: Admissions Office, 202 Wilson Hall, Oakland University, Rochester, Michigan 48063.

OHIO UNIVERSITY Athens, Ohio 45701   Tel. (614) 594-3811

Department of Linguistics
Marmo Soemarmo, Chairman
Degrees: MA, Interdisciplinary Ph.D. is available through Graduate College.
          Degrees Granted 1972-73: 20 MA. Majors: 27g. In Residence: 27g.

Four programs leading to a Master of Arts in Linguistics are available: Teaching English as a Second/Foreign Language (the largest), English Linguistics for High School; English Linguistics for College, and General Linguistics (for those who intend to go to Ph.D. study).
    Intensive English for foreign students is available through OPIE (Ohio Program in Intensive English), Dr. Robert Dakin, director.

All the staff has had some overseas experience in Asia, Africa, or Middle East. We have strong ties with International Studies that has Southeast Asia, Africa, and Latin America area studies, Hearing and Speech Sciences, English, Modern Languages, Black Studies Institute, Interpersonal Communication, and Psychology.

Students are involved in every aspect of the Departmental Committees, and have their own Graduate Linguistics Circle. Faculty and students publish their research activities in the Ohio University Informal Working Papers in Applied Linguistics.

COURSE OFFERINGS

Introductory, 2; Phonology, 4; Theoretical Models, 4; Semantics & Logic, 2; Sociolinguistics, 4; Dialectology, 1; Field Methods, 1; Applied Lx., 1; Psycholinguistics, 3; Historical Linguistics, 2; History of Linguistics, 1; Language Pedagogy, 5.

UNCOMMONLY-TAUGHT LANGUAGES

Chinese   Hausa   Indonesian   Swahili

STAFF

James Coady (Ph.D., Indiana, 1973; Asst Prof) Phonology, Sociolinguistics, Applied Linguistics.
Robert Dakin (Ph.D., Michigan, 1968; Assoc Prof) Dialectology, English as a Foreign Language.
John Dewees (Ph.D., Wisconsin, 1972; Asst Prof) African Linguistics, General Linguistics, Diachronic Linguistics.
Fonda Fry (MA, Ohio U., 1970) English for Foreign Students.
William Holschuh (MA, Ohio U., 1973) English for Foreign Students.
Rex Moser (Ph.D., Indiana, 1973; Asst Prof) Stylistics, African Linguistics, General Linguistics.
David Sjafiroeddin (MA, Ohio U., 1972) Indonesian Language and Literature.
Marmo Soemarmo (Ph.D., UCLA, 1970; Asst Prof) Syntax, Austronesin Linguistics, Psycholinguistics.

Support Available

Teaching assistantships in Linguistics, Teaching English to Foreign students, and Non-Western languages (Hausa, Swahili, Chinese) are available.

Tuition scholarship is also available for students who are qualified, as well as work study program.

Academic Calendar 1974-1975

Fall Quarter: September 26; Winter Quarter: January 6 - March 15; Spring Quarter: March 24 - June 7; Summer Session: First term: June 16 - July 19; Second term: July 21 - August 23. Deadline: August 4 for Fall.

DESCRIPTIVE MATERIAL: Write: Office of Admission, Chubb Hall, Ohio University, Athens, Ohio 45701.

OHIO STATE UNIVERSITY Columbus, Ohio 43210   Tel. (614) 422-4052

Department of Linguistics
Michael L. Geis, Chairman
Degrees: BA, MA, Ph.D. Degrees Granted 1972-73: 6 BA, 3 MA, 3 Ph.D. Majors: 32g. In Residence: 31g, 22u.

The undergraduate program gives students a general introduction to linguistics, intro-
ductions to the main subfields of linguistics -- phonetics, syntax, phonology, and historical linguistics -- and encourages students to broaden their education in languages
and other related fields. A wide range of course options are available beyond the basic
core courses.

The graduate program includes the core courses in the undergraduate program, and
a wide variety of elective courses. A thesis is required of MA candidates. Areas of
specialization at the Ph.D. level include phonetics, phonological theory, syntactic
theory, semantics, mathematical linguistics, psycholinguistics, Indian linguistics,
child language, sociolinguistics, the history of linguistics, anthropological linguistics, Amerindian linguistics, and Indo-European studies. The department has a strongly
theoretical orientation. Faculty members are largely concerned with the development
of an adequate universal theory of language and detailed accounts of the structure and
development of individual languages. Considerable emphasis is placed upon the construc-
tion and evaluation of arguments for and against various proposed ways of describing
and explaining grammatical facts.

Facilities include a departmental library and a well-equipped phonetics research
laboratory. Research done by the faculty and students is published in Working Papers
in Linguistics. Detailed information about the department and its programs is given
in an annual newsletter, available upon request.

COURSE OFFERINGS

Introductory, 8; Phonology, 5; Theoretical Models, 5; Semantics & Logic, 4; Sociolinguistics, 7; Dialectology, 2; Field Methods, 1; Psycholinguistics, 6; Math. & Comp.
Linguistics, 2; Historical Linguistics, 7; History of Linguistics, 1; Language Pedagogy,
3. Language Areas: Indic Lx. 1, Runic Norse 1, Gmc. 1, Hittite 1, Arabic 1, Chinese
9, French 7, German 5, Gothic 1, Greek 2, Hebrew 4, Italian 3, Japanese 4, Latin 3, Polish
5, Romance 1, Russian 12, OCS 2, Serbo-Croatian 5, Slavic 11, Spanish 6. Other: Lg.
& Music.

UNCOMMONLY-TAUGHT LANGUAGES

Arabic (g1 u4)	Gothic (g1)	Old Polish (g1)	Old Saxon (g1)
Chinese (g3 u6)	Greek (g2 u3)	Portuguese (u4)	Old Serbian (g1)
Class. Chinese (g1)	Hebrew (g3 u4)	Old Provencal (g1)	Serbo-Croatian
Old English (g1)	Japanese (g3 u6)	Rumanian (g1)	(g2 u4)
Old High German	Lake Miwok (g1)	Russian (g2 u4)	Old Church Slavonic
(g1)	Old Norse (g1)	Old Russian (g1)	(g1)
Mid. High German	Polish (g2 u4)	Sanskrit (g3)	Old Spanish (g1)
(g1)			Swahili (u4)

STAFF

Catherine A. Callaghan (Ph.D., Berkeley, 1963; Assoc Prof) Historical Linguistics,
    Descriptive Linguistics, American Indian Linguistics with Emphasis on California.
David R. Dowty (Ph.D., Texas, 1973; Asst Prof) Syntactic and Semantic Theory.
Sara S. Garnes (Ph.D., Ohio State, 1974; Visit. Asst Prof) Introductory Linguistics
    (3/4 time).
Olga K. Garnica (Ph.D., Stanford, 1974; Asst Prof) Psycholinguistics.
Michael L. Geis (Ph.D., M.I.T., 1970; Assoc Prof) Syntactic and Semantic Theory,
    Structure of English.
Robert J. Jeffers (Ph.D., Cornell, 1972; Asst Prof) Historical Linguistics, Indo-
    European Linguistics.
Ilse Lehiste (Ph.D., Michigan, 1959; Prof) Historical and Descriptive Phonology,
    Acoustic Phonetics, Language Contact and Language Change.
David L. Stampe (Ph.D., Chicago, 1973; Assoc Prof) Phonological, Semantic, and
    Esthetic Theory.
Arnold M. Zwicky (Ph.D., M.I.T., 1965; Prof) Syntactic and Phonological Theory.

Linguists in other Departments or Schools

Edward Allen (Ph.D., Ohio State; Prof). Humanities Education.
Donald Bateman (Ph.D., Ohio State; Assoc Prof) Humanities Education.
John W. Black (Ph.D., Iowa, 1935; Prof) Speech.

Steven Boer (Ph.D., Michigan, 1973; Asst Prof) Philosophy.
Alan K. Brown (Ph.D., Stanford; Assoc Prof) English.
H. William Buttelmann (Ph.D., North Carolina; Asst Prof) Computer and Information Science.
Frederic J. Cadora (Ph.D., Michigan, 1966; Assoc Prof) Arabic.
Johanna DeStefano (Ph.D., Stanford; Assoc Prof) Early and Middle Childhood Education.
Wolfgang Fleischhauer (Ph.D., Cologne, 1936; Prof) German.
Richard Garner (Ph.D., Michigan; Assoc Prof) Philosophy.
David A. Griffin (Ph.D., Chicago, 1956; Prof) Spanish Linguistics, Rumanian.
Dudley Hascall (Ed.D., Harvard, 1960; Assoc Prof) English Metrics.
Neal Johnson (Ph.D., Minnesota, 1961; Prof) Psychology.
Yehiel Hayon (Ph.D., Texas, 1969; Assoc Prof) Hebrew.
Maria Ibba (Ph.D., Georgetown, 1974; Asst Prof) Italian Linguistics.
Hans Keller (Ph.D., U. of Basel, Switzerland; Prof) French Linguistics.
Jasna Kragalott (Ph.D., Ohio State; Asst Prof) Slavic Languages.
William Lycan (Ph.D., Chicago, 1970; Assoc Prof) Philosophy.
Leroy Meyers (Ph.D., Syracuse; Assoc Prof) Mathematics.
Kenneth E. Naylor (Ph.D., Chicago, 1966; Assoc Prof) Slavic Languages.
Lawrence W. Newman (Ph.D., Harvard; Asst Prof) Russian and West Slavic Linguistics.
Hiroko Quackenbush (Ph.D., Michigan, 1970; Asst Prof) Japanese Linguistics.
David F. Robinson (Ph.D., Pennsylvania, 1964; Assoc Prof) East Slavic and Baltic Linguistics.
Charles Winthrop (Ph.D., Ohio State; Asst Prof) French Linguistics.
Frank J. Zidonis (Ph.D., Ohio State; Prof) Humanities Education.

Support Available

Financial aid to students consists of various fellowships and assistantships. Students may apply for NSF traineeships and University Fellowships. University fellows receive fellowship support in their first and fourth (dissertation) year and are guaranteed assistantships in their second and third year. Fellowships are usually given to beginning graduate students, whereas teaching and research assistantships are awarded to more advanced graduate students whose performance we have already had a chance to observe. There are also some special University Fellowships available for members of minority groups. The Department of Linguistics has no language teaching assistantships available; students interested in such assistantships should communicate directly with the appropriate language department. The deadline for fellowships is February 1.

Academic Calendar 1974-1975

Fall Quarter: September 30 - December 13; Winter Quarter: January 6 - March 21; Spring Quarter: April 1 - June 13; Summer Quarter: June 23 - August 29. Deadline: August 15 undergraduate, September 3 graduate.

DESCRIPTIVE MATERIAL: Write: Department of Linguistics, Ohio State University, 1841 Millikin Road, Columbus, Ohio 43210.

OKLAHOMA STATE UNIVERSITY Stillwater, Oklahoma 74074   Tel. (405) 372-6211, x7701

English Department Linguistics Program
John Battle, Co-ordinator of Linguistic Studies
Degrees: BA, BS, MA, MS, Ph.D., Ed.D. in English or other major with specialization in linguistics. Degrees Granted 1972-73: 2 MA/MS. Majors: 7g. In Residence: 7g, 1u.

Specialization in linguistics may be included in studies toward a bachelor's, master's, or doctor's degree in English or in some other field such as foreign languages, speech, sociology, psychology, or philosophy. Requirements call for a minimum of 30 hours from a list of 21 linguistics-related courses, including descriptive linguistics, structure of a language, and work in at least two foreign languages. The 30 hours may include previously earned hours, but not the hours given for master's thesis or doctoral dissertation.

COURSE OFFERINGS

Introductory, 2; Phonology, 1; Theoretical Models, 1; Semantics & Logic, 2; Sociolinguistics, 1; Psycholinguistics, 5; Historical Linguistics, 2; Linguistics & Literature, 2; Language Pedagogy, 1. Language Areas: OE, ME, French 1.

UNCOMMONLY-TAUGHT LANGUAGES

Chinese (u2)   Hebrew (u2)   Japanese (u4)

STAFF

John Battle (Ph.D., Texas, 1969; Asst Prof) Linguistic Theory, Descriptive and
   Comparative Linguistics, History and Structure of English.
Dennis E. Bertholf (Ph.D., New Mexico State, 1968) Mathematical Linguistics.
Burchard Carr (Ph.D., Ohio U., 1964; Prof) Applied Psycholinguistics, Phonology.
Larry Hochhaus (Ph.D., Iowa State, 1970; Asst Prof) Psycholinguistics.
Jennifer Kedney-Wells (Ph.D., Yale, 1974; Asst Prof) History and Structure of
   English.
Neil Luebke (Ph.D., Johns Hopkins, 1968; Assoc Prof) Symbolic Logic.
Jane Marie Luecke (Ph.D., Notre Dame, 1964; Prof) Old and Middle English, History
   of English.
D. Judson Milburn (Ph.D., Oklahoma, 1953; Prof) Applied Linguistics.
Robert T. Radford (Ph.D., Texas, 1970; Assoc Prof) Philosophy of Language.
John L. Schweitzer (MA, Michigan, 1957; Assoc Prof) French Linguistics.
Sherry Scott (Ph.D., Purdue, 1970; Asst Prof) Applied Psycholinguistics.
Robert F. Stanners (Ph.D., Iowa, 1963; Assoc Prof) Psychologyof Verbal Processes.
Genese Warr-Leeper (MA, Oklahoma, 1971; Asst Prof) Applied Psycholinguistics.

Support Available

Some scholarships and teaching assistantships are available in the participating departments. Stipends for 1974-5 for assistantships range from $2565 to $3060 per year.

Academic Calendar 1974-1975

Fall Semester: August 26 - December 21; Spring Semester: January 13 - May 9; Summer Session: June 2 - July 25. Deadline: For domestic students, 30 days before beginning of semester. For international students, 6 months before beginning of semester.

DESCRIPTIVE MATERIAL: Write: Registrar, Oklahoma State University, Stillwater, Oklahoma 74074.

UNIVERSITY OF OREGON   Eugene, Oregon 97403   Tel. (503) 686-3938

Interdisciplinary Committee on Linguistics
Clarence Sloat, Chairman
Degrees: BA, MA, in linguistics; Ph.D. in English with concentration in Linguistics.
        Degrees Granted 1972-73: 1 BA, 5 MA, 1 Other. Majors: 23g. In Residence:
        22g, 10u.

The BA and MA programs in linguistics are administered by the Interdisciplinary Committee on Linguistics. A wide range of courses is available in linguistics and in related disciplines. The BA program combines general linguistics coursework with the study of two or more foreign languages. The MA program includes prescribed courses in linguistic theory and methodology and offers a number of opportunities for specialization (e.g. phonology, syntax, semantics, philosophy of language, English linguistics, Northwest Indian languages, psycholinguistics, and computational linguistics). An MA thesis is optional.

The Ph.D. program is offered through the Department of English. A typical program will include the following fields: Old English, Middle English, History and Structure of English, Linguistic theory, one additional linguistics field, one field in English literature.

Facilities include the computer center and speech clinic. Numerous field work opportunities are available for American Indian languages of the Pacific Northwest.

COURSE OFFERINGS

Introductory, 2u; Phonology, 1g 1u; Theoretical Models, 1g 2u; Semantics & Logic, 2g 1u; Sociolinguistics, 3u; Dialectology, 1u; Psycholinguistics, 3g 2u; Math. & Comp. Linguistics, 1g; Historical Linguistics, 2g 3u. Language Areas: German 2g, Russian 1g, French 1u, Spanish 1u, German 1u, Russian 1u.

UNCOMMONLY-TAUGHT LANGUAGES

Chinese (u22)	Mid. High German	Japanese (u22)	Old Church Slavonic
Czech (u3)	(g3)	Norwegian (u6)	(g1)
Mid. English	Old High German	Polish (u3)	Old Spanish (g3)
(g4, u2)	(g2)	Old Saxon (g1)	Swedish (u6)
Old English (g3)	Gothic (g1)	Serbo-Croatian	Ukrainian (u3)
Old French (g6)	Old Icelandic (g3)	(u3)	

STAFF

James E. Hoard (Ph.D., Washington, 1967; Assoc Prof) English and American Indian Linguistics.
Derry L. Malsch (Ph.D., Wisconsin, 1971; Asst Prof) Historical Linguistics.
Clarence Sloat (Ph.D., Washington, 1966; Assoc Prof) English and American Indian Linguistics.

Linguists in other Departments or Schools

J. Fred Beebe (Ph.D., Harvard, 1958; Assoc Prof) Russian, Slavic Linguistics.
James L. Boren (Ph.D., Iowa, 1970; Asst Prof) English.
Stanley B. Greenfield (Ph.D., California, 1950; Prof) English.
Thomas R. Hart (Ph.D., Yale, 1952; Prof) Romance Linguistics.
Stoddard Malarkey (Ph.D., Oregon, 1964; Assoc Prof) English.
Clyde P. Patton (Ph.D., California, 1943; Prof) Geography.
Helmut R. Plant (Ph.D., Cincinatti, 1964; Assoc Prof) Germanic Linguistics.
Larry H. Reeker (Ph.D., Carnegie-Mellon, 1973; Asst Prof) Computer Science, Computational Linguistics.
Benson Schaeffer (Ph.D., California, 1969; Assoc Prof) Psychology.
Wayne Wickelgren (Ph.D., California, 1962; Prof) Psychology.

Support Available

Teaching assistantships regularly available; application deadline March 15.

Academic Calendar 1974-1975

Fall Quarter: September 30 - December 21; Winter Quarter: January 8 - March 22; Spring Quarter: April 2 - June 14; Summer Session: June 24 - August 15. Deadline: August 15.

DESCRIPTIVE MATERIAL: Write: Prof. James E. Hoard, Linguistics Committee, University of Oregon, Eugene, Oregon 97403.

Committee on Linguistics
Halvor P. Hansen, Director
Degrees: BA. Majors: 6. In Residence: 6u.

The linguistics major provides a program of language study and research for students
who wish to undertake an inter-collegiate and inter-disciplinary study of the systems
of language, including semantic, syntactical, morphological and phonological analysis;
historical and comparative linguistics; psycholinguistics and sociolinguistics; and
field linguistics. This program will prepare individuals for graduate level work in
one of the several areas of linguistic science or in such fields as anthropology,
communication, education, foreign language study, English language teaching, or teaching
English as a second language. The linguistics major could serve as an excellent complement for students with a primary major in an allied discipline.
     While each student's program will be planned individually, the major, consisting
of a minimum of eight courses, will include a core of four required courses in introductory linguistics, phonology, grammar, and linguistic field work. Depending on the
area of interest, the student, the Director of the Linguistics Program, and a faculty
advisor will establish the remaining requirements. At least an intermediate level
proficiency in a second language is also required. Such language proficiency will be
determined by the linguistic faculty.
     Institutes, Language & Area Centers, Research Programs include East Asian Program
(Otis Shao); Intercultural Communication Institute (Halvor P. Hansen); Laboratory for
Educational Research (Roger Reimer); Language Laboratory (John Wonder); Reading Clinic
(Heath Lowry); Speech and Hearing Clinic (Kenneth Perrin).

COURSE OFFERINGS

Introductory, 1; Phonology, 1; Theoretical Models, 1; Semantics & Logic, 1; Sociolinguistics, 3; Field Methods, 1; Psycholinguistics, 3; Historical Linguistics, 1; Language
Pedagogy, 3.

UNCOMMONLY-TAUGHT LANGUAGES

Japanese

STAFF

Nathan F. Cogan (Ph.D., U.C. Berkeley, 1971; Asst Prof) General Linguistics (1/2
     time).
Robert S. Cox (Ph.D., Indiana U., 1965; Assoc Prof) Historical Linguistics,
     Phonology, English Syntax (1/2 time).
Alberto G. Eraso (Ph.D., Universidad Pedagogica de Colombia, 1952; Assoc Prof)
     Applied Linguistics (1/2 time).
Lars Gantzel (Ph.D., Stanford, 1967; Assoc Prof) Anthropological Linguistics
     (1/2 time).
Halvor P. Hansen (Ph.D., Wisconsin, 1955; Prof) Language and Culture.
Barbara Z. Heiman (Ph.D., U.C. Berkeley, 1972; Asst Prof) Biological Foundations
     of Language, Linguistic Anthropology, Psycholinguistics (2/5 time).
John P. Wonder (Ph.D., Stanford, 1952; Prof) Hispanic Lit. and Cult., Spanish
     Linguistics (1/2 time).

Linguists in other Departments or Schools

Donald M. Decker (Ph.D., U.C.L.A., 1961; Prof) English as a Second Language.
Ruth Marie Faurot (Ph.D., U. North Carolina, 1953; Prof) English as a Second
     Language (1/3 time).
Randall E. Rockey (Ph.D., Cornell, 1970; Asst Prof) English as a Second Language.

Support Available

Teaching assistantships, university fellowships, research assistantships and various
loans are available.

Academic Calendar 1974-1975

Fall Semester: September 6; Spring Semester: February 5.

DESCRIPTIVE MATERIAL: Write: E. Les Medford, Dean of Admissions, University of the Pacific, Stockton, California 95204.

UNIVERSITY OF PENNSYLVANIA Philadelphia, Pennsylvania 19174   Tel. (215) 594-6046

243

Department of Linguistics
Leigh Lisker, Chairman
Degrees: BA, MA, Ph.D. Degrees Granted 1972-73: 2 BA, 9 MA, 3 Ph.D.

Instruction in the department of linguistics at Pennsylvania falls under six main divisions: historical and comparative linguistics, speech acoustics and phonetics, formal linguistics, structural and descriptive linguistics, ethno- and sociolinguistics, and mathematical logic. Associated with the department are two research projects, one in syntactic theory headed by Professors Z. Harris and H. Hiz, and the other in sociolinguistics under Professor W. Labov. A special relationship with the Haskins Laboratories in New Haven, Conn. exists through Professor L. Lisker, who is a research associate of that laboratory of experimental phonetics. The department also has a close relationship with the university's South Asia Regional Studies department, chaired by Professor R. Lambert, which offers a large number of courses on the languages and linguistics of modern south Asia, and with the Oriental Studies department, headed by Professor L. Rocher, offering instruction in languages of the near, middle and far east. This latter department includes a Near East Language and Area Center program directed by Dr. Thomas Naff.

COURSE OFFERINGS

Introductory, 1; Phonology, 7; Theoretical Models, 7; Semantics & Logic, 6; Sociolinguistics, 7; Dialectology, 1; Field Methods, 2; Math. & Comp. Linguistics, 4; Historical Linguistics, 3; History of Linguistics, 1. Language Areas: Indian Grammar, Structure of a Selected Natural Lg.

UNCOMMONLY-TAUGHT LANGUAGES

Akkadian	Old High German	Malayalam (g3)	Old Church Slavonic
Arabic (g2 u3)	(g1)	Marathi (g3)	(g1)
Aramaic (g3)	Gujarati (g1)	Nepali (g2)	Sumerian (g3)
Bengali (g2)	Hebrew (g4 u4)	Persian (g2 u2)	Tamil (g5)
Chinese (g2 u2)	Hindi (g4)	Polish (g2)	Telugu (g2)
Dutch (u2)	Hittite (g2)	Old Provencal (g1)	Tibetan (g2)
Egyptian (g3)	Old Icelandic	Sanskrit (g2 u2)	Turkish (g3 u2)
Mid. High German	(g1)	Old Saxon (g1)	Ukrainian (g1)
(g1)	Japanese (g3	Serbo-Croatian	Urdu (g4)
	u2)	(g1)	

STAFF

George Cardona (Ph.D., Yale, 1960; Prof) Historical-Comparative Linguistics;
    Indic Linguistic Theory.
John Fought (Ph.D., Yale, 1967; Prof) Phonological Theory; Ethnolinguistics.
Zellig Harris (Ph.D., U. of Pennsylvania, 1934; Prof) Syntactic Theory.
Henry Hiz (Ph.D., Harvard, 1948; Prof) Formal Linguistics: Mathematical Logic.
Henry Hoenigswald (Ph.D., U. of Florence, 1936; Prof) Historical; Comparative
    Linguistics.
Dell Hymes (Ph.D., Indiana U., 1955; Prof) Ethnolinguistics.

William Labov (Ph.D., Columbia U., 1964; Prof) Sociolinguistics.
Leigh Lisker (Ph.D., U. of Pennsylvania, 1949; Prof) Phonetics.
Anna Live (Ph.D., U. of Pennsylvania, 1959; Prof) The Teaching of English as a
    Second Language.
Ellen Prince (Ph.D., U. of Pennsylvania, 1974; Prof) Syntax and Transformation
    Grammar.
Richard Smaby (Ph.D., U. of Pennsylvania, 1968; Prof) Syntactic Theory: Formal
    Linguistics, Mathematical Logic.

Linguists in other Departments or Schools

Aravind K. Joshi (Prof) Electrical Engineering.
Lila R. Gleitman (Prof) Education.
Dell H. Hymes (Prof) Folklore and Linguistics.
James Liang (Asst Prof) Chinese.
Hiroshi Miyaji (Assoc Prof) Japanese.
Franklin C. Southworth (Assoc Prof) South Asian Linguistics.

Support Available

Two full-year and one half-year teaching assistantships are regularly available, these
awarded only to students of demonstrated ability who have had at least one year of work
in the department. About half a dozen fellowship/scholarships are awarded each year.
Applications for awards must be received, together with all supporting materials, by
the graduate school before February 1 of the academic year preceding that for which
the award is to be made.

Academic Calendar 1974-1975

Fall Semester: registration: September 4-5, classes: September 6 - December 11, examinations: December 14-22; Spring Semester: registration: January 14-15, classes: January
16 - April 30, exams: May 3-11. Deadline: July 16 (fall term), December 3 (spring term).

DESCRIPTIVE MATERIAL: Write: (Undergraduate) Office of Admissions, 1 College Hall;
                      (Graduate) Graduate School of Arts and Sciences, 133 Bennett
                      Hall; University of Pennsylvania, Philadelphia, Pennsylvania
                      19174.

PENNSYLVANIA STATE UNIVERSITY University Park, Pennsylvania 16802
Tel. (814) 865-6873

Linguistics Program
Simon Belasco, Chairman
Degrees: BA, MA, Ph.D. Degrees Granted 1972-73: 25 BA, 6 MA, 1 Ph.D. Majors:
        30g. In Residence: 18g, 40u.

COURSE OFFERINGS

Introductory, 1; Phonology, 5; Theoretical Models, 5; Semantics & Logic, 1; Sociolinguistics, 1; Psycholinguistics, 3; Historical Linguistics, 3; Language Pedagogy, 2;
Applied Ling. Language Areas: Greek 1, Latin 1.

UNCOMMONLY-TAUGHT LANGUAGES

Arabic (u)	Mod. Hebrew (u)	Japanese (u)	Turkish (u)
Dutch (u)	Hindi (u)	Swahili (u)	Vietnamese (u)
Mod. Greek (u)	Hungarian (u)	Swedish (u)	

Academic Calendar 1974-1975

Fall Quarter: September 9 - November 16; Winter Quarter: December 5 - February 26;
Spring Quarter: March 13 - May 21; Summer Quarter: June 11 - August 20.

DESCRIPTIVE MATERIAL: Write: Grad. School (for grad Program), The Pa. State
University, Kern Building; or: Admissions (for Undergrad.)
Shields Bldg., University Park, Pa. 16802.

UNIVERSITY OF PITTSBURGH Pittsburgh, Pennsylvania 15260   Tel. (412) 624-5900

Department of General Linguistics
Christina Bratt Paulston, Acting Chairman
Degrees: MA, Ph.D., TESOL Certificate. Degrees Granted 1972-73: 12 MA, 3 Ph.D.
  Majors: 27g.

The Department of General Linguistics, founded as a result of the University's interest
in expanding its international dimension, has a strong interest in the applied aspects
of linguistics, especially those related to language teaching and learning. Additionally
the offerings in theoretical linguistics are gradually being increased in number.
   A certificate in TESOL accompanies the MA in Linguistics provided the student selects
certain courses, and the Ph.D. to the regular doctoral program.
   An English Language Institute for foreign students of the English language gives
courses three times yearly. A Language Acquisition Institute for the individualized
study of the less frequently taught languages, and the University's Language Laboratory
are administratively attached to the Department.
   The Department has hosted for a number of years a fall term International Development
Education Program through the U. S. Office of Education, and has maintained a close
relationship and exchange program with a number of Thai universities.
   A developing relationship with the University Center for International Studies
features a strong TESOL publications program and the potential for more extensive non-
credit teacher training programs in the U.S. and abroad.

COURSE OFFERINGS

Introductory, 3; Phonology, 2; Theoretical Models, 7; Semantics & Logic, 2; Sociolinguistics, 1; Dialectology, 2; Field Methods, 1; Psycholinguistics, 2; Historical Linguistics, 2; History of Linguistics, 1; Linguistics & Literature, 1; Language Pedagogy, 6.

UNCOMMONLY-TAUGHT LANGUAGES

Afghan-Farsi   Hungarian (g4 u4)   Romanian (g2 u2)   Turkish (g4 u4)
  (g2 u2)   Indonesian (g2   Sinhalese (g2   Vietnamese (g2
Arabic (g4 u4)   u2)   u2)   u2)
Mod. Greek   Irish Gaelic   Swedish (g2 u2)   Welsh (g2 u2)
  (g4 u4)   (g2 u2)   Tagalog (g2 u2)   Yiddish (g4 u4)
Hebrew (g4 u4)   Korean (g2 u2)   Thai (g4 u4)   Yoruba (g2 u2)
Hindi (g4 u4)   Persian (Iranian)
                      (g2 u2)

STAFF

Edward M. Anthony (Ph.D., Michigan, 1954; Prof) TESOL, Thai Language, English
   Grammar.
Mary N. Bruder (MA, Pitt, 1969; Lecturer) TESOL, Sociolinguistics.
David E. Eskey (Ph.D., Pitt, 1969; Asst Prof) Applied Linguistics, Reading.
Robert T. Henderson (MA, Pitt, 1974; Lecturer) TESOL, Uncommonly-Taught Languages.
Adrian Palmer (Ph.D., Michigan, 1971; Visiting Asst Prof) Language Testing.

Robert L. Parslow (Ph.D., Michigan, 1967; Assoc Prof) Dialectology.
Christina Bratt Paulston (Ed.D., Columbia, 1966; Assoc Prof) Sociolinguistics,
    Applied Linguistics.
Richmond Thomason (Ph.D., Yale, 1965; Assoc Prof) Semantics, Philosophy and
    Language.
Sarah G. Thomason (Ph.D., Yale, 1968; Asst Prof) Historical Linguistics, Phonology,
    Language Classification.
Judy A. Vernick (MA, Pitt, 1973; Lecturer) TESOL, Language Laboratory.
Lois I. Wilson (MA, Pitt, 1970; Lecturer) TESOL, Reading & Writing.

Linguists in other Departments or Schools

Dayle Barnes, East Asian Languages & Literatures.
Roy A. Boggs, Germanic Languages & Literatures.
Lilyan Brudner, Anthropology Department.
Edwin D. Floyd, Department of Classics.
Herschel Frey, Hispanic Languages & Literatures.
Michio Hojo, East Asian Languages & Literatures.
Audrey Holland, Department of Speech.
Terrence Kaufman, Anthropology Department.
Diana Meriz, French & Italian Languages & Literatures.
Herbert Rubin, Department of Speech.
Rae Siporin, Department of English.

Support Available

A number of assistantships are available for study in the Department of Linguistics.
Most of these assistantships entail teaching in the English Language Institute and
require prior experience (although in remarkable cases exceptions are made) and native
knowledge of English. A very few assistantships in the Language Acquisition Institute
are available for foreign students.
    Deadline for applying is April 1.

Academic Calendar 1974-1975

Fall Quarter: September 4 - December 17; Winter Quarter: January 6 - April 22; Spring
Quarter: April 28 - August 13; Spring Semester: April 28 - June 18; Summer Quarter:
June 24 - August 13. Deadline: June.

DESCRIPTIVE MATERIAL: Write: Dr. Sarah G. Thomason, Department of General Linguistics,
                    University of Pittsburgh, Pittsburgh, Pennsylvania 15260.

C. W. POST COLLEGE OF LONG ISLAND UNIVERSITY   Greenvale, L. I., New York 11548
Tel. (516) 299-2385

Foreign Language Department
Dr. Rafael Rasco, Chairman
Degrees: BA in foreign languages with minor in linguistics.

COURSE OFFERINGS

Introductory, 2u; Theoretical Models, 1g; Sociolinguistics, 1g; Dialectology, 2u;
Applied Lx., 1u; Psycholinguistics, 1g; Historical Linguistics, 1g.

STAFF

William Anders (Ph.D., Sorbonne; Prof) Comparative Language, Germanic Linguistics,
    Historical Linguistics.

126

Richard Auletta (MA, S.U.N.Y. at Buffalo; Ph.D. cand. S.U.N.Y. Stony Brook) Linguistic Geography, Historical Linguistics, Applied Linguistics.
Gail Meadows (Ph.D., Harvard) Historical Linguistics, Comparative Language.
Bohus Jan Pissko (Ph.D., U. of Comenius (Bratislava)) Historical Linguistics, Sociolinguistics, Psycholinguistics.

Academic Calendar 1974-1975

Fall Semester: September 4 - December 20; Spring Semester: January 27 - May 20; Summer Session: June - July 5 wks.; July - August 5 wks.

DESCRIPTIVE MATERIAL: Write: Admissions office, C. W. Post College, Long Is. University, Greenvale, New York 11548.

PRINCETON UNIVERSITY Princeton, New Jersey 08540   Tel. (609) 452-5405

(Graduate) Program in Linguistics
William G. Moulton, Chairman
Degrees: Ph.D.; on special application, BA with independent major in linguistics.
            Degrees Granted 1972-73: 4 Ph.D. Majors: 10g. In Residence: 8g.

Although the university has no Department of Linguistics and no regular undergraduate major in linguistics, an undergraduate may request approval of "independent concentration" in linguistics. With the guidance of two faculty members, he then devises his own program of concentration. This typically consists of (1) the two regular undergraduate courses in linguistics (Descriptive Linguistics and Historical Linguistics); (2) linguistically oriented undergraduate courses in related fields (anthropology, philosophy, psychology); (3) graduate courses in linguistics (e.g. Phonology, Syntax, Dialectology, Field Methods); and (4) advanced foreign language courses. Like all undergraduates, he writes junior papers and a senior thesis. In 1973-74, six undergraduates were engaged in independent concentration in linguistics.
      The graduate Program in Linguistics functions as an independent department as far as the individual student is concerned. Its faculty consists of members of the departments of Anthropology, Classics, East Asian Studies, English, Germanic Languages, Philosophy, Psychology, Romance Languages, and Slavic Languages. With the aid of a faculty adviser, each student designs his own program of study. He typically takes (1) a small number of courses in linguistics, especially phonology, syntax, dialectology, and field methods; and (2) courses in the linguistics of a language or language family and/or courses in related fields such as anthropology, philosophy, psychology, or literature. Whereas many graduate programs place primary emphasis on linguistics as such, Princeton has chosen to emphasize the interconnections between linguistics and related fields, especially foreign languages.
      Facilities include strong library holdings in linguistics and in foreign languages (notably Arabic, Chinese, Classics, Germanic, Romance, and Slavic), and a cooperative Computer Center.

COURSE OFFERINGS

Introductory, 1u; Phonology, 1g; Theoretical Models, 1g; Semantics & Logic, 1g 1u; Sociolinguistics, 2u; Dialectology, 1g; Field Methods, 1g; Psycholinguistics, 1u; Historical Linguistics, 2g 1u; History of Linguistics, 1g; Linguistics & Literature, 1g. Language Areas: Romance 1g 1u, Slavic 1u, German 2g.

UNCOMMONLY-TAUGHT LANGUAGES

Arabic (8g 6u)	Old High German	Bib. Hebrew	Portuguese
Chinese (5g 14u)	(1g)	(2g 2u)	(2g 3u)
Old English	Mid. High German	Old Irish (1g)	Sanskrit (4g)
(2g 1u)	(2g)	Japanese (5g 12u)	Old Saxon (1g)
Mid. English (4g)	Gothic (1g)	Old Norse (1g)	Syriac (2g)
Old French (3g)	Hebrew (u6)	Persian (4g 4u)	Turkish (4g 4u)

STAFF

Hans C. Aarsleff (Ph.D., Minnesota, 1960; Prof) History of Linguistics.
Samuel D. Atkins (Ph.D., Princeton, 1935; Prof) Indo-European, Sanskrit, Hittite.
David W. Crabb (Ph.D., Columbia, 1962; Assoc Prof) Anthropology, Ethnography of
   Speech, West African Languages.
James M. Dunn (Ph.D., Michigan, 1970; Asst Prof) Germanic, Phonology.
Sam Glucksberg (Ph.D., New York U., 1960; Prof) Psychology.
Gilbert H. Harman (Ph.D., Harvard, 1964; Prof) Philosophy, Syntax and Semantics.
William G. Moulton (Ph.D., Yale, 1941; Prof) Dialectology, Germanic, Historical
   Phonology.
Charles E. Townsend (Ph.D., Harvard, 1962; Prof) Russian, Czech, Slavic Language
   and Linguistics.
Thomas R. Trabasso (Ph.D., Michigan State, 1961; Prof) Psychology.
Karl D. Uitti (Ph.D., Berkeley, 1959; Prof) Romance, Linguistics and Literary
   Theory.

Support Available

Students in linguistics are eligible for the usual university fellowships, which include
tuition and up to $2500 composed of loans and (depending on merit and need) stipends.
Students who have successfully passed the General Examination (normally after two years
of study) are eligible for assistantships, which include tuition and up to $3800.

Academic Calendar 1974-1975

Fall Semester: September 12 - January 25; Spring Semester: February 3 - June 4.
Deadline: January 15.

DESCRIPTIVE MATERIAL: Write: Princeton University, The Graduate School, Graduate
                       Admissions, Box 270, Princeton, New Jersey 08540.

PURDUE UNIVERSITY West Lafayette, Indiana 47907   Tel. (317) 749-2672

English Department
Jacob H. Adler, Head
Degrees: MA, Ph.D. Degrees Granted 1972-73: 4 MA, 4 Ph.D. Majors: 172g.

The linguistics program at the doctoral level is especially appealing to students because
of its flexibility and interdisciplinary possibilities. Working in close contact with
his advisory committee, each candidate prepares his own plan of study. The main preliminary examination covers the chief aspects of historical, descriptive, and theoretical
linguistics. All doctoral candidates take two collateral examinations. Students in
linguistics may choose to be examined in periods of literary study, in comparative
literature, or in a wide variety of programs in other disciplines. Doctoral disserta-
tions for linguistics students include such diverse investigations as field work in
areal and social divergences in contemporary English, the theoretical basis of case
grammar, and tagmemic analysis of Old English. The Master of Arts degree is a more
general one with more specific hourly and course requirements. At this level students

may take half their work in linguistics and half in a wide choice of literature options. The programs in English language and linguistics can be supplemented with instruction in a number of related disciplines in cooperating departments. Students may elect studies in more theoretical linguistics, psycho-linguistics, sociolinguistics, comparative literature, medieval culture, artificial computer languages, language acquisition, or the philosophy of language. Undergraduates, too, may design interdisciplinary programs making use of courses in various departments.

COURSE OFFERINGS

Introductory, 1; Theoretical Models, 3; Dialectology, 1; Historical Linguistics, 3; Linguistics & Literature, 1; Language Pedagogy, 1. Language Areas: OE, ME, O Norse.

STAFF

Helen Carlson (Ph.D., U. of New Mexico, 1959; Asst Prof) Linguistics, Language
   Development, Place Names.
Russell Cosper (Ph.D., U. of Michigan, 1948; Prof) English and Linguistics.
Irma Cunningham (Ph.D., U. of Michigan, 1970; Asst Prof) Introductory Linguistics,
   English Syntax, Regional & Social Dialectology.
Harwood Hess (Ph.D., U. of Michigan, 1962; Assoc Prof) Linguistic Field Work,
   English Linguistics, English as a Second Language.
Shaun Hughes (Ph.D., U. of Washington, 1972; Asst Prof) History of English, Medieval
   Language & Literature, Icelandic Metrical Romances.
Barnett Kottler (Ph.D., Yale U., 1953; Assoc Prof) Medieval Literature, English
   Linguistics.
Thomas Ohlgren (Ph.D., U. of Michigan, 1969; Asst Prof) English Literature &
   Language to 1500, Medieval Studies, Interdisciplinary Studies.
Keith Schap (Ph.D., Indiana U., 1972; Asst Prof) English Literature 1660-1790,
   English Linguistics, Stylistics.

Linguists in other Departments or Schools

Robert Freiden (Ph.D., Indiana U., 1970; Asst Prof) Syntax, Semantics, Neurolinguistics.
Robert Hammarbert (MA, U. of Chicago, 1970; Inst) Linguistics.
James H. Rose (Ph.D., U. of Michigan, 1969; Asst Prof) Syntax, Semantics, Lexical
   Structure.

Support Available

Graduate Assistantships are available in administration, instruction and research -- generally on a half-time basis. The beginning stipend for half-time assistants is $320 per month for the ten-month academic year with remission of all but $60 in fees a semester. Graduate research assistantships are often available for the advanced student in which all of the research applies toward his degree. With such a half-time appointment, the student receives full residence credit and a $220 per month stipend.

Academic Calendar 1974-1975

Fall Semester: August 29 - December 21; Spring Semester: January 13 - May 10;
Summer Session: June 16 - August 8.

DESCRIPTIVE MATERIAL: Write: Professor H. M. Reichard, 324 Heavilon Hall, Purdue
   University, West Lafayette, Indiana 47907.

Department of Linguistics
Charles E. Cairns, Chairman
Degrees: BA.

The undergraduate program provides a full range of courses in Linguistics. There
is a large survey course in which about 700 students enroll each semester. All majors
take a core program which consists of linguistic theory (syntax, phonology, semantics)
and historical linguistics. There are two tracks, a general linguistics major and a
major in English as a Second Language. In addition, there are a number of courses,
such as sociolinguistics, structures of uncommonly taught languages, etc., which are
available to all majors; some of these courses are taken by non-majors as well.

Although we do not have a graduate program at Queens College, we are affiliated with
the Doctoral Program at the CUNY Graduate Center.

COURSE OFFERINGS

Introductory, 3; Phonology, 3; Theoretical Models, 4; Semantics & Logic, 1; Sociolinguistics, 1; Field Methods, 1; Historical Linguistics, 3; History of Linguistics, 1;
Language Pedagogy, 3. Other: Writing Systems.

UNCOMMONLY-TAUGHT LANGUAGES

Arabic	Danish	Icelandic	Serbo-Croatian
Aramaic	Dutch	Polish	Swahili
Chinese	Greek	Portuguese	Yoruba
Czech	Hebrew		

STAFF

Stephen A. Antell (BA, Queens College 1972; Adj Lect).
Rochelle Berkovits (BA, Brooklyn College, 1971; Adj Lect).
Charles E. Cairns (Ph.D., Columbia, 1968; Assoc Prof) Linguistic Theory.
Peter DePaola (BA, Brooklyn College, 1969; Adj Lect).
Mark Feinstein (BA, Queens College, 1968; Adj Lect).
Robert Fiengo (Ph.D., M.I.T., 1974; Asst Prof) Linguistic Theory.
Rosario C. Gingras (MA, U.C.L.A., 1961; Inst) Bilingualism and English as a Second
    Language.
R.M.R. Hall (Ph.D., New York U., 1967; Assoc Prof).
Stephen Krashen (Ph.D., U.C.L.A., 1972; Asst Prof) Second Language Learning,
    Neuro-Linguistics.
Amy Myers (BA, U. of Rochester, 1965; Inst) African Languages.
Ricardo Otheguy (MA, City College, CUNY, 1973; Adj Lect).
Lawrence Sheerin (MA, Harvard U., 1972) (Part-time).
Alan Stevens (Ph.D., Yale, 1964; Assoc Prof).
Walter Stock (BS, Union College, 1957; Adj Lect) German Philology.
Juri Suksdorf (MA, Brooklyn College, 1972; Adj Lect).

Linguists in other Departments or Schools

John Moyne, Computer Science.

Support Available

Loans, grants, and a work-study program for full-time students are administered by the
Financial Aid Office of the Dean of Students' Office.
    Financial Aid available: Supplemental Educational Opportunity Grants: (Grants in
amounts from $200 to $1,000 a year are available to exceptionally needy full-time matriculated undergraduate students. These grants from federal government funds will be
matched by other sources of financial aid, such as loans and jobs, to enable the student
to meet his educational expenses. College Work-Study Program: This program established
under the Economic Opportunity Act of 1964, provides jobs for matriculated students
who need to work to pay their expenses. Part-time jobs are available both on campus
and in outside non-profit community service agencies during the academic year. National
Direct Student Loan Program: Queens College participates in the loan program sponsored
by the federal government. Both full-time and part-time matriculated graduate and

undergraduate students in need of funds for educational expenses may borrow substantial amounts and repay after they leave school.

Guaranteed Loan Plan of New York Higher Education Assistance Corporation, The Corporation provides guarantees for low-cost, long-term, delayed repayment loans to needy full-time and part-time students who are residents of New York State. The loans are made by participating lending institutions in New York State.

Student Loan Funds, These funds are supported by contributions from groups and individuals mainly from within the College. Students may borrow small amounts for emergency purposes on a no-interest, short-term basis.

Morris Morgenstern Student Loan Fund, Short-term loans are available to any deserving student, other than freshmen, in the College who is in need of temporary assistance.

Student Activities Financial Aid Fund, Students in need of assistance may apply for a partial grant or loan in order to participate in specific College-sponsored activities.

Basic Educational Opportunity Grants, Federal grants are available to full-time students whose first college enrollment was after April, 1973 and who are U.S. citizens or permanent residents. The amount of grant is based on family income, assets, and size of family. Applications must be submitted directly to the BEOG Program before February 1.

Academic Calendar 1974-1975

Fall Semester: September 10 - January 7; Spring Semester: February 3 - May 20. Deadline: For information about undergraduate courses, call or write to the Admissions Office, Queens College, Flushing, N.Y. You have to submit your application by October 15 for admission in January and by January 15 for admission in September.

DESCRIPTIVE MATERIAL: Write: University Application Processing Center, Box #148, Vanderveer Station, Brooklyn, New York 11210.

THE UNIVERSITY OF ROCHESTER   Rochester, New York 14627   Tel. (716) 275-4251

Department of Foreign Languages, Literatures and Linguistics
Donald G. Reiff, Director
Degrees: MA, Ph.D.

THE MASTER OF ARTS
The requirements are as follows: Plan A: Twenty-four hours beyond the BA, a thesis (6 hours of course 495), and an oral examination on the thesis. Plan B: Thirty hours beyond the BA and a written examination on selected topics in the area of concentration, or an essay with oral examination. All MA programs under Plan B, according to University regulations, must include 18 hours of credit taken at the 400-level or above.

Candidates for the MA in Linguistics must be able to demonstrate preparation in the following at the MA examination: language description (including phonetics, phonology, and grammar); and two of the following: historical-comparative linguistics; experimental linguistics; areal linguistics; theoretical linguistics; applied linguistics; history and structure of one language.

The Department offers a curriculum in World Languages for secondary-level teachers at the MA level in General Linguistics. While this program is subject to all regulations for the MA degree, it is oriented toward enabling public school teachers to provide instruction in general linguistics at the junior or seniorhigh level.

General Linguistics - DOCTOR OF PHILOSOPHY
The Department presents a curriculum whose framework represents major areas of professional activity in the field of linguistics. While flexibility is seriously intended, adequate coverage of certain professional competences is required.

In the first year of doctoral work, all students must enroll in a comprehensive, cooperatively taught, research methods course, in which they are provided the skills to do careful, independent study in all areas of linguistic investigation.

The remainder of doctoral work consists of seminars or internships, and other related course work to complete the program the student has arrived at with his committee. Each student must complete at least three seminars or internships of the following five: applied linguistics, linguistic theory, experimental linguistics, historical-comparative linguistics, areal linguistics.

Upon successful completion of three seminar/internships a student may take the Qualifying Examination and will be advanced to Candidacy for the doctorate on acceptance, by the Linguistics Section, of his or her proposal for dissertation research.

All candidates for the Ph.D. will be required to engage in supervised teaching. On completion of one year of teaching, students will receive credit for Linguistics 590: Supervised Teaching (5 hours). In lieu of supervised teaching, the student may substitute an additional Internship for one year.

To implement professional training, the Department maintains two research laboratories: the Phonetics Laboratory (co-directors, Professors Obrecht and Reiff) and the Verbal Behavior Laboratory (director, Professor Sapon). The Department maintains a Language Services Center (director, Mr. Cruz) in which language materials of a wide variety, both for instructional and research purposes, is available.

COURSE OFFERINGS

Introductory, 1; Phonology, 3; Theoretical Models, 2; Sociolinguistics, 3; Dialectology, 1; Psycholinguistics, 2; Neurolinguistics, 1; Historical Linguistics, 2. Language Areas: French 2, German 4, Spanish 2. Other Depts.: Sociolinguistics, 3; Psycholinguistics, 5; Neurolinguistics, 1; Historical Linguistics, 1.

UNCOMMONLY-TAUGHT LANGUAGES

Arabic	Hebrew	Japanese	Swedish
Chinese			

STAFF

Charles Carlton, Romance Linguistics, Romanian, Applied Linguistics.
Dennis Frengle, Generative Phonology, Romance Linguistics, Spanish Grammar.
Ronald V. Harrington, Description and Historical Development of Slavic Languages.
Antanas Klimas, Historical Linguistics, Indo-European Linguistics, Germanic.
Demetrius Moutsos, Indo-European Linguistics.
Dean Obrecht, Voice Identification, Acoustic Phonetics, Experimental Phonetics.
Donald G. Reiff, Phonetics, Grammatical Theory, Aphasiology.
Stanley M. Sapon, Psycholinguistics, the Experimental Analysis of Verbal Behavior.
Rama Sharma, Formal Theory of Grammar, Sociolinguistics, Paninian.
Ronald Werth, Historical Linguistics, Languages in Contact, Germanic Linguistics.

Linguists in other Departments and Schools

Christopher Day, Anthropological Linguistics.
Lyn Kypriotaki Haber, Psycholinguistics, Reading, Sociolinguistics.
Ralph Haber, Reading, Psycholinguistics.
Lynn Libben, Psychology of the Deaf, Psycholinguistics.
Matthew Marino, Theoretical Linguistics, English Syntax, History of English.
Carla Posnansky, Applied Linguistics, Psycholinguistics.
Kieth Rayner, Applied Linguistics, Psycholinguistics.
Patricia Siple, Psycholinguistics, Psychology of the Deaf.
Haiganooh A. Whitaker, Neurolinguistics, Psycholinguistics.
Harry A. Whitaker, Neurolinguistics, Psycholinguistics.

Support Available

Tuition Waiver and Teaching Assistants in French, German, Russian and Spanish; occasional Univ. fellowship support.

RUTGERS UNIVERSITY   New Brunswick, New Jersey 08903   Tel. (201) 932-7366

Linguistics Committee
William Derbyshire, Acting Chairman
Degrees: B.A. with minor in linguistics. Certificate granted.

The Program in Linguistics of Rutgers College has only been formally approved by the
faculty this year. It will go into effect in September of 1974. The program will grant
a Certificate to those students who complete a specified set of course offerings in
linguistics in conjunction with their formal major. We anticipate attracting students
from foreign language departments, English, philosophy, anthropology and sociology,
psychology, and mathematics.
    The core courses of our Certificate Program include an introductory course in lin-
guistics, specific courses in syntax, semantics, morphology and phonology. Advanced
courses include work in Slavic linguistics, African linguistics, Italian linguistics,
psycholinguistics, sociolinguistics and anthropological linguistics.

COURSE OFFERINGS

Introductory, 2; Theoretical Models, 2; Semantics & Logic, 1; Sociolinguistics, 2;
Psycholinguistics, 2; Math. & Comp. Linguistics, 1. Language Areas: African 1, Slavic
1, Romance 1.

UNCOMMONLY-TAUGHT LANGUAGES

Chinese	Hebrew	Polish	Russian
Hausa	Kiswahili	Portuguese	Waswahili
	Old English		Yiddish

STAFF

Adele Abrahamson (Ph.D., U. of California at San Diego) Psycholinguistics.
Joseph Barone (Ph.D., Princeton U.) Tranformational Grammar, English Phonology.
Anna Benjamin (Ph.D., U. of Pennsylvania) Classics.
Ann Bodine (Ph.D., Cornell U.) Sociology, Anthropology.
Robert Bolton (Ph.D., U. of Michigan) Philosophy of Language, Semantics.
Whitney Bolton (Ph.D., Princeton U.) English Grammar, History of English.
William Derbyshire (Ph.D., U. of Pennsylvania) Slavic Linguistics.
Patricia DiSilvio (MA, U. of Colorado; doctorate U. of Florence) Italian Lin-
    guistics, Syntax.
Ernest Dunn (Ph.D., Michigan State U.) African Linguistics, Tagmemics.
Bridget Lyons (Ph.D., Columbia University) English Grammar (Syntax).
Fay Yeager (Ed.D., Columbia U.) Speech and Phonetics.

Academic Calendar 1974-1975

Fall Semester: September 12 - December 20; Spring Semester: January 29 - May 13.

DESCRIPTIVE MATERIAL: Write: Office of Admissions, Rutgers University, New
                        Brunswick, New Jersey 08903.

SAN DIEGO STATE UNIVERSITY   San Diego, California 92115   Tel. (714) 286-5268

Department of Linguistics
Glendon F. Drake, Chairman
Degrees: MA in linguistics; Basic and Advanced Certificates in Applied Linguistics.
        Degrees Granted 1972-73: 3 MA. Majors: 23g. In Residence: 23g.

The Department of Linguistics at San Diego State University presently offers a Master's degree in linguistics and two certificates in applied linguistics. A bachelor's degree program is planned for 1975-76.

The graduate program includes core courses within the linguistics department in generative syntax and phonology, field methods, sociolinguistics, psycholinguistics, historical-comparative linguistics, and Indo- and non-Indo-European languages. The program also utilizes courses from related departments within the University, such as anthropology and the foreign languages. There are special opportunities for the study of Amerindian languages and for applied linguistics.

The certificate programs are offered in applied linguistics at the basic level (requiring a semester's commitment) and at the advanced level (requiring two semesters' commitment). Practicum programs are provided.

Facilities, in addition to extensive library holdings in most areas of linguistics, include affiliation with a social science laboratory-learning center. This center provides sophisticated audio, video, and computer equipment for the use of both students and faculty. The University is situated in a bi-lingual area. It is surrounded by a number of different Native American communities. The University is in close range of both urban and rural culture areas, containing a wide range of social varieties of several different languages.

COURSE OFFERINGS

Introductory, 3u; Phonology, 1g; Theoretical Models, 1u; Sociolinguistics, 2g 1u; Dialectology, 1u; Field Methods, 1g; Psycholinguistics, 1u; Historical Linguistics, 1g 1u; Language Pedagogy, 1u; Applied Lx., 1u. Language Areas: Eskimo 1g, Navaho 2g. Other Departments: Introductory, 1u; Semantics & Logic, 1g 1u, Sociolinguistics, 1g 1u; Psycholinguistics, 1g; Historical Linguistics, 1g. Language Areas: French 1g 1u, German 3g 3u, Russian 1g 2u, Spanish 2g 3u, Slavic 1g.

UNCOMMONLY-TAUGHT LANGUAGES

Old English	Eskimo (1g)	Lakota (2u)	Navaho (1g)
Mid. English	Kumeyaay (2u)	Nahuatl (1g)	Sanskrit (1g)

STAFF

Afia Dil (Ph.D., Stanford U., 1972; Lect) Sociolinguistics, Applied Linguistics,
    Asian Languages (part-time).
Thomas S. Donahue (Ph.D., Ohio State U., 1968; Assoc Prof) Historical English
    Dialects, Generative Phonology, Mathematical Linguistics.
Glendon F. Drake (Ph.D., U. of Michigan, 1973; Assoc Prof) Linguistic Attitudes,
    Sociolinguistics, Psycholinguistics.
Suzette Elgin (Ph.D., U. of Calif. at San Diego, 1973; Asst Prof) Transformational
    Syntax, Applied Linguistics, Navajo.
Leonard H. Frey (Ph.D., U. of Oregon, 1959; Prof) Old English, History of English,
    Indo-European.
Orin D. Seright (Ph.D., Indiana U., 1964; Assoc Prof) Poetic Syntax, Phonemics and
    Morphemics, History of English.
James N. Tidwell (Ph.D., Ohio State U., 1947; Prof) American Dialectology, History
    of English.
Robert Underhill (Ph.D., Harvard U., 1964; Asst Prof) Theoretical Phonology and
    Syntax, Turkish Linguistics, Eskimo Linguistics.

Linguists in other Departments or Schools

Clay B. Christensen (Ph.D., U. of Washington, 1968; Assoc Prof) Spanish Applied
    Linguistics, Transformational Analysis, Synchronic Studies.
Philip J. Greenfeld (Ph.D., Arizona, 1972; Asst Prof) Anthropological Linguistics.
Ronald S. Himes (Ph.D., U. of Hawaii, 1972; Assoc Prof) Anthropological Linguistics.
Ludek A. Kozlik (Ph.D., U. of Texas, 1965; Prof) Slavic Linguistics, Computational
    Linguistics.
Richard H. Lawson (Ph.D., UCLA, 1956; Prof) Germanic Linguistics, Historical
    Linguistics.
Guerard Piffard (Ph.D., Stanford U., 1957; Prof) Romance Linguistics.
Yoshio Tanaka (Ph.D., UCLA, 1965; Assoc Prof) Germanic Linguistics, Phonology.

James L. Walsh (Ph.D., U. of Illinois, 1963; Assoc Prof) Spanish Linguistics,
    Phonology.
Ronald R. Young (Ph.D., Illinois (Urbana), 1971; Asst Prof) Diachronic and
    Synchronic Spanish Linguistics.

Support Available

Graduate teaching assistantships are occasionally available in the foreign language
and literature departments. Information may be obtained from the head of the department.
Financial aid in the form of loans and part-time employment is available to qualified
applicants.

Academic Calendar 1974-1975

Fall Semester: August 14 - December 31; Spring Semester: January 8 - May 30.
Deadline: August 31 for Spring 1975; November 30 for Fall 1975.

DESCRIPTIVE MATERIAL: Write: Office of Admissions, San Diego State University,
                       San Diego, California 92021.

SAN FRANCISCO STATE UNIVERSITY San Francisco, California 94132   Tel. (415) 469-2264

English Department
Graham Wilson, Chairman
Thurston Womack, Vice Chairman, Linguistics
Degrees: B.A. with linguistics minor; MA in TEFL; MA in English with linguistic
          concentration.

COURSE OFFERINGS

Introductory, 3; Phonology, 1; Theoretical Models, 2; Semantics & Logic, 3; Sociolinguistics, 1; Field Methods, 1; Psycholinguistics, 1; Historical Linguistics, 2;
Linguistics & Literature, 2; Applied Linguistics, 4; Language Pathology, 4; Language
areas: Chinese, English, French, German, Japanese, Russian, Spanish.

UNCOMMONLY-TAUGHT LANGUAGES

Chinese-Cantonese	Old English	Hebrew	Sanskrit
Classical Chinese	Filipino	Old Italian	
Chinese-Mandarin	Old French	Japanese	

STAFF

Kenneth Croft (Prof) TEFL, Anthropological Linguistics.
Dorothy Danielson (Prof) TEFL, English Linguistics.
John Dennis (Prof) TEFL, English Linguistics.
Daniel Glicksberg (Prof) TEFL, English Linguistics.
Ray Grosvenor (Prof) Phonetics, General Linguistics.
Alton Hobgood (Assoc Prof) English, Semantics.
Jagdish Jain (Asst Prof) Theoretical Linguistics.
Niel Snortum (Prof) Historical Linguistics.
Graham Wilson (Prof) English Linguistics.
Lois M. Wilson (Prof) TEFL.
Thurston Womack (Prof) TEFL.

Linguists in Other Departments or Schools

Joseph Miksak (Prof) Phonetics.
Toshiko Mishima (Assoc Prof) Japanese.
Harry Osser (Assoc Prof) Psycholinguistics.
Clyde Stitt (Prof) Speech
Marvin Weinberger (Prof) French.

DESCRIPTIVE MATERIAL: Write: English Department, San Francisco State University, San Francisco, California 94132.

SAN JOSE STATE UNIVERSITY San Jose, California 95192   Tel. (408) 277-2802

Linguistics Program
Philip H. Cook, Acting Coordinator
Degrees: MA. Degrees Granted 1972-73: 8 MA. Majors: 31g. In Residence: 31g.

The Linguistics Program offers a Master of Arts degree in Linguistics, with a concentration in Applied Linguistics. The graduate courses are designed both for students in linguistics and for students in such disciplines as education, English, a foreign language, and psychology whose professional competence would be enhanced by an understanding of the structure of a language and the nature of a linguistic theory. The purpose of the Linguistics Program is to provide students with an opportunity for an interdisciplinary education in the art and science of language. The program is administered by an interdepartmental Linguistics Committee.

COURSE OFFERINGS

Introductory, 2; Phonology, 2; Theoretical Models, 4; Semantics & Logic, 1; Sociolinguistics, 3; Dialectology, 1; Field Methods, 1; Psycholinguistics, 2; Historical Linguistics, 1; Language Pedagogy, 1; Applied Lx., 1. Language Areas: French 2, German 1, Spanish 3.

UNCOMMONLY-TAUGHT LANGUAGES

Cantonese (u2)	Ilocano (u2)	Mandarin (u2)	Tagalog (u2)
Hebrew (u2)	Japanese (u6)	Swahili (u2)	Yoruba (u2)

STAFF

Richard B. Applegate (Ph.D., U.C., Berkeley, 1972; Lect) Sociolinguistics, Anthropological Linguistics.
Estrella Calimag (Ed.D., Columbia, 1965; Asst Prof) TESL, Philippine Languages.
Mary Ann Campbell (MA, U. of Chicago, 1971; Lect) Syntax, Dialectology.
Philip H. Cook (Ph.D., U. of Southern Calif., 1973; Asst Prof) Applied Linguistics, Syntax.
Edith Trager Johnson (Ph.D., U. of Pennsylvania, 1960; Prof) Phonology, Anthropological Linguistics.
John T. Lamendella (Ph.D., U. of Michigan, 1969; Asst Prof) Psycholinguistics, Neurolinguistics, Semantics.
Michael P. Noonan (MA, U.C.L.A., 1972; Lect) Diachronic Linguistics, Linguistic Theory.
Manjari Ohala (Ph.D., U.C.L.A., 1972; Lect) Phonology (1/2 time).

Linguists in other Departments or Schools

James J. Asher, Psychology, Second Language Learning.
Candace C. Brooks, Cultural Anthropology.

James L. Dolby, Computational Linguistics.
Roland Hamilton, Spanish Structure, Spanish Dialectology.
Jose Hernandez, History of Spanish, Spanish Dialectology.
Taras Lukach, German Linguistics.
John J. Meryman, Psychology.
G. Kingsley Noble, Anthropological Linguistics, Phonology.
Jack L. Ray, Theories of Meaning.
Michael F. Schmidt, Philosophy of Language.
J. Reid Scott, Spanish Phonology.
Frances Underwood, Anthropology.

Support Available

One graduate assistantship is available for continuing graduate student. Stipend averages $130 a month ($1,170/year).

Academic Calendar 1974-1975

Fall Semester: September 5 - December 20; Spring Semester: January 17 - May 23; Summer Session: June - August. Deadline: Open.

DESCRIPTIVE MATERIAL: Write: Admissions Office, San Jose State University, 125 South Seventh Street, San Jose, California 95192.

UNIVERSITY OF SOUTH FLORIDA   Tampa, Florida 33620   Tel. (813) 974-2446

Department of Linguistics
Roger W. Cole, Chairman
Degrees: BA in Anthropology, Foreign Languages, English with concentration in
      linguistics; MA in linguistics. Degrees Granted 1972-73: 8 BA, 4 MA.
      Majors: 72g. In Residence: 18g, 40u.

Undergraduate programs provide for a linguistics concentration with degree programs in Anthropology, Foreign Languages, or English. There is no BA in Linguistics as such.
   The graduate program permits complete specialization in Linguistics leading to the MA degree. The core provides courses in the usual phases of linguistic theory and practice (generally a generative orientation, with emphasis upon current trends), historical linguistics, and research methodology.
   The 1975 Linguistic Institute will be held on the campus from June 23 to August 29, 1975.

COURSE OFFERINGS

Introductory, 3; Phonology, 1; Theoretical Models, 4; Semantics & Logic, 2; Sociolinguistics, 2; Field Methods, 1; Applied Lx., 1; Psycholinguistics, 3; Historical Linguistics, 4; History of Linguistics, 1; Linguistics & Literature, 2; Language Pedagogy, 1.

UNCOMMONLY-TAUGHT LANGUAGES

Akkadian (g2)	Czech (g1)	Ancient Hebrew	Japanese (u2)
Arabic (u2)	Dutch (u2)	(u4)	Polish (u2)
Bulgarian (g1)	Old English (g2)	Mod. Hebrew (u2)	Sanskrit (g2)
Chinese (u1)	Mod. Greek (u2)	Hindi (u2)	Old Church Slavic
			(g2)

STAFF

John P. Broderick (Ph.D., Georgetown; Asst Prof) General Linguistics, Spanish
    Linguistics.
Jacob C. Caflisch (Ph.D., Indiana; Asst Prof) General Linguistics, Slavics.
Roger W. Cole (Ph.D., Auburn, Assoc Prof) General Linguistics, Psycholinguistics.
Ruth M. Dudley (Ph.D., SUNY Buffalo, Interim Rsch. Asst Prof) General Linguistics,
    Amerindian (1/3 time).
Albert M. Gessman (Ph.D., Vienna, Prof) Historical-Comparative Linguistics, Ro-
    mance, Indo-European.
Robert C. O'Hara (MA, Louisville; Prof) General Linguistics, Sociolinguistics,
    English Language.
Thomas A. Sebeok (Ph.D., Princeton; Distinguished Visiting Prof) General Lin-
    guistics, Semiotics (Quarter II, 1975).

Linguists in other Departments or Schools

Edward J. Neugaard (Ph.D., North Carolina; Assoc Prof) Romance Linguistics.
Malory Iles (Ph.D., Florida; Asst Prof) Experimental Phonetics.
Stuart I. Ritterman (Ph.D., Case-Western Reserve, Assoc Prof) Sociolinguistics,
    Psycholinguistics.
Charles E. Scruggs (Ph.D., Kentucky, Assoc Prof) French Linguistics.
Suart Silverman (Ph.D., Yeshiva, Assoc Prof) Psycholinguistics, Sociolinguistics,
    Pedagogical Applications.
J. Jerome Smith (Ph.D., Arizona; Asst Prof) Anthropological Linguistics.

Support Available

University Scholar Fellowships ($3600); Graduate Council Fellowships ($4000). Deadline:
March 1, 1975. Some teaching and research assistantships offered by the Department.

Academic Calendar 1974-1975

Fall Quarter: September - December; Winter Quarter: January - March; Spring Quarter:
March - May; Summer Session: 1975 Linguistics Institute to be here June 23 - August
29. Deadline: August 15.

DESCRIPTIVE MATERIAL: Write: Office of Graduate Admissions, University of South
                       Florida, Tampa, Florida 33620.

UNIVERSITY OF SOUTHERN CALIFORNIA   Los Angeles, California 90007
Tel. (213) 746-2003

Department of Linguistics
Edward Finegan, Chairman
Degrees: BA, MA, Ph.D., MA in Applied Linguistics, Ph.D. in Applied Linguistics.
        Degrees Granted 1972-73: 9 MA, 5 Ph.D. Majors: 45g. In Residence:
        40g, 12u.

The undergraduate program offers a full range of courses providing an excellent background for graduate or professional study in Anthropology, Foreign Languages, Law,
Linguistics, Philosophy, and Speech Communication.
    The graduate program offers a balanced curriculum in both theory and data analysis.
A full range of courses are offered in linguistic theory with emphasis on current issues
in syntax, semantics, and phonology. Courses in field methods dealing with unfamiliar
languages as well asurban minority dialects and sociolinguistic phenomena are also available. Specializations include applied linguistics, sociolinguistics, psycholinguistics,
African linguistics, Japanese linguistics, Slavic linguistics, and Romance linguistics.

Facilities include the American Language Institute, Communicative Disorders Clinics, Japanese Linguistics Workshop, East Asian Studies Center, Language Laboratories featuring computer aided instruction; student exchange program with UCLA; library privilege at UCLA and California Institute of Technology.

Departmental publications: <u>Southern California Occasional Papers in Linguistics</u>, <u>Papers in Japanese Linguistics</u>.

COURSE OFFERINGS

Introductory, 4; Phonology, 6; Theoretical Models, 6; Semantics & Logic, 4; Sociolinguistics, 7; Field Methods, 1; Applied Ling., 2; Psycholinguistics, 9; Math. & Comp. Linguistics, 2; Historical Linguistics, 4; History of Linguistics, 1; Language Pedagogy, 5. Language Areas: Slavic 1, Comp. Gmc. 1, Comp. Rom. 1, Comp. Slavic 2, Japanese 4, Chinese 2, OE 1, ME 1, French 2, German 1, Russian 4, Spanish 2.

STAFF

Eugene J. Briere (Ph.D., Washington, 1964; Assoc Prof) Psycholinguistics, Applied Linguistics.

Fraida Dubin (Ph.D., UCLA, 1971; Lecturer) Sociolinguistics, Bilingualism (part-time).

Gilles R. Fauconnier (Ph.D., California at San Diego, 1971; Asst Prof) Semantics, Syntax, Mathematical Linguistics.

Edward Finegan (Ph.D., Ohio, 1968; Assoc Prof) Sociolinguistics, Historical Linguistics, English Linguistics.

James T. Heringer (Ph.D., Ohio State, 1971; Asst Prof) Linguistic Theory, Syntax, Semantics.

Larry M. Hyman (Ph.D., UCLA, 1972; Assoc Prof) Phonology, Historical Linguistics, Field Linguistics.

Robert B. Kaplan (Ph.D., Southern California, 1963; Prof) Applied Linguistics.

Elinor O. Keenan (Ph.D., Pennsylvania, 1974; Asst Prof) Sociolinguistics, Anthropological Linguistics, Psycholinguistics.

Christine A. Montgomery (Ph.D., UCLA, 1966; Lecturer) Computational Linguistics, Field Linguistics (part-time).

Edward T. Purcell (Ph.D., Wisconsin at Madison, 1970; Asst Prof) Phonetics, Slavic Linguistics.

Philip J. Regier (Ph.D., Washington, 1973; Asst Prof) Semantics, Etymology, Indo-European.

Masayoshi Shibatani (Ph.D., California at Berkeley, 1973; Asst Prof) General Linguistics, Phonology, Japanese Linguistics.

June E. Shoup (Ph.D., Michigan, 1964; Adjunct Assoc Prof) Phonetics (part-time).

Linguists in other Departments or Schools

Jose R. Araluce (Ph.D.) Spanish-Portuguese.
Max Berkey (Ph.D., California at Berkeley) French-Italian.
William Brown (Ph.D.) English.
Thomas Frentz (Ph.D., Wisconsin) Speech Communication.
Charles W. Gay (Ph.D., Southern California) American Language Institute, Applied Linguistics.
Seymour Ginsburg (Ph.D.) Engineering.
Mieko Han (Ph.D., Texas) East Asian Languages, Japanese, Phonetics.
Ward Hansen (Ph.D.) Slavic.
Sumako Kimizuka (Ed.D., UCLA) East Asian Languages, Japanese, Applied Linguistics.
William Perkins (Ph.D.) Communicative Disorders, Phonetic, Speech Pathology.
William Rutherford (Ph.D., UCLA) American Language Institute, Syntax, Applied Linguistics.
Carmen Sadek (Ph.D., UCLA) Spanish-Portuguese, Applied Linguistics.
Jacqueline Schachter (Ph.D., UCLA) American Language Institute, Semantics, Applied Linguistics.
Henry Tiee (Ph.D., Texas) EAst Asian Languages, Chinese, Applied Linguistics.
Virginia Tufte (Ph.D.) English.
Dallas Willard (Ph.D.) Philosophy.
Ross Winterowd (Ph.D.) English.
Nancy Wood (Ph.D.) Communicative Disorders, Speech Pathology.

Support Available

University Fellowships, stipend $15,000 - $3,000 plus tuition; deadline for application, February 1 each year. Teaching assistantships in Linguistics, American Language
Institute, and language departments, stipend, $3,000 - $4,000 plus tuition. Roughly
85 percent of the linguistics graduate students are supported by fellowships and teaching
assistantships.

ACADEMIC CALENDAR 1974-1975

Fall Semester: September 10 - January 29. Spring Semester: February 3 - June 6. Summer
Session: June 16 - August 3. Deadline: flexible.

DESCRIPTIVE MATERIAL: Write: Department of Linguistics, University of Southern
                       California, University Park, Los Angeles, California 90007.

SOUTHERN ILLINOIS UNIVERSITY AT CARBONDALE Carbondale, Illinois 62901
Tel. (618) 536-3385

Department of Linguistics
Patricia Carrell, Chairman
Degrees: MA, MA in E.F.L. Degrees Granted 1972-73: 9 MA. Majors: 48g. In
        Residence: 43g, 13u.

Graduate courses in theoretical and applied linguistics are offered leading to the Master
of Arts degree in linguistics or in English as a foreign language. Both 400-and 500-
level courses are also offered for a minor in linguistics, and in English as a foreign
language.
   Applicants for admission to either program, besides meeting the general conditions
for admission to the Graduate School, must have an undergraduate average of at least
3.7 (on a 5.0 scale). In addition, students who are not native speakers of English
must have a TOEFL score of at least 550. An undergraduate background or work experience
in one of the following fields is desirable but not required: anthropology, English,
foreign languages, mathematics, philosophy, psychology, sociology.
   As a vital part of his graduate educational experience, each student must be engaged
in an appropriate research or teaching assignment each term. These assignments vary
according to the needs and professional goals of the student. They are designed to
supplement the formal course work with a variety of preprofessional activities in research
and teaching, under staff supervision. The amount of time required of the student varies
according to his progress, the type of assignment, etc. The purpose of these assignments
is to expose the student to some of the types of activities that he will ultimately be
engaged in after he receives his MA degree. Performance on these assignments is evalu-
ated.
   Toward the end of their coursework, students will take a written comprehensive examination covering the areas of their concentration. This examination may not be taken
more than twice. An overall gradepoint average of 4.0 in all graduate work included
in the master's degree program is required before the degree can be awarded. This is
a requirement of the Graduate School.

COURSE OFFERINGS

Introductory, 2; Phonology, 5; Theoretical Models, 6; Sociolinguistics, 1; Dialectology,
2; Historical Linguistics, 2; History of Linguistics, 1; Linguistics & Literature, 1;
Language Pedagogy, 9.

UNCOMMONLY-TAUGHT LANGUAGES

Arabic	Hebrew (u3)	Persian (u2)	Vietnamese (u6)
Cambodian (u3)	Lao (u2)	Swahili (u5)	

STAFF

Patricia Carrell (Ph.D., U. of Texas, 1968; Assoc Prof) Generative Syntax/Semantics,
   Phonology.
Glenn G. Gilbert (Ph.D., Harvard, 1963; Assoc Prof) Sociolinguistics, German
   Linguistics.
Beverly Konneker (Ph.D., U. of Texas, Austin, 1972; Asst Prof) Historical Linguis-
   tics, Indo-European.
Dinh-Hoa Nguyen (Ph.D., New York U., 1956; Prof) Vietnamese and Chinese Linguistics,
   EFL.
Charles Parish (Ph.D., U. of New Mexico, 1965; Prof) EFL Methodology, Hebrew,
   Italian.
James E. Redden (Ph.D., Indiana U., 1965; Prof) Anthropological Linguistics, EFL.
Raymond O. Silverstein (Ph.D., U.C.L.A., 1973; Asst Prof) Phonetics, Phonology,
   African Linguistics.

Linguists in other Departments or Schools

Marvin L. Bender (Asst Prof) Anthropology.
Stepehen Blache (Asst Prof) Speech Path. & Audiology.
David S. Clarke (Asst Prof) Philosophy.
Edwin A. Cook (Assoc Prof) Anthropology.
Edmund L. Epstein (Prof) English.
Howard P. French (Assoc Prof) Foreign Languages.
Steven L. Hartman (Asst Prof) Foreign Languages.
Dorothy Higginbotham (Prof) Speech.
Joel M. Maring (Assoc Prof) Anthropology.
Dennis Molfese (Asst Prof) Psychology.
Sue Ann Pace (Assoc Prof) Speech Path. & Audiology.
Raymond S. Rainbow, Jr. (Prof) English.
James H-Y Tai (Asst Prof) Foreign Languages.

Academic Calendar 1974-1975

Fall Semester: August 27; Spring Semester: January 20; Summer Session: June 16.

DESCRIPTIVE MATERIAL: Write: Department of Linguistics, Southern Illinois Uni-
                        versity, Carbondale, Illinois 62901.

UNIVERSITY OF SOUTHERN MISSISSIPPI Hattiesburg, Mississippi 39401
Tel. (601) 266-7353

English Department
Marice C. Brown, Chairman
Degrees: BA, MA or Ph.D. in English with special emphasis in linguistics. Degrees
        Granted 1972-73: 1 BA, 2 MA. Majors: 5 MA, 3 Ph.D. In Residence: 2g, 2u.

The Linguistics Program is interdisciplinary in nature and is drawn from the Departments
of Communication, English, Foreign Languages, and other departments offering linguistically related courses. It is primarily designed to undergird careers calling for proficiency in the use and/or analysis of languages: the teaching of languages (including
English either as a first or second language), government service, business with overseas
operation, and the area of international relations. Students pursuing this program
will be assigned an adviser by the director of the program.

COURSE OFFERINGS

Introductory, 2; Phonology, 2; Theoretical Models, 2; Sociolinguistics, 1; Historical
Linguistics, 1.

UNCOMMONLY-TAUGHT LANGUAGES

Chinese (g3 u3)   Choctaw (g3)   Swahili (g3 u3)

STAFF

Marice C. Brown (Ph.D., L.S.U., 1968; Prof) Descriptive English, Choctaw, Dia-
    lectology (1/3 time).
Walter K. Everett (Ph.D., U. of N.C., 1974; Asst Prof) OE and ME, Mod E descriptive.
Giovanni Fontecchio (MA, L.S.U., 1968; Asst Prof) Foreign Languages.
Donald George (L.S.U., 1960; Assoc Prof) Phonology, Dialectology, Communication.
Philip Kolin (Ph.D., Northwestern U., 1973; Asst Prof) English, descriptive.

Support Available

On-campus and off-campus employment, merit scholarships, service scholarships and
loan programs are available. Apply to Director of Student Aid and Scholarships.

Academic Calendar 1974-1975

Fall Quarter: September 9; Winter Quarter: December 3; Spring Quarter: March 11;
Summer Quarter: June 4. Deadline: March 15.

DESCRIPTIVE MATERIAL: Write: Department of English, Box 37, Southern Station,
                       Hattiesburg, Mississippi 39401.

UNIVERSITY OF SOUTHWESTERN LOUISIANA   Lafayette, Louisiana 70501
                                         Tel. (318) 233-3850, x566

Department of English
Frank Meriwether, Chairman
Degrees: BA, MA, Ph.D. in English with emphasis in linguistics.

The foreign language department maintains an audio-lingual laboratory.

COURSE OFFERINGS

Introductory, 1; Phonology, 3; Theoretical Models, 1; Semantics & Logic, 1; Psycholinguistics, 3; Historical Linguistics, 1; Linguistics & Literature, 2. Language Areas:
French 2, Spanish 1.

STAFF

Robert A. Byrne (MA, Tulane U., 1951; Asst Prof) Advanced Grammar, History of the
    English Language.
Frank C. Flowers (Ph.D., Louisiana State U., 1941; Prof) Semantics, Applied Lin-
    guistics.
Donald A. Gill (Ph.D., East Texas State U., 1970; Assoc Prof) Transformational
    Grammar, Historical Linguistics, Onomastics.
Lyle Williams (MA, Tulane U., 1929; Assoc Prof) Advanced Grammar.

Linguists in other Departments or Schools

William W. Ellis (MA, Louisiana State U., 1949; Assoc Prof) Phonetics and Lin-
    guistics Area in Speech.
Virginia Koenig (MA, McGill U., 1942; Assoc Prof) French and Spanish Linguistics.
Hosea Phillips (D.U.P., U. of Paris (Sorbonne)) French.

Academic Calendar 1974-1975

Fall Semester: August 19 - December 20; Spring Semester: January 15 - May 10;
Summer Session: June 3 - August 4.

DESCRIPTIVE MATERIAL: Write: Office of Admissions, University of Southwestern
                        Louisiana, Lafayette, Louisiana 70501.

STANFORD UNIVERSITY   Stanford, California 94305   Tel. (415) 497-4284

Committee on Linguistics
Clara N. Bush, Chairman
Degrees: MA, Ph.D., BA in Human Language. Degrees Granted 1972-73: 2 MA, 8 Ph.D.
        Majors: 43g. In Residence: 25g.

The program in Linguistics is offered in the School of Humanities and Sciences, with
the cooperation of affiliate faculty in the Schools of Education and Medicine. Although
a small program characterized by personal contact between faculty and students, it provides a full range of instruction in general and theoretical linguistics, with emphasis
on the interaction of theory and empirical investigation and on cross-disciplinary
applications.
    The interdisciplinary undergraduate major in Human Language emphasizes the role of
language in man's thinking and social behavior. It provides a broad general base appropriate to advanced study in a wide variety of fields. On the graduate level, specializations include African linguistics, child language development, computational linguistics, generative grammar, processes of language change (including pidgins and creoles),
second language acquisition, sociolinguistics (including language planning), philosophy
of language and universals of language.
    Linguistics sponsors research in Universals of Language, Phonological Archiving (J.H.
Greenberg and C.A. Ferguson) and Child Language (C.A. Ferguson, E.V. Clark), and publishes
Working Papers in Language Universals, Papers and Reports on Child Language Development
and Stanford Occasional Papers in Linguistics. Stanford also sponsors an annual Child
Language Forum. Facilities include the NDEA African Language and Area Center and the
Speech and Hearing Research Laboratories. Occasional special summer programs feature
advanced work in sociolinguistics or child language.

COURSE OFFERINGS

Introductory, 2; Phonology, 9; Theoretical Models, 11; Semantics & Logic, 1; Sociolinguistics, 5; Field Methods, 2; Psycholinguistics, 4; Math. & Comp. Linguistics, 4; His-
torical Linguistics, 2; History of Linguistics, 1; Language Pedagogy, 5. Language Areas:
Lgs. of the Middle East 1, Lgs. of Africa 2, Hausa 1, Lgs. of the Pacific 1. Other
Departments: Phonology, 3; Theoretical Models, 1; Semantics & Logic, 5; Sociolinguistics, 5; Field Methods, 1; Psycholinguistics, 7; Math. & Comp. Linguistics, 3; Historical
Linguistics, 3; Linguistics & Literature, 2; Language Pedagogy, 5. Language Areas:
OE 1, ME 1, O Norse 1, O Icelandic 1, Chinese 3, Japanese 1, Greek 2, Latin 1, French
4, Romance Lx. 1, German 7, Russian 6.

UNCOMMONLY-TAUGHT LANGUAGES

Amharic (3g)	Class. Hebrew	Navaho	Sioux
Arabic (6g)	(2g)	Norwegian (6g)	Slovenian
Cebuano	Mod. Hebrew (6g)	Polish	Swahili (6g)
Cherokee	Indonesian (6g)	Portuguese (7g)	Swedish (3g)
Czech (6g)	Mod. Irish (6g)	Romanian	Tagalog (3g)
Dutch (3g)	Korean	Sanskrit (2g)	Twi
Hausa (6g)	Latvian (6g)	Serbo-Croatian (6g)	Yiddish (6g)
			Yoruba (6g)

STAFF

Clara N. Bush (Ph.D., Stanford U., 1961; Assoc Prof) Articulatory Phonetics, Phonetic Theory, Applied Linguistics.

Eve V. Clark (Ph.D., Edinburgh, 1969; Asst Prof) Psycholinguistics, Language Acquisition, Semantics.

Charles A. Ferguson (Ph.D., Pennsylvania, 1945; Prof) Language Universals, Sociolinguistics, Child Language.

Joseph H. Greenberg (Ph.D., Northwestern U., 1940; Prof) Linguistic Theory, Language Universals, Language Change (1/3 time).

Eduardo Hernandez-Ch. (BA, U. of Nebraska, 1956; Acting Asst Prof) Bilingualism, Language Acquisition, Hispanic Dialectology.

Elaine Marlowe Kaufman (Ph.D., U. of California, Berkeley, 1968; Lecturer) African Language Teaching, African Linguistics.

William R. Leben (Ph.D., M.I.T., 1973; Asst Prof) Phonological Theory, African Languages, Suprasegmentals.

Richard T. Oehrle (MA, Columbia U., 1969; Asst Prof) Syntax, Semantics, Comparative Literature.

Frieda N. Politzer (Ph.D., Columbia, 1954; Lecturer) English for Foreign Students, Teacher Training, Methodology (3/4 time).

Elizabeth C. Traugott (Ph.D., U. of California, Berkeley, 1964; Assoc Prof) Linguistic Change, Stylistics, Grammatical Theory (2/3 time).

Thomas Wasow (Ph.D., M.I.T., 1972; Asst Prof) Generative Syntax, Mathematical Linguistics, Semantics (2/3 time).

Terry A. Winograd (Ph.D., M.I.T., 1970; Asst Prof) Computational Linguistics, Semantics (1/4 time).

Linguists in other Departments or Schools

Herbert H. Clark (Ph.D., Johns Hopkins U., 1966; Assoc Prof) Psycholinguistics, Semantics, Reasoning.

Dina B. Crockett (Ph.D., U. of Penna., 1966; Asst Prof) Syntax and Morphology of Modern Russian.

Andrew M. Devine (MA, Oxon., 1964; Assoc Prof) Latin Phonology, General and Classical Metrics (2/3 time).

James A. Fox (MA, Tufts, 1970; MA, Chicago, 1973; Asst Prof) Linguistics, Ethnology, Comparative Symbology.

Charles O. Frake (Ph.D., Yale, 1955; Prof) Anthropological Linguistics, Cognitive Anthropology, Comparative Austronesian.

Joseph H. Greenberg (Ph.D., Northwestern, 1940; Prof) Linguistics, Anthropological Theory, Cultural Anthropology (2/3 time).

Dorothy A. Huntington (Ph.D., U. Illinois, 1952; Assoc Prof) Experimental Phonetics, Speech Perception and Production.

Alphonse Juilland (Doctorat d'Etat, Sorbonne, Paris, 1951; Prof) General and Romance Linguistics, Rumanian, French.

Kung-yi Kao (Ph.D., Stanford, 1970; Asst Prof) Chinese Linguistics, Semantics, Language Teaching.

J.M.E. Moravcsik (Ph.D., Harvard, 1959; Prof) Philosophy of Language.

Robert L. Politzer (Ph.D., Columbia U., 1947; Prof) Second Language Acquisition, Bilingualism, Dialectology.

Orrin W. Robinson III (Ph.D., Cornell, 1972; Asst Prof) Comparative Germanic, Modern German, Language Change.

Michelle Z. Rosaldo (Ph.D., Harvard, 1972; Asst Prof) Symbolic Anthropology, Linguistics, Women.

Rosaura Sanchez (Ph.D., U. of Texas, 1974; Asst Prof) Romance Linguistics, Dialectology.

Richard Schupbach (Ph.D., UCLA, 1969; Asst Prof) Slavic Languages, Lexicology and Semantics.

Joseph A. Van Campen (Ph.D., Harvard, 1961; Prof) Slavic Languages, Computational Linguistics.

Support Available

A limited number of University graduate fellowships are available, providing opportunity for supervised experience in teaching and research as well as support for full-time graduate study.

Academic Calendar 1974-1975

Fall Quarter: September 23 - December 13; Winter Quarter: January 6 - March 21; Spring Quarter: March 31 - June 11; Summer Session: June 23 - August 16. Deadline: Graduate: (with aid) January 15; (without aid) May 1; Undergraduate: January 1.

DESCRIPTIVE MATERIAL: Write: Clara N. Bush, Chairman, Committee on Linguistics, Bldg. 100, Stanford University, Stanford, California 94305.

SYRACUSE UNIVERSITY Syracuse, New York 13210   Tel. (315) 423-3973

Department of Linguistics
J. Joseph Pia, Chairman
Degrees: BA, MA in linguistics. Ph.D. work is interdisciplinary. Degrees Granted 1972-73: 1 BA, 2 MA. Majors: 10g. In Residence: 3g, 2u.

Linguistics has been taught as a separate discipline since 1965. The University Senate authorized offering the MA in 1969. The program became a department in 1970, and in the summer of 1974, it became one of the units of the newly organized Faculty of Foreign Languages and Literatures, which in turn is a constituent of the College of Arts and Sciences.

The program operates on the notion that language is one of the information processing systems characteristic of Man. There are two ramifications. First, that system must necessarily be examined in the context of other perceptual and cognitive systems and of the "natural logic" by which they operate. Second, as a system language - or our knowledge of it - can be expected to share the properties of systems. These approaches, taken together, ought to lead to some suggestions for resolving some of the impasses which generative transformational grammar has revealed.

The undergraduate program was designed to serve primarily as a component of a liberal education rather than as preparation for graduate or professional school. While there is a year each of syntax and phonology available, the major emphasis is on understanding language as an information processing system. Consequently our courses bring to focus on the classical questions of language and mind material from a variety of fields of study. We find that the emergent systems approach proves quite useful both in liberally educating students and in preparing them for graduate education.

Graduate study begins as coursework leading to the MA degree. Work beyond the MA is distinctive in two respects. First, it is research and/or course and curriculum design. Second, it is multidisciplinary. The University is phasing out departmental doctorates in favor of interdisciplinary or broadly based programs. Students in linguistics enter either the Humanities program or the Systems and Information Science program. In some cases the intellectual substance is nearly identical but the degree requirements vary.

Degree programs are tailored to the student's interest. Currently people are taking cognate work in such fields as philosophy of science, history, theology, logic, philosophy of education, child development, and formal properties of artificial languages. We expect our students to appear in increasingly diverse fields as our student population grows.

MA theses and papers for advanced courses and working papers by faculty are published in Orange Papers: Syracuse Studies in Linguistics.

COURSE OFFERINGS

Introductory, 1g 2u; Phonology, 4g; Theoretical Models, 4g 2u; Psycholinguistics, 1g 1u. Other Departments: Semantics & Logic, 4g; Sociolinguistics, 1g; Psycholinguistics, 8g; Neurolinguistics, 3g; Math. & Comp. Linguistics, 4g; Historical Linguistics, 1g; Linguistics & Literature, 1g. Language Areas: German 3, Romance 4, Slavic 2.

UNCOMMONLY-TAUGHT LANGUAGES

Amharic (g2)	Mod. Hebrew (u4)	Portuguese (u2)	Somali (g2)
Bulgarian (u4)	Hindi (g4 u4)	Sanskrit (g2)	Swahili (g4 u4)
Old English	Japanese (g2 u2)	Serbo-Croatian (u4)	Ukranian (u4)

STAFF

Richard D. Molitor (BA, candidate for doctorate, Indiana; Inst) Phonology, African Languages.
Joseph J. Pia (Ph.D., Indiana, 1965; Assoc Prof) Phonology, Linguistics in the Humanities, African Languages.
William C. Ritchie (Ph.D., Michigan, 1969; Asst Prof) Syntax, Second Language Acquisition, Thai, Japanese.
Martin Rothenberg (Ph.D., Michigan, 1967; Assoc Prof) Speech Science, Phonetics.
Robert O. Swan (Ph.D., Pennsylvania; Prof) Hindi.

Linguists in other Departments or Schools

Agenhendanda Bharati (Acharya, Samyasi Mahadivalaya, India; Prof) Language and Culture, South Asia, Hindi.
Theodore Denise (Ph.D., Michigan; Prof) History of Philosophy, Logic.
Robert Gates (Ph.D., Iowa; Assoc Prof) English Linguistics, History of English, Stylistics.
Thomas E. Hart (Ph.D., Wisconsin; Assoc Prof) History of German, Beowulf.
Anne Howe (Ph.D., Texas at Austin; Assoc Prof) Philosophy of Science.
Jacob Hursky (Prof) Ukranian.
Nicholas Karateew (Ph.D., Cornell; Assoc Prof) Slavic Linguistics.
William J. Meyer (Ph.D., Syracuse; Prof) Child Development.
Murray S. Miron (Ph.D., Illinois; Prof) Psycholinguistics, Acoustics, Computer Analysis of Text.
Patricia Moody (Ph.D., Texas at Austin; Asst Prof) History of English, Dialects, Literary Studies.
Philip L. Peterson (Ph.D., Duke; Assoc Prof) Philosophy of Language, Logic.
Louis W. Roberts (Ph.D., SUNY-Buffalo; Assoc Prof) Classics, Latin, Logic.
Gerlinde Sanford (Ph.D., Vienna; Assoc Prof) History of German, Literary Studies.
Gerd Schneider (Ph.D., Washington, Seattle; Assoc Prof) Teaching German, Literary Studies.
Daniel W. Smothergill (Ph.D., Minnesota; Assoc Prof) Child Development.
James P. Soffietti (Ph.D., Columbia; Assoc Prof) Romance Linguistics, Foreign Language Education.
Joseph Sturr (Ph.D., Rochester; Prof) Perception, Vision.
Steward Thau (Ph.D., Michigan; Assoc Prof) Epistemology.
Susan Wadley (Ph.D., Chicago; Asst Prof) Language and Culture, South Asia.

Support Available

1. Assistantships. For 1974-75 the stipend is $2850 for a maximum of 20 hours per week with 24 hours of remitted tuition. Assignments involve work with the undergraduate program: teaching, grading papers, materials development, etc. No language teaching is involved.
2. Scholarships. These remit tuition but pay no stipend.
3. Fellowships. University Graduate Fellowships. These awards remit full tuition and pay a stipend of $4000 per academic year. No obligations are involved. GRE Aptitude Test scores in the 790's qualify one for the competition.
Federal: The University regularly has a small number of NDEA Title VI awards for students who plan to study Hindi or one of the African languages. GRE Verbal Aptitude scores in the 750's or above qualify one for the competition. These awards pay tuition and

a stipend, and there are no obligations beyond study. Students who hold graduate awards must agree to hold no other remunerative posts during the award period. The awards are not renewable, but students may re-enter the competition each year. Deadline for students seeking support is no later than February 1 each year. Earlier application can often be helpful.

Academic Calendar 1974-1975

Fall Semester: September 9 - December 23; Spring Semester: January 17 - May 7; Summer Session: 1st session, May 19 - June 27; 2nd session, June 30 - August 8. Deadline: February 1.

DESCRIPTIVE MATERIAL: Write: Graduate Admissions, Syracuse University, Syracuse, New York 13210.

UNIVERSITY OF TEXAS AT ARLINGTON   Arlington, Texas 76019   Tel. (817) 273-3161

Foreign Languages and Linguistics Department
Virgil L. Poulter, Chairman
Degrees: MA. Degrees Granted 1972-73: 7 MA. Majors: 43g. In Residence: 38g.

The University of Texas at Arlington in cooperation with the International Linguistics Center (Summer Institute of Linguistics) offers a program of study leading to the degree of Master of Arts in linguistics.

Candidates upon admission or early in the graduate program must present the following prerequisite undergraduate courses (or pass appropriate examinations): introduction to descriptive linguistics, introduction to historical and comparative linguistics, history of a language, advanced grammar of a language, two upper-level intensive courses in a non-Indo-European language (or four lower-level courses), a course in phonological analysis, and a course in grammatical analysis. Up to nine hours of these prerequisite courses may be taken for credit toward a graduate degree.

The program provides for thesis and non-thesis options.

COURSE OFFERINGS

Introductory, 1; Phonology, 4; Theoretical Models, 5; Dialectology, 1; Field Methods, 1; Applied Lx., 2; Psycholinguistics, 1; Neurolinguistics, 1; Math. & Comp. Linguistics, 2; Historical Linguistics, 4; Language Pedagogy, 1. Language Areas: Non-IE 1g, French 4, German 2, Spanish 4. Other: Metalinguistics.

STAFF

Sarah Gudschinsky (Ph.D., Pennsylvania, 1958; Adj Prof) Literacy, Grammar, Phonology.
George Huttar (Ph.D., Michigan, 1967; Adj Assoc Prof) Phonetics, Phonology, Guiana Languages.
William Jackson (MA, U.C.L.A., 1966; Adj Asst Prof) Phonetics, Phonology.
Alvin Jett (Ph.D., Texas, 1954; Assoc Prof) Metalinguistics, Semantic Theory, Historical Linguistics.
Ernest Lee (Ph.D., Indiana, 1966; Adj Prof) Literacy, Phonology, Grammar.
Robert Longacre (Ph.D., Pennsylvania, 1955; Adj Prof) Grammar, Grammar Theories, Discourse Analysis.
Marvin Mayers (Ph.D., Chicago, 1960; Adj Prof) Social Anthropology, Historical Linguistics, Phonology.
William Merrifield (Ph.D., Cornell, 1965; Adj Prof) General Linguistics, Cultural Anthropology, Chinantec.
Joyce Overholt (MA, Oregon, 1970; Adj Asst Prof) Field Methods, Spanish.
Charles Peck (Ph.D., Michigan, 1963; Adj Assoc Prof) Phonetics, New Guinea Languages.

Virgil Poulter (Ph.D., L.S.U., 1973; Assoc Prof) Phonology, Spanish Philology, Spanish Phonology.
Frank Robbins (Ph.D., Cornell, 1965; Adj Assoc Prof) Field Methods, Chinantec.
Lenard Studerus (Ph.D., Colorado, 1974; Visiting Asst Prof) Survey Descriptive Linguistics, Spanish Linguistics.
David Thomas (Ph.D., Pennsylvania, 1967; Adj Assoc Prof) Grammar Theory, Field Methods, Philippine Languages.

Linguists in other Departments or Schools

Duane Martin (Ph.D., Minnesota, 1955; Assoc Prof) Psycholinguistics.
Ernestine Sewell (Ph.D., T.C.U., 1968; Assoc Prof) History and Development of English.

Support Available

Some Graduate Teaching Assistantships are available in Linguistics for persons qualified to teach beginning courses in Chinese, Japanese, Portuguese, Russian, Latin, Greek, or English as a Foreign Language. Stipends are $2700 per academic year for teaching two sections. Applications are considered in April.

Some tuition scholarships are available in linguistics for qualified graduate students in the amount of $200 per semester or more. Applications should be submitted to the department chairman at the same time the application to graduate school is submitted.

Academic Calendar 1974-1975

Fall Semester: August 28 - December 20; Spring Semester: January 15 - May 16; Summer Session: May 30 - July 10; July 11 - August 12. Deadline: 60 days prior to beginning of semester.

DESCRIPTIVE MATERIAL: Write: Director of Admissions, The University of Texas at Arlington, Arlington, Texas 76019.

UNIVERSITY OF TEXAS AT AUSTIN   Austin, Texas 78712   Tel. (512) 471-5946

Department of Linguistics
Robert T. Harms, Chairman
Degrees: BA, MA, Ph.D. Degrees Granted 1972-73: 4 BA, 4 MA, 10 Ph.D. Majors:
        70g. In Residence: 61g, 33u.

The undergraduate major program provides a full range of courses, including both grammatical theory and work in a wide range of special topics.

The graduate program consists of a core program including phonological theory, grammatical theory, semantics, experimental phonetics and historical linguistics leading to the MA or Ph.D. Admission to the program does not require previous specialization in linguistics. Doctoral work is provided in a number of tracks: phonology, syntax and semantics, phonetics, historical linguistics, sociolinguistics, language acquisition and Indo-European; other programs of study may be set up by petition. (The program in applied linguistics is under the direction of the Foreign Language Education Center.)

Facilities include extensive library holdings in all areas of linguistics. The Department also maintains its own reference library. A modern phonetics laboratory allows for advanced research in experimental phonetics.

COURSE OFFERINGS

Introductory, 1; Phonology, 9; Theoretical Models, 8; Semantics & Logic, 3; Sociolinguistics, 7; Psycholinguistics, 4; Historical Linguistics, 5; History of Linguistics, 2; Linguistics & Literature, 2; Language Pedagogy, 2; Applied Linguistics, 3. Language Areas: MidEast 1, Gmc. 1, Latin & Italic 1, Arabic 3, Chinese 1, Hindi 1, Klamath 1, Russian 1, Japanese 1, Turkish 1, Dravidian 2, Sanskrit 1. Other Departments: Introductory, 3; Phonology, 9; Theoretical Models, 4; Semantics & Logic, 1; Sociolinguistics, 14; Dialectology, 6; Field Methods, 1; Psycholinguistics, 10; Neurolinguistics, 2; Math. & Comp. Linguistics, 2; Historical Linguistics, 8; History of Linguistics, 2; Language Pedagogy, 5; Applied Linguistics, 1. Language Areas: Gmc. 6, Latin & Italic 4, Arabic 8, Chinese 5, Hindi 3, Japanese 4, Middle America 1, South America 1, Mayan 1, Sanskrit 1, Greek 1, French 8, Italian 1, German 16, Dravidian 1, Bantu 1, Hebrew 5, Persian 2, Swahili 1, Czech 1, Russian 4, OCS 1, Slavic 3, Serbo-Croatian 1, Portuguese 10, Spanish 15.

UNCOMMONLY-TAUGHT LANGUAGES

Mod. Arabic (g2 u4)	Class. Chinese (u1)	Mod. Japanese (u5)	Quechua (g3)
Class. Arabic (g2)	Czech (u4)	Class. Japanese (g1)	Sanskrit (u4)
Cairo Arabic (g2)	Dutch (u4)	Mayan (g1)	Serbo-Croatian (u2)
Mod. Chinese (u7)	Mod. Greek (u5)	Norwegian (u4)	Swahili (u6)
	Mod. Israeli Hebrew (u7)	Persian (u4)	Swedish (u4)
	Hindi (u5)	Portuguese (u8)	Yiddish (u4)

STAFF

C. L. Baker (Ph.D., Harvard, 1968; Assoc Prof) Syntax.

Aaron Bar-Adon (Ph.D., Hebrew University, Jerusalem, Israel, 1959; Prof) Hebrew Language and Child Language (1/2 time).

Arlene Berman (Ph.D., Harvard, 1973; Asst Prof) Syntax.

John G. Bordie (Ph.D., U. of Texas, 1958; Prof) Applied Linguistics.

David DeCamp (Ph.D., U. of California, Berkeley, 1953; Prof) Sociolinguistics, English Grammar and Creoles (2/3 time). On leave.

Robert T. Harms (Ph.D., U. of Chicago, 1960; Prof) Phonology, Historical Linguistics, Uralic Languages.

A. A. Hill (Ph.D., Yale, 1927; Prof Emeritus) English Linguistics.

Lauri Karttunen (Ph.D., Indiana U., 1969; Assoc Prof) Syntax, Semantics.

Robert D. King (Ph.D., U. of Wisconsin, 1965; Prof) Phonology, Historical Linguistics.

W. P. Lehmann (Ph.D., U. of Wisconsin, 1941; Ashbel Smith Prof) Indo-European Linguistics, Historical Linguistics.

Peter F. MacNeilage (Ph.D., McGill U., 1962; Prof) Experimental Phonetics, Psycholinguistics (1/2 time).

Larry Nessly (Ph.D., U. of Michigan, 1974; Asst Prof) Phonology, Sociolinguistics.

P. Stanley Peters (SB, Massachusetts Institute of Technology, 1963; Assoc Prof) Mathematical Linguistics, Grammatical Theory.

Edgar C. Polome (Ph.D., Free U. of Brussels, 1949; Prof) Indo-European Linguistics.

Susan F. Schmerling (Ph.D., U. of Illinois, 1973; Asst Prof) Syntax, English Stress.

Royal J. Skousen (Ph.D., U. of Illinois, 1972; Asst Prof) Phonology, Language Acquisition.

Carlota S. Smith (Ph.D., U. of Pennsylvania, 1967; Assoc Prof) English Syntax, Psycholinguistics.

Harvey M. Sussman (Ph.D., U. of Wisconsin, 1970; Asst Prof) Psycholinguistics, Behavioral Cybernetics, Speech Science (1/2 time).

Linda K. Thomas (Ph.D., U. of Massachusetts, 1974; Asst Prof) Phonology, Slavic Linguistics (1/3 time).

Robert E. Wall (Ph.D., Harvard, 1961; Assoc Prof) Syntax, Mathematical Linguistics.

Robin B. White (Ph.D., U. of Washington, 1972; Asst Prof) Phonology, Historical Linguistics.

Sian L. Yen (Ph.D., U. of Illinois, 1965; Assoc Prof) Historical Linguistics, Sino-Japanese Linguistics.

Linguists in other Departments or Schools

Peter F. Abboud (Assoc Prof) Oriental and African Languages.
Lawrence J. Banchero (Asst Prof) English.
Ben Blount (Asst Prof) Anthropology.
Thomas Cable (Assoc Prof) English.
Donald J. Foss (Assoc Prof) Psychology.
Philip B. Gough (Prof) Psychology.
Ernest F. Haden (Prof) French, Italian.
David T. Hakes (Assoc Prof) Psychology.
Ian F. Hancock (Asst Prof) English.
Fritz Hensey (Assoc Prof) Spanish, Portuguese.
M. A. Jazayery (Prof) Oriental and African Languages.
S. M. Katre (Prof) Oriental and African Languages.
Mark Long (Asst Prof) French, Italian.
Marta Lujan (Asst Prof) Spanish, Portuguese.
Arthur Norman (Assoc Prof) English.
Thomas J. O'Hare (Assoc Prof) German.
Andrew Rogers (Inst) English.
Mary Sanches (Asst Prof) Anthropology.
Joel Sherzer (Asst Prof) Anthropology.
Andree Sjoberg (Assoc Prof) Oriental and African Languages.
James H. Sledd (Prof) English.
Brian M. Stross (Asst Prof) Anthropology.
Karla Trnka (Asst Prof) Slavic Languages.
Gary N. Underwood (Asst Prof) English.
Herman H. Van Olphen (Asst Prof) Oriental and African Languages.
Charlotte Webb (Asst Prof) Anthropology.
John Weinstock (Assoc Prof) German.
Stanley N. Werbow (Prof) German.

Support Available

University Fellowships ($3000 for academic year, not including tuition and fees; deadline February 1; nonrenewable); have been extremely limited. In the past few years at most two graduate students have received these.

Teaching Assistantships ($3000-$3500 for two semesters; deadline April 15). The Department has only 4-5 TA positions. We generally require the Ph.D. qualifying exam for these. They may be held only one year.

Research assistantships and work in the departmental library provide limited support for only a handful of students. Those who can qualify for federal "work-study" aid can generally be hired within the Department.

Academic Calendar 1974-1975

Fall Semester: August 27 - December 21; Spring Semester: January 8 - May 14; Summer Session: June 3 - July 13, July 15 - August 22. Deadline: 60 days prior to registration for the semester (or summer session) in which a student wishes to begin (former UT students may apply up to 30 days prior to the semester).

DESCRIPTIVE MATERIAL: Write: Department of Linguistics, University of Texas at Austin, Calhoun Hall 501, Austin, Texas 78712.

UNIVERSITY OF TEXAS AT EL PASO   El Paso, Texas 79968   Tel. (915) 747-5767

Department of Linguistics
Ray Past, Chairman
Degrees: MA in Applied English Linguistics. Degrees Granted 1972-73: 4 BA, 3 MA.
      Majors: 20g. In Residence: 20u.

The undergraduate program is probably standard, except that perhaps more emphasis is
given to Spanish than is generally found elsewhere. This is owing to the University's
location on the Mexican border, in a bilingual community. Also readily available for
students in both the graduate and undergraduate programs are a number of Amerindian
languages. Today the El Paso Southwest is placing much emphasis on bilingual education;
the program at U. T. El Paso has long been interested in it and offered courses in the
area.
      U. T. El Paso has a sizeable and growing ESL program for foreign students, providing
practical experience for a number of graduate students.

COURSE OFFERINGS

Introductory, 1; Phonology, 1; Theoretical Models, 4; Sociolinguistics, 2; Dialectology,
1; Psycholinguistics, 2; Math. & Comp. Linguistics, 1; Historical Linguistics, 2; History
of Linguistics, 1; Linguistics & Literature, 1; Language Pedagogy, 3. Language Areas:
Spanish 4, Amerindian lgs., Swahili 1, Japanese 1, Mandarin 1, Tarahumara. Applied
Lx.: Lx. in The Classroom.

STAFF

Edward L. Blansitt (Ph.D., U. T. Austin, 1963; Prof) Phonological Analysis, Lin-
   guistic Field Methods, Amerindian Linguistics.
Lurline H. Coltharp (Ph.D., U. T. Austin, 1964; Prof) Historical Linguistics,
   Dialectology, English as a Second Language.
Eleanor G. Cotton (Ph.D., U. of New Mexico, 1973; Asst Prof) Language Acquisition,
   English as a Second Language.
Charles G. Elerick (Ph.D., U. T. Austin, 1972; Asst Prof) Phonology, Generative
   Grammar, Semantics.
Diana S. Natalicio (Ph.D., U. of Texas at Austin, 1970; Assoc Prof) Psycholinguistics,
   Contrastive Linguistics, Ibero-Romance Languages.
Jacob Ornstein (Ph.D., U. of Wisconsin, 1940; Prof) Bilingualism, Sociolinguistics,
   Tagmemics.
Ray Past (Ph.D., U. T. Austin, 1950; Prof) Transformational Grammar, Contrastive
   Linguistics, English as a Second Language.
John M. Sharp (Ph.D., U. of Chicago, 1949; Prof) Spanish Linguistics, History of
   Linguistics, Historical Linguistics.
Charles F. Springstead (MA, U. T. El Paso, 1970; Asst Prof) English as a Second
   Language.

Linguists in other Departments or Schools

George W. Ayer (Ph.D., U. of Paris; Prof) Spanish Linguistics, Applied Linguistics.
Edmund Coleman (Ph.D., Johns Hopkins U.; Prof) Psycholinguistics.
Judith Goggin (Ph.D., U. of California at Berkeley; Assoc Prof) Psycholinguistics.
William M. Russell (Ph.D., U. of North Carolina; Assoc Prof) Romance Linguistics.

Support Available

There are a few teaching assistantships available, the number depending upon enrollment in the English for foreign students program. Stipends run about $2500.
Applications should be made by May for the following academic year.

Academic Calendar 1974-1975

Fall Semester: September 3 - December 20; Spring Semester: January 20 - May 16;
Summer Session: June 2 - July 8; 2nd Summer Session: July 11 - August 15.

DESCRIPTIVE MATERIAL: Write: Admissions Office, U. T. El Paso, El Paso, Texas
                 79968.

UNIVERSITY OF TEXAS AT SAN ANTONIO San Antonio, Texas 78285

Tel. (512) 732-2141, x218

College of Multidisciplinary Studies
Curtis W. Hayes, Chairman
Degrees: MA. Degrees Granted 1972-73: 2 M.A. Majors: 5g.

The University of Texas at San Antonio is open now for various graduate programs and
will open in 1975 (September) for Undergraduates. At the present time, we have an MA
in ESL Linguistics pending and expect to be adding more courses and programs at the
graduate and undergraduate levels in Linguistics.

COURSE OFFERINGS

Introductory, 1; Phonology, 1; Psycholinguistics, 1; Language Pedagogy, 1. Language
Areas: Spanish 3, Nahuatl 1.

UNCOMMONLY-TAUGHT LANGUAGES

Nahuatl

STAFF

R. Joe Campbell (Ph.D., Illinois; Assoc Prof) Phonetics and Phonology, Structure of
    Nahuatl.
Curtis W. Hayes (Ph.D., Texas; Assoc Prof) General Linguistics, Bilingualism,
    Linguistics and Literature.

Support Available

Work-study Grants.

Academic Calendar 1974-1975

Fall Semester: September 1 - December; Spring Semester: January - May.

DESCRIPTIVE MATERIAL: Write: Mr. Richard Lewis, Registrar, University of Texas at
                       San Antonio, San Antonio, Texas 78285.

TEXAS A&M UNIVERSITY College Station, Texas 77843   Tel. (713) 845-3452

Linguistics Program in the Department of English
Garland Cannon, Director
Degrees: MA, Ph.D. Majors: 4g. In Residence: 4g.

The graduate linguistics program offers work in grammatical analysis and theory, historical linguistics especially in English and other Germanic languages, applied linguistics
especially bilingualism and TESOL, and interdisciplinary studies such as sociolinguistics, stylistics, and applications to the theory and strategies of rhetoric and written
composition. Historical work in Indo-European, Old English, and Middle English is one
of the specialties. The other two specialties are in syntactic-semantic analysis of
the English language and in bilingualism-biculturalism-TESOL including the training
of future teachers and administrators of TESOL programs.
    There is an innovative sophomore-level course in language and communication which
is team-taught by members of five different disciplines bound around a linguistics center
which can provide opportunity for experimentation in undergraduate interdisciplinary
relations of language. A summer program for freshman Mexican-American students equivalent to the regular freshman English two-semester course can provide opportunity for
research, particularly in contrastive structures plus pedagogical-cultural features.
The regular freshman TESOL courses for international students can also provide

instructional opportunity under direction of an internationally known scholar. Various research proposals are in various stages of review, which may provide other opportunities for interested students.

COURSE OFFERINGS

Introductory, 2; Phonology, 1; Theoretical Models, 3; Sociolinguistics, 2; Dialectology, 1; Psycholinguistics, 1; Historical Linguistics, 3; Linguistics & Literature, 4; Language Pedagogy, 2. Language Areas: OE 1, ME 1.

UNCOMMONLY-TAUGHT LANGUAGES

Czech (u8)

STAFF

Paul Angelis (Ph.D., Georgetown, 1968; Asst Prof) TESOL, Applied Linguistics, French.
Garland Cannon (Ph.D., Texas, 1954; Prof) Structure of Present-Day English, Historical Linguistics, Sir William Jones (1746-94).
Chester C. Christian (Ph.D., Texas, 1967; Prof) Bilingual-bicultural Aspects of Second-Language Teaching for Spanish and English Speakers, Tests and the Theory of Testing.
Jack A. Dabbs (Ph.D., Texas, 1950; Prof) Spanish, Bengali, Historical Linguistics.
Helmut Esau (Ph.D., UCLA, 1971; Assoc Prof) Theoretical Linguistics, Germanic Philology, Stylistics.

Linguists in other Departments or Schools

Clessen Martin (Ph.D., Wayne State, 1963; Prof) Telegraphic Speech, Child Language, Psycholinguistics.
William Smith (Ph.D., Utah, 1960; Prof) Acoustics, Psycholinguistics.

Support Available

Teaching assistantships primarily in freshman English for native students, with a slight possibility of TESOL. Stipend of $3,150-3,600 for teaching two 3-hour courses for each of two semesters. Applications desired by late winter or early spring, to be sent to Head of Department of English, Dr. Harrison E. Hierth, with copy to G. Cannon.

Academic Calendar 1974-1975

Fall Semester: September 2 - December 20; Spring Semester: January 20 - May 17; Summer Session: June 3 - July 9; July 11 - August 15. Deadline: as early as possible.

DESCRIPTIVE MATERIAL: Write: Registrar, Texas A&M University, College Station, Texas 77843.

THE UNIVERSITY OF TOLEDO   Toledo, Ohio 43606   Tel. (419) 537-4111

Linguistics Program
Samir Abu-Absi, Director
Degrees: BA in linguistics; Graduate Minor. Degrees Granted 1972-73: 2 BA. In Residence: 3u.

The linguistics program is interdepartmental in the sense that its staff and some of its courses belong to other departments. The courses which are offered as strictly linguistics courses are the Introduction to Linguistics, Phonology, Syntax, and the

Structure courses. Other courses are offered by the Departments of English, Foreign Languages, Sociology and Anthropology, Psychology, and Philosophy.

The undergraduate program offers a full major leading towards a BA in Linguistics. However, most students opt for a joint major in one of the departments mentioned above. Also, Speech and Hearing majors find the core linguistics courses to be of particular relevance.

The graduate program offers a minor area of concentration for majors in other departments.

The Center for International Studies offers areas of concentration which include Asian, European, and Latin American Studies.

COURSE OFFERINGS

Introductory, 1; Phonology, 1; Theoretical Models, 3; Semantics & Logic, 1; Sociolinguistics, 1; Psycholinguistics, 1; Historical Linguistics, 1; Linguistics & Literature, 1. Language Areas: Russian 1, Arabic 1, Romance 1, Spanish 2.

UNCOMMONLY-TAUGHT LANGUAGES

Arabic (u4)

STAFF

Samir Abu-Absi (Ph.D., Indiana U., 1972; Asst Prof) Arabic, Syntax, Applied Linguistics.
Orlando M. Reyes-Cairo (Ph.D., U. of Michigan, 1970; Asst Prof) Spanish, Phonology, Stylistics.
Robert S. Rudolph (Ph.D., U. of Wisconsin, 1966; Assoc Prof) Dialectology, Historical Linguistics, Old and Middle English.
Jacques H. Transue (MA, Ohio State U., 1968; Inst) Theoretical Linguistics, Syntax, Phonology.

Support Available

None specifically for linguistics. For information concerning different types of financial aid available, write the University Financial Aid Office.

Academic Calendar 1974-1975

Fall Quarter: September 23 - December 13; Winter Quarter: January 7 - March 21; Spring Quarter: April 1 - June 13; Summer Session: I. June 17 - July 17, II. July 21 -August 22, III. June 17 - August 8.

DESCRIPTIVE MATERIAL: Write: College of Arts and Sciences, The University of Toledo, 3801 W. Bancroft, Toledo, Ohio 43606.

TRENTON STATE COLLEGE Trenton, New Jersey 08625   Tel. (609) 771-2297

English Department
Henry Beechhold, Chairman
Degrees: BA in English with a minor in linguistics.

Trenton State College offers a strong undergraduate minor in linguistics. There are three aspects to the program: one, basic education in linguistics and methods of teaching linguistics for students who plan to be elementary or secondary school teachers; two, research seminars and independent study in psycholinguistics, sociolingistics, and ethnography of communication for students from a variety of disciplines; and three, a core of courses including history, phonology, grammatical theory, and philosophy, as well as others, organized for students who will do graduate work in linguistics.

The emphasis on education for teachers who will teach young people about the structure and use of language is expressed not only in the course requirements for linguistics in education, but also in the fact that Trenton State College is the sponsoring institution for the New Jersey Linguistic Association, which has as its central purpose the discussion of issues in teacher education in linguistics. Students in the linguistics program may participate in the Association, which holds a fall and spring meeting, and publishes both summaries of papers given at the meetings, and occassional papers on linguistic pedagogy.

COURSE OFFERINGS

Introductory, 1; Phonology, 2; Theoretical Models, 2; Semantics & Logic, 1; Sociolinguistics, 2; Dialectology, 1; Psycholinguistics, 2; Historical Linguistics, 1.

STAFF

Henry F. Beechhold (Ph.D., Penn State University, 1955; Prof) Grammatical theory, Applied linguistics.
William Birnes (Ph.D., New York University, 1974; Inst) Historical linguistics.
Norman Heap (Ph.D., Louisiana State University, 1958; Assoc Prof) Phonology, Dialectology.
Lynn Waterhouse (Ph.D., University of Pennsylvania, 1972; Asst Prof) Psycholinguistics, Sociolinguistics, Ethnography of Communication.

Academic Calendar 1974-1975

Fall Semester: Sept 6, 1974 - Dec. 20, 1974; Spring Semester: January 28, 1975 - May 14, 1975; Summer Session: July 2, 1975 - August 20th.

DESCRIPTIVE MATERIAL: Write: Dr. Henry Beechhold, Trenton State College, Trenton, New Jersey 08625.

TRINITY UNIVERSITY   San Antonio, Texas 78222   Tel. (512) 736-7518

English Department
John D. Brantley, Chairman
Degrees: BA, MA in English with emphasis in linguistics.

Special work is available in sociolinguistics, comparative language structures, and language acquisition and development, also linguistic analysis of literature. Specialists conduct research and direct graduate study in bilingual education and related problems relative to the Mexican-American environment of south Texas. Specialists also have special strength in Japanese language and literature. Third U.S.-Japan Sociolinguistics Conference will be sponsored by Trinity University in September, 1974.

COURSE OFFERINGS

Introductory, u2; Phonology, u1; Theoretical Models, u2; Semantics & Logic, u1; Sociolinguistics, u1; Dialectology, u1; Psycholinguistics, u1; Historical Linguistics, u1; Linguistics & Literature, u1. Other: Studies in Eng. Lg. (g), Studies in Lx. (g), Problems (g).

STAFF

Scott Baird (Ph.D., U. of Texas at Austin; Asst Prof) Sociolinguistics, Comparative
    Language Structures, Structure of Written English.
Bates L. Hoffer (Ph.D., U. of Texas at Austin; Assoc Prof) Sociolinguistics,
    Linguistics and Literature, Comparative Language Structures.
Tetsuya Kunihiro (Visiting Prof of Linguistics, Spring Semester only, 1975) Socio-
    linguistics, Language Structures (1/3 time).

Linguists in other Departments or Schools

Sarah P. Burke (Ph.D., U. of Texas at Austin; Asst Prof) Russian.

Support Available

Graduate Assistantships available. For information write Dean of the Graduate School,
Trinity University.

Academic Calendar 1974-1975

Fall Semester: August 24 - December 20; Spring Semester: January 7 - May 13; Summer
Session: Two- five week terms probably beginning June 2. Deadline: For information
write Dean of Graduate School, Trinity University or (for undergraduates) Director of
Admissions, Trinity University.

DESCRIPTIVE MATERIAL: Write: Dean of the Graduate School, Trinity University,
                      715 Stadium Drive, San Antonio, Texas 78284.

TULANE UNIVERSITY   New Orleans, Louisiana 70118   Tel. (504) 865-5336

Anthropology Department
John L. Fischer, Chairman
Degrees: BA, MA, Ph.D. in Anthropology (Linguistics). Degrees Granted 1972-73:
        1 Ph.D. Majors: 3g. In Residence: 4g, 3u.

Within the Anthropology Department the program is designed to give students a general
competence in modern linguistics. The principal focus is on the languages of Middle
America. Yucatecan Maya is taught every other year with a native informant. Instruction
in Nahuatl will be initiated in 1973-74.

COURSE OFFERINGS

Introductory, 2; Theoretical Models, 2; Sociolinguistics, 1; Field Methods, 1; Psycholinguistics, 1; Historical Linguistics, 1. Language Areas: Yucatecan Maya 1, French 2.

UNCOMMONLY-TAUGHT LANGUAGES

Maya (yucatec) (g1, u1)   Nahuatl (g1, u1)

STAFF

Victoria R. Bricker (Ph.D., Harvard, 1968; Assoc Prof) Sociolinguistics, Tzotzil
    and Yucatecan Maya.
Munro S. Edmonson (Ph.D., Harvard, 1952; Prof) Ethnolinguistics, Quiche and Yucatecan
    Maya, Nahuatl.
John L. Fischer (Ph.D., Harvard, 1956; Prof) Sociolinguistics, Oceanic Languages,
    Japanese.
Francesca Merlan (Ph.D., New Mexico, 1974; Asst Prof) General Linguistics, Trans-
    formational-generative Grammar, Arikara.

Linguists in other Departments or Schools

Ann R. Arthur (Ph.D., North Carolina, 1964; Asst Prof) German, Historical Linguistics.
Paul W. Brosman, Jr. (Ph.D., North Carolina 1956; Prof) Indo-European, Historical
   Linguistics.
Robert Cook (Ph.D.; Assoc Prof) English, Historical Linguistics.
George Cummins (Ph.D., Harvard; Asst Prof) Russian, Theoretical Linguistics,
   Phonology.
Weber D. Donaldson, Jr. (Ph.D., Indiana, 1970; Asst Prof) French, Theoretical
   Linguistics.
Sanford Ethridge (Ph.D., Harvard) Sanskrit.
Frederick W. Koenig (Ph.D., Wisconsin, 1961; Prof) Psycholinguistics.
Thomas Montgomery (Ph.D., Wisconsin, 1955; Prof) Spanish, Historical Linguistics.
James E. Quick (Ph.D.; Asst Prof) English, Synchronic Linguistics, Structural and
   Applied Linguistics.
George W. Wilkins, Jr. (Ph.D., Tulane, 1961; Assoc Prof) Applied Linguistics,
   Spanish.
Daniel S. Wogan (Ph.D., North Carolina, 1939; Prof) Spanish, Dialectology.
William S. Woods (Ph.D., North Carolina, 1948; Prof) French, Historical Linguistics.

Support Available

Scholarships, grants, loans & campus employment are available. Minimum scholastic
standards must be met to qualify. Contact Director of Financial Aid.

Academic Calendar 1974-1975

Fall Semester: August 21 - December 18; Spring Semester: January 8 - May 13.

DESCRIPTIVE MATERIAL: Write: The Graduate School, Tulane University, New Orleans,
                        Louisiana 70118.

UNIVERSITY OF UTAH   Salt Lake City, Utah 84112   Tel. (801) 581-8047

Linguistics Program
Wick R. Miller, Chairman
Degrees: MA in linguistics; Ph.D. in Anthropology, English or Languages with major
         in linguistics. Degrees Granted 1972-73: 4 MA. Majors: 24g.

The Linguistics Program is interdepartmental, administered jointly through Anthropology, English and Languages. The program offers an MA in Linguistics. It also offers
a Ph.D. but it must be done through one of the three cooperating departments so that
the Ph.D. is in Anthropology-Linguistics, English-Linguistics or Languages-Linguistics.
An undergraduate major will be submitted for approval in the next academic year; in
the meantime, a student may work out a college major in which Linguistics is emphasized.
The courses in the core area of the program are offered in Linguistics; the remaining
courses are cross listed with one of the three cooperating departments as well as with
Psychology. The main area of strength is in applied linguistics, English as a second
language, American Indian linguistics, Spanish linguistics and languages in linguistics
of the Middle East.

COURSE OFFERINGS

Introductory, u1; Theoretical Models, g2, u/g3; Sociolinguistics, u1, u/g2, g1; Dia-
lectoloty, u/g1; Field Methods, g1; Psycholinguistics, u/g4; Historical Linguistics,
g1, u/g1; Language Pedagogy, g2, u/g1. Language Areas: N. Amerindian Lgs. 1u/g, Selected
Lg. 1u/g, Aztec 2g. Other Departments: Language Pedagogy, 1. Language Areas: Arabic
1, French 2, German 2, Russian 1, Comp. Slavic 1.

UNCOMMONLY-TAUGHT LANGUAGES

Arabic (g)	German (2g)	Persian (g)	Sanskrit (u)
French (2g)	Hebrew (g)	Russian (3g)	Old Church Slavic
			Turkish (g)

STAFF

Ray A. Freeze (Ph.D., U. of Texas at Austin, 1970; Asst Prof) Uto-Aztecan and Mayan Linguistics, Field Techniques, General Linguistics (3/4 time).
David E. Iannuci (Ph.D., Cornell U., 1972; Asst Prof) General Linguistics, Socio-linguistics, Black English (2/3 time).
Wick R. Miller (Ph.D., U. of Calif. at Berkeley, 1962; Prof) American Indian Linguistics (Uto-Aztecan), Child Language (1/5 time).
Mauricio J. Mixco (Ph.D., U. of Calif., Berkeley, 1971; Asst Prof) Romance Linguistics, North American Indian Languages, Language in Contact (1/2 time).
William R. Slager (Ph.D., U. of Utah, 1951; Prof) Applied Linguistics, English as a Second Language, Teacher Training and Materials Development (1/5 time).

Linguists in other Departments or Schools

Dan B. Chopyk (Ph.D.) Slavic Linguistics.
Charles Dibble (Ph.D.) Aztec Linguistics.
David Dodd (Ph.D.) Developmental and Psycholinguistics.
Harris Lenowitz (Ph.D.) Hebrew Linguistics.
Diana Major (Ph.D.) English Linguistics.
Mehdi Marashi (Ph.D.) Persian Linguistics.
Mary Taylor (Ph.D.) English Linguistics.

Support Available

Very limited support through teaching and research assistantships.

Academic Calendar 1974-1975

Fall Quarter: September 30; Winter Quarter: Mon. January 6; Spring Quarter: Mon. March 24; Summer Quarter: June 24. Deadline: July 16.

DESCRIPTIVE MATERIAL: Write: Admissions Office, Park Building, University of Utah, Salt Lake City, Utah 84112.

UNIVERSITY OF VERMONT Burlington, Vermont 05401   Tel. (802) 656-3056/7

Interdepartmental Linguistics Committee
Virginia P. Clark, Chairperson
Degrees: BA. In Residence: 3u.

Through its Individual Design Major option, the College of Arts and Sciences of the University of Vermont provides the opportunity for undergraduate students to major in linguistics or to combine a traditional departmental major with courses in linguistics (e.g., anthropology and linguistics, English and linguistics). The linguistics courses are coordinated by an Interdepartmental Linguistics Committee with members from all interested departments.

COURSE OFFERINGS

Introductory, 3; Phonology, 2; Theoretical Models, 1; Semantics & Logic, 2; Sociolinguistics, 2; Dialectology, 1; Field Methods, 1; Psycholinguistics, 6; Historical Linguistics, 1; Linguistics & Literature, 1. Language Areas: German 2, Slavic 1.

UNIVERSITY OF VERMONT (Continued)

UNCOMMONLY-TAUGHT LANGUAGES

Chinese (u4)	Mid. English	Japanese (u4)	Swahili (u2)
Old English	Hebrew (u4)	Serbo-Croatian (u4)	

Linguists in other Departments or Schools

Virginia P. Clark (Ph.D., U. of Conn., 1968; Assoc Prof) Syntax, Stylistics,
  History of English.
A. I. Dickerson (Ph.D., U. of North Carolina, 1968; Asst Prof) Old and Middle English.
Paul Eschholz (Ph.D., U. of Minnesota, 1971; Assoc Prof) Dialectology.
Joseph Hasazi (Ph.D., U. of Miami, 1970; Asst Prof) Language Acquisition.
William Lewis (Ph.D., U. of Florida, 1955; Prof) General Semantics.
Jon Lyon (Ph.D., U. of Colorado, 1973; Asst Prof) Phonetics & Phonology.
Wolfgang Mieder (Ph.D., Michigan State, 1968; Assoc Prof) Germanistics.
Kenneth Nalibow (Ph.D., U. of Pennsylvania, 1970; Assoc Prof) Historical Balto-
  Slavic Linguistics.
Linda Rodd (MA, U. of North Carolina, 1969; Instr) Language Acquisition.
John Weiger (Ph.D., U. of Indiana, 1965; Prof) Spanish Linguistics.
Mary Wilson (Ph.D., Northwestern, 1968; Assoc Prof) Language Acquisition, Syntax.
Peter Woolfson (Ph.D., U. of Buffalo, 1970; Assoc Prof) Field Linguistics.
Dharam Yadav (Ph.D., Michigan State, 1967; Asst Prof) Cross-cultural Communication.

Support Available

Scholarships, loans & employment are available.

Academic Calendar 1974-1975

Fall Semester: September 3 - December 18; Spring Semester: January 15 - May 9.
Deadline: March 15.

DESCRIPTIVE MATERIAL: Write: Admissions Office (Richard Steele, Director of Ad-
                       missions), 194 S. Prospect St., Univ. of Vermont, Burlington,
                       Vermont 05401.

UNIVERSITY OF VIRGINIA Charlottesville, Virginia 22903   Tel. (804) 924-7157

Interdepartmental Committee on Linguistics
John T. Roberts, Chairman
Degrees: B.A. with concentration in linguistics; M.A. in linguistics

COURSE OFFERINGS

Introductory, 3; Phonology, 1; Theoretical Models, 2; Sociolinguistics, 1; Field
Methods, 1; Psycholinguistics, 2; Historical Linguistics, 1; Applied Linguistics, 1;
Language Areas: French, Spanish, Slavic, Linguistics.

UNCOMMONLY-TAUGHT LANGUAGES

Arabic	Old High German	Japanese	Sanskrit
Chinese-Mandarin	Biblical Hebrew	Polish	Serbo-Croatian
Old English	Hindi	Portuguese	Old Spanish
Old French	Old Icelandic	Prakrit	Swedish

STAFF

Pierre F. Cintas (Ph.D, Asst Prof) French Linguistics.
James Deese (Ph.D, Prof) Psycholinguistics.
Hoyl N. Duggan (Ph.D, Asst Prof) English Linguistics.
John B.Jensen (Ph.D, Asst Prof) Romance Linguistics.
Robert L. Kellogg (Ph.D, Prof) Old Icelandic.
John T. Roberts (Ph.D, Assoc Prof) Indic Linguistics.
Marion Ross (Ph.D, Asst Prof) Sociolinguistics.
Gilbert W. Ray (Ph.D, Assoc Prof) East Asian Linguistics.

DESCRIPTIVE MATERIAL: Write: Professor John T. Roberts, Department of French
                        Literature and General Linguistics, University of Virginia,
                        Charlottesville, Virginia 22903.

WASHINGTON UNIVERSITY   St. Louis, Missouri 63130   Tel. (314) 863-0100, x 4668 or 4665

Linguistics Area Program
Marshall Durbin, Chairman
Degrees: BA, MA. Degrees Granted 1972-73: 2 BA, 1 MA. Majors: 4g. In Residence: 4g.

Students majoring in Linguistics generally come to the field with a background or interest in foreign languages. They are strongly encouraged to continue this involvement
by enrolling in further language courses and taking up the study of new languages, of
which a wide variety is available at the University. The traditional modern and classical languages are availablbe, including Russian and Hebrew. Among the less usual languages offered are Chinese and Japanese. Languages such as Sanskrit, Hindi, Ucatec
Maya, Swedish, Danish, and Swahili are offered on an irregular basis upon request.
Working with these and other languages, the student is introduced to the basic techniques
of linguistic science: linguistic analysis and description, theory and practice of
phonology and syntax, methods of comparison and reconstruction of protolanguages. At
the same time the student may take courses in other fields which are of close relevance
to linguistics, such as anthropology, mathematics, psychology, philosophy, sociology,
and speech and hearing.
    The Linguistics Area Program offers a small nucleus of courses from which the student
may branch out into a wide variety of associated fields, depending on particular interests. The rationale behind the program is to offer a major field to those students
in the College of Arts and Sciences who wish to study human language and its function
as a science in its own right.
    The Program is able to offer a strong emphasis on Chinese and Japanese. Both under-
graduate and graduate programs through the Ph.D. are offered in these languages. A
student may elect to also study in the Chinese Department, Japanese Department, or the
Asian Center while studying linguistics.
    The Program's main emphasis lies in its interest in Sociolinguistics, particularly
in Pidgins and Creoles. A project concerning the Creole languages of the Caribbean
is under way. Nearby are Creole languages such as German as spoken by the Amish and
Mennonites; French in a nearby community which is a blend of Canadian French, Cajun
French and Early American Colonial French; and a large community of Yiddish speakers.
Study in a wide variety of Native American Languages is also available, specifically
Athabascan, Mayan, and Carib.

COURSE OFFERINGS

Introductory, 1; Phonology, 4; Theoretical Models, 2; Semantics & Logic, 3; Sociolinguistics, 1; Field Methods, 1; Psycholinguistics, 2; Historical Linguistics, 1. Language areas: Japanese, Romance ling., Applied 1.

UNCOMMONLY-TAUGHT LANGUAGES

Chinese (u8 g8)   Japanese (u8 g8)   Hindi   Sanskrit (u g2)
                                                       Yucatec Maya (u2 g2)

STAFF

Mridula Adenwala, Asst Prof.
Marshall Durbin, Assoc Prof.
William Fisher, Asst Prof.
Ira J. Hirsh, Prof.
Randall Monsen, Asst Prof.
Carter Revard, Assoc Prof.
Marjorie Shaplin, Lect.

Academic Calendar 1974-1975

Spring Semester/Quarter: 1/17/75-5/14/75. Deadline: Feb. 15.

DESCRIPTIVE MATERIAL: Write: Dr. Marshall Durbin, Box 1117, Washington University,
                       St. Louis, Mo. 63130.

UNIVERSITY OF WASHINGTON Seattle, Washington 98195   Tel. (206) 543-2046

Department of Linguistics
Sol Saporta, Chairman
Degrees: MA, Ph.D. Degrees Granted 1972-73: 5 MA, 2 Ph.D. Majors: 40g. In Resi-
     dence: 39g.

The Department of Linguistics at the University of Washington offers a program of studies for graduate students leading to the degrees of Master of Arts and Doctor of Philosophy in linguistics. The program is administered by the faculty of the Department '
of Linguistics in cooperation with various other departments.
     In addition to syntax, phonology and historical linguistics, specialized course work
is available in various cooperating departments. Each student is expected to elect
an area of specialization and work out with the chairman of his supervisory committee
an appropriate program of courses supporting his regular work. The fields of specialization regularly available at this institution are the following (in cooperation with
the appropriate departments); Anthropological Linguistics, Chinese, English, Formal
Grammars, Germanic Linguistics, Japanese, Korean, Linguistics and Society, Linguistic
Philosophy, Psycholinguistics, Romance Linguistics, Scandinavian Linguistics, Semitic
Linguistics, Slavic Linguistics, Southeast Asian Linguistics, Speech and Phonetics.
     Before becoming a candidate for the doctoral degree, a student with a masters' degree
from another institution is required to satisfy our Master of Arts requirements, including the written masters' examination. After these requirements are met, a decision
will be made by the Masters' Examination Committee as to whether the student may proceed
directly to the Ph.D. program.
     The Department publishes a series, Studies in Linguistics and Language Learning,
available to interested individuals and institutions.

COURSE OFFERINGS

Introductory, 2; Phonology, 2; Theoretical Models, 5; Semantics & Logic, 1; Sociolin-
guistics, 2; Dialectology, 2; Psycholinguistics, 3; Math. & Comp. Linguistics, 1;
Historical Linguistics, 5; History of Linguistics, 1; Linguistics & Literature, 1;
Language Pedagogy, 3; Applied Lx.; Lx. & Related Disciplines. Language Areas: Indic
& IE 1, SE Asian Lx. 2, Comp. Altaic 1.

UNCOMMONLY-TAUGHT LANGUAGES

Akkadian (u6)	Mongolian (u4)	Swahili (u6)	Turkic (u1)
Arabic (u1)	Sanskrit (u9)	Tamil (u9)	Ugaritic (u3)
Hindi-Urdu (u9)	Serbo-croatian	Thai (u7)	Uzbek (u6)
Icelandic (u3)	(u6)	Tibetan (u6)	

STAFF

Ann Banfield (Ph.D., Wisconsin, 1973; Acting Asst Prof) English Syntax.
Michael Brame (Ph.D., M.I.T., 1970; Asst Prof) Phonology.
Heles Contreras (Ph.D., Indiana, 1961; Assoc Prof) Spanish Linguistics, Generative Grammar (2/3 time).
Frederick Newmeyer (Ph.D., Illinois, 1969; Asst Prof) Theoretical and English Syntax, Language and Society.
Emily Pope (Ph.D., M.I.T., 1972; Asst Prof) Philosophical Linguistics.
Sol Saporta (Ph.D., Illinois, 1955; Prof) Language and Society.
Larry Selinker (Ph.D., Georgetown, 1966; Asst Prof) Teaching English as a Second Language.

Linguists in Other Departments and Schools

Joseph Cooke (Ph.D., U.C. Berkeley, 1965; Assoc Prof) Thai Languages and Literature.
Philip Dale (Ph.D., Michigan, 1968; Assoc Prof) Language Development, Psycholinguistics, Cognitive Development (1/3 time).
Carol Eastman (Ph.D., Wisconsin, 1967; Assoc Prof) General Linguistics, Bantu Linguistics, Bantu Languages and Literature.
Miriam Lucian (Ph.D., Harvard, 1974; Asst Prof) Mathematical Logic and Formal Language Theory (1/2 time).
Fred Lukoff (Ph.D., Pennsylvania, 1954; Assoc Prof) Korean Language and Linguistics.
Lew Micklesen (Ph.D., Harvard, 1951; Prof) Slavic Linguistics.
Harold Schiffman (Ph.D., Chicago, 1969; Assoc Prof) Tamil Language and Linguistics.
Michael Shapiro (Ph.D., Chicago, 1970; Asst Prof) Hindi and Urdu Languages and Linguistics.
Kenneth Small (Ph.D., Chicago, 1974; Asst Prof) Semantic Theory and Logic.
Joseph Voyles (Ph.D., Indiana, 1965; Assoc Prof) Germanics and Linguistics.

Support Available

Teaching Assistantships: A limited number of teaching assistantships are available in the Department (five positions at present). Such positions pay a stipend of $1323 per quarter. Appointments are allocated on a one, two or three quarter basis.
Teaching Assistants give twenty hours of service a week, which includes three or five hours of teaching in the Department's programs in English for Foreign Students or four hours in the Introduction to Linguistics courses. Appointees carry a minimum of nine hours of graduate study per quarter.
Teaching assistantships in English for Foreign Students are usually limited to native speakers of English, and teaching assistantships in Linguistics are usually given to advanced graduate students. However, all applications are welcome and given full consideration.
Fellowships: The University may be eligible for fellowships for graduate students who are studying critical languages (generally these fellowships are limited to students who are citizens of the United States or have permanent residence status). In the past, students in the Department of Linguistics have received such fellowships for study in Chinese, Japanese, Mongolian, Russian, Spanish, Swedish, Tamil, Tibetan and Vietnamese.
For further information about these or other fellowships, one may write the Graduate School AD-30, Financial Aid Division, 1 Administration Building, University of Washington, Seattle, Washington 98195.
Other Financial Aids: For information about other financial aids or loans, one may write the Financial Aids Office PE-20, 105 Schmitz Hall, University of Washington, Seattle, Washington 98195.

Academic Calendar 1974-1975

Fall Quarter: September 30 - December 11; Winter Quarter: January 6 - March 14; Spring Quarter: March 31 - June 6; Summer Quarter: June 23 - July 23, July 24 -August 22. Deadline: April 1 (Fall), October 1 (Winter), January 1 (Spring), April 1 (Summer).

DESCRIPTIVE MATERIAL: Write: Sol Saporta, Department of Linguistics, GN-40, B5 E Padelford Hall, University of Washington, Seattle, Washington 98195.

WAYNE STATE UNIVERSITY Detroit, Michigan 48202   Tel. (313) 577-3034

Linguistics Program
Sol Rossman, Director
Degrees: MA. Majors: 15g. In Residence: 15g.

Students are required to do work in basic theory and methodology and to apply this work to a particular area of linguistic interest. Resources include the substantial linguistic holdings of the University Library, the Computer Laboratory, an acoustic phonetics laboratory, and the abundant field research possibilities of the metropolitan Detroit area. Cooperating Departments are Anthropology, English, Mathematics, Near Eastern and Asian Studies, Philosophy, Psychology, Romance and Germanic Languages, Slavic Languages, and Speech.

COURSE OFFERINGS

Introductory, 3; Phonology, 5; Theoretical Models, 2; Semantics & Logic, 2; Sociolinguistics, 3; Psycholinguistics, 3; Math. & Comp. Linguistics, 2; Historical Linguistics, 2. Language Areas: Semitic 1, French 5, Romance 1, German 4, Spanish 3, Russian 3, Slavic 1.

UNCOMMONLY-TAUGHT LANGUAGES

Arabic (g1 u9)	Mid. English	Hebrew (g1 u11)	Swahili
Armenian (u6)	Chinese (u3)	Polish (u11)	Ukrainian (u7)
Old English			

STAFF

Vladimir Bezdek (Ph.D., Charles U., Prague, 1939; Assoc Prof) Germanic Linguistics, Indoeuropean Linguistics, General Linguistics.
Thomas Z. Cassel (Ph.D., Duke U., 1971; Asst Prof) Developmental Sociolinguistics, Psycholinguistics, Ethnolinguistics.
Tatjana Cizevska (Ph.D., Harvard-Radcliffe, 1955; Prof) Church Slavonic, Old Russian, History of Russian.
Constance Joanna Gifvert (Ph.D., U. of Minnesota, 1971; Asst Prof) American Social and Ethnic Dialects, Bidialectalism in American Education.
Helen Hause (Ph.D., U. of Pennsylvania, 1948; Assoc Prof) Language and Culture, North African Ethnology, Social Anthropology.
Jane H. Hill (Ph.D., U. of California at Los Angeles, 1966; Assoc Prof) General Linguistics, Biological Foundations of Language, Language Variation.
John A. McClung (Ph.D., U. of Pittsburgh, 1970; Asst Prof) Speech Science, Anatomy and Physiology, Acoustic Phonetics.
Alan M. Perlman (Ph.D., U. of Chicago, 1973; Asst Prof) General Linguistics, English Language, Sociolinguistics.
Sol Rossman (Ph.D., U. of Michigan, 1969; Assoc Prof) Modern French Linguistics, Language and Literature.
Aleya Rouchdy (Ph.D., U. of Texas, 1970; Asst Prof) Syntax, Bilingualism, Field Methods.

Gary E. Eugene Scavnicky (Ph.D., U. of Illinois, 1969; Asst Prof) Spanish Linguistics, Latin-American Dialectology, General Linguistics.
Travis Trittschuh (Ph.D., Ohio State U., 1952; Assoc Prof) Historical Semantics, Linguistics and Literature.

Support Available

Graduate -Professional Scholarships (tuition awards) are available on a competitive basis. For information write Dean Frederic B. Burnham, Office of Graduate Studies, Wayne State University, Detroit, Michigan 48202.

Academic Calendar 1974-1975

Fall Quarter: September 9 - December 31; Winter Quarter: January 1 - March 30; Spring Quarter: May 31 - June 24; Summer Quarter: not yet available. Deadline: August 1 (Fall Quarter), November 15 (Winter Quarter), February 15 (Spring Quarter), May 15 (Summer Quarter).

DESCRIPTIVE MATERIAL: Write: Office for Graduate Admissions, Wayne State University, Detroit, Michigan 48202.

WESTERN MICHIGAN UNIVERSITY Kalamazoo, Michigan 49001   Tel. (616) 383-0064

Department of Linguistics
Robert A. Palmatier, Chairman
Degrees: BA, BS, MA in Teaching Linguistics in the Community College. Degrees
        Granted 1972-73: 6 BA. Majors: 14g. In Residence: 10g, 40u.

The Department offers an undergraduate major and minor in general linguistics, an undergraduate minor in one of eight critical languages (in cooperation with the Institute of International and Area Studies. A graduate major (leading to the unique MA degree in Teaching Linguistics in the Community College) in cooperation with the Teacher Education Department, and a graduate (cognate) minor.
    The undergraduate major consists of 30 semester hours: 20 in 5 "core" courses (the "minor" program), 3 in one applied course, and 7 in 2 or more cognate courses. The critical language minor consists of 20 hours: 4 in an introductory linguistics course and 16 in the target language. The graduate major consists of 31 hours: 16 in Linguistics, 7 in Education, 6 in related departments, and 2 in the Graduate College.
    Each summer the Department cooperates with the Division of Continuing Education to offer semi-intensive instruction in the Latvian language (Dr. Valdis Muiznieks, Coordinator) and with the Center for Korean Studies (Dr. Andrew C. Nahm, Director) to offer semi-intensive instruction in the Korean language. Each semester the Department publishes a newsletter, The Informant, which contains one or more scholarly articles by faculty or students.

COURSE OFFERINGS

Introductory, 3; Phonology, 1; Theoretical Models, 1; Sociolinguistics, 1; Dialectology, 1; Psycholinguistics, 1; Historical Linguistics, 1; Language Pedagogy, 1. Language Areas: African Lgs. 1, Asian Lgs. 1. Other Departments: Phonology, 2; Theoretical Models, 2; Semantics & Logic, 2; Sociolinguistics, 2; Dialectology, 1; Psycholinguistics, 7; Historical Linguistics, 1; Language Pedagogy, 2. Language Areas: French 1, German 1.

UNCOMMONLY-TAUGHT LANGUAGES

Arabic (g4 u4)	Hindi-Urdu (g4 u4)	Korean (g4 u4)	Mandarin (g4 u4)
Mod. Hebrew (g4 u4)	Japanese (g4 u4)	Latvian (g5 u5)	Swahili (g4 u4)

STAFF

Hyungsook Paik Chang (MA, Mich., 1965; Critical Language Teacher) Arabic (1/3 time).
Lilia Chen (BA, Catholic U., Peking, 1946; Critical Language Teacher) Mandarin (1/3 time).
D.P.S. Dwarikesh (Ph.D., Chicago, 1971; Assoc Prof) Critical Languages, Sociolin-
  guistics, Indic Linguistics.
Daniel P. Hendriksen (Ph.D., Mich., 1963; Assoc Prof) English as a Second Language,
  Psycholinguistics, Dialectology.
Samir F. Homsi (MA, Western Mich., 1973; Critical Language Teacher) Arabic (1/3 time).
Schiko I. Kido (BA, Western Mich., 1974; Critical Language Teacher) Japanese
  (1/3 time).
Jang H. Koo (Ph.D., Indiana, 1970; Visiting Prof) Korean (Summers).
Joseph Lelis (Ph.D., Harvard, 1961; Visiting Prof) Latvian (Summers).
Walter Mallya (BA, Kalamazoo, 1974; Critical Language Teacher) Swahili (1/3 time).
Lalita Muiznieks (MA, Western Mich., 1970; Visiting Prof) Latvian (Summers).
Joseph N. Muthiani (MA, Western Mich., 1971; Inst) African Languages, Sociolin-
  guistics, Comparative Bantu.
Robert A. Palmatier (Ph.D., Mich., 1965; Prof) Generative Grammar, Historical
  Linguistics, English Grammar.
Rachel Szmuszkovica (BA, Western Mich., 1974; Critical Language Teacher) Modern
  Hebrew (1/3 time).

Linguists in other Departments or Schools

William E. Buys (Ph.D., Wisconsin; Prof) Speech and Lang. Education.
Bernadine P. Carlson (Ed.D., Michigan; Asst Prof) Applied Linguistics, History
  of English.
Michael J. Clark (Ph.D., Michigan; Asst Prof) Speech and Lang. Development.
Benjamin Ebling (Ph.D., Ohio State; Prof) Applied Linguistics, French.
Arthur E. Falk (Ph.D., Yale; Assoc Prof) Philosophy and Lang., Logic.
Robert J. Griffin (Ph.D., Ohio State; Asst Prof) Applied Linguistics, Spanish.
Charles O. Houston (Ph.D., Columbia; Prof) Geolinguistics, Philippine Languages.
Theone Hughes (MA, Western Michigan; Asst Prof) Applied Linguistics, English.
Chester L. Hunt (Ph.D., Nebraska; Prof) Sociolinguistics, Philippine Languages.
Louise M. Kent (Ph.D., Iowa; Adjunct Asst Prof) Developmental Psycholinguistics.
Johannes A. Kissel (Ph.D., Michigan State; Asst Prof) Historical Linguistics,
  Applied Linguistics, German.
Jean Malmstrom (Ph.D., Minnesota; Prof) Applied Linguistics, Generative Gram.,
  American Dialects.
William J. McGranahan (Ph.D., Georgetown; Asst Prof) Slavic Languages, Applied
  Linguistics, Russian.
Arnold G. Nelson (Ph.D., Minnesota; Prof) Generative Gram., English Gram.
David G. Pugh (MA, Chicago; Assoc Prof) Generative Gram., English Gram.
George F. Osmun (Ph.D., Michigan; Prof) Indo-European, Classical Greek and Latin.
Constance Weaver (Ph.D., Michigan State; Assoc Prof) Generative Gram., American
  Dialects, Black English.
John P. Willis (MA, Chicago; Asst Prof) Anthropological Linguistics, Language in
  Culture.

Support Available

A few Teaching Assistantships are available each year for Critical Languages and English
as a Second Language. Contact the Chairman for details.

Academic Calendar 1974-1975

Fall Semester: September 3 - December 18; Winter Session: January 6 - April 26; Spring
Session: May 5 - June 25; Summer Session: July 1 - August 22. Deadline: Graduate: July
1 (Fall) (Foreign students: March 15); November 1 (Winter) (Foreign students: September
15); March 1 (Spring); May 1 (Summer).

DESCRIPTIVE MATERIAL: Write: Un.: Admissions Office; Gr: Graduate College, Western
                  Michigan University, Kalamazoo, Michigan 49001.

WESTERN WASHINGTON STATE COLLEGE Bellingham, Washington 98225

Interdepartmental Program in Linguistics
Robert A. Peters, Director
Degrees: BA in English, Foreign Languages, Sociology/Anthropology with minor in
        linguistics.

Minors in linguistics (general and applied) may be taken by candidates for the Bachelor
of Arts or the Bachelor of Arts in Education degrees. Minors are available in the
departments of English, foreign languages, and sociology/anthropology.

COURSE OFFERINGS

Introductory, 3; Phonology, 2; Theoretical Models, 2; Semantics & Logic, 2; Sociolinguistics, 2; Dialectology, 1; Psycholinguistics, 1; Math. & Comp. Linguistics, 1; Historical Linguistics, 2; Linguistics & Literature, 1; Applied Lx., 1. Language Areas:
German 1, French 1.

UNCOMMONLY-TAUGHT LANGUAGES

Chinese   Japanese   Portuguese

STAFF

Elizabeth Bowman (Ph.D., U. of Chicago, 1963; Assoc Prof) Applied English and Gen-
    eral Linguistics, Salishan Lummi.
Vladimor Milicic (MA, U. of Chicago, 1965; Asst Prof) Russian and General Linguistics.
Robert A. Peters (Ph.D., U. of Pennsylvania, 1961; Prof) Applied English and
    General Linguistics.
Colin E. Tweddell (Ph.D., U. of Washington, 1958; Lecturer) Anthropology and
    General Linguistics, Languages of Philippine Islands & SW China.

Support Available

Federal loans, Work-Study Programs and institutional scholarships are available. Apply
to Financial Aids Office by March 1. Parents Confidential Statement is required.

DESCRIPTIVE MATERIAL: Write: Director of Admissions, Western Washington State
                       College, Bellingham, Washington 98225.

UNIVERSITY OF WISCONSIN Madison, Wisconsin 53706   Tel. (608) 262-2292

Department of Linguistics
Sheldon Klein, Chairman
Degrees: BA, MA, Ph.D. Degrees Granted 1972-73: 7 BA, 5 MA, 5 Ph.D. Majors: 33g.
        In Residence 32g, 29u.

All students proposing to major or minor in Linguistics must consult the chairman, either
in person or in writing.
    Master's Degree: A Master's Degree in General Linguistics is offered to Ph.D. candi-
dates (applicants for a terminal MA are not normally admitted.). The requirements are
18 credits of graduate work with a GPA of 3.25, in addition to the equivalent of the
undergraduate major requirements.
    Ph.D. Degree: Three distinct options are available for those working toward a Ph.D.
in Linguistics: a. General Linguistics, b. Mathematical Linguistics, c. Comparative
Indo-European Linguistics. The basic language requirement, common to all options, is
minimal satisfactory competence in two languages out of the three: French, German,
Russian. Students are expected to satisfy this language requirement early in their
career.

The comprehensive preliminary examination, taken prior to work on a dissertation, emphasizes the subject matter of the appropriate option. Only those students will be admitted to candidacy for the Ph.D. who show clear evidence of ability to do independent work.

Major BA: All students proposing to major in linguistics must consult the chairman. Two options are availabe: (a) general linguistics; (b) mathematical linguistics. Both options have the following requirements in language: 1. Two years, or the equivalent, of each of two foreign languages and one year of a third foreign language, of which (a) one must be a non-Indo-European language and (b) no two may be in the same immediate language group (i.e., not two Romance languages); 2. A speaking and writing knowledge of one language equivalent to that gained in a third-year course in conversation and composition.

COURSE OFFERINGS

Introductory, 3; Phonology, 6; Theoretical Models, 3; Sociolinguistics, 1; Dialectology, 2; Math. & Comp. Linguistics, 5; Historical Linguistics, 5. Language Areas: Quechua 3, Skt. 1, O Irish 1, M Irish 1, Early Welsh 1, Comp. Celtic 1, Hittite 1, Altaic Lx. 1. Other Departments: Phonology, 3; Theoretical Models, 2; Semantics & Logic, 1; Sociolinguistics, 2; Psycholinguistics, 1; Neurolinguistics, 1; Math. & Comp. Linguistics, 2; Historical Linguistics, 3; Linguistics & Literature, 1; Language Pedagogy, 3; Applied Lx., 1. Language Areas: Chinese 2, Japanese 1, Greek 5, German 6, Portuguese 2, Russian 4, Scandinavian Lgs. 4, Spanish 10, Romance 1, Finnish 1, Serbo-Croatian 1, Slavic 1, Arabic 5, African Lgs. 5, Swahili 3, Xhosa 2, Hausa 2, Southern Sotho 2.

UNCOMMONLY-TAUGHT LANGUAGES

Arabic	Mid. English	Hindi	Southern Soto
Aramaic	Finnish	Japanese	Swahili
Bulgarian	Mid. High German	Persian	Tamil
Chinese	Old High German	Portuguese	Telugu
Czech	Hausa	Sanskrit	Xhosa
Old English	Hebrew	Serbo-Croatian	

STAFF

Murray Fowler (Ph.D., Harvard, 1940; Prof) Comparative Indo-European, Classics.
Sheldon Klein (Ph.D., U. of California, Berkeley, 1963; Prof) Computational Socio- and Anthropological Linguistics (1/3 time).
Peter Schreiber (Ph.D., NYU, 1968; Assoc Prof) English Syntax, Linguistics Theory.
Andrew L. Sihler (Ph.D., Yale, 1967; Assoc Prof) Comparative Indo-European, Historical Linguistics.
John Street (Ph.D., Yale, 1955; Prof) Comparative Altaic, Mongolian.
Manindra Verma (Ph.D., U. of Michigan, 1966; Prof) Linguistics Theory, Indic Linguistics, English Linguistics (1/3 time).
Valdis Zeps (Ph.D., Indiana U., 1961; Prof) Baltic (Latvian), Finno-Ugric (Cheremis), Slavic (Old Church Slavonic).

Academic Calendar 1974-1975

Fall Semester: August 26 - December 18; Spring Semester: January 13 - May 15; Summer Session: June 9 - August 2.

DESCRIPTIVE MATERIAL: Write: Office of Admissions, University of Wisconsin - Madison, Madison, Wisconsin 53706.

Department of Linguistics
Marvin D. Loflin, Acting Chairman
Degrees: BA. In Residence: 6u.

The Department of Linguistics provides a program leading to an undergraduate degree
in theoretical linguistics emphasizing the syntactic, phonological, and semantic analysis
of natural language. Courses in applied linguistics are also offered, such as Language
and Society, Linguistics in Education, Urban Dialects, etc. The department also participates in the degree programs of English linguistics and anthropological linguistics
as well as the Language and Literature degree programs. In cooperation with the School
of Education, the department teaches the required courses leading to the primary and
secondary certification in bilingual, bicultural, and foreign language instruction.
The Department of Linguistics takes an active part in fulfilling the university's urban
mission by administering instruction in three urban-related projects centered at the
University of Wisconsin-Milwaukee: the Native American Studies program (John Boatman,
Coordinator), the Experimental Program in Higher Education (Clara New, Director), and
the Spanish Speaking Outreach Institute (Gregorio Montoto, Acting Director). In fulfillment of another need, the Department teaches courses in modern languages and their
structure not taught in other departments (e.g., Chinese, Japanese). A further departmental activity is operation of the Language Laboratories as a teaching and research
unit which offers services to other academic units within the University, to other
educational institutions, and to the metropolitan Milwaukee community. These laboratories are used for foreign language instruction, preparation of pedagogical materials
in languages and linguistics, and linguistic research.
    The Department of Linguistics sponsors an annual symposium on topics of central
concern to the metatheory of linguistics. Topics have so far included the following:
Limiting the Domain of Linguistics, The Nature of Explanation in Linguistics, and Testing
Linguistic Hypotheses. A fourth symposium on The Nature of Linguistic Argumentation
is currently being planned for the spring of 1975. Papers from the first two symposia
are available in print and the third symposium papers are presently being prepared for
publication.

COURSE OFFERINGS

Introductory, 4; Phonology, 5; Theoretical Models, 6; Semantics & Logic, 8; Sociolinguistics, 5; Dialectology, 1; Field Methods, 1; Psycholinguistics, 2; Math. & Comp.
Linguistics, 1; Historical Linguistics, 2; Linguistics & Literature, 1; Language Pedagogy, 3; Applied Ling., 1. Language Areas: Chinese 1, Japanese 1, N. Amerindian 1,
Greek 1, Latin 1, French 3, German 6, Russian 2, Spanish 3.

UNCOMMONLY-TAUGHT LANGUAGES

Arabic (3u)	Mid. English	Native American	Serbo-Croatian
Aramaic (3u)	Hebrew (20u)	(3u)	(4u)
Chinese (2u)	Japanese (2u)	Polish (10u)	Swahili (4u)
Old English		Portuguese (8u)	Yiddish (2u)

STAFF

David Cohen (Ph.D., U. of Texas, 1971; Asst Prof) Historical and Philosophical
    Linguistics, Psycho/Neurolinguistics, Phonology.
Fred Eckman (Ph.D., Indiana U., 1972; Lect) Linguistics in Education, Historical
    Linguistics, Phonology.
Robert Hanson (Ph.D., U. of Texas, 1973; Asst Prof) Applied Linguistics, Compu-
    tational/Formal Linguistics, Phonetics (1/2 time).
Marvin Loflin (Ph.D., Indiana U., 1965; Assoc Prof) Indian Languages of South
    America, Finnish, Black American English (1/2 time).
Barbara Robson (Ph.D., U. of Texas, 1971; Lect) Applied Linguistics, Pidgins and
    Creoles, Phonology.
Jessica Wirth (Ph.D., U. of Minnesota, 1973; Asst Prof) Oriental Languages, Philo-
    sophical Linguistics, Syntax.

Linguists in other Departments or Schools

Sidney Greenbaum (Ph.D.) Stylistics.
Bruce Stark (Ph.D.) Old English, Stylistics.
John Taylor (Ph.D.) Stylistics.
William Washabaugh (Ph.D.) Sociolinguistics.

Academic Calendar 1974-1975

Fall Semester: September 3 - December 23; Spring Semester: January 13 - May 17; Summer Session: June 16 - August 9. Deadline: Graduate Application Deadlines are: December 6 for admission to Semester II, 1974-75; May 9 for admission to Summer, 1974-75; July 25 for admission to Semester I, 1975-76.

DESCRIPTIVE MATERIAL: Undergraduate: Office of Admissions, MEL 262; Graduate: Graduate School - Admissions, PUR 102; U. of Wisconsin-Milwaukee, Milwaukee, Wisconsin 53201.

YALE UNIVERSITY   New Haven, Connecticut 06520   Tel. (203) 436-1862

Department of Linguistics
Edward Stankiewicz, Chairman
Degrees: MA, Ph.D. Degrees Granted 1972-73: 2 Ph.D., 3 Other. Majors: 26 Ph.D.
In Residence: 16g, 5u.

The department offers doctoral programs in linguistic theory, comparative Indo-European, Malayopolynesian, Japanese, and Chinese. Students are cautioned that by normal Graduate School policy they can expect four years of financial support at most, so that if they need three years of course work they should plan on a dissertation topic that can be completed in one year. Students without previous training in linguistics will normally need three years to complete their course work, but those with previous training may need less time.

COURSE OFFERINGS

Introductory, 1; Phonology, 3; Theoretical Models, 6; Semantics & Logic, 2; Sociolinguistics, 1; Dialectology, 1; Psycholinguistics, 3; Math. & Comp. Linguistics, 2; Historical Linguistics, 7; History of Linguistics, 1. Language Areas: Comp. Greek & Latin 3, Greek 1, Latin 4, Oscan & Umbrian 1, Balto-Slavic 1, Lithuanian 1, Tocharian 1. Other Departments: Sociolinguistics, 2; Dialectology, 1; Field Methods, 2; Psycholinguistics, 1; Linguistics & Literature, 1. Language Areas: Gmc. 1, Slavic 9, Russian 2, Polish 1, Comp. Semitics 1, Sumerian 3, Anatolian 1, Chinese 5, Korean 1, Japanese 2, Javanese 1, Tagalog 1, Indonesian 1, Malayo-Polynesian 3, SE Asia 1, Mayan 1.

UNCOMMONLY-TAUGHT LANGUAGES

Akkadian	Old High German	Korean	Prakrit
Arabic	Mid. High German	Lithuanian	Sanskrit
Assyrian	Gothic	Luwian	Old Saxon
Chinese	Hebrew	Lithuanian	Old Church Slavic
Coptic	Hittite	Oscan	Sumerian
Old English	Hurrian	Pali	Tocharian
Mid. English	Indonesian	Old Persian	Umbrian
Egyptian	Japanese	Polish	Vietnamese
Ethiopic	Javanese	Portuguese	

STAFF

Guy Carden (Ph.D., Harvard, 1970; Asst Prof) Transformational Grammar.
Warren Cowgill (Ph.D., Yale, 1957; Prof) Indo-European Linguistics.
Isidore Dyen (Ph.D., U. of Penn., 1939; Prof) Comparative Linguistics and Austro-
    nesian Languages.
Rufus Hendon (Ph.D., Yale, 1960; Assoc Prof) Southeast Asian Languages, Computer
    Programming in Linguistics, Anthropological Linguistics.
Stanley Insler (Ph.D., Yale, 1963; Assoc Prof) Indo-Iranian.
Sydney M. Lamb (Ph.D., U. of Calif. Berkeley, 1948; Prof) Cognitive Linguistics.
Alvin M. Liberman (Ph.D., Yale, 1942; Prof) Acoustic Phonetics, Relation of Speech
    to Language.
Samuel E. Martin (Ph.D., Yale, 1940; Prof) Japanese, Korean Linguistics.
Edward Stankiewicz (Ph.D., Harvard, 1954; Prof) Slavic Linguistics.
Hugh M. Stimson (Ph.D., Yale; Prof) Chinese Linguistics.
Rulon Wells (Ph.D., Harvard, 1942; Prof) Synchronic Semantics.

Linguists in other Departments or Schools

Harold Conklin (Prof) Anthropology.
Franklin Cooper (Prof) Haskins Lab.
J. J. Finkelstein (Prof) Near Eastern Lang. and Lit.
E. David Francis (Asst Prof) Classics.
Howard Garey (Prof) French.
William W. Hallo (Prof) Near Eastern Lang. and Lit.
Alice Healy (Asst Prof) Psychology.
Harry Hoffner (Assoc Prof) Near Eastern Lang. and Lit.
Floyd G. Lounsbury (Prof) Anthropology.
Peter Richardson (Asst Prof) Germanic Lang. and Lit.
Franz Rosenthal (Prof) Near Eastern Lang. and Lit.
Alexander Schenker (Prof) Slavic Lang. and Lit.

Support Available

Yale fellowship, research assistantships, and loans.

Academic Calendar 1974-1975

Fall/Winter Semester: September 9 - December 21; Spring Semester: January 13 -
May 4. Deadline: January 20.

DESCRIPTIVE MATERIAL: Write: Admissions Office - Hall of Graduate Studies, Yale
                       University, New Haven, Connecticut 06520.

YESHIVA UNIVERSITY New York, New York 10003   Tel. (212) 255-5600

Educational Psychology Department
Lillian Zach, Chairman
Degrees: Ph.D. in Educ. Psych. with a concentration in either psychology or socio-
         logy of language. Degrees Granted 1972-73: 2 Ph.D. Majors: 4g. In Resi-
         dence: 4g.

The concentration in psychology or sociology of language provides an opportunity for
training in language-behavior with close contact with students and faculty specializ-
ing in various branches of psychological and educational research and practice. The
concentration requires course work in psychology, sociology and/or education in addition
to a core of linguistics and language-related courses. Students work closely with their
instructors and with each other, receive careful supervison, and are provided with

research guidance and, whenever possible, research assistantships. Recent faculty research has concentrated on language acquisition, language and cognition, bilingual education and language maintenance-language shift.

COURSE OFFERINGS

Introductory, 1; Sociolinguistics, 1; Psycholinguistics, 4; Language Pedagogy, 2.

UNCOMMONLY-TAUGHT LANGUAGES

Arabic (g4)	Judeo-Arabic	Judesmo	Yiddish (u4)
Hebrew (6u)	(g2 u2)	(g2 u2)	

STAFF

Moshe Anisfeld (Ph.D., McGill, 1964; Prof) Psycholinguistics: Acquisition of Grammar, Language and Memory, Language and Cognition.
Joshua A. Fishman (Ph.D., Columbia U., 1953; Prof) Sociology of Language, Bilingual Education.
Vivian Horner (Ph.D., Rochester, 1966; Assoc Prof) Bilingual Education, Language Acquisition, Teaching through Television.

Linguists in other Departments or Schools

Isaac Bacon (Ph.D., Maseryk U., Prof) German, Linguistics.
Irving Linn (Ph.D., New York U., Prof) English, Linguistics.
Abraham Tauber (Ph.D., Columbia U., Prof) Speech.

Support Available

Research assistantships available depending on faculty research needs and opportunities.

Academic Calendar 1974-1975

Fall Semester: October - January; Spring Semester: January - May; Summer Session: June - July. Deadline: September.

DESCRIPTIVE MATERIAL: Write: Director of Admissions, Ferkauf Grad School, Yeshiva University, 55 Fifth Avenue, New York, New York 10003.

YOUNGSTOWN STATE UNIVERSITY   Youngstown, Ohio 44503   Tel. (216) 746-1851

English (Linguistics is a sub-department)
Clyde Hankey, Coordinator for Linguistics
Degrees: BA in English with minor in linguistics.

The program provides, in addition to linguistics requirements for the English major, the option of a strictly linguistics minor for interested majors in English, foreign languages, sociology-anthropology, and perhaps others.

COURSE OFFERINGS

Introductory, u1; Theoretical Models, g1 u2; Semantics & Logic, g2; Sociolinguistics, u1; Dialectology, g1; Field Methods, u1; Historical Linguistics, g1 u1. Language Areas: German 1, Spanish 1.

UNCOMMONLY-TAUGHT LANGUAGES

Swahili (ul)

STAFF

Jerome Bunnag (Ph.D., Texas, 1967; Asst Prof) Transformational Grammar, Generative Semantics.

Clyde T. Hankey (Ph.D., Michigan, 1960; Prof) History and Structure of the English Language, Dialectology, Phonology.

Janet Schlauch Knapp (MA, Michigan, 1972; Asst Prof) Narrative Grammar, Case Grammar.

Robert H. Secrist (Ph.D., New York U., 1965; Assoc Prof) History of the English Language, Graphemics, Orthographic Reform.

Linguists in other Departments or Schools

Dominico Aliberti (D Litt, U. of Messina, Italy, 1959; Asst Prof) History of the Italian Language.

Luba Barna-Gulanich (Doplom Promovany' filolop, Institute of Charles U., Prague, 1960; MA, Case Western Reserve U., 1965; Asst Prof) Russian Phonetics.

Christine R. Dykema (MA, Western Reserve U., 1951; Prof) French Phonetics.

Margarita Metzger (D en Filosofia y Letras Castellanas, U. Jaime Balmes, Mexico, 1973; Assoc Prof) History of the Spanish Language.

Patricia Tway (Ph.D., Syracuse U., 1974; Instr) Anthropological Linguistics, Sociolinguistics (1/3 time).

Allan Viehmeyer (Ph.D., Illinois, 1971; Asst Prof) Comparative Germanic Linguistics, History of the German Language, Pennsylvania German.

Support Available

Undergraduate: Usually partial, usually based upon demonstrated needs; information available from Office of Financial Aids, YSU. Graduate: Teaching assistantships available ($3200 per annum, renewable, but no fee remission), but limited to students in English MA program. Admission to graduate school prerequisite to assistantship consideration.

Academic Calendar 1974-1975

Fall Quarter: Approx. September 19 - December 7; Winter Quarter: Approx. January 2 - March 19; Spring Quarter: Approx. March 27 - June 11; Summer Session: 1st half --approx. June 16; 2nd -- approx. July 22. Deadline: One month before beginning of classes, but increasingly flexible.

DESCRIPTIVE MATERIAL: Write: Admissions Officer, Youngstown State University, Youngstown, Ohio 44503.

UNIVERSITY OF ALBERTA Edmonton, Alberta T6G 2H1   Tel. (403) 432-3434

Department of Linguistics
C.I.J.M. Stuart, Head
Degrees: MS, Ph.D., BA Honors, BS Honors. Degrees Granted 1972-73: 2 MS, 1 Ph.D.,
     3 BA Hons. Majors: 8 MS, 7 Ph.D. In Residence: 14g, 5u.

The Department of Linguistics at the University of Alberta is established within the
Faculty of Science for the experimental study of language phenomena. Programs leading to the M.Sc. and the Ph.D. are offered in experimental linguistics. The department provides facilities for students to specialize either in investigations which
emphasize psychological parameters (psycholinguistics programs) or in those which
emphasize physiological parameters (physiological linguistics programs). In either
case, the current research interests of the staff enable the student to specialize in
problems of language ontogeny and pathology as well as in the normal language functions
of the adult. In addition, a limited number of students may be admitted who wish to
specialize in the foundations of linguistic theory.
   Laboratories are linked to the department's PDP-12A computer, permitting on-line
digitalization and analysis of data signals as well as stimulus generation and presen-
tation. Students also have access to the university IBM 360/67 computer. The instrumentation systems in the department laboratories permit a wide range of experimentation
in language physiology and acoustics, and a variety of subject-testing facilities is
available for psycholinguistic studies.

<u>COURSE OFFERINGS</u>

Introductory, 4; Phonology, 5; Theoretical Models, 5; Field Methods, 1; Psycholinguistics, 2; Math. & Comp. Linguistics, 3; Historical Linguistics, 2; History of Linguistics,
2.

<u>STAFF</u>

Wm. J. Baker (Ph.D., Fordham, 1963; Prof) Psycholinguistics, Experimental Design and
   Statistics.
Ann Cartwright Crawford (BA, Radcliffe, 1962; Asst Prof) Experimental Phonetics.
Bruce L. Derwing (Ph.D., Indiana, 1970; Assoc Prof) Language Ontogeny, Phonological
   Theory.
John T. Hogan (Ph.D., Georgetown, 1972; Asst Prof) Psychoacoustics, Mathematical
   Linguistics.
Mary Lois Marckworth (Ph.D., Brown, 1973; Asst Prof) Language Pathology.
Gary D. Prideaux (Ph.D., Texas, 1966; Assoc Prof) Psycholinguistics, Syntactic
   Theory.
Anton J. Rozsypal (Ph.D., Alberta, 1972; Asst Prof) Psychoacoustics, Engineering
   Theory.
C.I.J.M. Stuart (MA, Durham, 1960; Prof) Foundations of Linguistic Theory, Physio-
   logical Linguistics.
N.R. Thomas (Ph.D., Bristol; Hon Prof) Anatomy and Physiology.

<u>Linguists in other Departments or Schools</u>

Jo-Ann D. Creore (MA, U. of Washington; Assoc Prof) Romance Phonology.
Richard J.E. D'Alquen (Ph.D., Illinois; Assoc Prof) Dialectology.
Eugene Dorfman (Ph.D., Columbia; Prof) Historical Linguistics, Narrative Structure.
Kyril T. Holden (Ph.D., Texas; Asst Prof) Slavic Phonology.
Tom Priestly (Ph.D., Simon Fraser; Asst Prof) Historical Slavic Linguistics.
Bernard L. Rochet (Ph.D., Alberta; Asst Prof) Historical Romance Linguistics.
Gloria P. Sampson (Ph.D., Michigan; Sessional Lecturer) English as a Second Lan-
   guage.
Gunter H. Schaarschmidt (Ph.D., Indiana; Assoc Prof) Slavic Syntax.

<u>Support Available</u>

Graduate Teaching Assistantships and Graduate Service Assistantships are available
on a competitive basis, with stipends ranging from $1,899 to $3,600. Application
for support should be made to the Graduate Advisor, Department of Linguistics.

Academic Calendar 1974-1975

Term I: September 9 - December 14; Term II: January 6 - April 21; Spring Session (6 weeks): May 5 0 - June 13; Summer Session (6 weeks): July 2 - August 8. Deadline: August 15.

DESCRIPTIVE MATERIAL: Write: Faculty of Graduate Studies and Research, University of Alberta, Edmonton, Alberta T6G 2H1.

UNIVERSITY OF BRITISH COLUMBIA   Vancouver, B. C. V6T 1W5   Tel. (604) 228-4256

Linguistics Department
Robert J. Gregg, Head
Degrees: BA, MA, Ph.D. Degrees Granted 1972-73: 12 BA, 2 MA, 1 Ph.D. Majors:
     20g. In Residence: 12g, 20u.

We have five programs in Linguistics: the BA (major and honours); the MA (with or without thesis) and the Ph.D. We are also planning currently to give a Diploma in Applied Linguistics which would follow a bachelor's degree.
    The basic components in all programs are phonology, grammar and historical & comparative linguistics. The optional areas include American Indian languages, child language acquisition, contrastive linguistics, dialectology (especially Canadian English), experimental phonetics, Romance linguistics, and sociolinguistics.
    All programs (except the Ph.D.) may be taken part-time or full-time, and a limited number of courses are offered in night school during the winter session, as well as in Summer school and in intersession (night-school courses, given between winter and summer sessions).
    There are many possibilities for interdisciplinary programs with language departments and with the Faculty of Education. Graduate Students may also specialize in the teaching of English as a second language, and practical teaching experience as available for a limited number of Teaching Assistants in the Foreign Students' English Project.

COURSE OFFERINGS

Introductory, u2; Phonology, gl u3; Theoretical Models, gl ul; Semantics & Logic, gl; Sociolinguistics, gl ul; Dialectology, gl ul; Field Methods, gl; Psycholinguistics, ul; Historical Linguistics, gl ul; Language Pedagogy, gl ul. Language Areas: Romance Ling. ul, N. Amerindian Lgs. ul, Indian Lgs. of the Northwest gl.

UNCOMMONLY-TAUGHT LANGUAGES

Chinese	Scots Gaelic	Lituanian	Sankrit
Old English	Irish	Polish	Serbo-Croatian
Hebrew	Japanese	Old Provençal	Old Church
Hindi	Latvian	Old Prussian	Slavonic

STAFF

Ingrida Brenzinger (MA, U.B.C., 1967; Senior Inst) Comparative & Historical Linguistics, Phonology, General Linguistics.
Robert J. Gregg (Ph.D., Edinburgh, 1963; Prof) Contrastive Linguistics, Dialectology, Phonology.
David Ingram (Ph.D., Stanford, 1970; Asst Prof) Child Language Acquisition, Generative Phonology & Grammar.
M. Dale Kinkade (Ph.D., Indiana, 1963; Prof) American Indian languages, General Linguistics, Field Methods.
Bernard Saint-Jacques (Docteur de l'Universite de Paris, 1966; Assoc Prof) Sociolinguistics, Japanese Linguistics, Language and Culture.

Linguists in other Departments or Schools

Ronald Beaumont (Senior Inst) Germanic Linguistics, American Indian Languages.
Fred Bowers (Assoc Prof) T-G Grammar, Language & Law.
Alex P. Harshenin (Assoc Prof) Generative Phonology, Slavic Linguistics, Russian
    Dialectology.
Thomas E. Patton (Prof) Language & Philosophy.
Nicholas Pappe (Assoc Prof) Slavonic Linguistics.
James V. Powell (Asst Prof) Antrhopological Linguistics, American Indian Languages.
Edwin G. Pulleyblank (Prof) Historical Chinese Linguistics.
Lilita Rodman (Inst) T-G Grammar, Dialectology.
Matsuo Soga (Assoc Prof) Japanese Linguistics, T-G Grammar.
D. Roger Tallentire (Asst Prof) T-G Grammar, Linguistics & Stylistics.
Peter A. Taylor (Asst Prof) T-G Grammar.
Patricia M. Wolfe (Assoc Prof) T-G Grammar, Phonology, History of English Language.

Support Available

A limited number of teaching assistantships in the Foreign Students' English Project
are available to graduate students. Highly qualified applicants for Graduate Studies
may be nominated for fellowships if they apply early (in January) and send their transcripts and letters of recommendation.

Academic Calendar 1974-1975

Winter Session (1st term): September - December; Winter Session (2nd term): January
- May; Intersession: May - July; Summer Session: July - August. Deadline: Before the
end of January (if it is desired to apply for a fellowship) -- otherwise any time up
to August. The academic year begins the first week of September.

DESCRIPTIVE MATERIAL: Write: The Registrar's Office (undergraduates); Faculty of
                      Graduate Studies (graduate), University of B.C., 2075 Wesbrook
                      Place, Vancouver, B.C., Canada V6T 1W5.

THE UNIVERSITY OF CALGARY   Calgary, Alberta T2N 1N4   Tel. (403) 284-5469

Department of Linguistics
Head to be appointed; Ronald H. Southerland, Deputy Head
Degrees: BA, MA. Degrees Granted 1972-73: 5 BA, 5 MA. Majors: 9g.

The undergraduate programme (regular and Honours) requires completion of a set of core
courses and allows for sufficient options to permit specialization in any of several
areas (theoretical linguistics, historical linguistics, TESL, sociolinguistics, Amerindian).
    At the graduate level courses are offered in theoretical linguistics. Students may
specialize in this or other areas (as above) by writing a thesis of a particular topic.
    Special facilities include an excellently equipped phonetics laboratory and a depart-
mental library in addition to University holdings. Opportunities exist to do field
work in native languages of the area (Algonquian, Athapaskan, and Siouan) and in the
majority English-speaking community. Special strengths of the department, in terms
of research interests of individual staff members, include Amerindian, Romance linguistics, linguistic theory and historical linguistics.

COURSE OFFERINGS

Introductory, 3; Phonology, 4; Theoretical Models, 5; Semantics & Logic, 1; Sociolinguistics, 4; Field Methods, 1; Psycholinguistics, 1; Math. & Comp. Linguistics, 1; Historical Linguistics, 3; Language Pedagogy, 3. Other: Lexicography, 1. Language Areas:
Romance ling., Amerindian langs.

UNCOMMONLY-TAUGHT LANGUAGES

Blackfoot (u4)   Chinese (Mandarin) (u4)   Plains Cree (u4)   Stoney (u4)

STAFF

James M. Anderson (Ph.D., Washington, 1963; Assoc Prof) Romance, Historical Linguistics.
Eung-Do Cook (Ph.D., Alberta, 1968; Assoc Prof) Athapaskan, Korean, generative
    grammar.
Albert C. Heinrich (Ph.D., Washington, 1963; Prof) Ethnosemantics, anthropological
    linguisitcs, North America (1/3 time).
Herbert J. Izzo (Ph.D., Michigan, 1965; Assoc Prof) Romance, phonetics, history of
    linguistics.
Terry J. Klokeid (B.A., Victoria, 1968; Asst Prof) Syntactic theory,anthropological
    linguistics.
William C. McCormack (Ph.D., Chicago, 1956; Prof) Sociolinguistics (1/3 time).
Lili Rabel-Heymann (Ph.D., California, 1957; Assoc Prof) English, TEFL, Khasi.
R. Radhakrishnan (Ph.D., Chicago, 1970; Assoc Prof) Language acquisition & language
    disorders, Dravidian
B. H. Smeaton (Ph.D., Columbia, 1959; Prof) Lexicography, Arabic studies.
Ronald H. Southerland (Ph.D., Pennsylvania, 1970; Asst Prof) Sociolinguistics,
    languages of Scandinavia, historical linguistics.

Linguists in other Departments or Schools

Alexander Malycky (Ph.D., Cincinnati, 1961) Department of Germanic & Slavic.
Stephen P. Soule (Ph.D., Chicago, 1973) Department of Mathematics.
Robert X. Ware (D.Phil., Oxford, 1967) Department of Philosophy.

Support Available

Graduate Assistantships: (1) Teaching: $1500 - $3800. (2) Research: $1200 or $2400.
(Both with full or half remission of programme fees. Amount of award dependent upon
the availability of funds and qualifications of applicant).
    Other financial assistance available occasionally from members of staff who have
research grants.

Academic Calendar 1974-1975

Fall Session: 3 Sept. - 20 December; Winter Session: 9 Jan. - 29 April; Spring
Session: 15 May - June 28, 1975; Summer Session: 2 July - 16 August. Deadline: 29
August.

DESCRIPTIVE MATERIAL: Write: The Registrar's Office, The University of Calgary,
                       Calgary, Alberta, T2N 1N4.

CARLETON UNIVERSITY   Ottawa, Ontario K1S 5B6   Tel. (613) 231-5573

Department of Linguistics
William G. Cowan, Chairman
Degrees: BA, BA Honours, Certificate in TESL. Degrees Granted 1972-73: 6 BA.
        In Residence: 58u.

The Department offers comprehensive undergraduate programs including BA with a major
in Linguistics (a three-year program after grade 13) and BA with Honours in Linguistics
(a four-year program after grade 13). Combined majors and honours programs are offered
with other Departments in the University, including Classics, English, French, German,
Italian, Philosophy, Psychology, Russian, Sociology-Anthropology and Spanish.

In addition, there is a special combined honours degree in Russian and Linguistics emphasising professional training in translation.

As of 1974-75 the Department also offers a "Certificate in the Teaching of English as a Second Language." Admission to the certificate program usually requires a Baccalaureat degree, but the program, which involves one year full-time study or equivalent, does not have the status of a Master's degree.

Through Dr. Jean-Pierre Paillet the Department participates in the research programs of the Speech Research Group, along with members of the Department of Psychology and the Systems Department of the Faculty of Engineering. The Speech Research Group publishes a series of monographs, the Speech Research Monographs. So far six of these have appeared; copies may be obtained by writing to Dr. Paillet.

COURSE OFFERINGS

Introductory, 1; Phonology, 4; Theoretical Models, 2; Semantics & Logic, 1; Sociolinguistics, 1; Psycholinguistics, 2; Historical Linguistics, 2; Language Pedagogy, 3. Other Departments: Introductory, 1; Semantics & Logic, 3; Sociolinguistics, 2; Historical Linguistics, 1; Linguistics & Literature, 2. Language Areas: French 7, German 4, Russian 4, Spanish 2.

UNCOMMONLY-TAUGHT LANGUAGES

Arabic (u3)	Old English (u4)	Old Norse (u2)	Old Church Slavonic
Bulgarian (u2)	Mid. High German	Portuguese (u4)	(u2)
Czech (u2)	(u2)	Sanskrit (u4)	Swahili (u1)
	Hebrew (u4)		Ukrainian (u6)

STAFF

William G. Cowan (Ph.D., Cornell, 1960; Prof) Historical, Arabic, Algonquian.
Michael B. Dobrovolsky (MA, TEFL Cert., Pittsburgh, 1966; Asst Prof) Phonology, Intonation, E.S.L.
C. Stanley Jones (MA, Washington, 1966; Asst Prof) Phonology, Theory (1/2 time).
Jean-Pierre Paillet (Doctorat 3e. cycle, Aix-en-Provence, 1970; Assoc Prof) Syntax, Semantics, Eskimo.
Ian Pringle (MA, Auckland, 1963; Assoc Prof) Historical, Germanics, Austronesian (1/2 time).
Elaine Pressman (Ph.D., Ohio State, 1971; Asst Prof) Psycholinguistics, Speech (1/3 time).
Jaromira Rakusan (M. Lang. and Lit. Sci., Charles, 1964; Sessional Lecturer) Syntax, Slavics.
Stella Van Vlasselaer (MA, Ottawa, 1973; Sessional Lecturer) Language Didactics.

Linguists in other Departments or Schools

Florence Cousin (Doctorat 3e cycle, Paris; Assoc Prof) Theory, Phonology.
Jutta Goheen (Dr. Phil., Potsdam; Assoc Prof) German Stylistics, History of German.
V.I. Grebenschikov (Ph.D., Montreal; Prof) Theory, Slavics, Language Didactics.
Pierre Laurette (Doctorat d'univ., Strassbourg; Assoc Prof) French Stylistics, Lexicology.
Alan Moffitt (Ph.D., Minnesota) Language Acquisition.
Sinclair Robinson (MA, Rochester; Asst Prof) Sociolinguistics.
Pierre Van Rutten (Ph.D., Ottawa; Assoc Prof) French Stylistics.
Jean-Jacques Van Vlasselaer (MA, Ottawa; Senior Lect) Syntax, Semantics, Language Didactics.
Janice Yalden (MA, Michigan; Asst Prof) Language Didactics.

Academic Calendar 1974-1975

Fall Quarter: September 12 - December 6; Winter Quarter: January 6 - April 11; Spring Quarter: May 20 - August. Deadline: August 1.

DESCRIPTIVE MATERIAL: Write: The Admissions Office, Carleton University, Colonel By Drive, Ottawa, Ontario K1S 5B6.

Département de langues et linguistique
Albert Maniet, Chairman
Degrees: BA, MA, Ph.D. Degrees Granted 1972-73: 13 MA 5 Ph.D.

En plus des programmes qui mènant aux diplômes, l'université subventionne divers in-
stituts et centres, dont le Centre International de Recherches sur le Bilinguisme (Jean-
Guy Savard, directeur). Le Centre a en cours plusieurs projets de recherche et une
série de publications a déjà paru contenant les résultats des recherches antérieures.

COURSE OFFERINGS

Introductory, 1; Phonology, 5; Theoretical Models, 5; Semantics & Logic, 1; Sociolinguistics, 2; Applied Ling., 10; Psycholinguistics, 2; Math. & Comp. Linguistics, 1;
Historical Linguistics, 3; Linguistics & Literature, 1; Language Pedagogy, 5. Language
Areas: Romance ling. 3, French 18, Canadian French 4, Greek & Latin 1, English 9, Spanish
9, German 6. Other: Lexicology, 5; Translation, 5.

STAFF

Gerardo Alvárez (Doctorat, Professeur invité) Linguistique appliquée.
Lionel Boisvert (Doctorat, Adjoint) Philologie française.
André Boudreau (M.A., Adjoint) Didactique des langues.
Marcel Boudreault (Doctorat, Titulaire) Phonétique générale.
Conrad Bureau (Doctorat, Adjoint) Syntaxe et stylistique objective.
Michele Bussières (L. ès L., Assistant) Français aux nonfrancophones et phonétique.
Sandra Clarke (Doctorat, Professeur assistant) Grammaire anglaise.
Lysanne Coupal-Dorion (Doctorat, Adjoint) Phonétique de l'espagnol.
Jean Darbelnet (Agr. Fr., Titulaire) Semantique, grammaire et stylistique differen-
   tielle du français et de l'anglais.
Gaston Dulong (L. es L. Titulaire) Dialectologie francocandienne.
Elvire Eberthardt (Doctorat, Adjoint) Grammaire historique de l'allemand.
Adrien Favre (D.E.S., Agrégé) Traduction.
Jean-Denis Gendron (Doctorat, Titulaire) Phonétique generale.
Jacque Genest (L. ès L., Adjoint) Phonetique.
Walter Hirtle (Doctorat, Titulaire) Psychomécanique et grammaire de l'anglais moderne.
Cyrille Jauksch-Orlovski (Doctorat, Agrégé) Langue russe.
Marcel Juneau (Doctorat, Adjoint) Dialectologie galloromane.
Bruno Lafleur (L. ès L., Adjoint) Francais aux non-francophones.
Lorne Laforge (Doctorat, Titulaire) Didactique des langues.
Jean-Guy LeBel (Doctorat, Agrégé) Phonétique differentielle.
Claude LeFlem (L. ès L., Assistant) Grammaire française.
William F. Mackey (Doctorat, Titulaire) Didactique des langues et bilinguisme.
Albert Maniet, (Doctorat, Titulaire) Grammaire comparee des langues indo-europeennes.
Geneviève Mareschal (Lic. Trad., Assistant) Traduction.
Roger Maraschal (Lic. Trad. Adjoint) Didactique des langues.
Pierre Martin (Doctorat, Adjoint) Phonologie.
Michael Mepham (Doctorat, Agrégé) Automatisation linguistique.
Dolores Ortiz (Doctorat, Adjoint) Lexicologie espagnole.
Jacques Ouellet (D.E.S., Adjoint) Grammaire française.
Arthur Padley (Doctorat, Agrégé) Philologie anglaise.
Hélène Paléologue (M.A., Adjoint) Langue russe.
Annette Paquot-Maniet (Doctorat, Adjoint) Lexicologie at sémantique.
Frenão Perestrelo (Doctorat, Professeur invité) Portugais.
Guy Plante (D.E.S., Agrégé) Grammaire française.
Roda Roberts (Doctorat, Adjoint) Traduction.
Claude Rochette (Doctorat, Agrégé) Phonétique generale et experimentale.
Jean-Guy Savard (D.E.S., Agrégé) Lexicometrie.
Ilonka Schmidt-Mackey (Doctorat, Titulaire) Didactique des langues.
Ronald Sheen (MA, Adjoint) Grammaire anglaise.
Jean-Guy Ignacio Soldevila (Doctorat, Titulaire) Stylistique et lexicologie espagnoles.
Christine Tessier (M.A., Adjoint) Linguistique allemande.
Antonien Tremblay (Doctorat, Agrégé) Lexicologie espagnole.
Jean-Louis Tremblay (L. ès L, Assistant) Français aux non-francophones.
Roch Valin (L. ès L. Titulaire) Psychomécanique du langage.
Soulange Vouvé (D.E.S., Adjoint) Traduction.

Sylvia Weiser (M.A., Adjoint) Philologie espagnole.
Millicent Winston (MA, Adjoint) Phonétique de l'anglais.

Support Available

L'énumération et la description des differentes bourses et prêts font l'objet d'une
publication spéciale mise à la disposition des étudiants. Pour obtenir la publication "Aide financière", l'on voudra bien s'adresser au "Service des bourses et de
l'aide financière", Pavillon Pollack, Cité Universitaire, Québec, G1K 7P4.

DESCRIPTIVE MATERIAL: Write: Service de l'admission, Bureau du régistraire, Pavillon
                       de la Bibliothèque, Université Laval, Québec, Québec G1K 7P4.

UNIVERSITY OF MANITOBA   Winnipeg, Manitoba R3T 2N2   Tel. (204) 474-9361

Anthropology Department
W. D. Wade, Chairman
H. C. Wolfart, Coordinator, Linguistics Programme
Degrees: BA, MA (interdisciplinary) with minor in linguistics. Degrees Granted
         1972-73: 4 BA, 1 MA. Majors: 7g. In Residence: 5g, 4u.

The Linguistics Programme is one of the basic constituents of the Department of Anthropology. It emphasizes the testing of linguistic theory and the development of techniques
for describing complex speech communities. The languages of Manitoba, both indigenous
(Cree, Ojibwa, Chipewyan, Dakota, and Eskimo) and immigrant (for example, established
Icelandic, Mennonite Low German, and Ukrainian communities), provide ample opportunity
for field work in both these areas. (Students are strongly encouraged to take courses
in related fields).
    Current research concentrates on indigenous languages (especially the Algonquian
and Siouan languages) in combination with computer-assisted linguistic analysis and
automatic rule-testing.
    Research and training facilities include the archives of the Hudson Bay Company, the
University Computer Centre (IBM 370-158; COMIT-II, a Linguistic Data Control package),
and the first-rate recording facilities of the Linguistics Laboratory.
    Research reports appear in the University of Manitoba Anthropology Papers. A detailed
inventory of research completed and in progress is available on request.

COURSE OFFERINGS

Introductory, g1 u1; Phonology, g2; Theoretical Models, g1 u1; Semantics & Logic, g1
u1; Sociolinguistics, u1; Field Methods, g1; Math. & Comp. Linguistics, g1; Historical
Linguistics, g1. Language Areas: Native lgs. in N. America g1 u1, Cree g1.

UNCOMMONLY-TAUGHT LANGUAGES

Arabic (u2)	Hebrew (u10)	Polish (u4)	Ukrainian (u8)
Aramaic (u2)	Icelandic (u6)	Sanskrit (u2)	Yiddish (u4)
Gothic (u1)	Old Icelandic (u5)	Old Church Slavonic (u2)	

STAFF

Haraldur Bessason (Cand. Mag., Iceland, 1956; Adjunct Prof) Syntax, Old and Modern
    Icelandic, North American Icelandic.
Richard T. Carter, Jr. (Ph.D., New Mexico, 1974; Asst Prof) Theoretical Linguistics,
    American Indian Languages, Siouan.
Marilyn E. Jessen (Ph.D., Edinburgh, 1974; Post-Doctoral Fellow) Semantics, Syntax,
    Cree.

Paul H. Voorhis (Ph.D., Yale, 1967; Adjunct Prof) Descriptive Linguistics, Language Pedagogy, Algonquian.

H. Christoph Wolfart (Ph.D., Yale, 1969; Assoc Prof) General Linguistics, Linguistic Anthropology, Algonquian.

Linguists in other Departments or Schools

Language-oriented teaching and research is also carried out in several other departments, including computer science, education, philosophy, psychology, sociology and, of course, the language-and-literature departments.

Support Available

Canada Council Special MA Scholarship ($4,500 plus travel); University Fellowship ($3,600); Departmental (Teaching) Assistantship ($2,000); Research Assistantship (variable, up to $3,600 part-time); Provincial/federal bursaries and loans.

Academic Calendar 1974-1975

Academic Year: September - April; Summer Session: (approximately July 1 - August 15). Deadline: March 1 (July 1) (and later in exceptional cases).

DESCRIPTIVE MATERIAL: Write: Copies of the General Calendar must be ordered directly from: Office of the Registrar, University of Manitoba, Winnipeg, Manitoba R3T 2N2, Canada ($1; foreign mail: $2). All other correspondence should be sent directly to the Linguistics Programme.

McGILL UNIVERSITY   Montreal, Quebec H3A 1G5   Tel. (514) 392-4433

Department of Linguistics
C. Douglas Ellis, Chairman
Degrees: BA, MA, Ph.D.

The programme is designed to provide for study and research in key areas of the field of Linguistics. Course offerings are under constant review in terms of their relevance to the field as a whole, to the departmental programme and to the specific needs of students. There has evolved a general principle that no staff member will normally offer more than two graduate seminars in addition to undergraduate courses, and these will be given alternately. This restriction implies that the programme is built on a) core courses; b) special interests (staff and student).

Considerations relating to both a) and b) are weighed prior to modification of existing courses or proposal of new ones. The goal in all such cases is to bring the student to the cutting edge of research and to keep him/her near it. Where added weight or substance is required beyond that provided by the Department, this is handled through the use of one (or more) of the following: 1) comprehensive evaluations; 2] resources of related departments: e.g. Philosophy, Psychology, language departments; 3) resources of other Quebec universities.

The general tenor of linguistic offerings is necessarily heavily theoretical. As the department charged with the study of language as a phenomenon of human behaviour, our concerns are primarily of an analytical nature and the focus is on questions of theory not related elsewhere.

The Department has, for some time, been interested in developing a programme in Amerindian Linguistics, both in response to increased interest in Canadian Indian languages, and as an area of linguistic enquiry of value in its own right. The analysis of the various Amerindian languages is important, whether as salvage work or as a contribution to linguistic theory. As a training group in analytical techniques for our own students, these languages are unsurpassed.

Facilities include Phonetics Research Laboratory; Redpath, McLennan, Arctic Institute and Faculty of Education Library Holdings; School of Computer Science; Computing Centre; School of Human Communication Disorders; Centre for Northern Studies and Research, and collaboration with departments in related fields.

The Department also collaborates with l'Universite de Montreal and l"universite du Quebec in the publication of Montreal Working Papers in Linguistics.

COURSE OFFERINGS

Introductory, 2u; Phonology, 3g 3u; Theoretical Models, 2g 1u; Semantics & Logic, 3g; Sociolinguistics, 2g 2u; Field Methods, 1u; Psycholinguistics, 1g 2u; Math & Comp. Linguistics, 1g; Historical Linguistics, 2g 1u; Language Pedagogy, 1u. Language Areas: Indian lgs. of N. America 1u, Comp. Algonquian 1g.

UNCOMMONLY-TAUGHT LANGUAGES

Arabic	Estonian	Indonesian	Rumanian
Azerbaijani	Finnish	Japanese	Sanskrit
Bengali	Georgian	Kazakh	Serbo-Croat
Bulgarian	Mod. Greek	Latvian	Slovak
Chinese	Hebrew	Lithuanian	Swahili
Cree	Hausa	Malay	Turkish
Czech	Hindi	Persian	Ukrainian
Eskimo (Canadian)	Hungarian	Polish	Urdu
			Yiddish

STAFF

Irena Bellert (Doc. Habi., Warsaw, 1970; Vis. Asst Prof) Descriptions of Syntax and Semantics, Methodology, Theoretical Linguistics (1/2 time).
C. Douglas Ellis (Ph.D., McGill, 1954; Prof) Field Linguistics, Pedagogical Grammars, Development of Orthographies.
Myrna Gopnik (Ph.D., Penn., 1968; Assoc Prof) Linguistic Theory, Semantics, Computational Linguistics.
Jonathan D. Kaye (Ph.D., Columbia, 1970; Assoc Prof) Linguistic Theory, Historical and Comparative Linguistics, Phonology.
David W. Lightfoot (Ph.D., Michigan, 1971; Asst Prof) Historical and Comparative Grammar, Diachronic Syntax, Linguistic Theory.
Glyne L. Piggott (MA, Toronto, 1968; Asst Prof) Generative Phonological Theory, Historical and Comparative Grammar, Amerindian Linguistics.
André A. Rigault (D.E.S. D.Ph., Paris; Prof) General Phonetics, Acoustic Phonetics: Spectrographic Analysis and Speech Synthesis, Speech Perception.
Elizabeth Segalowitz (MA, Ateneo de Manila U., 1968; Sess. Lect.) Sociolinguistics, Bilingualism, Developmental Psycholinguistics.
Rose-Marie Weber (Ph.D., Cornell, 1965; Assoc Prof) Linguistics and Reading, Sociolinguistics, Developmental Psycholinguistics.

Linguists in other Departments or Schools

Marc Angenot (French).	John Nicholson (Russian).
Abbot Conway (English).	Michelangelo Picone (Italian).
Irvin Gopnik (English).	Albert Schachter (Classics).
Wilhelm Hempel (German).	Donald Theall (English).
Wallace Lambert (Psychology).	G. Richard Tucker (Psychology).
John MacNamara (Psychology).	David Williams (English).

Academic Calendar 1974-1975

Fall Semester: September - January; Spring Semester: January - April. Deadline: July 15.

DESCRIPTIVE MATERIAL: Write: Admissions Office, Faculty of Arts, McGill University, Box 6070, Station A, Montreal, Que., H3C 3G1.

Department of Linguistics
J. Hewson, Chairman
Degrees: BA, MA, M.Phil.   Degrees Granted 1972-73: 5 BA, 2 MA, 1 Other.   Majors: 10g.
          In Residence: 9g, 6u.

Regional language studies: Newfoundland English (dialectology), Micmac, Naskapi (algonkian), Eskimo. Facilities include sound archive of Newfoundland speech, files of
Newfoundland Dialect Dictionary (in progress) and field recordings and native informants
for Micmac, Naskapi and Eskimo, languages of the Province.
   R.L.S. (=Regional Language Studies) is published annually by the Department of English
under the editorship of Dr. W. J. Kirwin.

COURSE OFFERINGS

Introductory, 3; Phonology, 3; Theoretical Models, 2; Sociolinguisictics, 1; Dialectology, 2; Historical Linguistics, 4; Applied Linguistics, 20.   Language Areas: Franco-
Canadian, Romance Linguistics, Amerindian.

UNCOMMONLY-TAUGHT LANGUAGES

| Eskimo (3) | Cree (2) | Micmac (2) | Naskapi (2) |
| | | | Sanskrit |

STAFF

V. Bubenik (Ph.Dr., Brno 1967; Asst Prof) Historical, Indo-European, Semitic.
J. Hewson (D. de l'u., Laval 1964; Prof) General and Historical, Amerindian
   (Algonkian), Romance.
H. J. Paddock (Ph.D., London, 1960; Assoc Prof) Phonetics, English, English
   Dialectology.
F. W. Peacock (D. Litt., Memorial, 1971; Visiting Fellow) Eskimo.
L. R. Smith (M.A., Michigan, 1968; Asst Prof) Transformational Grammer, Eskimo.

Linguistis in other Departments or Schools

W. J. Kirwin (Ph.D., Chicago, 1961; Prof) English.

Support Available

University Fellowships ($3000), highly competitive.

Academic Calendar 1974-1975

Fall Semester: 6 Sept - 14 Dec; Winter Quarter: 9 Jan - 20 Apr; Spring Semester:
9 May - 17 Aug; Summer Session: 24 June - 8 Aug.

DESCRIPTIVE MATERIAL: Write: Registrar, Memorial University, St. John's, Nfld,
                        Canada.

UNIVERSITÉ DE MONTRÉAL Montréal 101, Québec   Tel. (514) 343-6221

Linguistique et Philologie
André Clas, Chairman
Degrees: BA, MA, Ph.D.   Degrees Granted 1972-73: 14 BA, 2 MA.   Majors: 149g.
         In Residence: 28g, 149u.

The undergraduate program offers a basic all round training in phonetics, semantics, morphology and syntax as well as initiation to more particular areas of specialization, language fields (romance, germanic, slavic, indo-european and amerindian), lexicography, stylistics and sociolinguistics).

The graduate program whilst offering increased specialization is so designed to accommodate students with first degrees in other fields. Seminars are held on a variety of specialized topics. Recent development in Syntactic Theory, North American French, Montagnais, Neurolinguistics and students are required to participate actively bringing to light in group discussion problems arising in the course of their dissertation research.

Post graduate study is closely linked with research projects persued within the department or at faculty or inter-university level. Many of the projects are funded by provincial, national or international organisations as well as by internal university grants and many students work part time on these projects which are at present situated in the following fields, phonetics, Canadian French, Contrastive English-French Syntax, Artificial Intelligence Mechanical Translation, Descriptive Algonquian and Haitian Creole, Romance Philology, Aphasia and Formal Semantics.

COURSE OFFERINGS

Introductory, 2; Phonology, 7; Theoretical Models, 5; Semantics & Logic, 1; Sociolinguistics, 2; Dialectology, 1; Psycholinguistics, 1; Math. & Comp. Linguistics, 1; Historical Linguistics, 3; Linguistics & Literature, 1; Language Pedagogy, 3. Other: Applied ling., Lexicology 2. Language Areas: Canadian French 2, NonIE Lg. 2, French 10, Romance lgs. 2, American French 1. Other Departments: Introductory, 2; Phonology, 1. Language Areas: German 3, Spanish 7, Greek 2, Latin 2, Russian 3.

UNCOMMONLY-TAUGHT LANGUAGES

Breton	Chinese	Greek	Japanese
Catalan	(Mandarin)	(Modern)	Quechua

STAFF

André Clas (Pr. agr.)
Guy Connolly (Ch. ens.)
Kathleen Connors-Pupier (Pr. adj.)
Alan Ford (Pr. adj.)
Richard Kittredge (Pr. adj.)
Rolf Max Kully (Pr. agr.)
Gilles Lefebvre (Pr. agr.)
Ghislaine Legendre (Pr. adj.)
Jean-Yves Le Guillo (Pr. agr.)
Nathan Ménard (Pr. adj.)
Bernard Moreux (Pr. agr.)
Yves Morin (Pr. adj.)
Antonio Querido (Pr. agr.)
John Reighard (Ch. ens.)
Laurent Santerre (Pr. agr.)
Emile Seutin (Pr. adj.)
Rajendra Singh (Pr. adj.)
Etienne Tiffou (Pr. agr.)

Support Available

The department offers no scholorships but a limited number of assistanships in phonetics and introductory linguistics are available for students having completed the MA credit requirement. Financial support from research projects is also available to qualified applicants.

Academic Calendar 1974-1975

Fall Quarter: September 4 - December 20; Winter Quarter: January 6 - April 25. Deadline: March 1.

DESCRIPTIVE MATERIAL: Write: Sécrétariat, Bureau du régistraire, Université de
Montréal, Case Postale 6128, Montréal 101, Québec.

UNIVERSITY OF OTTAWA Ottawa, Ontario K1N 6N5   Tel. (613) 231-4207

Department of Linguistics & Modern Languages
Guy Rondeau, Chairman
Degrees: BA, MA. Degrees Granted 1972-73: 6 BA, 10 MA. Majors: 56g. In
Residence: 15g.

The Department of Linguistics and Modern Languages offers an Honours BA in linguistics
alone; it also offers an honours degree with a Major in linguistics, in which the main
emphasis is on linguistics but permitting a Minor in another field such as a specific
language, in philosophy, or in some other field. It is also possible to combine a Minor
in linguistics with a Major in another field. The foregoing are four-year programs;
a three-year General BA is also obtainable with a concentration of six courses in linguistics.
The graduate degree of MA in Applied Linguistics is also offered. The student may
specialize in various fields; admission to the program requires an honours BA in linguistics. Students not having such a degree may be admitted to the graduate program
following a preparatory program comprising seven linguistics courses on the undergraduate
level.
The department has a very well-equipped phonetics laboratory. A publication entitled
Cahiers de linguistique d'Ottawa is produced two or three times a year with a collection
of papers written by department members and others. The department also houses a Linguistics Documentation Center which provides bibliographical services in addition to
providing facilities for research in data-processing in connection with linguistics.

COURSE OFFERINGS

Introductory, 2u; Phonology, 4g 3u; Theoretical Models, 2g 1u; Semantics & Logic, 2g
2u; Sociolinguistics, 4g 1u; Dialectology, 1g; Field Methods, 1g 2u; Psycholinguistics,
3g 1u; Neurolinguistics, 1u; Math. & Comp. Linguistics, 1g 1u; Historical Linguistics,
2u; History of Linguistics, 1g; Language Pedagogy, 8g 3u. Other: Applied Ling. 2.
Language Areas: Eskimo 2u, Chinese 2u, French 1g 1u, Canadian French 1g 1u, Romance
Ling. 1u.

UNCOMMONLY-TAUGHT LANGUAGES

Chinese (u4)   Cree (u4)   Eskimo (u4)

STAFF

J. Brunet (MA, Ottawa) Phonetics and Phonology of French.
P. Calve (M.Sc., Ottawa) Applied Linguistics, Comparative Grammar of French & English.
C. Germain (D. 3e cycle, Aix) Semantics, Applied Linguistics.
B. Harris (BA (Hons.) Lond.) Computational Linguistics, Machine Translation,
Retrieval.
P. C. Hauptman (Ph.D., Michigan) Applied Linguistics and Japanese Language.
T. S. T. Henderson (MA, Oxon.) Algonquian Studies.
T. R. Hofmann (MA, Illinois) Theories of Language; Meaning, Preception, and Writing;
Syntax.
L. G. Kelly (D.ès L., Laval) Translation Theory, Bilingualism, Theories of
Language.
A. Lapierre (D. 3e cycle, Strasbourg) Lexicography, Quantitative Lexicology, Can-
adian French.
R. Leblanc (D. 3e cycle, Aix) Applied Linguistics.
C. Lee (BA, Taiwan) Chinese (1/3 time).

G. Lefebvre (Ph.D., Montreal) French Ethnolinguistics and Dialectology, Algonquian (1/3 time).

G. Neufeld (Ph.D., University of California, Berkeley) Psycholinguistic Problems of Bilingualism, First and Second Language Acquisition.

P. G. Patel (Ph.D., Alberta) Language Acquisition, Language Pathology and Psycholinguistics in Relation to General Linguistics, Neurolinguistics.

T. Pavel (D. 3e cycle, Paris) Semantics, Semiotics, Contemporary Linguistic History.

M. L. Rivero (Ph.D., Rochester) Syntax, Semantics, Philosophy and Linguistics.

J. P. Rona (D. Lett., Rio Gr.) Theory of Language, Semantics, Sociolinguistics.

G. Rondeau (D. Ling., Nancy) Stylistics, Applied Linguistics.

C. Sammurtuq, Eskimo Language and Culture, Linguistics of Eskimo (2/3 time).

J. T. Tan (B.J., Hong Kong) Chinese (1/3 time).

D. C. Walker (Ph.D., University of California, San Diego) Phonological Theory, Romance Linguistics.

Support Available

1) Department Research Assistantships; 2) Teaching and Research assistantships with the Centre for Second Language Learning; 3) Various support from outside agencies (Ontario Government, Canada Council, etc.). Consult the granting body. Deadlines: for departmental support same as admission application; for outside agencies, consult the appropriate granting body. Stipend: maximum $3,000 per annum.

Academic Calendar 1974-1975

Fall Quarter: September - December; Winter Quarter: January- April; Spring Quarter: May - September; Summer Quarter: July 1 - August 15. Deadline: Undergraduate -- Beginning July for September, Beginning December for January, Beginning April for May, Mid-April for Summer Courses; Graduate -- Mid-August for September, Mid-November for January, Mid-March for May. All dates estimated until official calendars issued. One month earlier for applications from outside Canada.

DESCRIPTIVE MATERIAL: Write: Admissions Office, University of Ottawa, 550 Cumberland Street, Ottawa, Ontario, K1N 6N5. Applications for admission to Graduate School may be sent directly to the School of Graduate Studies, University of Ottawa, 110 Wilbrod St., Ottawa, Ont., K1N 6N5.

UNIVERSITÉ DU QUÉBEC À MONTRÉAL   Montréal, Québec H3C 3P8

Tel. (514) 876-3301

Départment de Linguistique
Monique Lemieux-Niéger, Chairman
Degrees: BA, MA. Degrees Granted 1972-73: 10 BA, 2 MA. Majors: 70g. In Residence: 52g, 75u.

The undergraduate program in Linguistics is offered by the Linguistics Council (Module Linguistique) and through the cooperation of participating Departments, (e.g.: Linguistics, Mathematics, Philosophy departments). There is a set of core courses to exemplify the application of the scientific method to the study of language.

Undergraduates may concentrate their studies in one of three fields: theoretical linguistics, psycholinguistics and sociolinguistics.

The MA program is offered by the Linguistics Department and has the same three orientations as the undergraduate program. It includes a set of courses and a thesis.

Facilities include extensive library holdings on Canadian French; a faculty exchange program with the Université de Paris VII; the Ecole Française d'Eté. The department publishes a journal (Cahiers de Linguistique, and co-edits with McGill University and l'Université de Montréal "The Montreal Working Papers in Linguistics".

COURSE OFFERINGS

Introductory, 1; Phonology, 3; Theoretical Models, 4; Semantics & Logic, 3; Sociolinguistics, 7; Dialectology, 1; Psycholinguistics, 4; Neurolinguistics, 1; Math. & Comp. Linguistics, 1; Historical Linguistics, 1; History of Linguistics, 1; Language Pedagogy, 13. Other: Lg. of Publicity, Lexicology. Language Areas: French 3, Quebecois 1.

UNCOMMONLY-TAUGHT LANGUAGES

Esquimau   Mohawk   Montagnais

STAFF

Pierre Andreani (Doctorat ès Lettres, U. libre de Bruxelles, 1974) Language Teaching.
Claire Asselin (Ph.D., U. de Chicago, 1968) Syntax.
Philippe Barbaud (Doctorat, U. de Vincennes, 1974) Syntax, Semantics, Teaching of French as a First Language.
Alain Beulieu (MA, U. de Montréal, 1970) Semiology, Syntax, Theoretical Linguistics.
Hentietta Cedergren (Ph.D., U. de Cornell, 1972) Sociolinguistics, French Canadian, Latin American Spanish.
Colette Dubuisson (MA, U. de Montréal, 1971) Syntax.
Jacques Duschesne (MA, U. de Montréal, 1971) Psycholinguistics, Speech Pathology.
André Dugas (Doctorat 3e cycle, U. de Grenoble, 1966) Syntax, Language Teaching.
Denis Dumas (MA, U. de Montréal, 1972) Phonology.
Hanny Feurer (MA, U. de Michigan, 1963) Sociolinguistics, Iroquois, Discourse Analysis.
Cheryl Goodenough (Ph.D., U. de Toronto, 1973) Neurolinguistics, Psycholinguistics.
Benoit Jacque (MA, U. de Montréal, 1971) Phonetics.
Guy Labelle (MA, U. de Montréal, 1970) Psycholoinguistics.
Jacques Labelle (MA, U. de Montréal, 1970) Phonetics, Syntax.
Jacqueline Lamothe (MA, U. de Montréal, 1968) Semantics.
René Matte (MA, Universite de Montréal, 1964) Spanish.
Monique Nieger (Doctorat d'Université, U. d'Aix-Marseille, 1966) Diachronic Linguistics, French Canadian, Syntax.
Roland Pelchat (Doctorat d'Université, U. de Strasbourg, 1960) Psycholinguistics.
Paul Pupier (Doctorat 3e cycle, U. de Paris X, 1970) Phonology, Sociolinguistics, Lexicology.
Madeleine Saint-Pierre (MA U. de Montréal, 1970) Sociolinguistics, French Canadian, Creole languages.
Bernard Tranel (Ph.D., U. de Californie, San Diego, 1974) Phonetics, Phonology, Psycholinguistics.

Linguists in other Departments or Schools

M. André Vidricaire, Département de Philosophie.
M. J.G. Meunier, Département de Philosophie.

Support Available

Auxiliaires d'enseignement; Chargés de cours.

Academic Calendar 1974-1975

Fall Semester: September 3rd - December 21; Spring Semester: January 6 - April 21. Deadline: November 1st for Spring Quarter; March 1st for Fall Quarter.

DESCRIPTIVE MATERIAL: Write: Bureau du Régistraire, Université du Québec à Montréal, C.P. 8888, Montréal, Québec H3C 3P8.

UNIVERSITY OF SASKATCHEWAN Saskatoon, Saskatchewan S7N 0W0

Tel. (306) 343-5040

Linguistics Committee
J. A. Mills, Chairman
Degrees: BA. In Residence: 5u.

The Major in Linguistics is an undergraduate programme taught by faculty from the
departments of Anthropology and Archaeology, English, French and Spanish, and
Psychology. The aim of the programme is to give general coverage of certain
basic topics in Linguistics.

COURSE OFFERINGS

Introductory, 3; Phonology, 1; Theoretical Models, 1; Sociolinguistics, 1; Psycholinguistics, 1; Historical Linguistics, 2. Language Areas: Amerindian Lgs. 1, Cree 1,
French 1, Spanish 1, German 1, Slavic 1.

UNCOMMONLY-TAUGHT LANGUAGES

Cree (u2)

STAFF

Mary C. Marino (Ph.D., Cal Berkeley, 1968; Asst Prof) Siouan Language-family (Dakota,
Winnebago), Descriptive Linguistics (2/3 time).
John A. Mills (Ph.D., Cape Town, 1965; Assoc Prof) Grammaticality, Application
of Chomskyan Theory to Psychology (1/3 time).
Robert I. Scott (Ph.D., State University of New York at Buffalo, 1964; Assoc
Prof) English Grammars, Semantics (1/3 time).
Curt J. Wittlin (Ph.D., Basle, 1965; Assoc Prof) Romance Philology (2/3 time).

Academic Calendar 1974-1975

Fall Semester: September 9 - December 3; Spring Semester: January 6 - April 4.
Deadline: June 15.

DESCRIPTIVE MATERIAL: Write: Dr. J. A. Mills, University of Saskatchewan, Saskatoon,
Canada 57N 0W0.

UNIVERSITÉ DE SHERBROOKE Sherbrooke, Québec   Tel. (819) 565-4699

Section de linguistique
Louis Painchaud, Chairman
Degrees: BA, MA, Ph.D. Degrees Granted 1972-73: 8 BA. Majors: 50g. In Residence:
6g, 34u.

Au premier cycle, le programme de linguistique veut assurer les bases de la discipline
tout en permettant à l'étudiant de bâtir un programme selon ses besoins. C'est un programme ouvert sur d'autres disciplines complémentaires. Il donne la possibilité
d'approfondir ses connaissances du français en tant que langue maternelle ou que
langue seconde et de se préparer a son enseignement. Les cours sont offerts durant
les trois sessions de l'année.
    Au deuxième et au troisème cycles, le français au Québec et la sociolinguistique
sont les principaux secteurs de recherche. Un programme d'études souple permet à
l'étudiant de travailler à fond son domaine de spécialisation. Un laboratoire de
phonétique est à sa disposition.
    Depuis quelques années, une équipe de professeurs et d'étudiants poursuivent des
enquêtes sur le parler régional. Les "Recherches sociolinguistique dans la région
de Sherbrooke" sont sous la direction de M. N. Beauchemin. Quatre documents de
travail on déjà paru.

COURSE OFFERINGS

Introductory, 3; Phonology, 2; Theoretical Models, 5; Semantics & Logic, 2; Socio-
linguistics, 3; Math. & Comp. Linguistics, 1; Historical Linguistics, 3; Linguistics
& Literature, 2. Language Areas: Québécois 3. Other: Lexicology, Quantitative
Study of Vocabulary. Other Departments: Introductory, 2; Semantics & Logic, 1;
Historical Linguistics, 2; Language Pedagogy, 3.

STAFF

Normand Beauchemin (D. d'U., Strasbourg, 1967; Agrégé) Phonétique générale et experimentale, linguistique générale, dialectologie romane.
Pierre Collinge (MA, Montréal, 1967; Adjoint) Grammaire normative du francais,
   grammaire transformationelle, lexicologie et terminologie.
Jean-Marie Doutreloux (L. Philologie romane, Louvain, 1957; Adjoint) Sémiologie
   générale, signification comme procès, axiomatique et systématique des com-
   portements sémiotiques.
Jean-Marcel Léard (D.E.S., Rennes, 1966; Chargé d'enseignement) Grammaire et syntaxe,
   moyen français, stylistique.
Pierre Martel (D. 3e cycle, Strasbourg, 1970; Adjoint) Statistique lexicale, langue
   française au Québec (vocabulaire), sociolinguistique.
Louis Painchaud (MA, Montréal, 1958; Adjoint) Grammaire descriptive, morphologie
   et lexicologie, franco-québécois.
Michel Théoret (D.E.S., Montréal, 1969; Chargé d'enseignement) Philologie, langues
   et civilisations anciennes.

Support Available

Quelques bourses d'assistant ($1000) offertes au début de septembre.

Academic Calendar 1974-1975

Fall Quarter: 9 sept. - 21 déc.; Winter Quarter: 6 janvier - 26 avril; Spring
Quarter: 5 mai - 27 juin; Summer Quarter: 2 juillet - 13 août. Deadline: Hiver:
ler novembre; Automne; ler mars.

DESCRIPTIVE MATERIAL: Write: Bureau de régistraire, Université de Sherbrooke,
                        Sherbrooke, Québec, J1K 2R1.

SIMON FRASER UNIVERSITY   Burnaby 2, British Columbia   Tel. (604) 291-3544

Department of Modern Languages
Dr. Ch. P. Bouton, Chairman
Degrees: BA, MA, Ph.D., MA in the teaching of French. Degrees Granted 1972-73:
      14 BA, 1 MA, 2 Ph.D. Majors: 18g. In Residence: 14g.

The Department offers instruction on the undergraduate level in the linguistics and
literature of French, Spanish, German, and Russian. Language-only courses are offered
in Chinese, Swahili, and Latin. The Department also offers a BA degree with a major
in linguistics. Interdisciplinary programs exist in African Studies, Latin-American
Studies, and Canadian Studies.
   On the graduate level the Department offers course work leading to the degrees of
MA and PhD in linguistics. A special feature of the graduate program is the MA in the
teaching of French offered during the July-August summer session.
   The Department publishes the linguistics journal GLOSSA.

COURSE OFFERINGS

Introductory, 3u; Phonology, 1g 4u; Theoretical Models, 2g 2u; Semantics & Logic, 1g
1u; Sociolinguistics, 1g 1u; Psycholinguistics, 1g; Historical Linguistics, 1g 1u; Language Pedagogy, 1u. Other: Applied linguistics.

UNCOMMONLY-TAUGHT LANGUAGES

Mandarin Chinese (u2)   Swahili (u2)

STAFF

Anneliese Altmann (Ph.D., Georgetown; Asst Prof) Theoretical and Applied Linguistics.
B. E. Bartlett (Ph.D., Simon Fraser; Asst Prof) French linguistics, History of
Linguistics, Linguistic Theory.
C. P. Bouton (Doctorat es Lettres, Sorbonne; Prof) Applied Linguistics and French
Linguistics.
G. L. Bursill-Hall (Ph.D., London; Prof) Linguistic Theory, History of Linguistics.
E. R. Colhoun (Ph.D., Cornell; Asst Prof) Caribbean and Latin-American Dialectology.
R. C. DeArmond (Ph.D., Chicago; Asst Prof) Slavic Linguistics, Modern Linguistic
Theory.
J. Foley (Ph.D., MIT; Assoc Prof) Phonological Theory.
P. Guiraud (Doctorat es Lettres, Sorbonne; Prof) Semantics, Stylistics, French
Linguistics.
H. M. Hammerly (Ph.D., Texas; Asst Prof) Applied Linguistics, Second Language
Teaching.
A. Hurtado (Doctorat es Lettres, Sorbonne; Asst Prof) Theoretical Linguistics.
Margret B. Jackson (Dr. Phil., Muenster; Asst Prof) Germanic Linguistics.
T. W. Kim (Ph.D., Michigan; Asst Prof) Romance Linguistics.
D. R. J. Knowles (Ph.D., London; Asst Prof) Syntactic Theory and Spanish Linguistics.
N. J. Lincoln (Ph.D., Cornell; Asst Prof) South Asian Studies, Typology.
B. E. Newton (MA, Oxford; Prof) Greek, Semantics, Phonology.
E. W. Roberts (Ph.D., Cambridge; Assoc Prof) Phonetics, Phonological Theory.
Marguerite Saint-Jacques (Docteur de troisieme cycle, Paris; Asst Prof) French
Linguistics, Creole French Dialects, Ethnolinguistics.
R. Saunders (Ph.D., Brown; Asst Prof) Russian Linguistics, Phonological Theory.
J. H. Wahlgren (Ph.D., California, Berkeley; Assoc Prof) Russian Linguistics,
Computational Linguistics.

Academic Calendar 1974-1975

Fall Semester: September - December; Spring Semester: January – April; Summer Semester:
May - August. Deadline: Application to graduate program may be at any time. For undergraduate program deadline for admission to fall semester is 1 August, for spring semester
is 1 December, for summer semester is 1 April.

DESCRIPTIVE MATERIAL: Write: Dr. Charles P. Bouton, Chairman, Department of
                        Modern Languages, Simon Fraser University, Burnaby,
                        British Columbia.

Dept. of Classics, Mod. Lgs., and Linguistics
Charles R. Barton, Executive Officer
Degrees: BA. Degrees Granted 1972-73: 3 BA. In Residence: 20u.

The University offers students interested in linguistics the option of(a) a full major
(9 courses) in Indo-European Linguistics or (b) a joint major (5 courses) in Linguistics
and another discipline.
   In addition to a general introductory course both programmes require upper-level
training in linguistic theory, non-IE structures (with a field work component) and Indo-
European.
   Various subjects are covered in "special topics" courses. These are determined in
consultation with advanced students in an attempt to meet their specific interests.
To date rather more emphasis has been placed on the study of specific languages and
their structures than on theory.

COURSE OFFERINGS

Introductory, 1; Theoretical Models, 1; Historical Linguistics, 2. Language Areas:
Non-IE Structures 1, Arabic 1. Other Departments: Phonology, 1; Theoretical Models,
1. Language Areas: French 2.

UNCOMMONLY-TAUGHT LANGUAGES

Arabic (u2)   Coptic (ul/2)   Swahili (ul/2)   Turkish (ul/2)

STAFF

Charles R. Barton (Ph.D., N.Y.U., 1965; Assoc Prof) Indo-European.
John D. Grayson (Ph.D., N.Y.U., Assoc Prof) Arabic, Spanish and Romance Linguistics,
   Descriptive Linguistics.

Academic Calendar 1974-1975

Fall Semester: September 9 - December 21; Spring Semester: January 6 – April 26.
Deadline: Marcy 10, 1975.

DESCRIPTIVE MATERIAL: Write: The Registrar, Sir George Williams University,
                        Norris Building, Montreal, Quebec.

Linguistics Studies Department
N. E. Collinge, Acting Chairman
Degrees: MA, Ph.D. Degrees Granted 1972-73: 6 MA, 3 Ph.D. Majors: 37g. In
         Residence: 30g.

Undergraduate courses are available in the core areas of the subject, with separate
coverage of anthropological, sociological, psychological and mathematical aspects.
Joint 'specialist programmes' are provided with several other disciplines.
   The graduate programme includes coverage of the transformational, neo-Bloomfieldian,
stratificational and systematic models of analysis. Specialities (in addition to those
given above) include neurolinguistics, immigrant language studies, field work on native
languages and linguistics in literature. There is cooperation with the Department of
Experimental Phonetics (P. Léon).
   The University offers a wide range of language teaching departments, clinical faci-
litiels for e.g. aphasia studies and extensive library holdings.
   Publications: 'Linguistic Series' (2 titles so far).

Organized joint research in: communication and the deaf (Reich); speech pathology and audiology (Rehabilitation Medicine); immigrant languages (Samarin); Canadian Indian languages (Kaye) (Eastern and Central).

COURSE OFFERINGS

Phonology, 1; Theoretical Models, 6; Semantics & Logic, 1; Sociolinguistics, 3; Field Methods, 1; Math. & Comp. Linguistics, 1; Historical Linguistics, 1; History of Linguistics, 1. Language Areas: Comp. Slavic 1, Japanese 1, French 1, Iroquoian 1, Modern Scots Gaelic 1. Other: Theories of Translation.

UNCOMMONLY-TAUGHT LANGUAGES

Hittite (g2)   Mohawk (Iroquoian) (g2)   Odawa (Ojibwa) (g2)

STAFF

B. Brainerd (Ph.D., Michigan, 1954; Prof) Mathematical Linguistics (1/3 time).
E. M. Burstynsky (Ph.D., Toronto, 1967; Assoc Prof) Romance Phonology.
J. K. Chambers (Ph.D., Alberta, 1970; Asst Prof) Transformational, English (2/3 time).
H. A. Gleason, Jr. (Ph.D., Hartford, 1946; Prof) Theoretical, English (1/2 time).
J. D. Kaye (Ph.D., Columbia, 1970; Assoc Prof) Transformational, Algonkian.
P. A. Reich (Ph.D., Michigan, 1970; Asst Prof) Stratificational, Psycholinguistics (2/3 time).
H. A. Roe (Ph.D., Harvard, 1965; Prof) Comparative, Indo-European, Germanic (1/3 time).
H. E. Rogers (Ph.D., Yale, 1967; Assoc Prof) Phonology, Gaelic (1/2 time).
W. J. Samarin (Ph.D., Berkeley, 1962; Prof) Sociolinguistics, African (1/2 time).

Linguists in other Departments or Schools

R. I. Binnick, Scarborough College, Humanities.
P. Bouissac, French.
Edmund Brent, Ed. Theory.
A. Cameron, English.
J. J. Chew, Jr., Anthropology.
L. Dolezel, Slavic.
D. G. Huntley, Slavic.
D. M. James, Scarborough, Humanities.
P. R. Léon, French.
P. Martin, French.
D. R. Olson, Ed. Theory.
P. H. Salus, Scarborough, Humanities.
H. G. Schogt, French.
F. Smith, Ed. Theory.
H. H. Stern, Ed. Theory.
J. D. Woods, Scarborough, Humanities.
S. A. Sper, Anthropology.
C. Yorio, Extension (Woodsworth College).

Support Available

Canada Council doctoral and masters' awards; Ontario Graduate Scholarships (only Canadian citizens and landed immigrants eligible). University of Toronto "open" graduate awards; Teaching and research assistantships, subject to annual budgeting.

Academic Calendar 1974-1975

Fall Semester: September 4 - December 20; Spring Semester: January 6 - May 20 (appros.): classes end in April. Summer Session: Variable. Deadline: Normally preceding April.

DESCRIPTIVE MATERIAL: Write: Graduate Secretary (graduate); Office of Admissions (undergraduate); University of Toronto, Dept. of Linguistic Studies, Toronto, Ontario M5S 1A1.

UNIVERSITY OF VICTORIA   Victoria, British Columbia V82 2Y2   Tel. (628) 477-6911

Linguistics Department
M. H. Scargill, Chairman
Degrees: BA, MA, Ph.D. Degrees Granted 1972-73: 12 BA, 4 MA. Majors: 20g.

The undergraduate and graduate programmes both provide for special work in Native Indian
Languages of British Columbia, T.E.S.L., Psycholinguistics, Canadian English, Experimen-
tal Phonetics, grammatical theory.
    With the Faculty of Education, the Linguistics Department offers a special diploma
Programme confined to native Indians and designed to help them teach their own languages
to their own people.
    The Department also offers a Summer English Language Institute for students from
Japan and Quebec who wish to learn English.

COURSE OFFERINGS

Introductory, 2; Phonology, 2; Dialectology, 1; Historical Linguistics, 1; Language
Pedagogy, 1. Language Areas: Indian Lgs. of British Columbia 1, Canadian English 1,
Japanese 1, Korean 1.

UNCOMMONLY-TAUGHT LANGUAGES

Cowichan Indian (u2, g2)   Korean (u2)

STAFF

J. Arthurs (MA, U. Victoria; Lecturer) Romance Linguistics.
B. F. Carlson (Ph.D., Hawaii; Asst Prof) Native Indian Languages, Anthropological
    Linguistics.
T. E. Hukani (Ph.D., Washington; Asst Prof) Generative Phonology, Grammatical Theory,
    Native Indian Languages.
J. F. Kess (Ph.D., Hawaii; Assoc Prof) Psycholinguistics.
G. N. O'Grady (Ph.D., Indiana; Prof) Austronesian Linguistics, Native Indian Languages.
M. H. Scargill (Ph.D., Leeds, 1940; Prof) Canadian English, History of English,
    Lexicology.
H. J. Warkentyne (Ph.D., London; Assoc Prof) Experimental Phonetics, T.E.S.L.,
    Japanese.

Support Available

Five Assistantships (c.$1600.00); Scholarships; and Fellowships ($1500.00 to
$3000.00). Sept. 1.

Academic Calendar 1974-1975

Winter Quarter: September - December; Spring Quarter: January - May; Summer Quarter:
July - August. Deadline: June 30.

DESCRIPTIVE MATERIAL: Write: Registrar, University of Victoria, Victoria, B.C.
                       V82-242, B.C. (for undergrad.). For grad.: Head, Dept. of
                       Linguistics, University of Victoria, Victoria, B.C. V82-
                       242.

UNIVERSITY OF WESTERN ONTARIO   London, Ontario N6A 3K7   Tel. (519) 679-3430

University Linguistics Committee
Lee Guemple, Chairman
Degrees: B.A. with Concentration in linguistics.

COURSE OFFERINGS

Introductory, 2; Phonology, 1; Semantics & Logic, 1; Sociolinguistics, 2; Psycholinguistics,3; Historical Linguistics, 2.   Language Areas: Structure of a NonIE Lg. 1, French 1, Russian 1.

STAFF

B. I. Bandeen (Ph.D., Radcliffe).
C. A. Creider (Ph.D., Minnesota).
J. P. Denny (Ph.D., Duke).
G. M. Eramian (Ph.D., Brown).
A. Goldschläger (L.es L., Brussels).
D. L. Guemple (Ph.D., Chicago).
D. J. Hockney (Ph.D., Cornell).
A. Marras (Ph.D., Duke).
A. U. Paivio (Ph.D., McGill).
Z. W. Pylyshyn (Ph.D., Saskatchewan).
M. Seguin (MA, Michigan).
S. Tuomi (Ph.D., Northwestern).
H. R. Wilson (Ph.D., Michigan).

Academic Calendar 1974-1975

Year begins Mid September, ends Mid May. Intersession: Mid May through third week in June. Summer Session: July 1 to mid August. Deadline: August 1.

DESCRIPTIVE MATERIAL: Write: Office of Admissions, Stevenson-Lawson Building,
                      University of Western Ontario, London, Ontario, N6A 3K7.

UNIVERSITY OF WINDSOR   Windsor, Ontario   Tel. (266) 253-4232

Program in Linguistics
Paul V. Cassano, Program Director
Degrees: BA.

COURSE OFFERINGS

Theoretical Models, 2; Sociolinguistics, 2; Psycholinguistics, 1; Historical Linguistics, 4; Linguistics & Literature, 1; Language Pedagogy, 1. Language Areas: Romance ling. 1.

STAFF

P. V. Cassano (Ph.D.; Assoc Prof) Romance Linguistics.
B. Harder (Ph.D.; Asst Prof) Transformational Grammar, Medieval Literature.
L. D. Majhanovich (MA; Lecturer) Slavic Linguistics.
J. A. Malone (Ph.D.; Prof) Psychology of Language.
D. G. McCasgill (MA; Asst Prof) Philosophy of Language.
L. Smedick (Ph.D.; Assoc Prof) English Philology.
W. Temelini (Ph.D.; Asst Prof) Italian Philology.
F. Wieden (Ph.D.; Assoc Prof) Germanic Philology.

Division of Language Studies
Robert Fink, Chairman
Degrees: BA.   In Residence: 10u.

The Division of Language Studies offers programmes in Linguistics leading to Ordinary, Combined Honours and General Honours BA degrees. In addition to a set of required core courses on grammatical theory, Honours students are required to complete a thesis and are encouraged to combine linguistics with a related field.

COURSE OFFERINGS

Introductory, 2; Phonology, 2; Theoretical Models, 1; Sociolinguistics, 1; Psycholinguistics, 2; Neurolinguistics, 1; Historical Linguistics, 2; Language Pedagogy, 1. Language Areas: French 1.

STAFF

Pedro Beade (Ph.D., Cornell, 1971; Asst Prof) Comparative Germanic, Sociolinguistics, Ojibwa.
Noel Corbett (Ph.D., Toronto, Assoc Prof) Comparative Romance (1/3 time).
Robert Fink (Ph.D., Rochester, 1969; Asst Prof) Language Acquisition, Psycholinguistics.
Michael L. Kay (MA, Oxford; Prof) Phonetics, Applied Linguistics (1/2 time).

Academic Calendar 1974-1975

Deadline: August 31. University does not operate on a semester system. Students may only enter in September.

DESCRIPTIVE MATERIAL: Write: Office of Student Programmes, S302 Ross Building, Downsview, Toronto, Ontario M3J 1P4.

APPENDIX A: Annual Summer Institutes

<u>Linguistic Institute of the Linguistic Society of America</u>. Since 1928, the Linguistic Institute, under the auspices of the Linguistic Society of America, has brought together scholars and students from various universities around the world for an intensive summer program in linguistics. The program and scholars vary annually; the host university for the Institute is decided upon by the LSA Executive Committee.

Course offerings usually include basic courses in descriptive, transformational, historical, and applied linguistics; more advanced courses on the theory of phonemic, morphological, and syntactical analysis, grammatical theory, experimental and articulatory phonetics, semantics, lexicology, dialectology, language typology, and field methods. Courses covering the newer linguistic disciplines such as sociolinguistics, psycholinguistics, neurolinguistics, etc. are also offered. A series of courses on the structure of individual languages, both ancient and modern, general courses in comparative linguistics, and intensive language courses are also usually available.

The 1975 Linguistic Institute will be held at the University of South Florida, Tampa; the 1976 Linguistic Institute at the State University of New York, Oswego; and the 1977 Linguistic Institute at the University of Hawaii, Honolulu. Further information on these Institutes is available by writing the Chairman of the Linguistics Department at these institutions or by writing the LSA Secretariat, 1611 North Kent Street, Arlington, Virginia 22209. A limited number of tuition fellowships are available for each of these Linguistic Institutes.

<u>Summer Institute of Linguistics</u>. Founded in 1934, the Summer Institute of Linguistics, which is affiliated with the Wycliffe Bible Translators, was organized with the aim of putting unwritten languages into written form for Bible translation. Literacy campaigns are an important part of the activity. During the summer, students are trained in linguistic analysis at several locations, among them, the Universities of Oklahoma, North Dakota, and Washington.

In the linguistics courses the concern is primarily with immediate practical implications of descriptive linguistics rather than pure theory. While the majority of students are missionaries en route to or on furlough from pre-literate groups, other students are commonly enrolled.

Inquiries should be addressed to SIL headquarters: Summer Institute of Linguistics, Box 1960, Santa Ana, California 92702.

<u>NDEA Intensive Language Programs</u>. Under Title VI of the National Defense Education Act, the U.S. Department of Health, Education, and Welfare supports language and area centers both during the academic year and during the summer.

Intensive language instruction in the "neglected" languages and related area studies is offered. Each of the host universities determines the standards for admission, academic credits, and fees for the programs it administers and selects the persons to receive NDEA graduate and undergraduate fellowships.

Inquiries about individual institutes or languages to be taught should be addressed to: Institute of International Studies, Division of Foreign Studies, Language and Area Centers Section, Department of Health, Education, and Welfare, Office of Education, Washington, D.C. 20202.

<u>Other Institutes</u>. Recently a number of smaller regional institutes, e.g. the California Summer Program in Linguistics, have taken place, and there are indications that this trend will continue. Information on regional programs can usually be obtained from the LSA Secretariat in the spring of each year.

APPENDIX B: Universities and Their Programs

	B.A./B.S.	M.A./M.S.	Ph.D.	Other
ARIZONA				
University of Arizona	-	•	•	-
Northern Arizona University	o	o	-	-
CALIFORNIA				
University of California-Berkeley	•	•	•	•
University of California-Davis	•	•	-	-
University of California-Irvine	•	-	-	-
University of California-Los Angeles	•	•	•	-
University of California-Riverside	•	-	-	-
University of California-San Diego	•	-	•	-
University of California-Santa Barbara	•	-	-	-
University of California-Santa Cruz	•	-	-	-
California State College-Dominguez Hills	o	o	-	-
California State College-Sonoma	o	-	-	-
California State University-Fresno	•	•	-	-
California State University-Fullerton	o	•	-	-
California State University-Long Beach	-	•	-	-
California State University-Los Angeles	o	o	-	-
California State University-Northridge	•	•	-	-
University of the Pacific	•	-	-	•
San Diego State University	-	•	-	o
San Francisco State University	o	•	-	-
San Jose State University	-	o	-	-
University of Southern California	•	•	•	-
Stanford University	o	•	•	-
COLORADO				
University of Colorado	•	•	•	-
CONNECTICUT				
Central Connecticut State College	o	o	-	-
University of Connecticut	-	•	•	-
University of Hartford	•	-	-	-
Yale University	-	•	•	-

Key to symbols: • Degree offered in Linguistics
  o Degree offered in another field with concentration in Linguistics
  - No degree or concentration offered in Linguistics

(See page 196 for explanation of symbols.)	B.A./B.S.	M.A./M.S.	Ph.D.	Other
DISTRICT OF COLUMBIA				
American University	-	●	-	-
Federal City College	o	o	-	-
Gallaudet College	o	o	-	-
George Washington University	-	●	-	-
Georgetown University	●	●	●	-
Howard University	-	●	●	-
FLORIDA				
University of Florida	-	●	●	-
Florida Atlantic University	●	●	-	o
University of South Florida	o	●	-	-
GEORGIA				
University of Georgia	-	●	●	-
HAWAII				
University of Hawaii	●	●	●	-
University of Hawaii, Hilo College	●	-	-	-
ILLINOIS				
University of Chicago	●	●	●	-
University of Illinois at Urbana/Champaign	-	●	●	-
University of Illinois at Chicago Circle	-	●	-	-
Illinois Institute of Technology	-	●	●	-
Northeastern Illinois University	●	●	-	-
Northern Illinois University	●	o	o	-
Northwestern University	●	●	●	-
Southern Illinois University	-	●	-	o
INDIANA				
Ball State University	-	●	-	-
Indiana University	●	●	●	-
Indiana State University	o	-	-	-
Marion College	o	-	-	-
Purdue University	-	●	●	-

(See page 196 for explanation of symbols.)	B.A./B.S.	M.A./M.S.	Ph.D.	Other
IOWA				
University of Iowa	o	●	-	-
Iowa State University	o	o	o	-
University of Northern Iowa	o	o	-	-
KANSAS				
University of Kansas	●	●	●	●
Kansas State University	●	●	-	-
KENTUCKY				
Morehead State University	o	o	-	-
LOUISIANA				
University of Southwestern Louisiana	o	o	o	-
Tulane University	o	o	o	-
MARYLAND				
University of Maryland	●	o	o	-
MASSACHUSETTS				
Boston College	●	●	-	-
Boston University	o	-	-	-
Brandeis University	o	-	o	-
Gordon College	o	-	-	-
Hampshire College	o	-	-	-
Harvard University	●	●	●	-
University of Massachusetts	-	●	●	-
Massachusetts Institute of Technology	-	-	●	-
MICHIGAN				
Andrews University	o	o	-	-
Central Michigan University	●	●	-	-
University of Detroit	o	o	-	-
University of Michigan	●	●	●	-
Michigan State University	●	●	●	-
Oakland University	●	-	-	-
Wayne State University	-	●	-	-
Western Michigan University	●	o	-	-

(See page 196 for explanation of symbols.)	B.A./B.S.	M.A./M.S.	Ph.D.	Other
MINNESOTA				
Bethel College	●	-	-	-
Macalester College	●	-	-	-
University of Minnesota at Minneapolis	●	●	●	-
University of Minnesota at Duluth	o	-	-	-
MISSISSIPPI				
University of Southern Mississippi	o	o	o	-
MISSOURI				
University of Missouri	●	●	o	-
Washington University at St. Louis	●	●	-	-
MONTANA				
University of Montana	o	o	-	-
NEBRASKA				
University of Nebraska	●	o	o	-
NEVADA				
University of Nevada	o	-	-	-
NEW JERSEY				
Drew University	o	o	o	-
Montclair State College	●	-	-	-
Princeton University	-	-	●	-
Rutgers University	o	-	-	-
Trenton State College	o	-	-	-
NEW HAMPSHIRE				
University of New Hampshire	o	o	-	-
NEW MEXICO				
University of New Mexico	●	o	o	-

(See page 196 for explanation of symbols.)

	B.A./B.S.	M.A./M.S.	Ph.D.	Other
NEW YORK				
Barnard College	●	-	-	-
City College, CUNY	●	-	-	-
Columbia University	-	●	●	●
Columbia University Teachers College	-	●	●	●
Cornell University	●	●	●	-
Graduate School of CUNY	-	-	●	-
Hofstra University	o	-	-	-
Herbert H. Lehman College of CUNY	●	-	-	-
New York University	●	●	●	-
C.W. Post College of Long Island University	o	-	-	-
Queens College, CUNY	●	-	-	-
University of Rochester	-	●	●	-
State University of New York-Binghamton	●	-	-	-
State University of New York-Buffalo	●	●	●	-
State University of New York-Stony Brook	●	●	-	-
State University of New York-College at Oswego	●	-	-	-
Syracuse University	●	●	o	-
Yeshiva University	-	-	o	-
NORTH CAROLINA				
Duke University	●	-	-	-
University of North Carolina	●	●	●	-
OHIO				
University of Cincinnati	●	●	●	-
Cleveland State University	o	o	-	-
Miami University	o	o	-	o
Ohio University	-	●	o	-
Ohio State University	●	●	●	-
University of Toledo	●	o	o	-
Youngstown State University	o	-	-	-
OKLAHOMA				
Oklahoma State University	o	o	o	o
OREGON				
University of Oregon	●	●	-	-

(See page 196 for explanation of symbols.)	B.A./B.S.	M.A./M.S.	Ph.D.	Other
PENNSYLVANIA				
University of Pennsylvania	●	●	●	-
Pennsylvania State University	●	●	●	-
University of Pittsburgh	-	●	●	o
PUERTO RICO				
Inter American University of Puerto Rico	o	-	-	-
RHODE ISLAND				
Brown University	●	●	●	-
TENNESSEE				
Nashville University Center	o	o	o	o
TEXAS				
East Texas State University	o	o	-	o
University of Houston	o	o	-	-
University of Texas-Arlington	-	●	-	-
University of Texas-Austin	●	●	●	-
University of Texas-El Paso	-	o	-	●
University of Texas-San Antonio	-	●	-	-
Texas A&M University	-	o	o	-
Trinity University	o	o	-	-
UTAH				
Brigham Young University	-	●	-	-
University of Utah	-	●	o	-
VERMONT				
University of Vermont	●	-	-	-
VIRGINIA				
Mary Washington College	o	-	-	-
University of Virginia	o	●	-	-

(See page 196 for explanation of symbols.)	B.A./B.S.	M.A./M.S.	Ph.D.	Other
WASHINGTON				
University of Washington	-	●	●	-
Western Washington State College	o	-	-	-
WISCONSIN				
University of Wisconsin-Madison	●	-	●	-
University of Wisconsin-Milwaukee	●	-	-	-
CANADA				
University of Alberta	●	●	●	-
University of British Columbia	●	●	●	-
University of Calgary	●	●	-	-
Carleton University	●	-	-	o
Université Laval	●	●	●	o
University of Manitoba	o	o	-	-
McGill University	●	●	●	-
Memorial University of Newfoundland	●	●	-	●
Université de Montréal	●	●	●	o
University of Ottawa	●	●	-	-
Université du Québec à Montréal	●	●	-	-
University of Saskatchewan at Saskatoon	●	-	-	-
Université de Sherbrooke	●	●	●	-
Simon Fraser University	●	●	●	o
Sir George Williams University	●	-	-	-
University of Toronto	-	●	●	-
University of Victoria	●	●	●	-
University of Western Ontario	o	-	-	-
University of Windsor	●	-	-	-
York University	●	-	-	-

APPENDIX C: Other Institutions

Included in this appendix are institutions which have some courses in linguisitics, but do not qualify for the main listing; institutions which requested not to be listed in the main text because their programs were in transition; and institutions which were listed in the previous edition and did not complete the questionnaire for the present work.

ALABAMA

Auburn University
Auburn, Alabama   36830

ARIZONA

Arizona State University
Tempe, Arizona   85281

CALIFORNIA

California Institute of Technology
Pasadena, California   91109

California State College, Hayward
Hayward, California   94542

California State University, Sacramento
Sacramento, California   95819

Pacific Union College
Angwin, California   94508

Simpson College
San Francisco, California   94134

COLORADO

Colorado State University
Fort Collins, Colorado   80521

University of Northern Colorado
Greeley, Colorado   80631

DELAWARE

University of Delaware
Newark, Delaware   19711

DISTRICT OF COLUMBIA

George Washington University
Washington, D. C.   20006

GEORGIA

Emory University
Atlanta, Georgia   30322

Georgia Southern College
Statesboro, Georgia   30458

HAWAII

Church College of Hawaii
Laie, Hawaii   96762

ILLINOIS

Southern Illinois University (Edwardsville)
Edwardsville, Illinois   62025

INDIANA

Earlham College
Richmond, Indiana   97374

IOWA

Central College
Pella, Iowa   50219

Drake University
Des Moines, Iowa   50311

KANSAS

Wichita State University
Wichita, Kansas   67208

KENTUCKY

University of Kentucky
Lexington, Kentucky   40506

Transylvania University
Lexington, Kentucky   40508

LOUISIANA

Centenary College of Louisiana
Shreveport, Louisiana   71104

Louisiana State University
Baton Rouge, Louisiana   70803

MAINE

University of Maine at Orono
Orono, Maine   04473

MARYLAND

Frostburg State College
Frostburg, Maryland   21532

University of Maryland, Baltimore County
Baltimore, Maryland   21228

MASSACHUSETTS

Assumption College
Worcester, Massachusetts 01609

College of the Holy Cross
Worcester, Massachusetts 01610

Southeastern Massachusetts University
North Dartmouth, Massachusetts 02747

MICHIGAN

Hope College
Holland, Michigan 49423

MINNESOTA

Mankato State College
Mankato, Minnesota 56001

MISSISSIPPI

Mississippi State University
Mississippi State, Mississippi 39762

MISSOURI

Central Missouri State College
Warrensburg, Missouri 64093

NEW MEXICO

Eastern New Mexico University
Portales, New Mexico 88130

NEW JERSEY

St. Peter's College
Jersey City, New Jersey 07306

NEW YORK

Adelphi University
Garden City, L. I., New York 11530

Hunter College of CUNY
New York, New York 10021

Rensselaer Polytechnic Institute
Troy, New York 12181

SUNY, College at Cortland
Cortland, New York 13045

SUNY, College at New Paltz
New Paltz, New York 12561

OHIO

University of Akron
Akron, Ohio 44304

Case Western Reserve University
Cleveland, Ohio 44106

OKLAHOMA

University of Oklahoma
Norman, Oklahoma 73069

OREGON

University of Oregon
Eugene, Oregon 97403

PENNSYLVANIA

Duquesne University
Pittsburgh, Pennsylvania 15219

Temple University
Philadelphia, Pennsylvania 19122

TEXAS

North Texas State
Denton, Texas 76203

Rice University
Houston, Texas 77001

Texas Tech University
Lubbock, Texas 79409

WASHINGTON

Central Washington State College
Ellensburg, Washington 98926

Washington State University
Pullman, Washington 99163

CANADA

Brandon University
Brandon, Manitoba

University of Guelph
Guelph, Ontario

Lakehead University
Thunder Bay, Ontario

Laurentian University
Sudbury, Ontario

Loyola of Montréal
Montréal, Québec

University of New Brunswick
Fredericton, New Brunswick

École Normal Notre Dame de Foy
Cap-Rouge, Québec

Université du Québec à Trois-Rivières
Trois-Rivières, Québec

Queen's University
Kingston, Ontario

AFGHAN-FARSI Pittsburgh.
AFRIKAANS Cal-San Diego.
AKAN Northwestern.
AKKADIAN Arizona, Brandeis, Brigham
  Young, Brown, Cal-Berkeley, Columbia,
  Harvard, Indiana, Mass-Amherst, Minne-
  sota, New York, Pennsylvania, South
  Florida, Washington, Yale.
ALBANIAN Cal-San Diego.
AMHARIC Bethel C, Cal-Santa Barbara,
  Howard, SUNY-Binghamton, Northwestern,
  Stanford, Syracuse.
ARABIC Arizona, Brigham Young, Cal-
  Berkeley, Cal-Irvine, Cal State-Los
  Angeles, Cal State-Fullerton, Carleton,
  Central Conn State C, Cleveland State,
  Colorado, Columbia, Georgetown, Harvard,
  Howard, Illinois-Chicago Circle,
  Illinois-Urbana-Champaign, Indiana,
  Kansas, Manitoba, Mass-Amherst, McGill,
  Michigan, Minnesota, New York, SUNY-
  Binghamton, North Carolina-Chapel Hill,
  Northeastern Illinois, Northern Illi-
  nois, Northwestern, Ohio State, Penn-
  sylvania, Penn State, Pittsburgh,
  Princeton, Queens C, Rochester, Sir
  George Williams, South Florida, South-
  ern Illinois, Stanford, Texas-Austin,
  Toledo, Utah, Virginia, Washington,
  Wayne State, Western Michigan, Wiscon-
  sin-Madison, Wisconsin-Milwaukee, Yale,
  Yeshiva.
ARABIC-CAIRO Texas-Austin.
ARABIC-CLASSICAL Harvard, Texas-Austin.
ARABIC-EASTERN Cal-San Diego.
ARABIC-EGYPTIAN Cal-San Diego.
ARABIC-IRAQI Cal-San Diego.
ARAMAIC Brigham Young, Harvard, Indiana,
  Manitoba, Minnesota, New York, Pennsyl-
  vania, Queens C, Wisconsin-Madison,
  Wisconsin-Milwaukee.
ARMENIAN Columbia, Harvard, Mass-Amherst,
  Wayne State.
ARMENIAN-CLASSICAL Boston C, Harvard.
ARMENIAN-MEDIEVAL Harvard.
ASSYRIAN Yale.
AVESTAN Boston C, Harvard.
AYMARA Florida.
AZERBAIJANI McGill.

BAMBARA UCLA.
BASQUE Cal-San Diego, Nevada-Reno.
BENGALI Cal-San Diego, Chicago, Hawaii,
  McGill, Minnesota, Pennsylvania.
BERBER Howard, Michigan.
BLACKFOOT Calgary.
BRETON Montreal.
BULGARIAN Cal-San Diego, Cal-Berkeley,
  Carleton, Chicago, Harvard, McGill,
  SUNY-Stony Brook, Northern Iowa, South
  Florida, Syracuse, Wisconsin-Madison.
BURMESE Cal-San Diego, Cornell, Hawaii,
  Illinois-Urbana-Champaign, Michigan.

CAMBODIAN Cornell, Hawaii, Southern
  Illinois.
CATALAN Montreal.
CEBUANO Bethel C, Cornell, Stanford.
CELTIC North Carolina-Chapel Hill.
CHEROKEE Stanford.
CHINESE American, Boston, British Colum-
  bia, Cal-Irvine, Cal State-Fresno, Cal
  State-Fullerton, Cal State-Long Beach,
  Cal State-Los Angeles, Cal State-North-
  ridge, Central Conn State C, Cincinnati,
  Cleveland State, Columbia, Duke, Federal
  City C, Florida, Harvard, Georgetown,
  Herbert H. Lehman C, Hofstra, Illinois-
  Chicago Circle, Illinois-Urbana-
  Champaign, Indiana, Iowa, Mass-Amherst,
  McGill, Miami U-Ohio, Michigan, Michigan
  State, Minnesota, Montana, New York,
  SUNY-Binghamton, SUNY-Stony Brook, North
  Carolina-Chapel Hill, Northwestern, Oak-
  land, Ohio, Ohio State, Oklahoma State,
  Oregon, Ottawa, Pennsylvania, Princeton,
  Queens C, Rutgers, South Florida, South-
  ern Mississippi, Texas-Austin, Vermont,
  Washington-St Louis, Wayne State, West-
  ern Wash State C, Wisconsin-Madison,
  Wisconsin-Milwaukee, Yale.
CHINESE-AMOY Cal-San Diego.
CHINESE-CANTONESE Bethel C, Cal-Berkeley,
  Cal-Davis, Cal-San Diego, Cornell,
  Hawaii, San Francisco State, San Jose
  State.
CHINESE-CLASSICAL Cal-Berkeley, Harvard,
  Ohio State, San Francisco State, Texas-
  Austin.
CHINESE-HOKKIEN Cornell.
CHINESE-LITERARY Chicago.
CHINESE-MANDARIN Brown, Calgary, Cal-
  Berkeley, Cal-Davis, Cal-San Diego,
  Cornell, Marion C, Maryland, Montreal,
  Northern Illinois, San Francisco State,
  San Jose State, Simon Fraser, Virginia,
  Western Michigan.
CHIPPEWA Minnesota-Duluth.
CHOCTAW Southern Mississippi.
CHUVASH Harvard, Indiana.
COPTIC Brigham Young, Cal-Berkeley, Sir
  George Williams, Yale.
COWICHAN Victoria.
CREE Calgary, McGill, Ottawa, Saskatch-
  ewan-Saskatoon, Newfoundland.
CZECH American, Boston C, Brown, Cal-
  Berkeley, Cal-San Diego, Carleton,
  Chicago, Columbia, Houston, Indiana,
  McGill, Michigan, SUNY-Stony Brook,
  Oregon, Queens C, South Florida, Stan-
  ford, Texas-Austin, Texas A&M, Wiscon-
  sin-Madison.

DAKOTA Minnesota.
DANISH Cal-Berkeley, Cal-San Diego,
  Indiana, Mass-Amherst, Minnesota, SUNY-
  Stony Brook, Northern Iowa, Queens C.

DUTCH Cal-Berkeley, Cal-San Diego, Columbia, Duke, Indiana, Mass-Amherst, Michigan, Minnesota, New Hampshire, Pennsylvania, Penn State, Queens C, South Florida, Stanford, Texas-Austin.

EFIK Cal-San Diego.
EGYPTIAN Brigham Young, Brown, Cal-Berkeley, Pennsylvania, Yale.
EGYPTIAN-ANCIENT Minnesota.
OLD ENGLISH Boston C, British Columbia, Brown, Cal-Berkeley, Cal-Davis, Carleton, Chicago, Cincinnati, Illinois-Urbana-Champaign, Indiana, Iowa, Michigan, Minnesota, Nebraska, Nevada-Reno, New Hampshire, Ohio State, Oregon, Princeton, Rutgers, San Diego State, San Francisco State, South Florida, Syracuse, Vermont, Virginia, Wayne State, Wisconsin-Madison, Wisconsin-Milwaukee, Yale.
MIDDLE ENGLISH Boston C, Cal-Davis, Cincinnati, Illinois-Urbana-Champaign, Indiana, Michigan, Minnesota, Nebraska, Nevada-Reno, Oregon, Princeton, San Diego State, Vermont, Wayne State, Wisconsin-Madison, Wisconsin-Milwaukee, Yale.
ESKIMO Bethel C, McGill, Ottawa, Quebec-Montreal, San Diego State, Newfoundland.
ESTONIAN Indiana, McGill.
ETHIOPIC Yale.
ETHIOPIC-CLASSICAL Harvard.
FILIPINO San Francisco State.
FINNISH Cal-San Diego, Columbia, Indiana, Minnesota, McGill, Wisconsin-Madison.
OLD FRENCH Boston C, Harvard, Illinois-Urbana-Champaign, Minnesota, Nebraska, Oregon, Princeton, San Francisco State, Virginia.
OLD FRISIAN New Hampshire.

GAELIC-IRISH British Columbia, Harvard, Pittsburgh, Stanford.
GAELIC-SCOTS/SCOTTISH British Columbia, Cincinnati, Harvard, Michigan.
GEORGIAN Chicago, Indiana, McGill.
GEORGIAN-CLASSICAL Harvard.
MIDDLE HIGH GERMAN Brown, Cal-Davis, Carleton, Cincinnati, Harvard, Illinois-Urbana-Champaign, Indiana, Iowa, Michigan, Minnesota, Nebraska, New Hampshire, SUNY-Stony Brook, Ohio State, Oregon, Pennsylvania, Princeton, Wisconsin-Madison, Yale.
OLD HIGH GERMAN Cal-Berkeley, Cal-Davis, Harvard, Illinois-Urbana-Champaign, Indiana, Iowa, Michigan, Minnesota, Nebraska, New Hampshire, SUNY-Stony Brook, Ohio State, Oregon, Pennsylvania, Princeton, Wisconsin-Madison, Yale.
GOTHIC Cal-Berkeley, Cal-Davis, Harvard, Illinois-Urbana-Champaign, Iowa, Mass-Amherst, Manitoba, Minnesota, Nebraska, New Hampshire, SUNY-Stony Brook, Ohio State, Oregon, Princeton, Yale.
GREEK American, Cal-San Diego, Columbia, Florida, Indiana, Illinois-Urbana-Champaign, Mary Washington C, Maryland, Mass-Amherst, McGill, Minnesota, Montreal, SUNY-Binghamton, North Carolina-Chapel Hill, Northern Illinois, Northern Iowa, Ohio State, Penn State, Pittsburgh, Queens C, South Florida, Texas-Austin.
GUJARATI Pennsylvania.

HAITIAN CREOLE Cal-San Diego, Indiana.
HAUSA Cal-San Diego, Columbia, Teachers C/Columbia, UCLA, Howard, Indiana, Iowa State, McGill, Michigan State, North Carolina-Chapel Hill, Northwestern, Ohio, Rutgers, Stanford, Wisconsin-Madison.
HAWAIIAN Cal-San Diego, Hawaii, Hilo C.
HEBREW American, Arizona, Boston C, Boston U, Brandeis, British Columbia, Brown, Cal-Berkeley, Cal-Irvine, Cal-San Diego, Cal State-Fresno, Cal State-Long Beach, Cal State-Los Angeles, Cal State-Northridge, Carleton, Cincinnati, Colorado, Columbia, Florida, Grad School of CUNY, Hartford, Harvard, Hofstra, Houston, Illinois-Urbana-Champaign, Illinois-Chicago Circle, Indiana, Kansas, Manitoba, Marion C, Mass-Amherst, McGill, Miami U-Ohio, Michigan, Minnesota, New York, SUNY-Binghamton, SUNY-Stony Brook, North Carolina-Chapel Hill, Northern Illinois, Northwestern, Oakland, Ohio State, Oklahoma State, Pennsylvania, Penn State, Pittsburgh, Princeton, Rochester, Rutgers, San Francisco State, San Jose State, Southern Illinois, South Florida, Stanford, Syracuse, Texas-Austin, Utah, Vermont, Western Michigan, Wayne State, Wisconsin-Madison, Wisconsin-Milwaukee, Yale, Yeshiva.
HEBREW-BIBLICAL Boston C, Brown, Harvard, Illinois-Urbana-Champaign, North Carolina-Chapel Hill, SUNY-Stony Brook, Princeton, South Florida, Stanford, Virginia.
HINDI American, Arizona, Boston, British Columbia, Cal-San Diego, UCLA, Cal State-Long Beach, Cal State-Sonoma, Chicago, Hartford, Hawaii, Illinois-Urbana-Champaign, Kansas State, McGill, Minnesota, Missouri-Columbia, Pennsylvania, Penn State, Pittsburgh, South Florida, Syracuse, Texas-Austin, Virginia, Washington-St Louis, Wisconsin-Madison.
HINDI-URDU Cal-Berkeley, Columbia, Cornell, Duke, Michigan, Oakland, Washington, Western Michigan.
HITTITE Boston C, Cal-Berkeley, Harvard, Illinois-Urbana-Champaign, New Hampshire, North Carolina-Chapel Hill, Pennsylvania, Yale, Toronto.
HOPI Arizona, Northern Arizona.
HUNGARIAN Cal-Berkeley, Cal-San Diego, Cleveland State, Columbia, Indiana, McGill, Michigan, SUNY-Binghamton, SUNY-Stony Brook, Penn State, Pittsburgh.

HURRIAN Yale.

ICELANDIC Cal-San Diego, Manitoba,
  Minnesota, Nebraska, SUNY-Stony Brook,
  Queens C, Washington.
OLD ICELANDIC Brown, Cal-Berkeley, Cal
  State-Dominguez Hills, Indiana, Mass-
  Amherst, Manitoba, Nebraska, Oregon,
  Pennsylvania, Virginia.
IGBO Cal-San Diego, Cal State-Northridge,
  Iowa State, Michigan State.
ILOCANO Hawaii, San Jose State.
INDONESIAN Cornell, Hawaii, Illinois-
  Urbana-Champaign, McGill, Michigan,
  Northern Illinois, Ohio, Pittsburgh,
  Stanford, Yale.
IRANIAN Columbia.
OLD IRANIAN Cal-Berkeley.
IRISH (See GAELIC-IRISH)
MIDDLE IRISH Harvard, Indiana.
OLD IRISH Harvard, Indiana, Princeton.
OLD ITALIAN San Francisco State.

JAPANESE American, Boston, British
  Columbia, Brown, Cal-Berkeley, Cal-
  Davis, Cal-Irvine, Cal-San Diego,
  Cal State-Fullerton, Cal State-Long
  Beach, Cal State-Los Angeles, Cal
  State-Northridge, Cincinnati, Columbia,
  Cornell, Duke, Georgetown, Harvard,
  Hawaii, Hilo C, Hofstra, Illinois-
  Urbana-Champaign, Indiana, Iowa, Mary
  Washington C, Maryland, Mass-Amherst,
  McGill, Miami U-Ohio, Michigan State,
  Michigan, Minnesota, Montreal, New
  Hampshire, New York, SUNY-Binghamton,
  North Carolina-Chapel Hill, Northern
  Illinois, Ohio State, Oklahoma State,
  Oregon, U of the Pacific, Pennsylvania,
  Penn State, Princeton, Rochester, San
  Francisco State, San Jose State, South
  Florida, Syracuse, Texas-Austin, Ver-
  mont, Virginia, Washington-St Louis,
  Western Michigan, Western Wash State C,
  Wisconsin-Madison, Wisconsin-Milwaukee,
  Yale.
JAPANESE-CLASSICAL Chicago, Harvard,
  Texas-Austin.
JAVANESE Cornell, Yale.
JUDEO-ARABIC Yeshiva.
JUDESMO Yeshiva.

KASHAYA POMO Cal State-Sonoma.
KASHMIRI Illinois-Urbana-Champaign.
KAZAKH McGill.
KHALKHA Harvard.
KISWAHILI Rutgers.
KOREAN Cal-Berkeley, Cal-San Diego,
  Columbia, Harvard, Hawaii, Illinois-
  Urbana-Champaign, Indiana, Pittsburgh,
  Stanford, Victoria, Western Michigan,
  Yale.
KRIO Northwestern.
KUMEYAAY San Diego State.
KURDISH Harvard, Michigan.

LAKOTA Colorado, San Diego State.
LAO Hawaii, Southern Illinois.

LATVIAN American, British Columbia,
  McGill, Stanford, Western Michigan.
LINGALA Howard.
LITHUANIAN British Columbia, Illinois-
  Chicago Circle, McGill, Michigan,
  Northern Iowa, Yale.
LUGANDA Cal-San Diego.
LUWIAN Yale.

MACEDONIAN SUNY-Stony Brook.
MALAY Cal-San Diego, McGill, SUNY-
  Binghamton, Northern Illinois.
MALAYALAM Chicago, Pennsylvania.
MANDARIN (See CHINESE-MANDARIN)
MANDE Northwestern.
MANDINGO Indiana.
MAORI Cal-San Diego.
MARATHI Chicago, Hawaii, Michigan,
  Minnesota, Pennsylvania.
MAYA (YUCATEC) Texas-Austin, Tulane,
  Washington-St Louis.
MICMAC Newfoundland.
MIWOK-LAKE Ohio State.
MOHAWK Quebec-Montreal, Toronto.
MONGOLIAN Cal-Berkeley, Harvard, Indiana,
  Washington.
MONGOLIAN-CLASSICAL Harvard, Indiana.
MONGOLIAN-MIDDLE Harvard.
MONTAGNAIS Quebec-Montreal.

NAHUATL Cal State-Northridge, San Diego
  State, Texas-San Antonio, Tulane.
NASKAPI Newfoundland.
NAVAJO Brigham Young, Cal-San Diego,
  UCLA, New Mexico, Northern Arizona,
  San Diego State, Stanford.
NEPALI Cal-San Diego, Pennsylvania.
OLD NORSE Carleton, Cincinnati, Harvard,
  Illinois-Urbana-Champaign, Iowa, Mass-
  Amherst, Minnesota, Nevada-Reno, Ohio
  State, Princeton.
NORWEGIAN Cal-Berkeley, Cal-San Diego,
  Harvard, Michigan, Minnesota, Northern
  Iowa, Oregon, Stanford, Texas-Austin.

OJIBWA Michigan, Minnesota, Toronto.
OSCAN-UMBRIAN Columbia, Minnesota, Yale.

PALI Cal State-Long Beach, Harvard,
  Hawaii, Michigan, Yale.
PANJABI Cal-San Diego.
PAPAGO Arizona.
PASHTO Harvard.
PERSIAN Arizona, Cal-Berkeley, Cal-San
  Diego, Columbia, Grad School of CUNY,
  Harvard, Illinois-Urbana-Champaign,
  Indiana, Mass-Amherst, McGill, Michigan,
  Minnesota, New York, SUNY-Binghamton,
  Pennsylvania, Pittsburgh, Princeton,
  Southern Illinois, Texas-Austin, Utah,
  Wisconsin-Madison.
MIDDLE PERSIAN Harvard.
OLD PERSIAN Boston C, Harvard, Michigan,
  Minnesota, Yale.
PIDGIN-NIGERIAN Cal-San Diego, Michigan
  State.
PIDGIN-NEW GUINEA Bethel C.
PIDGIN-SIGN ENGLISH Gallaudet C.

POLISH American, British Columbia, Cal-Berkeley, Cal-San Diego, Chicago, Cleveland State, Florida, Harvard, Illinois-Urbana-Champaign, Indiana, Manitoba, McGill, Michigan, Minnesota, SUNY-Binghamton, SUNY-Oswego C, SUNY-Stony Brook, Ohio State, Oregon, Pennsylvania, Queens C, Rutgers, South Florida, Stanford, Virginia, Wayne State, Wisconsin-Milwaukee, Yale.
OLD POLISH Ohio State.
PORTUGUESE Boston C, Brown, Cal-Berkeley, Cal-Irvine, Cal-San Diego, Carleton, Cornell, Federal City C, Georgetown, Harvard, Hilo C, Iowa, Mass-Amherst, Michigan, Minnesota, Nevada-Reno, SUNY-Binghamton, SUNY-Stony Brook, Northern Illinois, Oakland, Ohio State, Princeton, Queens C, Rutgers, Stanford, Syracuse, Texas-Austin, Virginia, Western Wash State C, Wisconsin-Madison, Wisconsin-Milwaukee, Yale.
PRAKRIT Chicago, Hawaii, Michigan, Virginia, Yale.
PROVENÇAL Boston C.
OLD PROVENÇAL British Columbia, Cal-Berkeley, Cal-Davis, Minnesota, Ohio State, Pennsylvania.
OLD PRUSSIAN British Columbia.

QUECHUA Cornell, UCLA, Gordon C, Indiana, New Mexico, Montreal, Texas-Austin.

RAJASTHANI Chicago.
ROMANIAN Boston C, Columbia, Harvard, Indiana, McGill, Ohio State, Pittsburgh, Stanford.
OLD RUSSIAN Boston C, Harvard, SUNY-Stony Brook, Ohio State.

SANSKRIT Boston C, Boston U, British Columbia, Brown, Cal-Berkeley, Cal State-Fullerton, Cal State-Long Beach, Cal State-Los Angeles, Cal State-Sonoma, Carleton, Chicago, Colorado, Columbia, Harvard, Hawaii, Illinois-Urbana-Champaign, Indiana, Manitoba, Maryland, McGill, Michigan State, Michigan, Minnesota, Missouri-Columbia, Newfoundland, New Hampshire, New York, SUNY-Binghamton, SUNY-Stony Brook, North Carolina-Chapel Hill, Northern Iowa, Ohio State, Pennsylvania, Princeton, San Diego State, San Francisco State, South Florida, Stanford, Syracuse, Texas-Austin, Utah, Virginia, Washington, Washington-St Louis, Wisconsin-Madison, Yale.
OLD SAXON Cal-Berkeley, Cal-Davis, Iowa, Mass-Amherst, Michigan, Minnesota, Ohio State, Oregon, Pennsylvania, Princeton, Yale.
OLD SERBIAN Ohio State.
SERBO-CROATIAN, SERBO-CROAT Boston C, British Columbia, Brown, Cal-Berkeley, Cal-San Diego, Chicago, Columbia, Harvard, Illinois-Chicago Circle, Illinois-Urbana-Champaign, Indiana, McGill,

Michigan, Minnesota, SUNY-Binghamton, SUNY-Stony Brook, Ohio State, Oregon, Pennsylvania, Queens C, Stanford, Syracuse, Texas-Austin, Vermont, Virginia, Washington, Wisconsin-Madison, Wisconsin-Milwaukee.
SIGN LANGUAGE, AMERICAN Gallaudet C.
SINHALESE Cornell, Pittsburgh.
SIOUX Stanford.
MEDIEVAL SLAVIC Harvard.
OLD CHURCH SLAVONIC/SLAVIC Boston C, British Columbia, Cal-Davis, Carleton, Harvard, Illinois-Urbana-Champaign, Indiana, Manitoba, Mass-Amherst, Michigan, SUNY-Stony Brook, Ohio State, Oregon, Pennsylvania, South Florida, Utah, Yale.
SLOVAK McGill, SUNY-Stony Brook.
SLOVENIAN SUNY-Stony Brook, Stanford.
SOGDIAN Harvard.
SOMALI Syracuse.
SOTHO Howard, Wisconsin-Madison.
OLD SPANISH Boston C, Illinois-Urbana-Champaign, Iowa, Nebraska, Ohio State, Oregon, Virginia.
STONEY Calgary.
SUMERIAN Cal-Berkeley, Columbia, Harvard, Minnesota, New York, Pennsylvania, Yale.
SWAHILI Brandeis, Brown, UCLA, Cal-San Diego, Cal State-Fullerton, Cal State-Northridge, Carleton, Cincinnati, Cleveland State, Columbia, Teachers C/Columbia, Duke, Federal City C, Florida, Herbert H. Lehman C, Hofstra, Houston, Howard, Illinois-Chicago Circle, Illinois-Urbana-Champaign, Indiana, Iowa State, Maryland, Mass-Amherst, McGill, Michigan State, Minnesota, Montclair State C, SUNY-Binghamton, North Carolina-Chapel Hill, Northern Illinois, Northwestern, Oakland, Ohio, Ohio State, Penn State, Queens C, San Jose State, Simon Fraser, Sir George Williams, Southern Illinois, Southern Mississippi, Stanford, Syracuse, Texas-Austin, Vermont, Washington, Wayne State, Western Michigan, Wisconsin-Madison, Wisconsin-Milwaukee, Youngstown State.
SWEDISH Cal-Berkeley, Cal-Davis, Cal-San Diego, Cincinnati, Cornell, Harvard, Mass-Amherst, Minnesota, SUNY-Binghamton, SUNY-Stony Brook, Northern Iowa, Oregon, Penn State, Pittsburgh, Rochester, Stanford, Texas-Austin, Virginia.
SYRIAC Brigham Young, Columbia, Harvard, Minnesota, Princeton.

TAGALOG Bethel C, Cal-San Diego, Cornell, Hawaii, Pittsburgh, San Jose State, Stanford.
TAMIL Boston C, Boston U, Cal-Berkeley, Chicago, Cornell, Hawaii, Kansas State, Pennsylvania, Washington, Wisconsin-Madison.
TAMIL-CLASSICAL Chicago.
TELEGU Cornell, Pennsylvania, Wisconsin-Madison.
THAI American, Bethel C, Brigham Young, Cal-San Diego, UCLA, Cornell, Hawaii, Illinois-Urbana-Champaign, Michigan,

Northern Illinois, Pittsburgh, Washington.
TIBETAN Cal-Berkeley, Cal-San Diego, Columbia, Indiana, SUNY-Stony Brook, Pennsylvania, Washington.
TIBETAN-CLASSICAL Harvard.
TOCHARIAN Yale.
TSWANA Howard.
OLD TURKIC Harvard, Indiana.
MIDDLE TURKIC Harvard.
TURKISH Brigham Young, Brown, Cal-Berkeley, Cal-San Diego, Columbia, Harvard, Indiana, Mass-Amherst, McGill, Michigan, Minnesota, New York, Pennsylvania, Penn State, Pittsburgh, Princeton, Sir George Williams, Utah, Washington.
TURKISH-RUNIC Boston C.
TWI Cal-San Diego, Howard, Iowa State, Northeastern Illinois, Stanford.

UGARITIC Brandeis, Brigham Young, Columbia, Drew, Harvard, New York, Washington.
OLD UIGHUR Harvard.
UKRANIAN Carleton, Chicago, Florida, Harvard, Illinois-Urbana-Champaign, Indiana, Manitoba, McGill, Michigan, SUNY-Stony Brook, Oregon, Pennsylvania, Syracuse, Wayne State.
URDU Chicago, Illinois-Urbana-Champaign, Kansas State, McGill, Minnesota, Pennsylvania.
URDU-CLASSICAL Harvard.
UZBEK Columbia, Indiana, Washington.

VEDIC Chicago.
VIETNAMESE Cal-San Diego, Cornell, Harvard, Hawaii, Penn State, Pittsburgh, Southern Illinois, Yale.

WASWAHILI Rutgers.
WELSH Grad School of CUNY, Pittsburgh.
EARLY WELSH Harvard.

XHOSA UCLA, Cal State-Northridge, Wisconsin-Madison.

YIDDISH Brandeis, Cal-San Diego, Columbia, Manitoba, McGill, Michigan, Minnesota, SUNY-Binghamton, SUNY-Stony Brook, Pittsburgh, Rutgers, Stanford, Texas-Austin, Wisconsin-Milwaukee, Yeshiva.
YORUBA UCLA, Cal-San Diego, Howard, Herbert H. Lehman C, Illinois-Urbana-Champaign, Iowa State, Michigan State, Pittsburgh, Queens C, San Jose State, Stanford.

ZULU UCLA, Howard.
ZUNI Northern Arizona.

Aarsleff, Hans C.; Princeton
Abler, W.; Illinois Inst of Tech
Abrahamson, Adele; Rutgers
Abramson, Arthur S.; Connecticut
Abu-Absi, Samir; Toledo
Adenwala, Mridula; Washington-St Louis
Agard, F.B.; Cornell
Aissen, Judith; Harvard
Akmajian, Adrian; Mass-Amherst
Alatis, James E.; Georgetown
Algeo, John T.; Georgia
Allen, Doris A.; Columbia, Teachers C
Allen, Robert L.; Columbia, Teachers C
Allen, Walter P.; Houston
Alleyne, Mervyn C.; SUNY-Buffalo
Altmann, Anneliese; Simon Fraser
Alvarez, Gerardo; Laval
Amneus, Daniel A.; Cal State-Los Angeles
Anders, William; C.W. Post C
Anderson, Earl; Cleveland State
Anderson, Edmund A.; Bethel C
Anderson, Geraldine; Cal State-Fullerton
Anderson, James M.; Calgary
Anderson, Stephen R.; Harvard
Andreani, Pierre; Québec-Montreal
Andrews, J. Richard; Nashville U Ctr
Angelis, Paul; Texas A&M
Anisfeld, Moshe; Yeshiva
Anshen, Frank; SUNY-Stony Brook
Antell, Stephen A.; Queens C
Anthony, Edward M.; Pittsburgh
Anttila, Raimo; UCLA
Appleby, Jane; Georgia
Applegate, Richard B.; San Jose State
Apte, Mahadeo L.; Duke
Arbini, Ronald A.; Cal-Davis
Arenas, Marco A.; Central Conn State C
Arletto, Anthony T.; Harvard
Armagost, James L.; Kansas State
Aronoff Mark; SUNY-Stony Brook
Aronson, Howard I.; Chicago
Arthurs, J.; Victoria
Asselin, Claire; Québec-Montreal
Atkins, Samuel D.; Princeton
Auletta, Richard; C.W. Post C
Aurbach, Joseph; Herbert H. Lehman C
Austerlitz, Robert; Columbia

Babby, L.H.; Cornell
Bach, Emmon; Mass-Amherst, Hampshire C
Bahl, Kali; Chicago
Bailey, Beryl; Grad School of CUNY
Bailey, Dudley; Nebraska
Baird, Rey L.; Brigham Young
Baird, Scott; Trinity
Baker, C.L.; Texas-Austin
Baker, Wm.J.; Alberta
Bandeen, B.I.; Western Ontario
Banfield, Ann; Washington
Bar-Adon, Aaron; Texas-Austin
Barbaud, Philippe; Quebec-Montreal
Barnes, Lewis; Morehead State
Barnes, Marie C.; Florida Atlantic
Barnes, Ruth; Morehead State
Baron, Naomi S.; Brown

Barone, Joseph; Rutgers
Barrutia, Richard; Cal-Irvine
Barthelmess, James; Cleveland State
Bartlett, B.E.; Simon Fraser
Barton, Charles R.; Sir George Williams
Bartz, Wayne; Iowa State
Baslaw, Annette; Columbia, Teachers C
Bastian, Jarvis R.; Cal-Davis
Battison, Robbin M.; Gallaudet C
Battle, John; Oklahoma State
Bauer, Luanne; Andrews
Baumhoff, Martin A.; Cal-Davis
Beade, Pedro; York
Beatie, Bruce; Cleveland State
Beauchemin, Normand; Sherbrooke
Beaver, Joseph C.; Northeastern Illinois
Beck, Richard C.; Brown
Becker, Alton L.; Michigan
Becker, Edward F.; Nebraska
Bedell, George; UCLA
Beechhold, Henry F.; Trenton State C
Beeler, Madison S.; Cal-Berkeley
Bell, Alan E.; Colorado
Bellert, Irena; McGill
Beltramo, Anthony; Montana
Bender, Byron W.; Hawaii
Bendix, Edward; Grad School of CUNY
Benjamin, Anna; Rutgers
Benware, Wilbur A.; Cal-Davis
Berger, Marshall D.; City C of CUNY
Berkovits, Rochelle; Queens C
Berman, Aaron S.; Cal State-Sonoma
Berman, Arlene; Texas-Austin
Berry, Jack; Northwestern
Bertholf, Dennis E.; Oklahoma State
Bessason, Haraldur; Manitoba
Beulieu, Alain; Québec-Montréal
Bever, Thomas; Columbia
Bevington, Gary; Northeastern Illinois
Beym, Richard; Cal State-Dominguez Hills
Bezdek, Vladimir; Wayne State
Bhatt, Sooda; Boston
Bickerton, Derek; Hawaii
Bills, Garland; New Mexico
Binkert, Peter J.; Oakland
Bird, Charles S.; Indiana
Bird, Donald A.; Cal State-Los Angeles
Birnes, William; Trenton State C
Blair, Robert W.; Brigham Young
Blanco, Walter; Herbert H. Lehman C
Blansitt, Edward L.; Texas-El Paso
Blanton, M.J.V.; Illinois Inst of Tech
Blasedell, Richard; Iowa
Blaubergs, Maija; Georgia
Blumstein, Sheila E.; Brown
Boardman, Phillip C.; Nevada-Reno
Bodine, Ann; Rutgers
Bodman, N.C.; Cornell
Bohn, Roshni; Cal State-Sonoma
Boisvert, Lionel; Laval
Bokamba, E. Georges; Illinois-Urbana-
  Champaign
Bolton, Robert; Rutgers
Bolton, Whitney; Rutgers
Bone, Robert A.; Columbia, Teachers C

Bordie, John G.; Texas-Austin
Borkin, Ann H.; Michigan
Borowiec, E.J.; Cal State-Long Beach
Bouma, Lowell; Georgia
Boudreau, André; Laval
Boudreault, Marcel; Laval
Bouton, C.P.; Simon Fraser
Bowers, J.S.; Cornell
Bowers, John W.; Iowa
Bowman, Elizabeth; Western Wash State C
Boyd, John A.; Nebraska
Brainerd, B.; Toronto
Brame, Michael; Washington
Brandeau, John; Hampshire C
Brend, Ruth M.; Michigan State
Brengelman, Frederick H.; Cal State-Fresno
Bresnan, Joan; Mass-Amherst
Bright, Elizabeth S.; Cal State-Sonoma
Bright, William; UCLA
Brenzinger, Ingrida; British Columbia
Bricker, Victoria R.; Tulane
Briere, Eugene J.; Southern Cal
Broadbent, Sylvia; Cal-Riverside
Broderick, John P.; South Florida
Brodkey, Dean; New Mexico
Bronstein, Arthur; Grad School of CUNY
Bronstein, Arthur J.; Herbert H. Lehman C
Brown, A. Delores; Arizona
Brown, Cecil H.; Northern Illinois
Brown, H. Douglas; Michigan
Brown, Marice C.; Southern Mississippi
Bruder, Mary N.; Pittsburgh
Brunet, J.; Ottawa
Bubenik, V.; Memorial U of Newfoundland
Bunnag, Jerome; Youngstown State
Bureau, Conrad; Laval
Burkart, Edward; American
Burling, Robbins; Michigan
Bursill-Hall, G.L.; Simon Fraser
Burstynsky, E.M.; Toronto
Bush, Clara N.; Stanford
Bussieres, Michele; Laval
Butters, Ronald R.; Duke
Byrd, Donald; Grad School of CUNY
Byrne, Robert A.; Southwestern Louisiana

Caflisch, Jacob C.; South Florida
Cairns, Charles; Grad School of CUNY,
  Queens C
Cairns, Helen; Grad School of CUNY
Calimag, Estrella; San Jose State
Callaghan, Catherine A.; Ohio State
Callary, Robert E.; Northern Illinois
Calve, P.; Ottawa
Campbell, Mary Ann; San Jose State
Campbell, R. Joe; Texas-San Antonio
Campbell, Thomas P.; Cal-Davis
Cannon, Garland; Texas A&M
Cano, Juan; Boston
Cantrall, William R.; Northern Illinois
Capp, Michael; Detroit
Carden, Guy; Yale
Cárdenas, Daniel; Cal State-Long Beach
Cardona, George; Pennsylvania
Carlson, B.F.; Victoria
Carlson, Charles; East Texas State
Carlson, Helen; Purdue

Carlton, Charles R.; Cal State-North-
  ridge, Rochester
Carmony, Marvin; Indiana State
Carnicelli, Thomas A.; New Hampshire
Carpenter, Martha; Cal State-Sonoma
Carrell, Patricia; Southern Illinois-
  Carbondale
Carter, Marion; Gordon C
Carter, Richard T., Jr.; Manitoba
Carr, Burchard; Oklahoma State
Casagrande, Jean; Florida
Cassel, Thomas Z.; Wayne State
Casson, Ronald W.; Duke
Castleman, Alan S.; Columbia
Catford, John C.; Michigan
Cedergren, Henrietta; Québec-Montréal
Chafe, Wallace L.; Cal-Berkeley
Chambers, J.K.; Toronto
Chan, Marie C.; Brown
Chandola, Anoop C.; Arizona
Chang, Hyungsook Paik; Western Michigan
Chanover, Susan; SUNY-Stony Brook
Chapin, Paul G.; Cal-San Diego
Chapman, Robert; Drew
Chavarria-Aguilar, O.L.; City C of CUNY
Cheek, John H.; Nashville U Ctr
Chen, Lilia; Western Michigan
Chen, Matthew Y-Ch; Cal-San Diego
Cheng, Chin-chuan; Illinois-Urbana/Cham.
Chevalier, Carmen; Inter American
Chisholm, William; Cleveland State
Chomsky, Noam; MIT
Chreist, Fred; New Mexico
Christian, Chester C.; Texas A&M
Christian, Herbert O.; Inter American
Ch'u, Chauncey C.; Florida
Cintas, Pierre F.; Virginia
Civil, Miguel; Chicago
Cizevska, Tatjana; Wayne State
Clark, Eve V.; Stanford
Clark, Richard C.; Macalester C
Clarke, Nona H.; Federal City C
Clarke, Sandra; Laval
Clas, André; Montréal
Clubb, Merrel D., Jr.; Montana
Coady, James; Ohio
Cogan, Nathan F.; Pacific
Cohen, Daniel R.; Herbert H. Lehman C
Cohen, David; Wisconsin-Milwaukee
Cole, Peter; Illinois-Urbana-Champaign
Cole, Roger W.; South Florida
Coleman, Robert; Nashville U Ctr
Colhoun, E.R.; Simon Fraser
Collinge, Pierre; Sherbrooke
Coltharp, Lurline H.; Texas-El Paso
Condax, Iovanna D.; Hawaii
Conner, J. Wayne; Florida
Connolly, Michael J.; Boston C
Connolly, Guy; Montréal
Connors-Pupier, Kathleen; Montréal
Contreras, Heles; Washington
Cook, Eung-Do; Calgary
Cook, Mary Jane; Arizona
Cook, Philip H.; San Jose State
Cook, Walter A., S.J.; Georgetown
Cooke, Benjamin; Howard
Cooke, Faye Vaughn; Federal City C

Cooley, Marianne; Cal-Davis
Cooper, Franklin S.; Connecticut
Cooper, June; Cal State-Long Beach
Cooper, Russell E.; Marion C
Corbett, Noel; York
Cortes, Eileen; Inter American
Cortés, Julio; No. Carolina-Chapel Hill
Cosper, Russell; Purdue
Costa, Rachel M.; Michigan State
Costello, John R.; New York
Cotton, Eleanor G.; Texas-El Paso
Coupal-Dorion, Lysanne; Laval
Courtenay, Karen; UCLA
Cowan, William G.; Carleton
Cowgill, Warren; Yale
Cox, Keith D.; Ball State
Cox, Robert S.; Pacific
Cox, Soren F.; Brigham Young
Crabb, David W.; Princeton
Crawford, Ann Cartwright; Alberta
Crawford, James M.; Georgia
Creider, C.A.; Western Ontario
Crenshaw, James L.; Nashville U Ctr
Crist, Larry S.; Nashville U Ctr
Crockett, Harry J.; Nebraska
Croft, Kenneth; San Francisco State
Culicover, Peter; Cal-Irvine
Cunningham, Irma; Purdue
Curtis, James F.; Iowa

Dabbs, Jack A.; Texas A&M
Dakin, Robert; Ohio
Daly, Saralyn R.; Cal State-Los Angeles
Danielson, Dorothy; San Francisco State
Danielson, J. David; Hartford
Dammann, James E.; Colorado
Darbelnet, Jean; Laval
Darden, Bill J.; Chicago
Dato, Daniel P.; Georgetown
Davis, A.L.; Illinois Inst of Tech
Davis, Robert M.; New Hampshire
Davison, Alice; SUNY-Stony Brook
Dearin, Ray D.; Iowa State
DeArmond, R.C.; Simon Fraser
DeCamp, David; Texas-Austin
Decker, Henry; Cal-Riverside
Deese, James; Virginia
D'Eloia, Sarah G.; City C of CUNY
deGorog, Ralph; Georgia
Dellinger, David W.; Northern Illinois
Dembowski, Peter F.; Chicago
Demers, Richard A.; Mass-Amherst
Den Ouden, Bernard; Hartford
Dennis, John; San Francisco State
Denny, J.P.; Western Ontario
DePauola, Peter; Queens C
deQueljoe, David H.; Northern Illinois
Derbyshire, William; Rutgers
DeRemer, Franklin L.; Cal-Santa Cruz
Der-Houssiakian, Haig; Florida
Derwing, Bruce L.; Alberta
Deshpande, Madhav M.; Michigan
Dew, Donald D.; Florida
Dewees, John; Ohio
Diamond, Robert E.; Nevada-Reno
Diffloth, Gerard; Chicago
Dil, Afia; San Diego State
Diller, Karl C.; New Hampshire

Dingwall, William Orr; Maryland
Dinneen, David A.; Kansas
Dinneen, Francis P., S.J.; Georgetown
Dinnsen, Daniel; Indiana
Di Pietro, Robert J.; Georgetown
DiSilvio, Patricia; Rutgers
Disraeli, A. Stephen; Mary Washington C
Diver, William; Columbia
Dobrovolsky, Michael B.; Carleton
Donahue, Thomas S.; San Diego State
Dorman, Michael F.; Herbert H. Lehman C
Dougherty, Ray C.; New York
Douglass, Thomas; Iowa
Doutreloux, Jean-Marie; Sherbrooke
Downing, Bruce T.; Minnesota
Dowty, David R.; Ohio State
Drake, Glendon F.; San Diego State
Dronenfeld, David; Cal-Riverside
Dubin, Fraida; Southern Cal
Dubuisson, Colette; Quebec-Montreal
Dudley, Ruth M.; South Florida
Dugas, Andre; Quebec-Montreal
Duggan, Hoyt N.; Virginia
Dulong, Gaston; Laval
Dumas, Denis; Québec-Montréal
Duncan, Caroline; Cal State-Dominguez
  Hills
Dunn, Ernest; Rutgers
Dunn, James M.; Princeton
Durbin, Marshall; Washington
Durham, S.P.; Cornell
Duschesne, Jacques; Québec-Montréal
Dusek, R. Valentine; New Hampshire
Dwarikesh, D.P.S.; Western Michigan
Dyen, Isidore; Yale

Eaton, Dannis; Columbia, Teachers C
Eberthardt, Elvire; Laval
Echols, J.M.; Cornell
Eckert, Penelope; Michigan
Eckman, Fred; Wisconsin-Milwaukee
Edmonson, Munro S.; Tulane
Ehlers, Henry J.; Minnesota-Duluth
Ehri, Linnea C.; Cal-Davis
Ekeleme, Adaihudma Rosaline; Nashville
  U Ctr
Elbert, Samuel H.; Hawaii
Elder, Marjorie; Marion C
Elerick, Charles G.; Texas-El Paso
Elgin, Suzette; San Diego State
Elliott, C.E.; Cornell
Elliott, Dale E.; Cal State-Dominguez
  Hills
Ellis, C. Douglas; McGill
Ellison, Emily; Northeastern Illinois
Elphick, Harold; Inter American
Emonds, Joseph; UCLA
Engel, James E.; Nashville U Ctr
Epstein, Steven; Columbia, Teachers C
Eramian, G.M.; Western Ontario
Eraso, Alberto G.; Pacific
Erazmus, Edward; Kansas
Erway, Ella; Columbia, Teachers C
Esau, Helmut; Texas A&M
Eskey, David E.; Pittsburgh
Estarellas, Juan; Florida Atlantic
Eulenberg, John B.; Michigan State
Evans, Robert E.; Ball State

Everett, Walter K.; Southern Mississippi
Evica, George M.; Hartford

Fairbanks, Gordon H.; Hawaii
Falk, Julia S.; Michigan State
Faneslow, John; Columbia, Teachers C
Farnsworth, Maryruth Bracy; Brigham
  Young
Fasold, Ralph W.; Georgetown
Fauconnier, Gilles R.; Southern Cal
Favre, Adrien; Laval
Feindler, Joan; Columbia, Teachers C
Feinstein, Mark; Queens C
Ferentz, Elizabeth W.; Herbert H. Leh-
  man C
Ferguson, Charles A.; Stanford
Fetting, Hans; Central Michigan
Feurer, Hanny; Québec-Montréal
Fidelholtz, James Lawrence; Maryland
Fiengo, Ribert; Queens C
Fifield, Merle; Ball State
Figueroa, Zulma; Inter American
Fillmore, Charles J.; Cal-Berkeley
Filonov, Antonina; Nashville U Ctr
Finegan, Edward; Southern Cal
Fink, Robert; York
Fischer, John L.; Tulane
Fisher, William; Washington-St Louis
Fishman, Joshua A.; Yeshiva
Flaxman, Erwin; Columbia, Teachers C
Fleshler, Helen; Herbert H. Lehman C
Flint, Aili; Columbia
Flórez, Gloria; Columbia, Teachers C
Flowers, Frank C.; Southwestern Louisiana
Fodale, Peter; Michigan
Fodor, Janet Dean; Connecticut
Foley, J.; Simon Fraser
Fontecchio, Giovanni; Southern
  Mississippi
Forbes, Gerald; Hartford
Ford, Alan; Montreal
Ford, Gordon B., Jr.; Northern Iowa
Forman, Donald; SUNY-Binghamton
Forman, Michael L.; Hawaii
Forsdale, Louis; Columbia, Teachers C
Fort, Marron C.; New Hampshire
Foster, Joseph F.; Cincinnati
Foster, Rand B.; New Hampshire
Fought, John; Pennsylvania
Fowkes, Robert A.; New York
Fowler, Murray; Wisconsin
Frajzyngier, Zygmunt; Colorado
Francis, W. Nelson; Brown
Franks, Jeffrey J.; Nashville U Ctr
Freed, Alice F.; Montclair State C
Freeman, Donald C.; Mass-Amherst
Freeze, Ray A.; Utah
Frengle, Dennis; Rochester
Frey, Leonard H.; San Diego State
Friedrich, Paul W.; Chicago
Fries, Peter; Central Michigan
Fromkin, Victoria; UCLA
Fry, Fonda; Ohio
Fuentes, Carlos; Drew
Fujimura, Kumiko; Columbia, Teachers C
Fuller, Helene R.; Miami
Fullmer, Daniel H.; Oakland
Furbee-Losee, Louanna; Missouri-Columbia

Gaeng, Paul; Cincinnati
Gair, J.W.; Cornell
Gale, Irma F.; Ball State
Galyon, Aubrey E.; Iowa State
Gammon, Edward R.; Cal State-Fresno
Gantzel, Lars; Pacific
Garcia, Erica C.; Herbert H. Lehman C,
  Grad School of CUNY
Gardiner, Cynthia; Iowa
Gariona, Carmelo; Cal State-Northridge
Garnes, Sara S.; Ohio State
Garnica, Olga K.; Ohio State
Garvin, Paul L.; SUNY-Buffalo
Gates, J. Edward; Indiana State
Gaumer, Mahlon C., III; Cal State-
  Northridge
Gay, Thomas; Connecticut
Gedney, William J.; Michigan
Gefvert, Constance Joanna; Wayne State
Geis, Michael L.; Ohio State
Geissal, Mary Ann; Northeastern Illinois
Gelb, Ignace J.; Chicago
Gellinek, Christian; Florida
Gendron, Jean-Denis; Laval
Genest, Jacque; Laval
George, Donald; Southern Mississippi
Germain, C.; Ottawa
Gerstman, Louis J.; City C of CUNY
Gertner, Michael; Cincinnati
Gessman, Albert M.; South Florida
Gibb, Daryl K.; Brigham Young
Gibbon, William B.; Nebraska
Gibson, James; Nebraska
Giddings, Elaine; Andrews
Gilbert, Glenn G.; Southern Illinois-
  Carbondale
Giles, Anthony S.; New Hampshire
Gill, Donald A.; Southwestern Louisiana
Gingiss, Peter Judson; Houston
Gingras, Rosario C.; Queens C
Givón, Talmy; UCLA
Glasser, Marc; Morehead State
Glazov, Yuri; Boston C
Gleason, H.A., Jr.; Toronto
Glicksberg, Daniel; San Francisco State
Glucksberg, Sam; Princeton
Goddard, R.H. Ives, III; Harvard
Goffe, Lewis C.; New Hampshire
Golab, Zbigniew; Chicago
Goldschläger, A.; Western Ontario
Goodell, Ralph J.; Central Connecticut
  State C
Goodenough, Cheryl; Québec-Montréal
Goodman, Morris; Northwestern U
Goodman, Ralph M.; Northern Iowa
Goossen, Irvy W.; Northern Arizona
Gopnik, Myrna; McGill
Gorrell, Robert M.; Nevada-Reno
Grace, Eugene C.; Northeastern Illinois
Grace, George W.; Hawaii
Grady, Michael W.; Northern Illinois
Gragg, Gene B.; Chicago
Grayson, John D.; Sir George Williams
Green, Eugene; Boston C
Green, Georgia; Illinois-Urbana-Champaign
Greenberg, Joseph H.; Stanford
Gregersen, Edgar; Grad School of CUNY
Gregg, Robert J.; British Columbia

Grimes, J.E.; Cornell
Grinder, John T., Jr.; Cal-Santa Cruz
Grossman, Lois S.; New Hampshire
Grosvenor, Ray; San Francisco State
Grundt, Alice W.; Cal-San Diego
Gudschinsky, Sarah; Texas-Arlington
Guemple, D.L.; Western Ontario
Guidry, Loyd; East Texas State
Guiraud, P.; Simon Fraser
Gulstad, Daniel E.; Missouri-Columbia
Gunnerson, Dolores A.; Northern Illinois
Guterbock, Hans G.; Chicago
Guyer, Byron; Cal State-Los Angeles
Guzman, Avelino; Inter American

Haas, Mary R.; Cal-Berkeley
Hackenberg, Robert G.; Nashville U Ctr
Hacker, David; Iowa
Hafner, Mamie; East Texas State
Hale, Kenneth; MIT
Hall, Beatrice L.; SUNY-Stony Brook
Hall, R.A., Jr.; Cornell
Hall, R.M.R.; Grad School of CUNY,
  Queens C
Halle, Morris; MIT
Haller, Robert; Nebraska
Halliday, Michael A.K.; Illinois-Chicago
  Circle
Halverson, John; Cal-Santa Cruz
Hammerly, H.M.; Simon Fraser
Hamp, Eric P.; Chicago
Hankamer, Jorge; Harvard
Hankey, Clyde T.; Youngstown State
Hannah, Elaine; Cal State-Northridge
Hansen, Halvor P.; Pacific
Hanson, Allen; Hampshire C
Hanson, Robert; Wisconsin-Milwaukee
Harder, Jayne C.; Florida
Hardman-de-Bautista, Martha; Florida
Harman, Gilbert H.; Princeton
Harmon, Robert; Cal State-Long Beach
Harms, Robert T.; Texas-Austin
Harrah, David; Cal-Riverside
Harrington, Ronald V.; Rochester
Harris, B.; Ottawa
Harris, David P.; Georgetown
Harris, James W.; MIT
Harris, Zellig; Pennsylvania
Harsh, Wayne; Cal-Davis
Harvey, Gina; Northern Arizona
Harvey, William J.; East Texas State
Haslam, Gerald W.; Cal State-Sonoma
Hatten, John T.; Minnesota-Duluth
Haugen, Einar; Harvard
Hauptman, P.C.; Ottawa
Hause, Helen; Wayne State
Hausmann, Robert B.; Montana
Hawkins, Alice; Cal State-Northridge
Hayes, Curtis W.; Texas-San Antonio
Hays, David G.; SUNY-Buffalo
Heap, Norman; Trenton State C
Heard, Betty Ruth; Hawaii-Hilo, Hilo C
Heiman, Barbara Z.; Pacific
Heinrich, Albert C.; Calgary
Heiser, Mary; Cleveland State
Held, Warren H., Jr.; New Hampshire
Helke, Michael; New York
Heller, Louis G.; City C of CUNY

Henderson, Robert T.; Pittsburgh
Henderson, T.S.T.; Ottawa
Hendon, Rufus; Yale
Hendrickson, Richard; Cal State-Sonoma
Hendriksen, Daniel P.; Western Michigan
Heny, Frank W.; Mass-Amherst
Heringer, James T.; Southern Cal
Hernandez-Chavez, Eduardo; Stanford
Hertz, Robert M.; Cal State-Long Beach
Herzog, Marvin I.; Columbia
Hess, Harwood; Purdue
Hewson, J.; Memorial U of Newfoundland
Hieke, Adolf E.; Northern Iowa
Higgens, F. Roger; Indiana
Hill, A.A.; Texas-Austin
Hill, Clifford A.; Columbia, Teachers C
Hill, Jane H.; Wayne State
Hill, Kenneth C.; Michigan
Hillman, Larry N.; Cal-Davis
Hilsen, Linda R.; Minnesota-Duluth
Hinnebusch, Thomas; UCLA
Hirsh, Ira J.; Washington-St Louis
Hirtle, Walter; Laval
Hiż, Henry; Pennsylvania
Hoard, James E.; Oregon
Hobgood, Alton; San Francisco State
Hochhaus, Larry; Oklahoma State
Hock, Hans Henrich; Illinois-Urbana-
  Champaign
Hockett, C.F.; Cornell
Hockney, D.J.; Western Ontario
Hodge, Carleton T.; Indiana
Hodgman, Robert S.; Cal State-Los Angeles
Hoenigswald, Henry; Pennsylvania
Hoffer, Bates L.; Trinity
Hofmann, T.R.; Ottawa
Hogan, John T.; Alberta
Hollow, Robert C.; North Carolina-Chapel
  Hill
Hols, Edith J.; Minnesota-Duluth
Holschuh, William; Ohio
Homsi, Samir F.; Western
  Michigan
Honeck, Richard; Cincinnati
Hook, Peter E.; Michigan
Hooper, Joan B.; SUNY-Buffalo
Hooper, Nancy; Nevada-Reno
Hopkins, Jerry D.; Cal State-Fresno
Hopper, Paul J.; SUNY-Binghamton
Horner, Vivian; Yeshiva
Hornik, John; Hampshire C
Houck, Charles L.; Ball State
Houlihan, Kathleen; Minnesota
Householder, F.W.; Indiana
Howard, Irwin; Hawaii
Howell, Richard W.; Hawaii-Hilo, Hilo C
Howie, John M.; Missouri-Columbia
Howren, Robert; Iowa
Hozeski, Bruce W.; Ball State
Hsu, Robert W.; Hawaii
Hubbell, Robert D.; Arizona
Huberman, Gisela; American
Huffman, F.E.; Cornell
Huffman, Herbert; Drew
Hughes, Shaun; Purdue
Hukani, T.E.; Victoria
Hull, Alexander; Duke
Huntley, Jackson; Minnesota-Duluth

Hurtado, A.; Simon Fraser
Hutchinson, Larry G.; Minnesota
Huttar, George; Texas-Arlington
Hyman, Larry M.; Southern Cal
Hymes, Dell; Pennsylvania

Iannucci, David E.; Utah
Ilardo, Joseph A.; Herbert H. Lehman C
Illwitzer, Robert P.; Northeastern Illinois
Ingemann, Frances; Kansas
Ingram, David; British Columbia
Inniss, John L.; Columbia
Inostroza, Raul; Cal State-Long Beach
Insler, Stanley; Yale
Irvin, Bruce E.; Northern Illinois
Irwin, Betty J.; Georgia
Isaacson, Norman; Herbert H. Lehman C
Izzo, Herbert J.; Calgary

Jackendoff, Ray S.; Brandeis
Jackson, Margret B.; Simon Fraser
Jackson, William; Texas-Arlington
Jacobs, Roderick A.; Hawaii
Jacobsen, William H., Jr.; Nevada-Reno
Jacobson, Lars-Alvar; Columbia, Barnard C
Jacque, Benoit; Québec-Montréal
Jaffe, Hilda; Houston
Jain, Jagdish; San Francisco State
Jakofsky, Klaus; Minnesota-Duluth
Jamison, Stephanie; North Carolina-Chapel
  Hill
Jasanoff, Jay; Harvard
Jauksch-Orlovski, Cyrille; Laval
Jeffers, Robert J.; Ohio State
Jegers, Benjamin; Northern Illinois
Jensen, Frede; Colorado
Jensen, John B.; Virginia
Jenson, Paul J.; Florida
Jessen, Marilyn E.; Manitoba
Jett, Alvin; Texas-Arlington
John-Steiner, Vera; New Mexico
Johnson, Bruce C.; North Carolina-Chapel
  Hill
Johnson, C. Douglas; Cal-Santa Barbara
Johnson, Charles R.; Macalester C
Johnson, Edith Trager; San Jose State
Johnson, Falk S.; Illinois-Chicago Circle
Johnson, Quentin G.; Iowa State
Johnson, Valdon L.; Northern Iowa
Jones, C. Stanley; Carleton
Jones, Lawrence G.; Boston C
Jones, R.B., Jr.; Cornell
Jorden, E.H.; Cornell
Jorgensen, Peter; Cal-Riverside
Josephs, Lewis S.; Hawaii
Juhasz, Francis J.; Columbia
Juneau, Marcel; Laval

Kac, Michael B.; Minnesota
Kachru, Braj B.; Illinois-Urbana-Champaign
Kachru, Yamuna; Illinois-Urbana-Champaign
Kahane, Henry; Illinois-Urbana-Champaign
Kamil, Michael L.; Minnesota-Duluth
Kantor, Marvin; Northwestern
Kaplan, Milton A.; Columbia, Teachers C
Kaplan, Robert B.; Southern Cal
Karch, Dieter; Nebraska
Karttunen, Lauri; Texas-Austin

Kaske, R.E.; Cornell
Katz, Eli; Cal State-Sonoma
Katz, Jerrold; Grad School of CUNY
Kaufman, Elaine Marlowe; Stanford
Kay, Alan S.; Cal State-Fullerton
Kay, Michael L.; York
Kaye, Jonathan D.; McGill, Toronto
Kazazis, Kostas; Chicago
Kedney-Wells, Jennifer; Oklahoma State
Keenan, Elinor O.; Southern Cal
Keller-Cohen, Deborah; Michigan
Kelley, G.B.; Cornell
Kellogg, Robert L.; Virginia
Kelly, L.G.; Ottawa
Keeney, Terrence; Cal-Riverside
Kenstowicz, Michael; Illinois-Urbana-
  Champaign
Kerek, Andrew; Miami
Kerr, David; Hampshire C
Kess, J.F.; Victoria
Key, Harold; Cal State-Long Beach
Key, Mary Ritchie; Cal-Irvine
Keyser, Samuel Jay; Mass-Amherst
Kido, Schiko I.; Western Michigan
Killean, Carolyn G.; Chicago
Kim, Chin-W; Illinois-Urbana-Champaign
Kim, T.W.; Simon Fraser
Kimball, John; Indiana
Kimura, Tadashi; Hawaii-Hilo, Hilo C
King, Robert D.; Texas-Austin
Kinkade, M. Dale; British Columbia
Kinman, Leon; Cincinnati
Kiparsky, Paul; MIT
Kirk, Paul L.; Cal State-Northridge
Kirshenblatt-Gimblett, Barbara; Columbia
Kisseberth, Charles; Illinois-Urbana-
  Champaign
Kittredge, Richard; Montréal
Kitzgerald, Dale K.; Herbert H. Lehman C
Klammer, Thomas; Nebraska
Klein, Jared; Georgia
Klein, Sheldon; Wisconsin
Kligerman, Jack; Herbert H. Lehman C
Klima, Edward S.; Cal-San Diego
Klimas, Antanas; Rochester
Klokeid, Terry J.; Calgary
Knapp, Janet Schlauch; Youngstown State
Knecht, Mathilda S.; Montclair State C
Knee, David I.; Hofstra
Knowles, D.R.J.; Simon Fraser
Kolin, Philip; Southern Mississippi
Kollian, Vera S.; Hofstra
Kolodny, Annette; New Hampshire
Konneker, Beverly; Southern Illinois-
  Carbondale
Koo, Jang H.; Western Michigan
Koplin, James; Hampshire C
Kotey, Paul A.; Florida
Kottler, Barnett; Purdue
Koutsoudas, Andreas; Indiana
Kozelka, Paul; Columbia, Teachers C
Kozlowski, Edwin; Iowa
Krashen, Stephen; Grad School of CUNY,
  Queens C
Kreidler, Charles W.; Georgetown
Kretschmer, Richard; Cincinnati
Krolak, Patrick D.; Nashville U Ctr
Krulee, Gilbert; Northwestern

Kufner, H.L.; Cornell
Kully, Rolf Max; Montréal
Kunihiro, Tetsuya; Trinity
Kuroda, Sige-Yuki; Cal-San Diego
Kuznets, Lois R.; Herbert H. Lehman C

Labelle, Guy; Québec-Montréal
Labelle, Jacques; Québec-Montréal
LaBelle, Joseph L.; Northern Illinois
Labov, William; Pennsylvania
Ladefoged, Peter; UCLA
Lado, Robert; Georgetown
Lafleur, Bruno; Laval
Laforge, Lorne; Laval
Laird, Charlton G.; Nevada-Reno
Lakoff, George P.; Cal-Berkeley
Lakoff, Robin T.; Cal-Berkeley
Lamb, Sydney M.; Yale
Lamendella, John T.; San Jose State
Lamothe, Jacqueline; Québec-Montréal
Landar, H.; Cal State-Los Angeles
Langacker, Ronald W.; Cal-San Diego
Langdon, Margaret H.; Cal-San Diego
Langedoen, D. Terence; Grad School of CUNY
Langr, Bernard J.; Minnesota-Duluth
Lapierre, A.; Ottawa
Larkin, Donald; Georgetown
Larsen, Eric V.; Columbia, Teachers C
Larson, Donald N.; Bethel C
Lasher, William; Cincinnati
Lasley, Marion M.; Florida
Lasnik, Howard; Connecticut
Latin, Janos; Columbia
Lattimore, David; Brown
Lavigne, Jean-Claude; Québec-Montréal
Lawler, John M.; Michigan
Lawton, David L.; Central Michigan
Léard, Jean-Marcel; Sherbrooke
LeBel, Jean-Guy; Laval
Leben, William R.; Stanford
Leblanc, R.; Ottawa
Lee, Berta; Indiana State
Lee, C.; Ottawa
Lee, Donald W.; Houston
Lee, Ernest; Texas-Arlington
Lee, Motoko; Iowa State
Lee, P. Gregory; Hawaii
Lee, Patricia A.; Hawaii
Leed, R.L.; Cornell
Lefebvre, G.; Ottawa
Lefebvre, Gilles; Montréal
LeFlem, Claude; Laval
Legendre, Ghislaine; Montréal
Legendre, Louis-Joseph; Laval
le Guillo, Jean-Yves; Montréal
Lehiste, Ilse; Ohio State
Lehmann, W.P.; Texas-Austin
Lejneiks, Valdis; Nebraska
Lelis, Joseph; Western Michigan
Lesage, René; Laval
LeTourneau, J.J.; Hampshire C
Levi, Judith; Northwestern
Levin, Jules F.; Cal-Riverside
Levin, Samuel; Grad School of CUNY
Levine, David; Nebraska
Levine, Lewis; New York
Li, Charles; Cal-Santa Barbara
Li, Fang-Kuei; Hawaii

Liberman, Alvin M.; Yale
Lieberman, Philip; Brown
Liebert, Burt; Cal-Davis
Lightfoot, David W.; McGill
Limber, John E.; New Hampshire
Lincoln, N.J.; Simon Fraser
Lindenfeld, Jaqueline; Cal State-Northridge
Lisker, Leigh; Pennsylvania
Live, Anna; Pennsylvania
Livoti, Paul; Inter American
Lockwood, David G.; Michigan State
Loflin, Marvin; Wisconsin-Milwaukee
Long, William J.; Nebraska
Longacre, Robert; Texas-Arlington
Love, Russell; Nashville U Ctr
Lowe, P., Jr.; Cornell
Lubow, Neil B.; New Hampshire
Luchenbach, Sidney; Cal State-Northridge
Luebke, Neil; Oklahoma State
Luecke, Jane Marie; Oklahoma State
Lyon, Richard; Hampshire C
Lyons, Bridget; Rutgers
Lyovin, Anatole V.; Hawaii
Lytle, Eldon G.; Brigham Young

Macdonald, R. Ross; Georgetown
Mackey, William F.; Laval
Maclay, Howard; Illinois-Urbana-Champaign
MacNeilage, Peter F.; Texas-Austin
Madsen, Harold S.; Brigham Young
Maher, J. Peter; Northeastern Illinois
Makkai, Adam; Illinois-Chicago Circle
Makkai, Valerie Becker; Illinois-Chicago Circle
Maling, Joan M.; Brandeis
Malkiel, Yakov; Cal-Berkeley
Mallya, Walter; Western Michigan
Malone, Joseph L.; Columbia, Barnard C
Malsch, Derry L.; Oregon
Mancill, Grace; American
Maniet, Albert; Laval
Maran, LaRaw; Indiana
Maraschal, Roger; Laval
Marckworth, Mary Lois; Alberta
Mareschal, Geneviève; Laval
Marino, Mary C.; Saskatchewan-Saskatoon
Markel, Norman M.; Florida
Markey, Thomas; Michigan
Markowicz, Harry; Gallaudet C
Markstein, Victoria; Herbert H. Lehman C
Marras, A.; Western Ontario
Marsh, William; Hampshire C
Martel, Pierre; Sherbrooke
Martin, Joan M.; Arizona
Martin, Larry W.; Iowa
Martin, Pierre; Laval
Martin, Samuel E.; Yale
Mathiot, Madeleine; SUNY-Buffalo
Matisoff, James A.; Cal-Berkeley
Matte, René; Québec-Montréal
Matthies, Barbara; Iowa State
Mattina, Anthony; Montana
Mattingly, Ignatius G.; Connecticut
Mayers, Marvin; Texas-Arlington
Maxwell, Edward R.; Northeastern Illinois
McAllister, Teresa Ann; Nashville U Ctr

McA'nulty, Judith; Québec-Montréal
McCawley, James D.; Chicago
McCawley, Noriko A.; Chicago
McClung, John A.; Wayne State
McCone, R. Clyde; Cal State-Long Beach
McCormack, William C.; Calgary
McCoy, J.; Cornell
McCullough, Gloria G.; Cal State-Long Bch.
McDavid, Raven I.; Chicago
McIntyre, B. Barton; Columbia, Teachers C
McKaughan, Howard P.; Hawaii
McLaughlin, John C.; Iowa
McLendon, Sally; Grad School of CUNY
McNeill, G. David; Chicago
McQuown, Norman; Chicago
McRae, Michael H.; Hawaii-Hilo, Hilo C
Meacham, J.D.; Northern Illinois
Meadows, Gail; C.W. Post C
Medish, Vadim; American
Megennery, William; Cal-Riverside
Meinecke, Fred Kalanianoeo; Hawaii-Hilo,
  Hilo C
Ménard, Nathan; Montreal
Mendelsohn, Richard L.; Herbert H. Lehman C
Mepham, Michael; Laval
Merkel, Gottfried; Cincinnati
Merlan, Francesca; Tulane
Merrifield, William; Texas-Arlington
Merrill, Peter C.; Florida Atlantic
Merrill, Robert W.; Nevada-Reno
Mertin-Barber, Laura; Cleveland State
Meskill, Robert H.; Brown
Messing, G.M.; Cornell
Meyerstein, R.S.; Cal State-Northridge
Michaels, David; Connecticut
Miksak, Joseph; San Francisco State
Milburn, D. Judson; Oklahoma State
Milic, Louis; Cleveland State
Milicic, Vladimir; Western Wash State C
Miller, Gary D.; Florida
Miller, Robert L.; Montclair State C
Miller, Royce W.; Gordon C
Miller, Wick R.; Utah
Mills, John A.; Saskatchewan-Saskatoon
Millward, Celia; Boston
Mims, Howard; Cleveland State
Mink, Walter D.; Macalester C
Miranda, Rocky V.; Minnesota
Mishima, Toshiko; San Francisco State
Mistry, P.J.; Cal State-Fresno
Mitchell, Stephen; Hampshire C
Mixco, Mauricio J.; Utah
Miyazaki, Akira; Cal State-Long Beach
Moelleken, Wolfgang W.; Cal-Davis
Mohr, Burckhard; Cal State-Dominguez Hills
Moles, Jerry A.; Cal-Davis
Molinsky, Steven; Boston
Molitor, Richard D.; Syracuse
Moloi, Alosi; UCLA
Monane, Tazuko Ajiro; Hawaii-Hilo, Hilo C
Monsen, Randall; Washington-St Louis
Montgomery, Christine A.; Southern Cal
Morenberg, Max; Miami
Moreux, Bernard; Montréal
Morgan, Jeannette P.; Houston
Morgan, Jerry; Illinois-Urbana-Champaign
Morgan, William; New Mexico
Morin, Yves; Montréal
Morter, Vivian C.; Nashville U Ctr

Moschetti, Gregory; Cincinnati
Moser, Rex; Ohio
Moses, Rae; Northwestern
Moshinsky, Julius; City C of CUNY, Grad
  School of CUNY
Moskowitz, Breyne; UCLA
Moulton, William G.; Princeton
Moutsos, Demetrius; Rochester
Moyne, John; Grad School of CUNY
Muckley, Robert L.; Inter American
Mueller, Hugo J.; American
Muiznieks, Lalita; Western Michigan
Muller, Richard; Hampshire C
Muthiani, Joseph N.; Western Michigan
Myers, Amy; Queens C
Myers, Dale; Columbia, Teachers C

Nash, Jeffrey E.; Macalester C
Natalicio, Diana S.; Texas-El Paso
Nessly, Larry; Texas-Austin
Neufeld, G.; Ottawa
Newmark, Leonard; Cal-San Diego
Newmeyer, Frederick; Washington
Newton, B.E.; Simon Fraser
Ngunjiri, Ngari N.; Montclair State C
Nguyen, Dinh-Hoa; Southern Illinois-
  Carbondale
Nieger, Monique; Québec-Montréal
Niblitt, J.S.; Cornell
Noonan, Michael P.; San Jose State
Norman, Linda; Indiana
Norris, Nelida G.; Florida Atlantic
Null, Peggy M.; Kansas State
Nunberg, Geoffrey; Herbert H. Lehman C
Nuñez, Theron A.; Florida
Nygard, Holger O.; Duke

O'Barr, William; Duke
Obrecht, Dean; Rochester
O'Brien, Richard J., S.J.; Georgetown
O'Bryan, Margie; Illinois-Urbana-Champaign
O'Donnell, Roy C.; Georgia
Odum, Penelope B.; Nashville U Ctr
Oehrle, Richard T.; Stanford
Oflager, Norman W.; Hartford
Ogle, Richard; Cal-Davis
O'Grady, G.N.; Victoria
Oh, Choon-Kyu; Kansas
Ohala, John J.; Cal-Berkeley
Ohala, Manjari; San Jose State
O'Hara, Robert C.; South Florida
Ohlgren, Thomas; Purdue
Oliphant, Robert T.; Cal State-Northridge
Oller, John; New Mexico
Olmsted, David L.; Cal-Davis
Olson, Paul; Nebraska
O'Neill, Joseph; Inter American
Opubor, Alfred E.; Michigan State
Ornstein, Jacob; Texas-El Paso
Ortiz, Dolores; Laval
Osser, Harry; San Francisco State
Otheguy, Ricardo; Queens C
Oullet, Jacques; Laval
Overholt, Joyce; Texas-Arlington

Pace, Donald; Columbia, Teachers C
Paddock, H.J.; Memorial U of Newfoundland
Padley, Arthur; Laval
Paige, Arnold; Florida

Paillet, Jean-Pierre; Carleton
Painchaud, Louis; Sherbrooke
Paivio, A.U.; Western Ontario
Paléologue, Hélène; Laval
Palmatier, Robert A.; Western Michigan
Palmer, Adrian; Pittsburgh
Palmer, Rupert E., Jr.; Nashville U Ctr
Paquot-Maniet, Annette; Laval
Paper, Herbert H.; Michigan
Parish, Charles; Southern Illinois-
  Carbondale
Parrish, Huguette H.; Florida Atlantic
Parslow, Robert L.; Pittsburgh
Partee, Barbara Hall; Mass-Amherst
Partmann, Gayle H.; Oakland
Past, Ray; Texas-El Paso
Patel, P.G.; Ottawa
Patte, Daniel M.; Nashville U Ctr
Paulston, Christina Bratt; Pittsburgh
Pavel, T.; Ottawa
Pawley, Andrew K.; Hawaii
Peacock, F.W.; Memorial U of Newfoundland
Peck, Charles; Texas-Arlington
Pelchat, Roland; Québec-Montréal
Pelfrey, Charles; Morehead State
Percival, W. Keith; Kansas
Perestrelo, Fernão; Laval
Perlman, Alan M.; Wayne State
Perlmutter, David; MIT, Brown
Peters, Ann M.; Hawaii
Peters, P. Stanley; Texas-Austin
Peters, Robert A.; Western Wash State C
Petersen, Jean D.; Minnesota
Peterson, David L.; Illinois-Urbana-
  Champaign
Peterson, Thomas H.; Cal State-Los Angeles
Pfaff, Carol W.; Cal State-Fresno
Pia, Joseph J.; Syracuse
Pierce, Robert F.; Minnesota-Duluth
Piggott, Glyne L.; McGill
Pike, Kenneth L.; Michigan
Pissko, Bohus Jan; C.W. Post C
Plante, Guy; Laval
Politzer, Frieda N.; Stanford
Polome, Edgar C.; Texas-Austin
Pope, Emily; Washington
Post, John F.; Nashville U Ctr
Poston, Lawrence; Nebraska
Poulter, Virgil; Texas-Arlington
Pound, Glen; Indiana State
Presby, Leonard; Herbert H. Lehman C
Pressman, Elaine; Carleton
Pride, Richard A.; Nashville U Ctr
Prideaux, Gary D.; Alberta
Prince, Ellen; Pennsylvania
Pringle, Ian; Carleton
Pritsak, Omelijan; Harvard
Pupier, Paul; Québec-Montréal
Purcell, Edward T.; Southern Cal
Pyle, Charles R.; Michigan
Pylyshyn, Z.W.; Western Ontario

Querido, Antonio; Montréal
Quinones, Julia; Inter American
Quinting, Gerd; Georgetown

Rabel-Ceymann, Lili; Calgary
Radetsky, Michael; Hampshire C
Radford, Robert T. Oklahoma State

Radhakrshnan, R.; Calgary
Raeth, Claire J.; Miami
Rakusan, Jaromira; Carleton
Raman, Carol J.; SUNY, C at Oswego
Ramanujan, A.K.; Chicago
Raney, George W.; Cal State-Fresno
Rangel, Vicente H.; Florida Atlantic
Rankin, Robert; Kansas
Raphael, Lawrence J.; Herbert H. Lehman C
Rardin, Robert; Hampshire C
Ratner, Lawrence; Nashville U Ctr
Raun, Alo; Indiana
Redden, James E.; Southern Illinois-
  Carbondale
Reddick, Robert J.; Ball State
Reddy, Michael J.; Columbia
Reed, David; Northwestern
Regier, Philip J.; Southern Cal
Reich, P.A.; Toronto
Reid, Lawrence A.; Hawaii
Reiff, Donald G.; Rochester
Reighard, John; Montréal
Reiner, Erica; Chicago
Reklaitis, Janine K.; Illinois-Chicago
  Circle
Rensky, Miroslav; Grad School of CUNY
Resnick, Melvyn C.; Florida Atlantic
Revard, Carter; Washington
Reyes-Cairo, Orlando M.; Toledo
Reynolds, Audrey L.; Northeastern Illinois
Richardson, Irvine; Michigan State
Richert, Hans-Georg; Cincinnati
Rigault, André A.; McGill
Rigsby, Bruce; New Mexico
Ringen, Catherine; Iowa
Ritchie, William C.; Syracuse
Ritter, John T.; Michigan State
Rivero, M.L.; Ottawa
Robbins, Frank; Texas-Arlington
Roberts, E.W.; Simon Fraser
Roberts, John T.; Virginia
Roberts, Roda; Laval
Robinett, Betty Wallace; Minnesota
Robson, Barbara; Wisconsin-Milwaukee
Rochette, Claude; Laval
Rockas, Leo; Hartford
Rodman, Robert D.; North Carolina-Chapel
  Hill
Rodriguez, Aurora; Inter American
Roe, H.A.; Toronto
Roeper, Tom; Mass-Amherst
Rogers, Cecil A., Jr.; Arizona
Rogers, H.E.; Toronto
Rolfe, O.W.; Montana
Romeo, Luigi; Colorado
Rona, J.P.; Ottawa
Rondeau, G.; Ottawa
Ronning, Royce; Nebraska
Rood, David S.; Colorado
Rosenbaum, Peter S.; Columbia, Teachers C
Ross, Charles; Cal State-Fullerton
Ross, Janet; Ball State
Ross, John R.; MIT, Brown
Ross, Marion; Virginia
Ross, Steve; Cal State-Long Beach
Rossman, Sol; Wayne State
Rothenberg, Martin; Syracuse
Rouban, John C.; New Hampshire
Rouchaleau, Yves; Florida

Rouchdy, Aleya; Wayne State
Roufs, Timothy; Minnesota-Duluth
Roy, Gilbert W.; Virginia
Rozsypal, Anton J.; Alberta
Rubin, Gerald M.; Brown
Rubin, Mordecai S.; Columbia, Teachers C
Rudolph, Robert S.; Toledo
Rudorf, E. Hugh; Nebraska
Runge, Richard; Iowa
Rystrom, Richard; Georgia

Sabatelli, Philip J.; New Hampshire
Sachs, Jacqueline; Connecticut
Saciuk, Bohdan; Florida
Sacks, Sheldon; Chicago
Sadock, Jerrold; Chicago
Sager, Naomi; New York
Saint-Jacques, Bernard; British Columbia
Saint-Jacques, Marguerite; Simon Fraser
Saint-Pierre, Madeleine; Québec-Montréal
Saitz, Robert; Boston
Sales, Bruce; Nebraska
Samarin, W.J.; Toronto
Sammurtuq, C.; Ottawa
Sandberg, Barbara; Columbia, Teachers C
Sandberg, Karl C.; Macalester C
Sanders, Gerald A.; Minnesota
Santerre, Laurent; Montréal
Santucci, James A.; Cal State-Fullerton
Sapon, Stanley M.; Rochester
Saporta, Sol; Washington
Sara, Solomon, S.J.; Georgetown
Saunders, R.; Simon Fraser
Savard, Jean-Guy; Laval
Saville-Troike, Muriel R.; Georgetown
Sawyer, Janet; Cal State-Long Beach
Sawyer, Jesse O.; Cal-Berkeley
Sayward, Charles W.; Nebraska
Scargill, M.H.; Victoria
Scavnicky, Gary E. Eugene; Wayne State
Schach, Paul; Nebraska
Schachter, Paul; UCLA
Schaechter, Mordkhe; Columbia
Schane, Sanford A.; Cal-San Diego
Schap, Keith; Purdue
Schiller, Andrew; Illinois-Chicago Circle
Schindler, Jochem; Harvard
Schmerling, Susan F.; Texas-Austin
Schmidt-Mackey, Ilonka; Laval
Scholes, Robert J.; Florida
Schramm, Gene; Michigan
Schreiber, Peter; Wisconsin
Schumsky, Donald A.; Cincinnati
Schütz, Albert J.; Hawaii
Schwab, William; Oakland
Schwartz, Arthur; Cal-Santa Barbara
Schweitzer, John L.; Oklahoma State
Scott, Robert I.; Saskatchewan-Saskatoon
Scott, Sherry; Oklahoma State
Seaman, P. David; Northern Arizona
Seaton, Jerome P.; North Carolina-Chapel
  Hill
Sebeok, Thomas A.; Indiana
Secrist, Robert H.; Youngstown State
Sedelow, Sally Y.; Kansas
Seegmiller, Milton S.; Montclair State C
Segalowitz, Elizabeth; McGill
Seguin, M.; Western Ontario

Seigel, Don M.; Northeastern Illinois
Selinker, Larry; Washington
Selkirk, Lisa; Mass-Amherst
Seright, Orin D.; San Diego State
Seutin, Emile; Montréal
Seward, Thomas; Cincinnati
Shah, Iris S.; Cal State-Northridge
Shaplin, Marjorie; Washington-St Louis
Sharifi, Hassan; Nebraska
Sharma, Rama; Rochester
Sharp, John M.; Texas-El Paso
Shawl, James R.; Northern Illinois
Sheen, Ronald; Laval
Sheerin, Lawrence; Queens C
Sheldon, Amy L.; Minnesota
Shelley, Harry; Nebraska
Sherman, James L.; New Hampshire
Sherman, Robert; Hartford
Shevelov, George Y.; Columbia
Shibatani, Masayoshi; Southern Cal
Shipley, William F.; Cal-Santa Cruz
Shister, Neil; Hampshire C
Shoup, June E.; Southern Cal
Shrum, William; Nebraska
Shukla, Shaligram; Georgetown
Shulman, Harold; Herbert H. Lehman C
Shuy, Roger W.; Georgetown
Sibley, Willis; Cleveland State
Sies, Luther; Herbert H. Lehman C
Sihler, Andrew L.; Wisconsin
Silver, Shirley; Cal State-Sonoma
Silverstein, Michael; Chicago
Silverstein, Raymond O.; Southern
  Illinois-Carbondale
Singer, Harry; Cal-Riverside
Singh, Rajendra; Iowa State
Singh, Rajendra; Montréal
Sjafiroeddin, David; Ohio
Skaggs, Merrill; Columbia, Teachers C
Skousen, Royal J.; Texas-Austin
Slager, William R.; Utah
Sloat, Clarence; Oregon
Smaby, Richard; Pennsylvania
Smeaton, B.H.; Calgary
Smith, Carlota S.; Texas-Austin
Smith, Donald L.; Georgia
Smith, Ernie A.; Cal State-Fullerton
Smith, L.R.; Memorial U of Newfoundland
Smith, Raoul; Northwestern U
Smith, Sara; Cal State-Long Beach
Smith, Steven B.; Cal-Riverside
Smith, Timothy S.; Cal-San Diego
Snortum, Niel; San Francisco State
Snyder, Owen; Marion C
Snyder, William J.; SUNY-Binghamton
Soemarmo, Marmo; Ohio
Solá, D.F.; Cornell
Soldevila, Ignacio; Laval
Solon, Peter C.; Cal State-Fullerton
Song, Seok C.; Michigan State
Soudek, Lev I.; Northern Illinois
Southerland, Ronald H.; Calgary
Spears, Arthur K.; Cal-Santa Cruz
Spears, Richard; Northwestern
Spolsky, Bernard; New Mexico
Spores, Ronald; Nashville U Ctr
Spradley, James P.; Macalester C
Springstead, Charles F.; Texas-El Paso

Stageberg, Norman C.; Northern Iowa
Stampe, David L.; Ohio State
Stankiewicz, Edward; Yale
Stanners, Robert F.; Oklahoma State
Stark, Donald; Gordon C
Starosta, Stanley; Hawaii
Steele, R.D.; Cornell
Steele, Susan; New Mexico
Steinmetz, Donald B.; Macalester C
Stephenson, Edward A.; Georgia
Stern, Arthur A.; Columbia, Teachers C
Stern, Henry R.; Duke
Stevens, Alan; Grad School of CUNY,
  Queens C
Stevens, Cj; Herbert H. Lehman C
Stewart, Michael F.; Ball State
Stewart, William A.; Columbia, Teachers C
Stick, Sheldon; Nebraska
Stillings, Neil; Hampshire C
Stimson, Hugh M.; Yale
Stitt, Clyde; San Francisco State
Stock, Walter; Queens C
Stockwell, Robert; UCLA
Stokoe, William C., Jr.; Gallaudet C
Stoll, Anita; Cleveland State
Stone, Edith; Andrews
Stone, Edward J.; Illinois-Chicago Circle
Stowasser, Karl; Georgetown
Street, John; Wisconsin
Stroud, R. Vernon; Cincinnati
Stryker, William G.; Cal State-Northridge
Stuart, C.I.J.M.; Alberta
Studerus, Lenard; Texas-Arlington
Su, Stanley Y.W.; Florida
Suci, G.J.; Cornell
Suksdorf, Juri; Queens C
Sullivan, William J.; Florida
Suner, M.A.; Cornell
Susi, Janet; Montclair State C
Sussman, Harvey M.; Texas-Austin
Swan, Robert O.; Syracuse
Sweeney, Dan; Inter American
Szmuszkovica, Rachel; Western Michigan

Tallman, Janet; Hampshire C
Tan, J.T.; Ottawa
Tarpley, Fred; East Texas State
Taylor, Allan R.; Colorado
Taylor, Harvey M.; Michigan
Taylor, Orlando; Howard
Teeter, Karl V.; Harvard
Teghtsoonian, Martha; Hampshire C
Temko, Philip O.; Cal State-Sonoma
Tenney, Yvette; Hampshire C
Terbeek, Dale; Chicago
Terrell, Tracy; Cal-Irvine
Teschner, Richard; Iowa
Tessier, Christine; Laval
Tharp, George W.; Northern Iowa
Théoret, Michel; Sherbrooke
Thogmartin, Clyde; Iowa State
Thomas, David; Texas-Arlington
Thomas, Earl W.; Nashville U Ctr
Thomas, Linda K.; Texas-Austin
Thomas, Lindsey; Cal State-Long Beach
Thomas, M.K.; Morehead State
Thomas, N.R.; Alberta
Thomason, Richmond; Pittsburgh

Thomason, Sara G.; Pittsburgh
Thompson, Laurence C.; Hawaii
Thompson, Roger M.; Florida
Thompson, Sandra; UCLA
Tidwell, James N.; San Diego State
Tiffou, Etienne; Montréal
Tikku, G.L.; Illinois-Urbana-Champaign
Timm, Lenora; Cal-Davis
Ting, Ho; Iowa
Todd, William; Cincinnati
Tlumak, Jeffrey S.; Nashville U Ctr
Topping, Donald M.; Hawaii
Townsend, Charles E.; Princeton
Trabasso, Thomas R.; Princeton
Trager, George L.; Northern Illinois
Trammell, Robert L.; Florida Atlantic
Tranel, Bernard; Québec-Montreal
Tranell, Bernard; Cal-Irvine
Transue, Jacques H.; Toledo
Traugott, Elizabeth C.; Stanford
Travis, Ann; Inter American
Tremblay, Antonien; Laval
Tremblay, Jean-Louis; Laval
Trinidad, Francisco; Cal State-Long Beach
Trittschuh, Travis; Wayne State
Truex, Gregory; Cal State-Northridge
Tsiapera, Maria; North Carolina-Chapel
  Hill
T'sou, Benjamin K.; Cal-San Diego
Tsuzaki, Stanley M.; Hawaii
Tullai, Gerald J.; Central Conn State C
Tunstall, George C.; Kansas State
Tuomi, S.; Western Ontario
Turner, Paul R.; Arizona
Tweddell, Colin E.; Western Wash State C
Twyford, Charles W.; Iowa State U

Uitti, Karl D.; Princeton
Underhill, Robert; San Diego State

Vago, Robert; Grad School of CUNY
Vail, James; Cincinnati
Valdes, H. Joyce Merrill; Houston
Valdman, Albert; Indiana
Valian, Virginia; Grad School of CUNY
Valin, Roch; Laval
Valk, Melvin E.; Florida
Vallier, Fred; Iowa State
van Coetsem, F.; Cornell
Van Metre, Patricia Downer; Arizona
Van Vlasselaer, Stella; Carleton
Vargas, Eduardo; Inter American
Velez, Jeannette; Inter American
Vennemann, Theo; UCLA
Verma, Manindra; Wisconsin
Vernick, Judy A.; Pittsburgh
Vigorita, J.F.; Cornell
Voegelin, Charles F.; Indiana
Voeltz, Erhard; Indiana
Voge, Wilfreid; Cal-Irvine
Von Glasersfeld, Ernst; Georgia
von Raffler Engel, Walburga; Nashville U
  Ctr
Vontsolos, Nicholas; Arizona
Voorhis, Paul H.; Manitoba
Vouvé, Soulange; Laval
Vroman, William V.; Cal-Santa Cruz

Wachal, Robert; Iowa
Wachsmann, Klaus; Northwestern
Wagner, Frank; Cincinnati
Wahlgren, J.H.; Simon Fraser
Wald, Benji; UCLA
Walker, D.C.; Ottawa
Wall, Carol; Cal-Davis
Wall, Robert E.; Texas-Austin
Wallacker, Benjamin; Cal-Davis
Walters, Theodore W., S.J.; Detroit
Wang, James P.; Michigan State
Wang, Peter C.; Cal State-Fresno
Wang, William S-Y.; Cal-Berkeley
Ward, Jack H.; Hawaii
Ward, Ralph; Grad School of CUNY
Wardhaugh, Ronald; Michigan
Warkentyne, H.J.; Victoria
Warren, David; Cal-Riverside
Warren, Dennis M.; Iowa State
Warr-Leeper, Genese; Oklahoma State
Wasow, Thomas; Stanford
Wasserman, Harvey; Hampshire C
Waterhouse, Lynn; Trenton State C
Watkins, Calvert; Harvard
Watt, William; Cal-Irvine
Waugh, L.; Cornell
Webber, Edwin; Northwestern
Weber, Rose-Marie; McGill
Weinberger, Marvin; San Francisco State
Weiner, Lynda; Herbert H. Lehman C
Weiser, Ernest L.; Florida Atlantic
Weiser, Sylvia; Laval
Weitzman, Raymond S.; Cal State-Fresno
Wells, Rulon; Yale
Welmers, William; UCLA
Welsh, Paul; Duke
Werner, Oswald; Northwestern
Wershow, Irving R.; Florida
Werth, Ronald; Rochester
Wescott, Roger; Drew
Wexler, Kenneth; Cal-Irvine
Wheeler, Daniel; Cincinnati
Whipp, Leslie; Nebraska
White, Robert; New Mexico
White, Robin B.; Texas-Austin
Whittier, Duane H.; New Hampshire
Wilderman, Raymond D.; Northern Illinois
Wilkinson, Robert; Northwestern
Williams, George W.; SUNY-Buffalo
Williams, Joseph M.; Chicago
Williams, Lyle; Southwestern Louisiana
Williams, Ronald; Federal City C
Williams, Theodore; Miami
Wilson, Glen M.; Macalester C
Wilson, Graham; San Francisco State
Wilson, Lois M.; San Francisco State
Wilson, H.R.; Western Ontario
Wilson, Lois I.; Pittsburgh
Winograd, Terry A.; Stanford
Winston, Millicent; Laval
Wirth, Jessica; Wisconsin-Milwaukee
Witherspoon, Christopher; Hampshire C
Wittlin, Curt J.; Saskatchewan-Saskatoon
Witucki, Jeanette R.; Cal State-Los Angeles
Wohl, Milton; Cal State-Fresno
Wojcik, Richard H.; Columbia
Wolf, Meyer L.; Michigan State
Wolfart, H. Christoph; Manitoba

Wolff, J.U.; Cornell
Wolfram, Walt; Federal City C
Wölck, Wolfgang; SUNY-Buffalo
Womack, Thurston; San Francisco State
Wonder, John P.; Pacific
Woodell, Thomas M.; Houston
Woods, David; Howard
Woods, H. Jennings; Nevada-Reno
Woodward, James C., Jr.; Gallaudet C
Woodward, Mary F.; Cal State-Los Angeles
Woolley, Dale E.; Illinois-Chicago Circle
Woolum, Sandra J.; Minnesota-Duluth
Wrenn, James J.; Brown

Yamamoto, Akira; Kansas
Yavener, Symond; Central Conn State C
Yeager, Fay; Rutgers
Yen, Sian L.; Texas-Austin
Young, Robert; New Mexico
Young, Rodney; New Mexico
Youmans, Gilbert C.; Iowa State
Yngve, Victor H.; Chicago

Zarechnak, Michael; Georgetown
Zeldis, Jack B.; Cal State-Fresno
Zeman, J. Jay; Florida
Zeps, Valdis; Wisconsin
Zide, Norman H.; Chicago
Zimmer, Karl E.; Cal-Berkeley
Zintz, Miles; New Mexico
Zwicky, Arnold M.; Ohio State

Abboud, Peter F; U Texas - Austin
Abdel-Messih, Ernest T; Michigan
Abernathy, Robert; Colorado
Afendras, Evangelos; Hawaii
Alani; Indiana
Allen, Edward; Ohio State
Aliberti, Dominico; Youngstown State
Allen, Edward; Ohio State
Allen, Harold B; Minnesota
Allen, J.H.D.; Illinois Urbana-Champaign
Allen, Robert L; Columbia
Aller, Wayne; Indiana State
Amerman, James D.; Missouri
Angenot, Marc; McGill
Anshen, Frank; SUNY - Stony Brook
Antonsen, Elmer; Illinois - Urbana Champaign
Aoki, Hauro; U Cal - Berkeley
Applegate, Joseph; Howard
Araluce, Jose R.; USC
Arbib, Michael; Massachusetts
Aronoff, Mark; SUNY - Stony Brook
Arthur, Ann R.; Tulane
Asher, James J.; San Jose State
Ashworth, David E.; Hawaii
Aston, Katharine; Illinois - Urbana Champaign
Attinasi, John; Columbia
Ayer, George W.; U Texas - El Paso

Bacon, Isaac; Yeshiva
Bailey, Richard W.; Michigan
Baker, D.; Maryland
Baldwin, Lawrence; Miami
Baltaxe, Christiane A.M.; UCLA
Bana, F.; Indiana
Banchero, Lawrence J.; U Texas - Austin
Barch, Abram; Michigan State
Barker, M.A.R.; Minnesota
Barna-Gulanich, Luba; Youngstown State
Barnes, Dayle; Pittsburgh
Barrett, Ralph; Michigan State
Barthel, John W.; Oakland
Basso, Keith H.; Arizona
Bateman, Donald; Ohio State
Beasley, Daniel; Michigan State
Beaumont, Ronald; British Columbia
Beebe, J. Fred; Oregon
Beeman, William; Brown
Bender, Marvin; Southern Illinois - Carbondale
Bergquist, Sidney; Northwestern
Berkey, Max; USC
Berlin, Brent; U Cal - Berkeley
Berr, Samuel; SUNY - Stony Brook
Berrent, Gerald; North Carolina
Bharati, Agenhendanda; Syracuse
Bickley, Verner; Hawaii
Biggar, Raymond G.; Boston C
Bilbao, Jon; Nevada - Reno
Binnick, R.I.; Toronto
Birnbaum, Henrik; UCLA
Blache, Stephen; Southern Illinois - Carbondale
Black, John W.; Ohio State
Blasedell, Richard; Iowa
Blatchford, Charles; Hawaii
Bloch, Ariel; U Cal - Berkeley
Bloom, Lois; Columbia

Bloomfield, Morton W.; Harvard
Blount, Ben; U Texas - Austin
Boer, Steven; Ohio State
Boggs, Roy A.; Pittsburgh
Bohannan, Laura; Illinois - Chicago Circle
Borden, Gloria; City Coll of CUNY
Boren, James L.; Oregon
Borker, R.; Cornell
Bosco, Frederick J.; Georgetown
Boswell, Richard; SUNY - Binghamton
Bouissac, P.; Toronto
Bouton, Lawrence; Illinois - Urbana Champaign
Bowen, J. Donald; UCLA
Bowerman, Melissa; Kansas
Bowers, Fred; British Columbia
Bowers, John W.; Iowa
Bowie, G. Lee; Michigan
Boyd, Julian; U Cal - Berkeley
Boyd-Bowman, Peter; SUNY - Buffalo
Braine, Martin D.; New York
Brandon, Elizabeth; Houston
Brandt, Elizabeth A.; Illinois - Chicago Circle
Brecht, Richard; Harvard
Brent, Edmund; Toronto
Bresler, Marilyn; Mary Washington Coll
Broen, Patricia S.; Minnesota
Bromberger, Sylvain; MIT
Brooks, Candace; San Jose State
Brosman, Paul W.; Tulane
Brown, Alan K.; Ohio State
Brown, Thomas; Marion Coll
Brown, William; USC
Brudner, Lilyan; Pittsburgh
Buccalleti, Georgio; UCLA
Burke, Sarah P.; Trinity
Burke, William; Kansas State
Burkhardt, Klaus; SUNY - Oswego
Burton, Benjamin B.; CSU - Fresno
Buttelmann, H. William; Ohio State
Buys, William E.; Western Michigan

Cable, Thomas; U Texas - Austin
Cadora, Frederic J.; Ohio State
Cameron, A.; Toronto
Cameron, George G.; Michigan
Cameron, H. Don; Michigan
Campbell, Russell N.; UCLA
Canfield, Robert; SUNY - Oswego
Carew, Jan R.; Northwestern
Carlson, Bernadine P.; Western Michigan
Carnes, Robert D.; SUNY - Oswego
Carroll, John B.; North Carolina
Carroll, Vern; Michigan
Carr, Denzl; U Cal - Berkeley
Carterette, Edward C.; UCLA
Cartledge, Samuel; CSU - Fullerton
Carton, Aaron; SUNY - Stony Brook
Casagrande, Joseph; Illinois - Urbana Champaign
Casteneda; Indiana
Catlin, J.; Cornell
Cathey, James E.; Massachusetts
Cazajou, Jean; Miami
Celarier, James; Maryland

Chan, Stephen; U Cal - Berkeley
Chang, Kun; U Cal - Berkeley
Chao, Y.R.; U Cal - Berkeley
Chapman, Kenneth G.; UCLA
Chatman, Seymour; U Cal - Berkeley
Chavarria-Aguilar, O.L.; CUNY
Cheng, Robert; Hawaii
Chew, J.J., Jr.; Toronto
Chin, Tsung; Maryland
Chomsky, Carol; Harvard
Chopyk, Dan B.; Utah
Christensen, Clay B.; San Diego State
Christensen, Lawrence; CSU - Fullerton
Christie, William M., Jr.; Arizona
Churchill, Lindsey; CUNY
Civikly, Jean; New Mexico
Clark, Herbert H.; Stanford
Clark, Michael J.; Western Michigan
Clark, Virginia P.; Vermont
Clarke, David S.; Southern Illinois
  Carbondale
Clegg, J. Halvor; Brigham Young
Clifton, Charles; Massachusetts
Clough, Carmen P.; CSU - Fresno
Coffin, Edna; Michigan
Coleman, Edmund; U Texas - El Paso
Collins, Tom J.; Arizona
Conant, Jonathan B.; Brown
Conklin, Harold; Yale
Conrad, Carole; New Mexico
Conway, Abbot; McGill
Cook, Edwin A.; Southern Illinois -
  Carbondale
Cook, Robert; Tulane
Cooke, Joseph; Washington
Cooper, Franklin; Yale
Coppola, Carlo; Oakland
Corcoran, John P.; SUNY - Buffalo
Correll, Thomas C.; Bethel Coll
Cousin, Florence; Carleton
Covey, Delvin; Gordon C
Craddock, Jerry; U Cal - Berkeley
Creore, Jo-Ann D.; Alberta
Cressey, William W.; Georgetown
Crockett, Dina B.; Stanford
Cross, Frank M.; Harvard
Crossgrove, William; Brown
Crothers, Edward J.; Colorado
Crymes, Ruth; Hawaii
Cumbee, Jack A.; Oakland
Cummins, George; Tulane
Currie, Winifred; Gordon C
Curtis, James F.; Iowa

Dale, Philip; Washington
D'Alquen, Richard J.E.; Alberta
Davis, Charles E.; Arizona
Davis, Jack Emory; Arizona
Dawson, Clayton L.; Illinois - Urbana Champaign
Day, Christopher; Rochester
Day, Richard; Hawaii
Decker, Donald M.; U of the Pacific
DeFrancis, John; Hawaii
Denise, Theodore; Syracuse
DeRemer, Franklin L.; U Cal - Santa Cruz
DeStefano, Johanna; Ohio State
Detrich, Dean; Michigan State
Devine, Andrew M.; Stanford

Dew, James E.; Michigan
Dibble, Charles; Utah
Dickerson, A.I.; Vermont
Dickerson, Wayne B.; Illinois - Urbana
  Champaign
Dixon, Paul W.; Hilo C, U Hawaii - Hilo
Dodd, David; Utah
Doherty, Paul C.; Boston C
Dolby, James L.; San Jose State
Dolezel, L.; Toronto
Donaldson, Weber D., Jr.; Tulane
Donato, Eugenio; SUNY - Buffalo
Donchenko, Adele; Minnesota
Donnellan, Keith S.; UCLA
Dorfman, Eugene; Alberta
Dóstal, Antonín; Brown
Douglass, Thomas; Iowa
Dow, Sterling; Boston C
Downer, James W.; Michigan
Dunatov, Rasio; Illinois - Urbana Champaign
Dunningan, Timothy; Minnesota
Dutton, Brian; Illinois - Chicago Circle
Dwyer, David; Michigan State
Dykema, Christine R.; Youngstown State
Dykstra, Gerald; Hawaii

Eastman, Carol; Washington
Ebert, Robert; Chicago
Eblen, Roy; Northern Iowa
Ebling, Benjamin; Western Michigan
Edmunson, H.; Maryland
Edwards, Thomas J.; SUNY - Buffalo
Ehret, Christopher; UCLA
Ellis, William W.; U Southwestern Louisiana
Eliot, John; Maryland
Epstein, Edmund L.; Southern Illinois -
  Carbondale
Ervin-Tripp, Susan; U Cal - Berkeley
Erwin, Wallace; Georgetown
Eschholz, Paul; Vermont
Ethridge, Sanford; Tulane

Falk, Arthur E.; Western Michigan
Faraci, Mary E.; Florida Atlantic
Farrell, Michael P.; SUNY - Buffalo
Faurot, Ruth Marie; U of the Pacific
Feinberg, Larry; North Carolina
Feldstein, Ronald; SUNY - Binghamton
Ferrell, James O.; Michigan
Filter, Maynard; Central Michigan
Findler, Nicholas; SUNY - Buffalo
Finkelstein, J.J.; Yale
Firestone, Robert T.; Colorado
Firestone, Ruth H.; Missouri
Fisher, Hilda; Northwestern
Fisher, John C.; SUNY - Oswego
Fleischhauer, Wolfgang; Ohio State
Flier, Michael S.; UCLA
Floyd, Edwin D.; Pittsburgh
Fodor, Jerry A.; MIT
Folsom, Marvin H.; Brigham Young
Foss, Donald J.; U Texas - Austin
Fowler, Catherine S.; Nevada - Reno
Fox, James A.; Stanford
Fox, Robert; American
Frake, Charles O.; Stanford
Francis, E. David; Yale
Frantz, Charles; SUNY - Buffalo

Franzblau, Daniel; Miami
Fraser, Bruce; Boston
Fraser, Russell A.; Michigan
Freeman, Jerry M.; Oakland
Freeman, Michael W.; Harvard
French, Howard P.; Southern Illinois -
  Carbondale
Frentz, Thomas; USC
Frey, Herschel; Pittsburgh
Frieden, Robert; Purdue
Friedman, Joyce B.; Michigan
Frye, Richard N.; Harvard
Fullerton, G. Lee; SUNY - Buffalo

Garcia, Rodolfo; Colorado
Garcia, Sandra J.; UCLA
Gardiner, Cynthia; Iowa
Gardner, R. Allen; Nevada - Reno
Garey, Howard; Yale
Garner, Richard; Ohio State
Garrett, Merrill F.; MIT
Garver, Newton; SUNY - Buffalo
Gates, H. Phelps; North Carolina
Gates, Robert; Syracuse
Gay, Charles W.; USC
Gettier, Edmund L.; Massachusetts
Gibson, Robert; Hawaii
Ginsburg, Seymour; USC
Gladney, Frank; Illinois - Urbana Champaign
Glanzer, Murray; New York
Gleitman, Lila R.; Pennsylvania
Goggin, Judith; U Texas - El Paso
Goheen, Jutta; Carleton
Goldin, M.; Indiana
Goldman, Iva R.; Hilo Coll, U Hawaii - Hilo
Goldman, Robert; U Cal - Berkeley
Gopnik, Irvin; McGill
Gordon, Alice; North Carolina
Gough, Philip B.; U Texas - Austin
Gradman, H.; Indiana
Grandstaff, Harvey L.; Miami
Grebenschikov, V.I.; Carleton
Greenbaum, Sidney; Wisconsin - Milwaukee
Greenberg, Joseph H.; Stanford
Greenblatt, Daniel; Missouri
Greenfeld, Philip J.; San Diego State
Greenfield, Stanley B.; Oregon
Gregory, O. Dean; Kansas
Grice, Paul; U Cal - Berkeley
Griffin, David A.; Ohio State
Griffin, Robert J.; Western Michigan
Grimes, Larry M.; Minnesota
Grimshaw, A.; Indiana
Grindell, Robert; Kansas State
Grosjean, Glen; U Cal - Berkeley
Grun, Ruth; Indiana State
Guitart, Jorge; SUNY - Buffalo
Guitarte, Guillermo; Boston C
Gumperz, John; U Cal - Berkeley

Haber, Lyn Kypriotaki; Rochester
Haber, Ralph; Rochester
Haden, Ernest F.; U Texas - Austin
Hadlich, Roger; Hawaii
Hagiwara, Michio P.; Michigan
Hakes, David T.; U Texas - Austin
Hall, Larry; Howard

Hall, Ross; North Carolina
Hallo, William W.; Yale
Halverson, John; U Cal - Santa Cruz
Hamilton, Roland; San Jose State
Hamilton, William S., Jr.; SUNY - Buffalo
Hammarbert, Robert; Purdue
Hammond, Mac S.; SUNY - Buffalo
Han, Mieko; USC
Hancock, Ian F.; U Texas - Austin
Hankley, William; Kansas State
Hansen, Ward; USC
Harnish, Robert M.; Arizona
Harris, Katherine; CUNY
Harris, Richard; Kansas State
Harrison, Ann; Michigan State
Harshenin, Alex P.; British Columbia
Hart, Thomas E.; Syracuse
Hart, Thomas R.; Oregon
Hartman, James; Kansas
Hartman, Steven L.; Southern Illinois -
  Carbondale
Hasazi, Joseph; Vermont
Hascall, Dudley; Ohio State
Hasselmo, Nils; Minnesota
Hatch, Evelyn R.; UCLA
Hawkins, Emily; Hawaii
Hayon, Yehiel; Ohio State
Healy, Alice; Yale
Hempel, Wilhelm; McGill
Hensey, Fritz; U Texas - Austin
Hernandez, Jose; San Jose State
Hetzron, Robert; U Cal - Santa Barbara
Higa, Masanori; Hawaii
Higgenbotham, James; Columbia
Higginbotham, Dorothy; Southern Illinois -
  Carbondale
Hildum, Donald C.; Oakland
Hill, David; Northwestern
Hilrich, John; New Mexico
Himes, Ronald S.; San Diego State
Hockings, Paul; Illinois - Chicago Circle
Hoffner, Harry; Yale
Hoijer, Harry; UCLA
Hojo, Michio; Pittsburgh
Holden, Kyril T.; Alberta
Holland, Audrey; Pittsburgh
Honeycutt, Ben F.; Missouri
Horner, Winifred B.; Missouri
Horton, David; Maryalnd
Houston, Charles O.; Western Michigan
Howard, Thomas; Gordon C
Howe, Anne; Syracuse
Hsieh, Hsin-I; Hawaii
Hubbell, Allan F.; New York
Hughes, Theone; Western Michigan
Hunt, Chester L.; Western Michigan
Huntington, Dorothy A.; Stanford
Huntley, D.G.; Toronto
Huntsman, K.; Indiana
Hursky, Jacob; Syracuse
Huttenlocher, Janellen B.; Columbia
Hymes, Dell H.; Pennsylvania

Ibba, Maria; Ohio State
Iles, Malory; South Florida
Imhoof, M.; Indiana
Iodice, Don R.; Oakland
Irvine, Judith; Brandeis
Ives, Sumner A.; New York

Jackson, Kenneth; Hawaii
Jakobovits, Leon; Hawaii
James, D.M.; Toronto
Jarvis, Donald K.; Brigham Young
Jazayery, M.A.; U Texas - Austin
Jenkins, Frederick; Illinois - Urbana
 Champaign
Jenkins, James J.; Minnesota
Jensen, Keith; Miami
Jochnowitz, George; CUNY
Johnson, Neal; Ohio State
Joshi, Aravind K.; Pennsylvania
Juilland, Alphonse; Stanford
Junghare, Indira Y.; Minnesota
Juntune, Thomas; Michigan State

Kadler, Eric; Central Michigan
Kane, Harold J.; Colorado
Kane, Kenneth B.; Miami
Kanno, Leila L.; Hilo Coll, U Hawaii - Hilo
Kao, Kung-yi; Stanford
Karateew, Nicholas; Syracuse
Kaschube, Dorothea V.; Colorado
Katre, S.M.; U Texas - Austin
Kaufman, Terrence; Pittsburgh
Kay, Paul; U Cal - Berkeley
Keller, Gary; City Coll CUNY
Keller, Hans; Ohio State
Kelley, D.; Montclair State
Kennard, Edward A.; Nevada - Reno
Kent, Louise M.; Western Michigan
Khanna, Satendra; Michigan
Kiddle, Lawrence B.; Michigan
Kimizuka, Sumako; USC
King, Harold V.; Michigan
Kintsch, Walter; Colorado
Kiraithe, Jacqueline; CSU - Fullerton
Kirsner, Robert S.; UCLA
Kirwin, W.J.; Memorial U Newfoundland
Kispert, Robert; Illinois - Chicago Circle
Kissel, Johannes A.; Western Michigan
Kitagawa, Chisato; Massachusetts
Kjolseth, J. Rolf; Colorado
Klammer, Thomas; CSU - Fullerton
Klein, Flora; Georgetown
Klein, Harriet; Montclair State
Kleinjans, Everett; Hawaii
Knudsig, Glenn; Michigan
Kochman, Thomas M.; Illinois - Chicago
 Circle
Koekkoek, Byron J.; SUNY - Buffalo
Koen, Frank M.; Michigan
Koenig, Frederick W.; Tulane
Koenig, Virginia; Southwestern Louisiana
Koenigsknecht, Roy; Northwestern
Korn, David; Howard
Koslow, Arnold; CUNY
Kozlik, Ludek A.; San Diego State
Kozlowski, Edwin; Iowa
Kragalott, Jasna; Ohio State
Kroch, Anthony; Connecticut
Krohn, Robert; Hawaii
Kučera, Henry; Brown
Kuhn, Sherman M.; Michigan
Kusanagi, Yutaka; Hawaii
Kyes, Robert L.; Michigan

Lackner, James; Brandeis
La Driere, Mimi; Detroit
Lambdin, Thomas O.; Harvard
Lambert, Wallace; McGill
Lance, Donald M.; Missouri
Lane, Eugene N.; Missouri
Lange, Roland A.; Columbia
Laughlin, Charles D., Jr.; SUNY - Oswego
Laurette, Pierre; Carleton
Lawson, Richard H.; San Diego State
Leap, William J.; American
Lee, Laura; Northwestern
Lehman, F.K.; Illinois - Urbana Champaign
Leis, Nancy; Central Michigan
Lelis, Joseph; Howard
Lencek, Rado L.; Columbia
Lenneberg, E.; Cornell
Lenowitz, Harris; Utah
Léon, P.R.; Toronto
Leonard, Clifford S.; Michigan
Leslau, Wolf; UCLA
Lester, Mark; Hawaii
Levin, Saul; SUNY - Binghamton
Levitt, Harry; CUNY
Lewis, Brian A.; Colorado
Lewis, William; Vermont
Li, Ying-Che; Hawaii
Liang, James; Pennsylvania
Libben, Lynn; Rochester
Liberman, Alvin M.; Connecticut
Lieberman, Dena; Missouri
Light, Timothy; Arizona
Lilja, Linnea; Missouri
Liljeblad, Sven S.; Nevada - Reno
Lindholm, James M.; Chicago
Linn, Irving; Yeshiva
Loesch, Katherine; Illinois - Chicago Circle
Lofstedt, Bengt; UCLA
Long, Mark; U Texas - Austin
Longhurst, Thomas; Kansas State
Lounsbury, Floyd G.; Yale
Lourie, Margaret; Michigan
Loveless, Owen R.; Minnesota
Lozano, Anthony G.; Colorado
Lucash, Frank S.; Nevada - Reno
Lucian, Miriam; Washington
Lujan, Marta; U Texas - Austin
Lukach, Taras; San Jose State
Lukoff, Fred; Washington
Lunt, Horace G.; Harvard
Luthy, Melvin J.; Brigham Young
Lycan, William; Ohio State
Lyon, Jon; Vermont

MacKay, Donald G.; UCLA
Macleish, Andrew; Minnesota
MacNamara, John; McGill
Mack, Dorothy; Michigan
Magnuson; Indiana
Major, Diana; Utah
Makino, Seiichi; Illinois - Urbana Champaign
Malarkey, Stoddard; Oregon
Malecot, Andre; U Cal - Santa Barbara
Malmstrom, Jean; Western Michigan
Malycky, Alexander; Calgary
Manis, Melvin; Michigan
Mann, Lydia S.; Mary Washington C
Manolis, John C.; Mary Washington C

Mantini, Lawrence C.; Minnesota
Marashi, Mehdi; Utah
Maratsos, Michael P.; Minnesota
Marchand, James; Illinois - Urbana Champaign
Maring, Joel M.; Southern Illinois - Carbondale
Marino, Matthew; Rochester
Marlin, Marjorie; Missouri
Martin, Clessen; Texas A & M
Martin, Duane; U Texas - Arlington
Martin, James; Maryland
Martin, Nancy; New Mexico
Martin, P.; Toronto
Martin, Richard; Northwestern
Masica, Colin P.; Chicago
Mason, H.E.; Minnesota
Matejka, Ladislav; Michigan
Mathiesen, Robert; Brown
Matson, Daniel S.; Arizona
Mazzola, M.; Indiana
McCarus, Ernest N.; Michigan
McCaskey, Michael; Georgetown
McClaran, Marlys; UCLA
McCormick, Terrence; Connecticut
McDermott, Charlene; New Mexico
McEvoy, J. Edward; SUNY - Oswego
McGloin, Naomi; Michigan
McGlone, Robert E.; SUNY - Buffalo
McGranahan, William J.; Western Michigan
McIntosh, Lois; UCLA
McKay, Janet; Federal City C
McKay, June Rumery; U Cal - Berkeley
McLain, Richard; SUNY - Binghamton
McMunn, William; Connecticut
McSparran, Frances; Michigan
Mehan, H.; Indiana
Meltzer, Bernard; Central Michigan
Menyuk, Paula; Boston
Meriz, Diana; Pittsburgh
Meryman, John J.; San Jose State
Metzger, Margarita; Youngstown State
Meunier, J.G.; Quebec - Montreal
Meyer, Edgar N.; Colorado
Meyer, William J.; Syracuse
Meyers, Leroy; Ohio State
Meyerson, Marion D.; CSU - Fresno
Micklesen, Lew; Washington
Mieder, Wolfgang; Vermont
Migliazza, Earnest; Maryland
Miksak, Joseph; San Francisco State
Millar, Michael; Northern Iowa
Miller, Carol; Kansas State
Miller, Mary; Maryland
Miron, Murray S.; Syracuse
Mishima, Toshiko; San Francisco State
Mitchell, J. Lawrence; Minnesota
Miyaji, Hiroshi; Pennsylvania
Moffitt, Alan; Carleton
Molfese, Dennis; Southern Illinois - Carbondale
Montgomery, Edward D., Jr.; North Carolina
Montgomery, Thomas; Tulane
Moody, Patricia; Syracuse
Moore, Marcia; SUNY - Oswego
Moravcsik, J.M.E.; Stanford
Morgan, David; Northern Iowa
Morgan, Raleigh, Michigan
Moyne, John; Queens C - CUNY
Munsell, Paul; Michigan State

Nagara, Susumu; Michigan
Nalibow, Kenneth; Vermont
Napoli, Donna Jo; North Carolina
Naremore, R.; Indiana
Naroll, Raoul; SUNY - Buffalo
Narvaez, Ricardo A.; Minnesota
Nasjleti, David; Harvard
Naylor, Kenneth E.; Ohio State
Nelms, Ben F.; Missouri
Nelson, Arnold G.; Western Michigan
Nelson, Frank G.; Hilo C; U Hawaii - Hilo
Neugaard, Edward J.; South Florida
Newman, Lawrence W.; Ohio State
Nichols, Johanna; U Cal - Berkeley
Nicholson, John; McGill
Nicolaisen, Wilhelm; SUNY - Binghamton
Niyekawa-Howard, Agnes; Hawaii
Noble, G. Kingsley; San Jose State
Nodarse, Samuel; Northern Iowa
Nolan, Rita D.; North Carolina
Norman, Arthur; U Texas - Austin
Nuessel, Frank; Indiana State

Oates, Michael; Northern Iowa
Odwarka, Karl; Northern Iowa
O'Hare, Thomas J.; U Texas - Austin
Ohtani, Taketo; Mary Washington C
Oinas, F.; Indiana
Olson, D.R.; Toronto
Olson, Gary; Michigan State
O'Neil, Wayne A.; MIT
Oro, Cesar; Howard
Osgood, Charles; Illinois - Urbana Champaign
Osmun, George F.; Western Michigan
Osser, Harry; San Francisco State
Otero, C.P.; UCLA
Ottenheimer, Harriet; Kansas State

Pace, George B.; Missouri
Pace, Sue Ann; Southern Illinois - Carbondale
Paden, Bill; Northwestern
Pak, Tae-Yong; Hawaii
Papalia, Anthony; SUNY - Buffalo
Pappe, Nicholas; British Columbia
Parisi, Gino; Georgetown
Parsons, Terry; Massachusetts
Patton, Clyde P.; Oregon
Patton, Thomas E.; British Columbia
Penchoen, Thomas G.; UCLA
Penzl, Herbert; U Cal - Berkeley
Perkins, William; USC
Peterson; Indiana
Peterson, Philip L.; Syracuse
Phillips, Hosea; Southwestern Louisiana
Phillips, Robert N.; Miami
Pialorsi, Frank; Arizona
Picone, Michelangelo; McGill
Piffard, Guerard; San Diego State
Pisonit; Indiana
Pitkin, Harvey; Columbia
Plant, Helmut R.; Oregon
Plum, Thomas; SUNY - Binghamton
Politzer, Robert L.; Stanford
Posnansky, Carla; Rochester
Powell, James V.; British Columbia

rator, Clifford H.; UCLA
ray, Bruce; U Cal - Berkeley
riestly, Tom; Alberta
rost, Jack; Illinois - Chicago Circle
ugh, David G.; Western Michigan
uhvel, Jean; UCLA
ulgrum, Ernst; Michigan U
ulleyblank, Edwin G.; British Columbia

afisheh, Hamdi A.; Arizona
uackenbush, Hiroko; Ohio State
uick, James E.; Tulane
uist, Raymond; Indiana State

acine, Marie M.; Federal City C
ahimi, Morteza; Michigan State
ainbolt, Harry; Kansas State
ainbow, Raymond S.; Southern Illinois -
  Carbondale
ameh, Clea; Georgetown
ammuny, Raji; Michigan
amos, Teresita; Hawaii
and, Earl; UCLA
au, Gilbert G.; Central Michigan
auch, Irmengard; Illinois - Urbana
  Champaign
ay, Jack L.; San Jose State
ayner, Keith; Rochester
eed, Carroll E.; Massachusetts
eeker, Larry H.; Oregon
egelson, Stanley; SUNY - Stony Brook
ehg, Kenneth; Hawaii
eidy, John; Michigan
einhardt, Karl J.; Houston
enehan, Robert F.; Boston C
ey, Alberto; Howard
eynolds, Janice; Central Michigan
eynolds, Larry; Central Michigan
hyne, James B.; Houston
ichardson, Peter; Yale
iegel, Klaus F.; Michigan
ieger, Charles; Maryland
itterman, Stuart I.; South Florida
oberts, Kelyn H.; UCLA
oberts, Louis W.; Syracuse
obinson, David F.; Ohio State
obinson, Jay L.; Michigan
obinson, Orrin W., III; Stanford
obinson, Sinclair; Carleton
ochet, Bernard L.; Alberta
ockey, Randall E.; U of the Pacific
odd, Linda; Vermont
odman, Lilita; British Columbia
ogers, Andrew; U Texas - Austin
ohsenow, Hill; Central Michigan
ojas, J. Nelson; Nevada - Reno
ooney, Timothy; Northern Iowa
oot, Michael; Minnesota
osaldo, Michelle Z.; Stanford
ose, Edward; Colorado
ose, James H.; Purdue
osen, Karl M.D.; Kansas
osenbaum, Peter; Columbia
osenberg, Sheldon; Illinois - Chicago
  Circle
osenthal, Franz; Yale
othstein, Robert A.; Massachusetts
ubin, Herbert; Pittsburgh

Ruder, Kenneth; Kansas
Runge, Richard; Iowa
Ruplin, Ferdinand; SUNY - Stony Brook
Russell, William M.; U Texas - El Paso
Russom, Geoffrey; Brown
Rutherford, William; USC
Ryan, William; New Mexico

Sadek, Carmen; USC
Sadovski, Otto; CSU - Fullerton
Salus, P.H.; Toronto
Salzmann, Zdenek; Massachusetts
Sampson, Gloria P.; Alberta
Sanches, Mary; U Texas - Austin
Sanchez, Rosaura; Stanford
Sands, Donald B.; Michigan
Sanford, Gerlinde; Syracuse
Sas, Louis F.; City Coll CUNY
Satarelli, Mario; Illinois - Urbana
  Champaign
Sauer, Keith; CSU - Fresno
Schaarschmidt, Gunter H.; Alberta
Schachter, Albert; McGill
Schachter, Jacqueline; USC
Schaeffer, Benson; Oregon
Scheer, Richard; Kansas State
Schegloff, Emanuel A.; UCLA
Schenker, Alexander; Yale
Schiffman, Harold; Washington
Schmidt, Michael F.; San Jose State
Schneider, Gerd; Syracuse
Schnerr, Walter J.; Brown
Schogt, H.G.; Toronto
Schulman, Samuel; Central Connecticut
  State Coll
Schultz; Indiana
Schulz, Muriel; CSU - Fullerton
Schupbach, Richard; Stanford
Schvanveldt, Roger W.; SUNY - Stony Brook
Schwartz, Martin; U Cal - Berkeley
Schwartz, Rosaline; City Coll CUNY
Schwarz, Jerold; Montclair State
Scollon, Ronald; Hawaii
Scott, J. Reid; San Jose State
Scruggs, Charles E.; South Florida
Searle, John; U Cal - Berkeley
Segal, Erwin M.; SUNY - Buffalo
Seligson, Gerda; Michigan
Semmel, M.; Indiana
Sewell, Ernestine; U Texas - Arlington
Seymour, Richard; Hawaii
Shaklee, Margaret E.; UCLA
Shanks, Susan J.; CSU - Fresno
Shankweiler, Donald; Connecticut
Shapiro, Michael; UCLA
Shapiro, Michael; Washington
Sharpe, Lawrence A.; North Carolina
Shaterian, Alan; U Cal - Berkeley
Shen, Yao; Hawaii
Sherzer, Joel; U Texas - Austin
Shetter, N.; Indiana
Shopay-Morton, Olga C.; Missouri
Shulman, Lee; Michigan State
Silverman, Suart; South Florida
Simonelli, Maria; Boston C
Sing Lien, Cheng; Central Connecticut
  State Coll
Siple, Patricia; Rochester

Siporin, Rae; Pittsburgh
Sjoberg, Andree; U Texas - Austin
Slayton, Paul C.; Mary Washington C
Sledd, James H.; U Texas - Austin
Slobin, Dan; U Cal - Berkeley
Small, Kenneth; Washington
Smith, Arthur L.; SUNY - Buffalo
Smith, Douglas; Central Michigan
Smith, F.; Toronto
Smith, J. Jerome; South Florida
Smith, Sidney, Jr.; North Carolina
Smith, William; Texas A&M
Smothergill, Daniel W.; Syracuse
Soffietti, James P.; Syracuse
Soga, Matsuo; British Columbia
Sohn, Ho-min; Hawaii
Soule, Stephen P.; Calgary
Southworth, Franklin C.; Pennsylvania
Speaks, Charles E.; Minnesota
Spendal, Ralph J.; Detroit
Sper, S.A.; Toronto
Springer, Sally; SUNY - Stony Brook
Staal, J.D.; U Cal - Berkeley
Stalker, James; Michigan State
Staneslow, Paul; Minnesota
Stark, Bruce; Wisconsin - Milwaukee
Steinberg, Danny; Hawaii
Steinmann, Martin; Minnesota
Stern, H.H.; Toronto
Stewart, William; Columbia
Stich, Stephen P.; Michigan
Stilo, Donald; UCLA
Stitt, Clyde; San Francisco State
Stone, H. Reynolds; Arizona
Straight, H. Stephen; SUNY - Binghamton
Stross, Brian M.; U Texas - Austin
Sturr, Joseph; Syracuse
Sugita, Hiroshi; Hawaii
Sullivan, Patrick; SUNY - Oswego
Swanson, Donald C.; Minnesota
Sweet, Waldo; Michigan

Tai, James H-Y; Southern Illinois -
    Carbondale
Takahara, Kumiko; Colorado
Tallentire, D. Roger; British Columbia
Tanaka, Yoshio; San Diego State
Tauber, Abraham; Yeshiva
Taylor, John; Wisconsin - Milwaukee
Taylor, Mary; Utah
Taylor, Peter A.; British Columbia
Teng, Shou-Hsin; Massachusetts
Teschner, Richard; Iowa
Thau, Steward; Syracuse
Theall, Donald; McGill
Thomas, Ian B.; Massachusetts
Thomas, O.; Indiana
Thompson, Carl L.; Houston
Thompson, David L.; Marion C
Tiee, Henry; USC
Tienson; Indiana
Tietze, Andreas; UCLA
Timberlake, Alan H.; UCLA
Ting, Ho; Iowa
Trnka, Karla; U Texas - Austin
Trombly, Thelma; Missouri
Tucker, G. Richard; McGill
Tufte, Virginia; USC

Turvey, Michael T.; Connecticut
Tway, Patricia; Youngstown State

Ullrich, John; New Mexico
Underwood, Frances; San Jose State
Underwood, Gary N.; U Texas - Austin

Valette, Rebecca; Boston C
Van Campen, Joseph A.; Stanford
VanDyk, Oebele; SUNY - Oswego
van Nooten, Berend; U Cal - Berkeley
Van Olphen, Herman H.; U Texas - Austin
Van Rutten, Pierre; Carleton
Van Vlasselaer, Jean-Jacques; Carleton
Vater, H.; Indiana
Vidricaire, Andre; Quebec-Montreal
Viehmeyer, Allan; Youngstown State
von Schooneveld, C.; Indiana
Van't Hul, Bernard; Michigan
Voyles, Joseph; Washington

Wadley, Susan; Syracuse
Waengler, Hans-H.; Colorado
Walker, Howard; SUNY - Oswego
Wallace, John; Minnesota
Wallenmaier, Thomas; Detroit
Wallentine, Virgil; Kansas State
Walsh, Harry H.; Houston
Walsh, James L.; San Diego State
Wang, Stephen S.; Minnesota
Wanner, Dieter; Illinois - Urbana
    Champaign
Ware, Robert X.; Calgary
Washabaugh, William; Wisconsin - Milwaukee
Watt, William; U Cal - Irvine
Weaver, Constance; Western Michigan
Webb, Charlotte; U Texas - Austin
Wedge, George; Kansas
Weiger, John; Vermont
Weil-Malherbe, Rosanne; Howard
Weinberg, Herbert; Indiana State
Weinberger, Marvin; San Francisco State
Weinstock, John; U Texas - Austin
Weiss, Curtis E.; Nevada - Reno
Weiss, Rita S.; Colorado
Werbow, Stanley N.; U Texas - Austin
Wexler, Kenneth; U Cal - Irvine
Whitaker, Haiganooh A.; Rochester
Whitaker, Harry A.; Rochester
White, Raymond M.; Miami
Whitfield, F.J.; U Cal - Berkeley
Wickelgren, Wayne; Oregon
Wilbur, Terence H.; UCLA
Wilder, Hugh T.; Miami
Wilkins, George W., Jr.; Tulane
Willard, Dallas; USC
Williams, David; McGill
Willis, John P.; Western Michigan
Wilson, Mary; Vermont
Wilson, Robert; UCLA
Windfuhr, Gernot; Michigan
Wing, Nathaniel; Miami
Winterowd, Ross; USC
Winthrop, Charles; Ohio State
Wogan, Daniel S.; Tulane
Wolfe, David L.; Michigan
Wolfe, Patricia M.; British Columbia
Wood, Barbara; Illinois - Chicago Circle